I0814029

Priest Under Fire

UNIVERSITY PRESS OF FLORIDA

Florida A&M University, Tallahassee
Florida Atlantic University, Boca Raton
Florida Gulf Coast University, Ft. Myers
Florida International University, Miami
Florida State University, Tallahassee
New College of Florida, Sarasota
University of Central Florida, Orlando
University of Florida, Gainesville
University of North Florida, Jacksonville
University of South Florida, Tampa
University of West Florida, Pensacola

Priest Under Fire

Padre David Rodríguez, the Catholic Church, and El Salvador's Revolutionary Movement

Peter M. Sánchez

UNIVERSITY PRESS OF FLORIDA
Gainesville / Tallahassee / Tampa / Boca Raton
Pensacola / Orlando / Miami / Jacksonville / Ft. Myers / Sarasota

Printed in the United States of America on acid-free paper

This book may be available in an electronic edition.

20 19 18 17 16 15   6 5 4 3 2 1

Library of Congress Cataloging-in-Publication Data

Sánchez, Peter Michael, 1954– author.
Priest under fire : Padre David Rodríguez, the Catholic Church, and El Salvador's revolutionary movement / Peter M. Sánchez.
pages cm
Includes bibliographical references and index.
ISBN 978-0-8130-6119-1
1. Rodríguez Rivera, José David. 2. Catholic Church—El Salvador—Clergy—Biography. 3. Insurgency—El Salvador—History. 4. El Salvador—History. I. Title.
BX4705.R628S26 2015
282.092—dc23
[B]
2015029221

The University Press of Florida is the scholarly publishing agency for the State University System of Florida, comprising Florida A&M University, Florida Atlantic University, Florida Gulf Coast University, Florida International University, Florida State University, New College of Florida, University of Central Florida, University of Florida, University of North Florida, University of South Florida, and University of West Florida.

University Press of Florida
15 Northwest 15th Street
Gainesville, FL 32611-2079
http://www.upf.com

To the poor of El Salvador, in hopes that their future will be better than their past.

Contents

Illustrations

Figures

Map

Table

Preface and Acknowledgments

I met David Rodríguez Rivera in November 2006 when he was giving a guest lecture at the Jesuit-run Universidad Centroamericana "José Simeón Cañas" (University of Central America) in San Salvador. I was visiting a history class taught by Gene Palumbo, a journalist who had been living in El Salvador since the early 1980s, when he reported on the civil war. Rodríguez had already finished serving his second term as a deputy (elected representative) in El Salvador's Legislative Assembly and had time on his hands, so he was Gene's guest lecturer on that particular day. As I sat there and listened to "Padre David," as he is almost universally known, recount his life story, I could not take notes fast enough. I was captivated by this priest who had taken the bold step to join the guerrillas and had now been elected to public office. I was intrigued mostly by his apparent sincerity and commitment to social justice. Even before the class was over, I had decided to jettison my existing research project if he would agree to let me write a book about his seemingly epic life. To my delight, Rodríguez agreed quickly to my proposal. A few months later, in May 2007, I flew him to Chicago, and in a period of two weeks he narrated to me his remarkable life story.

Before he came to Chicago, I began to look into his past. I quickly discovered that, surprisingly enough, very little had been written about him. A number of books and articles briefly identified him as an important religious leader in El Salvador's popular, Christian movement, but no one had written about Rodríguez exclusively, detailing his contributions to the liberationist church, the popular movement, the revolutionary movement, and the democratization of El Salvador. One book is a compilation of interviews with a number of former revolutionary leaders, and Rodríguez is one of those who is interviewed.[1] He is also mentioned in a number of newspaper articles, but again very little information is provided. In a short 1983 *New York Times* article he is erroneously credited with leading fifteen hundred guerrillas in an assault that brought about the taking of a small town during the civil war. The Salvadoran press, of course, mentioned "Padre David" often, particularly in the 1970s, owing to his important role in that decade as a progressive religious leader who butted heads with the oligarchy and the state. A number of times, he was accused of "inciting" the peasantry to violence. What I quickly discovered was that Rodríguez's central role in El Salvador's tumultuous 1970s and 1980s had not been adequately told.

The more I learned about Padre Rodríguez, the more I also wanted to see the places in El Salvador that were important in his life. So, a few months after I finished my interviews with him in Chicago, I flew to El Salvador to talk with people who knew him and to visit a number of key locations, camera in hand. I returned from El Salvador with ninety-five personal interviews, five interviews conducted by Alex Bonilla (Rodríguez's driver), lots of photos, and a much greater appreciation for the land and people of El Salvador. The most illuminating aspect of the interviews was the almost universal love and admiration that people expressed for Padre Rodríguez. When people speak of him they light up. When he enters a room they immediately turn to him. It may be hard to define charisma, but when you see how Salvadorans react to Padre David Rodríguez you can feel its presence. His magnetism was evident to me in 2008 when he was sixty-seven years old, so I can only imagine his effect on people in the 1970s when he was in his early thirties, the age of most revolutionary leaders. Even those who had lost a great deal because of their involvement in the civil war saw Rodríguez as a person who always did what he could to help the poor. One of my interviews was with a relative who did not agree with his cousin's progressive views and involvement with the armed guerrillas. Despite the disagreement, his relative conceded that Padre David had been motivated solely by his desire to help the Salvadoran peasant, a sentiment that was nearly universal in the interviews that I conducted.

In addition to these interviews, Rodríguez turned over to me the files of his parish in Tecoluca that Father Rafael Barahona, a key figure whom we will meet later in the book, had safeguarded. Father Barahona copied the files from the parish in 1980 when he fled the country,[2] as many priests did after the assassination of Archbishop Óscar Romero. The files contain extensive information about the establishment of Christian base communities, the conflicts between the government and the church, and the divisions within the church, as played out in one Salvadoran parish. This was no ordinary parish, however, since it was home to the first massacre of peasants in the country, in November 1974, and lay within El Salvador's key economic zone. The files also contain the pastoral plans that Rodríguez and Barahona devised in the early 1970s. Most likely no one other than those two men has seen these documents since the late 1970s. The interviews and files, along with El Salvador's historical record, serve as witness to the unique life experience of Padre David Rodríguez.

Although I have written the text, this book is the work of many. First and foremost, I am enormously indebted to David Rodríguez Rivera, "Padre David," who generously gave up his time to teach me about El Salvador and tell me about his exploits. It has been a uniquely educational experience to get to know him, as well as a great pleasure. While I was in El Salvador, Gene Palumbo and Alex Bonilla were also of immeasurable help. Gene helped to set up my research trip and provided a great deal of information and contacts. Alex was my driver, my tour guide, and eventually he became my assistant on the trip, to a point where he would remind me of things I had forgotten to do or ask. I hope he still has my Panama hat. Mercedes Henríquez, also known as "Merci" but particularly as "Flor," and "Padre David's" *compañera,* recounted to me much of Rodríguez's personal life. Ana Ruth, their daughter, also opened up a more personal view and turned over to me many family photos (some included in this book) that helped me to get a better visual feel for Rodríguez's past. I am extremely grateful to the many individuals whom I spoke with in El Salvador, since they filled in some gaps, added personal tidbits, and provided a better feel for how "Padre David" was, and continues to be, perceived. I have decided to keep their names out of the story to ensure their safety. Some of them are well-known figures, so I apologize in advance for omitting their names.

In addition to those I must thank in El Salvador, other people and organizations helped me with this book. At Loyola University Chicago, the Joan and Bill Hank Center for the Catholic Intellectual Heritage, and its director at the time, Mike Schuck, provided the initial funding for this project, allowing me to fly Rodríguez to Chicago for the interviews. Katie O'Donnell, also at the Hank Center, helped me with much of the planning and paperwork. I am very grateful to the Jesuit community at Loyola University, and particularly Father Dan Hartnett, S. J., who arranged for Rodríguez to stay at the Jesuit residence on campus while I interviewed him. The Office of Research Services at Loyola awarded me a generous book subvention and additional funds for my trip to El Salvador in 2008, as well as for the transcription of all of the interviews I conducted with Padre Rodríguez. I am indebted to Maria "Viki" Cano, who expertly transcribed the interviews. At the University Press of Florida I would like to thank Erika Stevens, who took on the project in midstream and helped me bring it to fruition. I particularly want to thank copy editor Jonathan Lawrence, who went through the manuscript with a fine-tooth comb.

I am grateful to a number of colleagues who read earlier parts of the manuscript and made useful suggestions: Deina A. Abdelkader, David Pion-Berlin, Peter Schraeder, and J. D. Trout. I would also like to thank the three reviewers that the press chose to review the initial manuscript, Ana Peterson, Yvon Grenier, and particularly Leigh Binford who provided many detailed comments and suggestions. A number of students at Loyola helped me in various ways: Aaron Martin, Jaime Vaca, Nate Gest, Nelson Wainwright, Sarah Newberger, and Kirstie Dobbs. I want to also mention the University of Santa Clara's Casa de la Solidaridad program in El Salvador. Santa Clara invited professors from various Jesuit universities to visit their program in San Salvador, and I gladly took advantage of this opportunity. Without this invitation I would never have met Padre David Rodríguez, and I would have worked on a very different, much less fascinating project. I also want to thank Curt's Café, in Evanston, Illinois, and its executive director, Susan Trieschmann, for providing such a wonderful and inspiring place to finish my work on this book.

Finally, I thank my wife, Kathleen Adams, who was always enthusiastic about this book's potential; and my daughter, Danielle, who met "Padre David" when she was six years old and drew a sketch of him wearing a beret.

Abbreviations

ACUS	Acción Católica Universitaria Salvadoreña (Salvadoran Catholic University Action)
ANEP	Asociación Nacional de la Empresa Privada (National Association of Private Enterprise)
ARENA	Alianza Republicana Nacionalista (Nationalist Republican Alliance)
BPR	Bloque Popular Revolucionario (Popular Revolutionary Bloc)
CEB	comunidad eclesial de base (Christian base community)
CEDES	Conferencia Episcopal de El Salvador (Episcopal Conference of El Salvador)
CELAM	Consejo Episcopal Latinoamericano (Latin American Episcopal Council)
COFIN	Comisión Financiera (Finance Commission of the FMLN)
CONAFIN	Comisión Nacional de Finanzas (National Finance Commission of the FPL)
CONIP	Coordinadora Nacional de la Iglesia Popular (National Coordination of the Popular Church)
CRM	Coordinadora Revolucionaria de Masas (Revolutionary Coordination of the Masses)
ERP	Ejército Revolucionario del Pueblo (People's Revolutionary Army)
FAL	Fuerzas Armadas de Liberación (Armed Forces of Liberation, the Communist Party's politico-military organization)
FAPU	Frente de Acción Popular Unificada (United Popular Action Front)
FARO	Frente Agrario de la Región Oriental (Eastern Region Agrarian Front)

FDR	Frente Democrático Revolucionario (Democratic Revolutionary Front)
FDS	Frente Democrático Salvadoreño (Salvadoran Democratic Front)
FECCAS	Federación Cristiana de Campesinos Salvadoreños (Christian Federation of Salvadoran Peasants)
FMLN	Frente Farabundo Martí para la Liberación Nacional (Farabundo Martí National Liberation Front)
FPL	Fuerzas Populares de Liberación "Farabundo Martí" (Popular Liberation Forces)
FTC	Federación de Trabajadores del Campo (Federation of Rural Workers)
ISTA	Instituto Salvadoreño de Transformación Agraria (Salvadoran Institute of Agrarian Transformation)
MERS	Movimiento Estudiantil Revolucionario de Secundaria (Revolutionary Secondary Student Movement)
MNR	Movimiento Nacional Revolucionario (National Revolutionary Movement)
MOR	Movimiento Obrero Revolucionario (Revolutionary Worker Movement)
MPSC	Movimiento Popular Social Cristiano (Popular Social Christian Movement)
ORDEN	Organización Democrática Nacionalista (Nationalist Democratic Organization)
PCN	Partido de Conciliación Nacional (National Conciliation Party)
PCS	Partido Comunista de El Salvador (Communist Party of El Salvador)
PDC	Partido Demócrata Cristiano (Christian Democratic Party)
PPLs	poderes populares locales (local popular powers)
PRTC	Partido Revolucionario de Trabajadores Centroamericanos (Revolutionary Party of Central American Workers)
RN	Resistencia Nacional (National Resistance)
UDN	Unión Democrática Nacionalista (Nationalist Democratic Union)
UNO	Unión Nacional Opositora (National Opposition Union)
UTC	Unión de Trabajadores del Campo (Union of Agricultural Workers)

1

A Man and Questions for All Seasons

Leaders and Ideas in Contentious Politics

Padre David Rodríguez drove his dusty jeep down a narrow dirt road on a cool, brisk day in February. The young priest had just celebrated mass with a fellow cleric in the canton of Los Laureles, located on the skirt of the majestic San Vicente volcano. The summit commands the vistas of the central region of El Salvador, rising to almost 7,200 feet. The aboriginal Nahuatl people called it Chinchontepec, meaning twin breasts, owing to its double peaks. Padre Rodríguez knew the volcano well, as he had spent much of his life in its shadows. He had grown up on his father's sugar plantation just to the northeast, and later he served as a priest in three different parishes to the north, east, and southeast of the volcano. Almost everyone called him "Padre David" with great affection and respect, and those who knew him well called him "Chele David," the nickname in El Salvador for light-skinned people. Some, as a fellow priest recalls, even called him "Chele Kennedy" since they saw in him facial features of the former U.S. president.

Rodríguez had grown up the son of a landowner, Lisandro Rodríguez, who made a good living but who was not one of the so-called "fourteen families" that constituted the country's powerful oligarchy. In addition to being a well-liked priest, Rodríguez was an excellent soccer player as well as a skilled guitarist and a singer of popular songs, writing a number of lyrics himself. His ability to enliven a church service with music enriched his role as a priest. For a charismatic and talented young man in a traditionally Catholic country, being a priest was enviable. As Padre Rodríguez snaked his jeep down the verdant slope of the volcano, probably singing to himself, dodging cattle, and waving to parishioners and friends he passed along the way, we can envision an idyllic pastoral setting; but this was El Salvador in

1977, a country at the cusp of a bloody civil war, and Padre David Rodríguez was no ordinary priest.

When he arrived at his parish church in the town of Tecoluca, Rodríguez took a large number of oranges out of his jeep, gifts from the people who worked in the *finca* (a farm or estate) of Los Laureles, where he had just celebrated mass. Parishioners often offered fruits of their labor to their priest in appreciation for the sacraments they performed or just out of sheer respect. Padre Rodríguez wanted to share his good fortune, so he distributed the oranges among the people in the market of Tecoluca, conveniently located directly in front of his church. For the rural poor of El Salvador, an orange was a generous offering. Rodríguez recalls that, as he shared the oranges, his assistant at the church, the sacristan, came up to him visibly shaken and pleaded, "Go inside, Padre, go inside, the son of Atilio Cañas is around here with a big pistol wanting to kill you!"[1] Atilio Cañas, the former mayor of Tecoluca, had been murdered earlier that day at a nearby produce market, but now some witnesses who claimed to have seen the killing were testifying that it was "Padre David," disguised as a woman, who had fired the deadly shot. At the time of the murder, however, Rodríguez had been saying mass at Los Laureles and recalls, "I didn't even know that Atilio had been killed."

Padre Rodríguez, ever prudent, quickly disappeared inside his church. Almost immediately, a number of National Guardsmen poured into the plaza that contained the market. The commanding officer demanded to know the whereabouts of the "fugitive priest," but he was almost immediately surrounded by parishioners. Those present in the market who spoke with the guardsmen insisted that Rodríguez had not been near the crime scene when Atilio Cañas had been shot. They pointed out that their priest had been saying mass at Los Laureles at the time of the murder. Rodríguez had an iron-clad alibi, with many witnesses. Higher authorities, however, had instructed the guardsmen to arrest him for the murder of Atilio Cañas, and they would follow their orders. As this exchange transpired, Rodríguez had already dispatched his sacristan to carry word of what was happening to Zacatecoluca, the capital of the department of La Paz, and only seven miles southwest from Tecoluca.

In Zacatecoluca, Father Rufino Bugitti, a Franciscan priest from Italy, knew exactly what to do. The prelate raced to Tecoluca, a trip that can take less than ten minutes if caution is thrown to the wind. When he arrived, he cleverly parked his car next to the parish house where Rodríguez lived, which was located alongside the church. The guardsmen were now pounding on the church door, impatient to make an arrest, but upon seeing Father Bugitti they turned their attention to him. The cleric implored the commanding officer to allow him entry to the church in order to talk with Padre David. When Bugitti entered the church, he rushed Rodríguez to the entrance of the parish house, the sacristan opened the door, and they put Rodríguez inside the trunk of Bugitti's car. Bugitti then exited the church, told the commanding officer that Padre David was not inside, and said that he needed to return to Zacatecoluca. The guardsmen were suspicious, but they focused on the church. And, thus, the Italian priest got into his car and sped away with the fugitive priest in the trunk. When the sacristan then agreed to let the guardsmen enter the church, they searched everywhere in vain. They would have to report to their commanding officer that the most wanted priest in El Salvador had eluded their grasp.

Father Bugitti raced back to Zacatecoluca with Rodríguez in the trunk of his car, but upon arriving they realized that the National Guard would most likely search for the fugitive priest there, since Bugitti had been inside the church in Tecoluca when Rodríguez had mysteriously disappeared. The priests then decided that the safest place to hide would be in the home of the bishop of the diocese of San Vicente, Pedro Arnoldo Aparicio y Quintanilla. Aparicio was Rodríguez's bishop, and he also happened to be one of the most conservative, traditional bishops in El Salvador. The bishop was also a "very strict and rigid" priest, according to Rodríguez. Years earlier, when Aparicio had served as the director of discipline in a Catholic school, the students had nicknamed him "Tamagás," after a deadly local snake.

Bishop Aparicio, as Bugitti and Rodríguez knew, was not at his home in San Vicente, so they were able to enter the house without having to engage with the prelate. Rodríguez also knew that Aparicio had "good relations" and "lots of credibility with the authorities." If anyone could help him out of a jam with the government, Tamagás could. Once the bishop returned, Padre Rodríguez was able to convince him of his innocence. It was clear that he had a solid alibi, and despite the bishop's growing frustrations with the young priest, Aparicio knew that Padre David was no murderer. Bishop Aparicio, however, was at the end of his rope, certain that this young, rebellious priest was "preaching communism rather than Christianity." So, although he eventually convinced the authorities that Rodríguez had not murdered Atilio Cañas, Bishop Aparicio removed him and the other parish priest, Padre Rafael Barahona, from the parish of Tecoluca, leaving the parishioners without a priest. Padre Rodríguez, his life in danger, decided to go completely into hiding. In fact, two years earlier, Padre Rodríguez had joined ("become incorporated into") the Fuerzas Populares de Liberación "Farabundo Martí" (FPL; Popular Liberation Forces), the largest of the revolutionary politico-military organizations in El Salvador. He made the right decision by going underground and "leading a clandestine life." In the next several years, the Salvadoran government and right-wing death squads would terrorize the Catholic Church, killing a number of priests, including the country's beloved archbishop, Óscar Romero. The political right would also carry out disappearances, tortures, and bombings to a point that, by 1980, death squads and government forces would kill or disappear about a thousand people each month.[2] Many of those who were arrested, tortured, disappeared, and killed were lay Christian leaders, trained by Padre Rodríguez and other religious leaders, who had embraced a new pastoral mission that focused on liberating the poor from their misery.

Enduring Questions

The narrative above, one of many remarkable events in David Rodríguez's life, is testimony to the extent to which some religious leaders engaged themselves in El Salvador's political crisis of the 1970s and 1980s. In fact, many Catholic leaders—nuns and priests alike—became leading figures in forming the country's Christian and popular organizations. These liberationist firebrands clashed with all those who wanted to preserve the status quo, who thought that the Catholic Church's new pastoral mission was too political and radical, namely, conservative church leaders, the oligarchy, the state and its security apparatus, and eventually the United States.

This book uses Padre David Rodríguez's life story to help answer a number of fundamental questions that arise from El Salvador's explosive political history, particularly how the Catholic Church helped to give rise to the country's contentious political mobilization in the 1970s. Cynthia McClintock has pointed out that not enough research has been devoted to revolutionary organizations and their leaders simply because it is very "difficult" to study them.[3] This book attempts to look into the actions of one key leader and his role in several organizations that were important to the rise of the Salvadoran Christian, popular, and revolutionary movements. The life of one leader will always be somewhat idiosyncratic, but by examining how one leader helped to mobilize peasants with a large number of grievances we can begin to more fully understand the origins of contentious politics and social mobilization. Also, if we can show that the work of one leader was not an isolated case but part of a much larger process of ideological renewal and contentious political activity, as we will see in the chapters that follow, then the life of one leader can help us to reach more detailed and general conclusions about social movements and their outcomes.

The Political Process of Social Movements

Perhaps the key questions in the study of contentious and revolutionary political behavior are, Why would people engage in life-threatening collective behavior, and why does this risky political behavior occur at a particular historical moment? To examine the impact that David Rodríguez and other religious leaders had in the rise of El Salvador's popular movement, I will use the framework articulated by Doug McAdam[4] and applied by Christian Smith in his study of liberation theology in Latin America.[5] The basic model posits that grievances alone do not explain the emergence of broad-based contentious political behavior. Instead, people contest an unjust status quo when opportunities for organization arise, when avenues exist for contentious organizations to develop strength, and when an insurgent consciousness emerges and moves people toward contentious or rebellious behavior. *Priest Under Fire* proposes to make a key contribution to this model by showing that contentious politics flowers at a particular point in history when revolutionary ideas emerge and new leaders employ those ideas to mobilize segments of the population with long-standing grievances, mostly the poor and marginalized. If the proper conditions are present—opportunities, organizational strength, and a viable insurgent consciousness—then new political entrepreneurs will be able to more effectively and more widely mobilize those with grievances, and leaders and masses can collectively form a powerful popular or social movement. Whether or not a movement can succeed in achieving its goals, however, depends upon a number of factors that we will also examine in this book.

What is most remarkable about El Salvador's political and revolutionary crisis of the 1970s and 1980s is that the Catholic Church was at the heart of much of the contentious political activity that mushroomed in the 1970s. As we will see, Catholic leaders embraced a progressive doctrine that motivated them to assist poor Christians to express their grievances and organize themselves in a manner that enhanced their ability to make political and economic demands. The church therefore provided extensive opportunities for those who were critical of the system. While the revolutionary groups (the politico-military organizations) operated clandestinely, in constant fear of being captured, for several years Christians were able to meet and mobilize in safe spaces—Catholic schools, training centers, seminaries, convents, and churches. These safe places allowed the Christian movement to grow exponentially for one decade. At the same time, the traditional political opposition lost its ability to effectively contest political power, since vote fraud became widespread. In the first half of the 1970s, religious engagement was the only safe manner in which to discuss grievances and organize the poor. The climate changed dramatically by the mid-1970s, but the Christian movement had already acquired so many followers that even the onset of state repression was unable to stem its strength. In effect, the Christian movement that commenced in 1970 gave "the aggrieved population the opportunity for successful insurgent action."[6] Clearly, El Salvador's initial phase of political mobilization resulted from the church's efforts at providing opportunities for carrying out political organization, while the state repressed the small rebel groups and the traditional political opposition.

Political opportunity alone, however, cannot guarantee that contention will grow into a national movement. Organizational strength is needed for contentious political behavior to expand broadly enough to become a viable social movement. No doubt sporadic contentious political behavior can be found almost at all times in many societies where serious grievances exist. Only when political contention becomes widespread and sustained over a reasonably long period of time, however, can a more sizable and important opposition to the status quo emerge. A sustained challenge to the system, in the form of a social movement, cannot occur, therefore, unless contentious groups have sufficient organizational strength to accomplish their goals and threaten the status quo. In the early 1970s, in El Salvador, the politico-military organizations were very weak, with few members and limited resources. The Catholic Church, on the other hand, provided a treasure trove of resources for religious leaders who desired to organize the peasantry and the urban poor. As Smith points out, powerful "organizations contribute five key resources to a social movement: members, leaders, a communication network, solidarity incentives, and 'enterprise tools,' such as meeting places, mimeograph machines, lawyers, office supplies, telephones, secretarial help."[7] In addition to these resources provided by the church, poor Salvadorans also had access to a number of formal and informal courses that would aid their empowerment. Political organizing via the church was a literal godsend, since Salvadorans with grievances all at once enjoyed access to a multitude of resources once they joined the Christian movement. Since the peasants of El Salvador were poor they were already used to working together, in solidarity, to survive. However, the liberationist movement gave them a much broader purpose to work together. Rather than working as a community for the sake of survival, they now had a reason to work collectively for a better future.

The third component of the political process model is the notion that an insurgent consciousness is necessary in order to convince large numbers of people to engage in risky collective action. As Smith argues, "insurgent consciousness is *a collective state of understanding which recognizes that social change is both imperative and viable*."[8] In a sense, organizational strength and a climate of opportunity are necessary but not sufficient conditions for the emergence of a social movement. Only when large numbers of people are convinced that change is urgently necessary and possible can a powerful and potentially successful movement emerge. We will see that new ideas embraced by the Catholic Church, and that eventually diffused to El Salvador, generated an insurgent consciousness among poor Christians. Religious leaders like Padre Rodríguez, however, served as the principal "transmission belts" for those revolutionary ideas.[9] While the political process model often sees leaders as just one element of organizational strength, the actions of Padre Rodríguez and other religious leaders suggest that leaders are vital for the formulation and introduction of an insurgent consciousness, and thus essential for the onset of widespread risky, contentious political behavior. The model also seems to focus more on the factors that facilitate the emergence of a social movement rather than on those that initiate the contentious behavior in the first place. Below I will expand on the role of leaders and their importance in creating an insurgent consciousness, since both elements are essential for the emergence of contentious political behavior at a specific historical moment. In essence, my argument is that widespread contention is generated only when a few political entrepreneurs, who operate in an unjust society, decide to risk their lives by challenging the status quo, and that they are most likely to be effective when they develop or use new, revolutionary ideas that generate a broad-based insurgent consciousness.

Why and When Will a Priest or a Peasant Engage in Rebellion?

Knowing why individuals engage in contentious political behavior is important, because a contentious movement cannot take place unless large numbers of people decide to take risks. A key argument that I make in this book is that contention begins when leaders act first and then convince many others—perhaps other leaders, but mostly followers—to do the same. Padre Rodríguez had a promising life before him. If he had simply followed the wishes of his bishop, Pedro Aparicio, he would most likely have been poised to become a bishop himself. Although scholars have found that those at the lower end of the social pyramid seldom rebel, it is easy to imagine that a poor peasant in a desperate situation with almost nothing to lose might choose to rebel. Padre Rodríguez, however, had much to lose. As our story unfolds we will see that although important grievances are a necessary condition for the emergence of political contention, large numbers of disaffected citizens will decide to challenge their government only after an "injustice frame" (insurgent consciousness) is created and broadly accepted, both by leaders and followers.[10] An objective condition of economic desperation such as the one that was present in El Salvador for many decades will not on its own necessarily move people to engage in risky political action, especially when facing a powerful state willing to repress its citizens. Rebellion most often requires that a number of leaders emerge who frame the existing injustices and grievances into a clear picture of who is to blame for people's suffering and how the current unjust social condition can best be altered. As we will see, in the early 1970s in El Salvador, many priests and nuns were instrumental in forging such an insurgent consciousness by crafting an injustice frame that moved the poor to engage in contentious political action.

Those who have written about the role of the Catholic Church in the development of El Salvador's revolutionary movement have identified what they term the consciousness-raising that was performed by priests and nuns in the early 1970s.[11] These scholars have convincingly argued that the poverty-stricken peasants, although living in a perennial condition of injustice, did not rise up until they were "awakened" by religious leaders.[12] In fact, almost everyone I interviewed for this book, including Padre Rodríguez, other priests, and former lay Christian leaders, mentioned *concientización* (awakening or consciousness-raising) as an essential step for the creation of the Christian and popular movements in El Salvador and for the crystallization of their own political awareness. This view, however, presents *campesinos* (peasants) as fatalistic and inert individuals who do not know why they are suffering and thus almost blindly accept their lot in life. Thus, for some scholars, the church awakened the Salvadoran peasantry and transformed them from fatalistic campesinos into liberated men and women.

What is missing in this long-standing explanation is the awakening of the religious leaders themselves. In El Salvador prior to the 1970s, priests and nuns went about their daily lives in the midst of poverty but, while certainly performing works of charity, did not challenge the unjust status quo and certainly did not call for revolutionary change. Padre Rodríguez refers to this type of ministry as "talking about the little birds and angels."[13] The priests and nuns who decided to awaken the poor were not illiterate peasants but mostly educated members of the middle and upper middle class, so their fatalism was not based on poverty or lack of education. Even those priests who came from relatively poor homes—like Padre Rutilio Grande, a Jesuit who was murdered—received an education with a cosmopolitan perspective via their religious training as priests. What happened in El Salvador was that some Catholic leaders were *themselves* awakened by the new, revolutionary ideas emanating from their church and from well-known theologians. The awakening of religious leaders then *preceded* the awakening of the peasants, and it is likely that peasants engaged in risky contentious politics because they now had strong allies they had never had before—highly respected priests and nuns who in the past had been part of the unjust system. It would be perfectly rational for peasants to think that, with the Catholic Church on their side, positive change would be possible in the near future. It would be completely reasonable for peasants to believe that if the church asked for reforms, the state and oligarchy would perhaps consider changing the status quo. The actions of religious leaders in El Salvador, as the life story of David Rodríguez suggests, support the notion that ideas and leaders are of paramount importance in explaining the timing of political contention in an unjust social context. In essence, contention is unlikely unless ideas and leaders give rise to a tipping point toward rebellion. As Malcolm Gladwell has put it, "Ideas . . . and behaviors spread just like viruses do."[14]

Doctrinal Changes in Catholicism: The New, Revolutionary Ideas

The first element for the emergence of a tipping point toward contentious political action is the introduction of new ideas that construct an acceptable injustice frame in a society already suffering from injustices and replete with grievances. For religious leaders in El Salvador, the notion that the status quo was corrupt and needed to be changed fundamentally as quickly as possible originated, ironically enough, in the Vatican. Much of the literature on the church's role in Latin America has rightly labeled the doctrinal changes that occurred during the Second Vatican Council a paradigmatic change in Catholicism.[15] The doctrinal changes were of immense importance to a large extent because of the new ideas—a new liberationist pastoral mission—that the bishops of the world proposed, approved, and then began to embrace.

In the early 1960s, many Catholic bishops and theologians had concluded that the Church of Saint Peter had become an anachronistic institution on the verge of irrelevance. As the world modernized, the pontiffs and the Vatican seemed stuck in antiquity. Padre Rodríguez jests that when he was ordained a priest in 1963, he may have been "the last priest of the Council of Trent" (held during 1545–63). As new ideas and organizations that beckoned to the masses emerged in the twentieth century, Catholics throughout Latin America turned their attention elsewhere, believing that the church was no longer relevant to their lives. To the surprise of many, Pope John XXIII, the "Good Pope," announced in 1962 that he would convene the Second Vatican Council.[16] This second council, the pope stated, would "open the windows" of the church and "let in some fresh air." What the council did was to put Catholicism on the side of the world's dispossessed, at least doctrinally if not in actual practice. The council dealt with many things, some of which had little to do with the secular world, but one key document, *Gaudium et spes,* begins with these lines: "The joys and the hopes, the griefs and the anxieties of the men of this age, especially those who are poor or in any way afflicted, these are the joys and hopes, the griefs and anxieties of the followers of Christ."[17] Many Catholics perceived *Gaudium et spes* as a particularly authoritative constitution of the church, since almost all of the world's bishops—more than two thousand—developed and approved the document. When the final vote on this church constitution was taken (yes, the bishops voted), 2,309 voted yes, while a mere 75 voted no.[18] Never in the history of the church had such an important, transformative document been formulated and blessed by nearly all of the bishops in the Catholic realm.

Earlier papal encyclicals, starting with Pope Leo XIII's *Rerum Novarum* (literally, Of Revolutionary Change; commonly known as Rights and Duties of Capital and Labor), had already started to give the church a more visible role in political and economic matters. As a result, in the 1900s, Catholic Action and Christian Democratic parties were established, closely linking the church and its social doctrine to civic and political organizations. In the 1960s, the pace accelerated and a number of progressive encyclicals, and Vatican II, led to a dramatically new pastoral mission that focused on the poor. The new ideas that emerged could have remained in documents that simply fluttered in the halls of the Vatican and theological centers were it not for the fact that two popes, hundreds of bishops, and countless priests and nuns embraced them and diligently tried to put them into practice.

Progressive bishops in Latin America not only welcomed the new posture of the church but wanted to ensure that the new ideas were applied to the region as quickly as possible. The result was the second Consejo Episcopal Latinoamericano (CELAM; Latin American Episcopal Council), at Medellín, Colombia, in 1968, where the bishops of the region met to consider how they could best implement the new pastoral that would put their dioceses at the service of the poor and dispossessed. This conference produced a final document with three important sections, titled "Poverty of the Church," "Peace," and "Justice," that spoke directly to the church's newly polished social doctrine and the conditions of injustice in Latin America. The document concerning the poverty of the church stated:

> The Lord's distinct commandment to "evangelize the poor" ought to bring us to a distribution of resources and apostolic personnel that effectively gives *preference to the poorest* and most needy sectors and to those segregated for any cause whatsoever, animating and accelerating the initiatives and studies that are already being made with that goal in mind.[19]

This passage yielded a powerful catchphrase—*the preferential option for the poor*—that came to define the liberationist movement in the Latin American church.

The "Peace" and "Justice" segments likewise provided ammunition for a more radical interpretation of the church's social doctrine. "Peace" promoted the notion of "structural violence." This concept was highly controversial in that it had important doctrinal and institutional ramifications for the church. For centuries, Catholicism in Latin America had been telling the poor that their lot in life was God's will and that if they accepted their fate and did not sin they would reap rich rewards in heaven. There was also the implicit suggestion that their lot in life might be due to their own personal sins. By embracing the idea of structural violence, the bishops of Latin America affirmed that poverty was *not* the result of personal sin on the part of the poor but rather "because of a structural deficiency of industry and agriculture, of national and international economy, of cultural and political life."[20] Thus, the poor were poor because the world's politico-economic structures were unjust. Moreover, it was the social sin of the wealthy and powerful that had led to these unjust structures. To fix the problem, the Latin American bishops asserted: "This situation demands all-embracing, courageous, urgent and profoundly renovating transformations."[21] The bishops did not call for revolution, but *profoundly renovating transformations* sure sounded like revolution to those who held economic and political power.

Perhaps the most important outcome of the Medellín Conference, however, was the imperative of a "new pastoral." For the pope and Vatican, the Mother Church had been principally a teacher, not a doer, except when it came to charity. For the Latin American bishops, the condition of the poor in Latin America necessitated immediate action, since they recognized that Catholicism shared some responsibility for the plight of the poor. As part of the power structure for hundreds of years, the church had been at least partly responsible for the structural violence perpetrated against the poor. An unstated rationale for the need for action was that the Latin American prelates, like the Vatican, feared that the poor were succumbing to Marxism and Protestantism, meaning that the church stood to lose its position as the champion of the downtrodden, the majority in the region. Yet, despite the fear of Marxism, the economic ideas that the Medellín bishops and even the Vatican had used to explain the state of the poor were similar to the dependency theory that Latin American scholars, who were highly critical of capitalism and sympathetic to socialism, had developed. Eventually, Catholic theologians used the progressive ideas promoted by Catholic social doctrine, Vatican II, papal encyclicals, and the Medellín Conference to craft what became known as liberation theology, or liberationism.[22] This new theology not only urged that the church side with the poor but argued that capitalism was savage and that socialism would better serve the interests of the poor. Despite the alarmist warnings emanating from those who were highly critical of this new theology, the vast majority of liberationists were neither Marxists nor proponents of violence. Liberationists, however, had certainly, and with good reason, become skeptical of reformism and advocated fundamental changes, which made them susceptible to charges of supporting revolution. Ironically, the liberationists called for the same changes that the recent papal encyclicals and *Gaudium et Spes* proposed, but the liberationists put a premium on action.

The ideational changes found in *Gaudium et Spes,* the papal encyclicals of the 1960s, and the documents of the Medellín Conference are quite complex, but the *preferential option for the poor* has been identified as perhaps the simplest way to summarize their key content. By the late 1960s, the Catholic Church chose to disassociate itself from the traditional elite (with which it had aligned itself since the colonial period) and side with the interests of the poor. In a sense, the church developed a new doctrine toward the poor, thus beginning the process of constructing an injustice frame that clearly explained why poverty and suffering existed in Latin America. The rich and powerful were guilty of "social sin" and structural violence, Christ favored the poor, and Christ fought for the poor and desired their integral—spiritual and secular—liberation.[23] If this new injustice frame was to move anyone to action and lead to an insurgent consciousness, leaders would have to embrace it and promulgate it with conviction. Consequently, the presence and formation of committed leaders would be the next step in the process of generating widespread political contention.

The Lack of Leadership in the Literature on Contentious Politics

Ideas alone cannot incite contention, since they must first be crafted into an injustice frame and then promulgated widely. Consequently, leaders are vital for the packaging and dissemination of an injustice frame and for the subsequent mobilization of people who have serious grievances. An important debate in the vast literature on social and revolutionary movements is whether contentious politics is the product of structural conditions or of the actions of key activists.[24] This sort of chicken-and-egg argument seems somewhat futile, since, like the chicken and egg, both elements are essential to the outcome: the emergence of a mass, contentious political movement requires the presence of both structural conditions *and* committed individuals. It is clear that followers, collective action, opportunities, resource mobilization, and an injustice frame are all necessary conditions for the emergence and success of contentious movements.[25] Leaders are also vital, however, and may even be the principal agents in helping to explain the precise moment at which contentious political action arises, yet most of the academic literature underplays the role of leadership.

Many scholars have lamented the fact that the study of contentious political movements has tended to focus on the structural conditions that lead people to challenge the status quo, rather than on the actions of leaders. Eric Selbin notes: "The study of social revolution has been dominated by structuralist conceptualizations that fail to recognize that social revolutions are creative acts, concrete episodes in which people pursue goals."[26] Likewise, Colin Barker, Alan Johnson, and Michael Lavalette write: "There is something of a black box in social movement studies, in that leadership has been under-theorised."[27] More recently, Marshall Ganz has bemoaned the fact that "social movement scholars have, with few exceptions, eschewed the [leadership] project."[28] This bias toward structural explanations has continued with the rise of newer models that focus on opportunity structures, resource mobilization, and the framing of grievances, such as the political process model.[29] Although they consider leadership, the new models mostly relegate leadership to a secondary or minimal place in the politics of contention. Leaders are often seen as a product of movements rather than as the creators or initiators of contention. For many scholars, therefore, much more needs to be done to understand the impact of leaders on the emergence and growth of contentious movements. The case of Padre Rodríguez suggests that these criticisms are warranted, since the actions of religious leaders in El Salvador, as we will see, help to explain the dramatic rise of contentious political behavior in that country in the early 1970s.

As stated above, the creation of an injustice frame is essential for insurgent consciousness to emerge, but who helps to package and disseminate the injustice frame that convinces people to express their grievances? Thomas R. Rochon posits that leaders turn ideas into "ideological frames."[30] While members of a large social movement may not share the same ideology,[31] leaders who helped to construct that movement are likely to embrace a somewhat homogeneous and precisely defined set of ideas. By way of definition, David A. Snow and Robert D. Benford assert that movement leaders "frame, or assign meaning to and interpret relevant events and conditions in ways that are intended to mobilize potential adherents and constituents, to garner bystander support, and to demobilize antagonists."[32] If revolution, or contention, begins in the mind, then we should try to understand in whose mind it first rears its head. Once we know where it is born, we can pinpoint those individuals who initiated the ideological framing for the movement, since they are the ones most likely to have started the process of political contention.

In addition to promoting an injustice frame, how else do leaders encourage the rise of a contentious political movement? Aldon D. Morris and Suzanne Staggenborg define leaders as "strategic decision-makers who inspire and organize others to participate in social movements"; more specifically, leaders "inspire commitment, mobilize resources, create and recognize opportunities, devise strategies, frame demands, and influence outcomes."[33] Consequently, leaders are essential for contentious movements in that they are active agents in most of the factors that promote political contention, social mobilization, and rebellion. Leaders are able to motivate and organize principally because they possess certain skills or advantages—charisma, organizational acumen, or official positions.[34] Even if we agree that leaders are important, where do we draw the line that separates leaders from followers? Those scholars who study leaders tend to focus solely on the heights of power, examining the principal leaders of a movement or organization.

For example, Clifford Bob and Sharon Erickson Nepstad look at how killing a leader can affect a movement by examining the murder of Archbishop Óscar Romero in El Salvador.[35] They find that when a leader is killed, a movement's strength can either be cut short or it can actually gain strength, as happened in El Salvador. The difficulty is in discovering why these contradictory outcomes occur. Perhaps the death of Archbishop Romero produced a stronger movement in the case of El Salvador not just because of his martyrdom but because, as we will see below, the Christian movement was already at a strong, mature state with the presence of countless young, committed leaders by the time the archbishop was murdered in 1980. When Romero was assassinated, liberationist priests and nuns had been organizing and "awakening" the poor for an entire decade. In fact, Morris has warned against devoting too much attention to key leaders and argues that we must examine what he calls "leadership configurations."[36] Moreover, Ganz suggests that "social movements are organized by identifying, recruiting, and developing leadership at all levels."[37] And, Leigh Binford notes that the strength of the church in El Salvador was to a large extent manifested through the "army of lay peasant and worker catechists" that priests and nuns trained in the 1970s.[38]

Leaders, therefore, not only help to initiate contention and to mobilize followers but also to facilitate and foment the training of other leaders, who become essential for the continued growth and strengthening of a movement. While no doubt a fountain of inspiration for the popular movement in the late 1970s, Archbishop Romero was in fact of no support for the emergence of the contentious political movement that commenced in the early 1970s.[39] The study of leadership should go well beyond examining those at the pinnacle of power and include the behavior of lower-level leaders, since the latter are often crucial to the rise, continuation, and ultimate strength of a movement. Salvadoran nuns and priests were precisely the ones who helped to start and fuel El Salvador's popular movement, so that, by 1980, when state repression was at its worst, the organizational strength of the Christian movement was at its height and thus could not be easily stymied even by intense state repression and the murder of a religious icon.

Padre David Rodríguez's life story will demonstrate in detail the salience of ideas and leadership in the birth and growth of El Salvador's peasant mobilization that began in the early 1970s. While his story does not include the mobilization of Salvadoran workers, other priests and nuns were involved in organizing the working poor. Nevertheless, El Salvador's civil war was principally a peasant rebellion, and thus the mobilization of the campesino is of utmost importance.

Why Did Traditional Catholicism Become Politically Engaged, and How Did This Choice Affect the Church?

The Salvadoran turmoil of the 1970s and 1980s also raises some important questions concerning the Catholic Church, since it was the doctrinal changes emanating from the Vatican that led to a liberationist injustice frame that inspired so many Salvadorans to action. Christianity started inauspiciously as the "church of the catacombs," referring to its early period when the Roman Empire tried to eliminate what it considered a dangerous cult. Those who followed the teachings of Christ hid in catacombs to protect themselves from the persecution of the authorities. Christians would meet in small groups, in simple, private homes. No grand basilicas or cathedrals existed; neither popes nor bishops led the faithful. When Constantine the Great converted to Christianity and made it the empire's official religion, Christians emerged from the catacombs and the church was transformed. Once the church was no longer in hiding, magnificent houses of worship were built, bishops lived in villas, and popes not only led all Christians but also served as the secular rulers of earthly domains, at times carrying out military campaigns. In fact, when popes were elected they were also crowned, a practice that did not end until the 1960s. The former church in hiding soon became the powerful and wealthy transnational Roman Catholic Church that we know today.[40] In Latin America the church was a stalwart defender of conservatism, supporting the hierarchical, elitist social order from the time of colonization in the early 1500s until its paradigmatic change in the 1960s, when its new doctrine led it to challenge the status quo and side with the poor.

Religions have not been strangers to political involvement. History is replete with tales of religious leaders who have questioned the status quo in order to create a better social order (or for less noble reasons). In the early 1500s, the Dominican friar (and future bishop) Bartolomé de Las Casas pleaded before the Spanish monarchs, Ferdinand and Isabella, for colonial authorities to treat the indigenous peoples of the New World more justly. At times the colonists in the Americas threatened Friar de Las Casas, since his admonitions to the crown hurt their financial interests.[41] Priests also inspired the independence movements in Mexico and El Salvador by calling for an end to Spanish colonialism. In Nazi Germany, Pastor Dietrich Bonhoeffer at first simply resisted National Socialism's ideology, but later became involved in the conspiracy to assassinate Adolf Hitler. Pastor Bonhoeffer believed, as did Padre Rodríguez, that "the church must question the state, help the state's victims, and work against the state, if necessary."[42] Another man of the collar who embraced political action was Robert Frederick Drinan, a Jesuit priest from Boston who ran for the U.S. Congress in 1970 and was elected to five consecutive terms.[43] Drinan's motivation to enter the political arena lay in his opposition to U.S. military involvement in Vietnam, although he was also a progressive who supported social programs. These religious leaders challenged not only their governments but eventually their churches as well. The examples from the United States and Germany suggest that the political involvement of religious leaders is not a phenomenon of the "developing world" or of non-Christian religions. For good or ill, religion will continue to be a sociopolitical force in the world, producing ideological and real conflict. Inevitably, religious leaders will at times become community and national leaders who will challenge unjust situations either directly or indirectly. In fact, religious leaders have enormous potential for political action owing to their respected calling and their assumed proximity to higher morality and authority. Challenges to the status quo will, most likely, often meet resistance from those who stand to gain the most from the existing order. Consequently, progressive religious leaders will invariably come into conflict with governments and entrenched interests when those leaders become engaged in promoting change.

The church had played a conservative role for centuries, so why did Pope John XXIII convene the Second Vatican Council in 1962 in an effort to dramatically alter the church's role in the world? It is clear that the Vatican would not have undertaken fundamental doctrinal changes if it was not confronted by a serious crisis—a crisis arising in developing countries, but most importantly in Latin America, home to the largest Catholic population in the world. John O'Malley has noted that two years before Vatican II, Pope John XXIII asked the world's bishops for their input and they "registered widespread concern about Communism."[44] In the early 1960s, the Vatican was worried that the church was going to lose Latin America, since the extant injustices in the region made secular ideologies and Protestantism more appealing to the poor.[45] The church, therefore, had to do more to help its faithful, most of whom were poor and destitute. Without the existence of a patently unjust context and the institutional crisis in the church, it is unlikely that the Vatican would have taken bold steps at the Second Vatican Council. Thus, most likely, the church's doctrinal change was inspired both by its concerns for the poor in Latin America and its commitment to institutional preservation. While ideas and leaders inspired contention in El Salvador in the early 1970s, those new ideas emerged from a church that was worried about the unjust conditions in which the poor lived, meaning that injustice remains the principal, necessary condition for the advent of contention.

In addition to understanding the motivations for the church's doctrinal changes that gave rise to the new pastoral, we will also want to know how the spread of liberationism affected the church itself. Since the church furnished ideas and opportunities for the development of the Christian movement in El Salvador, the strength and direction of that movement would depend upon the church's continued promotion of the new pastoral. We will see, however, that the liberationist undertaking eventually led to deep divisions within the church and to an ideological move away from the progressive ideas of Vatican II and the Medellín Conference. These changes, along with state repression, forced many organized Christians in El Salvador to join popular and revolutionary organizations, since the church no longer provided opportunities for political organization. Once the state began to attack progressive Christians, the followers of the liberationist cause joined forces with those who advocated the use of force against the state. Eventually, the safe spaces that allowed the Christian movement to germinate and flower in the 1970s were closed abruptly by the state at the end of the decade and eventually by the church itself in the mid-1980s.

Did the Actions of Liberationists Like Padre Rodríguez Help to Produce a More Just Society in El Salvador?

Similar to the lack of research on leaders, social movement scholars for decades neglected to study fully the consequences or outcomes of mass collective action.[46] More recently, a number of studies have surfaced on this topic, but nevertheless, "much work remains to be done."[47] This study hopes to contribute to this neglected line of research by identifying the reasons for both the accomplishments and the failures of the Christian movement that eventually became part of the revolutionary movement in El Salvador.

As we will see, the Christian movement that liberationists helped to create and mobilize focused on what religious leaders like Rodríguez called "redemptive demands." For the most part, the Salvadoran peasants and their religious advocates simply wanted access to land, better wages, and other benefits, such as credit and access to water for irrigation. Some wanted more, such as access to health care and education. The demands were minimal and reasonable rather than revolutionary, and the methods used for making these demands were peaceful and mostly non-confrontational.

These reformist efforts resulted in state repression, instigated principally by the landed oligarchy. Once the state repressed the Christian movement, many of the members of the movement became radicalized and engaged in more confrontational tactics; some chose to join the politico-military organizations. This shift from reformism to radicalism supports the notion promoted by some scholars that, in addition to the injustice frame that helps to convince people to become engaged in contentious political behavior, moral "outrage," revenge, and protection are also motivating factors for those who decided to engage in rebellion.[48] As political opportunities began to collapse, especially after the murder of Archbishop Romero, the only option for those who desired to continue challenging the state, or simply wanted to protect themselves, was to join the guerrilla organizations. Most Christians ended up joining either the FPL or the Ejército Revolucionario del Pueblo (ERP; People's Revolutionary Army), the second-largest politico-military organization. In effect, the Christian movement failed to achieve its reformist goals in the 1970s, because the state chose to respond to the minimal demands of organized Christians with repression. In early 1980, after a military coup, the government hurried to carry out a land-reform program, but by then the reforms constituted too little too late, particularly since the civil war had already started.[49]

At this point, the Christian movement's goals essentially became part of the goals of the Frente Farabundo Martí para la Liberación Nacional (FMLN; Farabundo Martí National Liberation Front), formed in late 1980 and composed of the five politico-military organizations that existed at the time. Organized Christians then fought for twelve years under the aegis of the rebel front. The FMLN, supported by an amalgam of opposition parties in exile and defunct popular movements, fought against the U.S.-supported Salvadoran state until a peace treaty ended the war in 1992. At first the FMLN grew in power substantially, but after 1983, under U.S. tutelage, the Salvadoran military mushroomed in size and strength and became more "professional." During the entire war, Padre Rodríguez worked with the FMLN in various ways in hopes that victory would liberate the poor. The FMLN, however, even with the help of organized Christians, and some nuns and priests, like Rodríguez, was not able to defeat the Salvadoran armed forces. As Jeff Goodwin proposes, and as we will see below, a state-centric analysis, while not fully adequate, goes a long way in helping us to understand why the Salvadoran state was able to fend off the largest revolutionary movement in Latin America.[50] After a faulty start, the Salvadoran state became more unified, and with support from a wealthy oligarchy and a superpower it was able to prevent the FMLN from winning the war.

Although the FMLN was not victorious, the peace accords that the two sides signed in Mexico City in 1992 did bring about a number of key changes to El Salvador. The Salvadoran government accepted that the FMLN represented a sizable segment of the population and thus agreed that it should become a legal political party. In essence, the government finally agreed to allow for full political contestation and participation, the hallmarks of democratic government.[51] The most notorious elements of the security apparatus, such as the National Guard, were eliminated, and the armed forces were reduced in size and purged of some of the officers who had violated human rights. As a result of the peace accords, Salvadorans hoped that the state would no longer torture, kill, or disappear its own citizens simply for expressing their political beliefs. Finally, former combatants—both soldiers and guerrillas—were given some land, but the extensive kind of land reform that the church and then the FMLN had called for was never carried out. The FMLN, via the twelve-year civil war, forced the demilitarization of El Salvador, helped to bring about the democratization of the political system, and won the right to become a legal political actor. These were solid accomplishments that could not have been achieved without the assistance of the Christian movement. Moreover, the FMLN was optimistic, as was Padre Rodríguez, that the right to participate politically would eventually yield other important changes, such as land reform and economic justice. Padre Rodríguez attempted to return to the priesthood after the end of the war, but eventually he became engaged politically once more, and was elected four times as a representative in El Salvador's Legislative Assembly. We will thus see whether or not his efforts to bring greater justice to El Salvador via the democratic process succeeded.

In trying to assess the successes and failures in Rodríguez's quest for a more just society after the end of the civil war, we will examine the actions of the FMLN as a political party, the stance of the church, and the quality of El Salvador's democratic system. As Paul Burstein has pointed out, democracy will tend to undermine the goals of social movements either because of its flaws or because of the way it works.[52] Although Padre Rodríguez is still close to and very attentive to the church, he now has constituents rather than parishioners. Instead of focusing on what the church should do, he says, "We need to make state institutions work for poor people." For him, the state should adopt the preferential option for the poor.

Why El Salvador, Padre David Rodríguez, and the Parish of Tecoluca?

If we want to understand the precise origin of a contentious movement, we need to know who did what and when in a country where a strong popular and revolutionary movement emerged. El Salvador is an excellent case study for a number of reasons, since the popular and revolutionary movements that developed in the 1970s were the most powerful that ever emerged in Latin America.[53] El Salvador is also a country where the structural conditions for revolution were clearly present, owing to the existence of a patently unjust political and economic system and the absence of any sort of land reform.[54] If any country in the world in the twentieth century exhibited the objective conditions for the emergence of rebellion, it was El Salvador. In fact, in 1932 the country was rocked by a mass uprising, led by

Farabundo Martí, a founder of the Partido Comunista de El Salvador (PCS; Communist Party of El Salvador). The results were tragic: the government killed around ten thousand people, including Martí, and passed a law that prohibited the peasantry from organizing, while the coffee-growing oligarchy turned political power over to the armed forces, which kept hold of that power with few exceptions until 1992.[55] El Salvador had all the conditions for the emergence of serious grievances and thus for rebellion: a repressive, undemocratic government; a landed oligarchy that maintained a patently unjust land-tenure system; and extensive poverty both in rural and urban areas. Nevertheless, decades went by before another rebellion emerged, to a large extent because of the state's willingness to use repression. If leadership appears to be important in the rise of contention in El Salvador, where structural conditions were begging for rebellion, then leadership is probably always important, since it could then be more important in cases where objective conditions and grievances are less conducive for contention to emerge.

The economic and political conditions for Salvadorans, however, became particularly acute in the early 1970s, with increasing land scarcity and rising inflation,[56] and thus there can be little doubt that contention was more likely to emerge during that period, especially since the state provided the political opposition with new opportunities to contest political power in the 1960s.[57] As the economic and political situation changed, a number of organizations and opposition groups emerged—some calling for reforms, others for dramatic social transformation—and this also greatly increased the likelihood that large-scale collective action would emerge. Peasant organizations, though "illegal" at the time, were formed. Small groups of leaders founded the first two politico-military organizations, the FPL and the ERP, in 1970. Opposition parties contested political power, most notably the Partido Demócrata Cristiano (PDC; Christian Democratic Party) and the Movimiento Nacional Revolucionario (MNR; National Revolutionary Movement), a social democratic party. And, the Catholic Church instituted its "new pastoral," inspired by Vatican II and the Medellín Conference. This appearance of opposition groups, highly conducive for the flowering of contentious politics, allows us to examine the historical timing of the rise of El Salvador's Christian, popular, and revolutionary movements to see which actors or organizations seem to be most prominent in fomenting the social mobilization that eventually became a strong, amalgamated rebellious movement in the early 1980s. The contentious social context of the late 1960s and early 1970s witnessed not only the growth and strengthening of popular organizations and political parties but also the rise of a number of influential opposition leaders from a variety of sectors.

Padre David Rodríguez was one of those new leaders who called for fundamental change in El Salvador. Paul Almeida writes that "the 1967–1972 protest wave generated a number of new oppositional figures from the labor, educational, and church sectors," and he names ten such leaders, including Rodríguez.[58] A number of other authors have mentioned Rodríguez as an influential liberationist priest and a key leader in the popular movement.[59] Phillip Berryman not only mentions him as one of the most active priests but also points out that the "parishes [of these priests] were later to become battle sites: Aguilares, Suchitoto, Rosario de Mora, Guazapa, Quetzaltepeque, Zacatecoluca, Tecoluca, Arcatao, Cojutepeque."[60] In 1969, Rodríguez became the parish priest of Tecoluca, an especially important parish to the church and to El Salvador, since it was geographically expansive, included large fincas and *haciendas* (ranches), and was in the country's para-central region, containing the most productive lands in El Salvador. The parishes of Suchitoto and Aguilares have attracted a great deal of attention owing to the well-known liberationist work of Fathers Rutilio Grande and José Inocencio "Chencho" Alas[61]—yet the parish of Tecoluca, led by Padre Rodríguez, and then jointly by him and Padre Rafael Barahona, was at the heart of the Salvadoran storm that commenced in 1970. The first peasant massacre in El Salvador, in November 1974, occurred in the hamlet called La Cayetana, in Rodríguez's parish of Tecoluca. Landowners in the area justified the killings by saying that the parish priests, Rodríguez and Barahona, had "indoctrinated" the peasants.[62] In the early 1980s, a fellow priest said that Rodríguez was "a great theologian . . . a prophet . . . [and] the most persecuted."[63]

In the narrative that follows, we will see that Padre David Rodríguez became an important spiritual and political leader in El Salvador: he was a key liberationist priest, was instrumental in helping to build the Christian and popular movement, was an important mid-level leader in the revolutionary front, and, after the war, became a leading political figure. Rodríguez's actions as a liberationist priest will give us a rich insight into how religious leaders helped to promulgate an injustice frame that mobilized peasants. During the war, his efforts will help us to understand the challenges that revolutionary and religious leaders faced in the armed conflict and the importance of state power and unity for the success of a revolutionary movement. And after the war, Rodríguez's role as an elected representative in El

Salvador's Legislative Assembly will highlight the difficulty that leaders and movements face when trying to bring about reforms via the democratic process.

A Note on Methodology

This book is a detailed case study of the life of one Salvadoran religious leader who played an important role in his country during a tumultuous historical period. The actions of Padre Rodríguez, however, while exceptional, were not idiosyncratic, since many priests and nuns and then lay workers carried out similar activities that helped to form a powerful Christian movement. Thus by examining the life of one key leader, particularly one who was there at the beginning and center of the political crisis, we can gain important insight into how religious leaders in El Salvador helped to mobilize citizens to engage in collective action. In a sense, the life of Padre Rodríguez provides a sort of smoking gun that uncovers the role of ideas and leadership in the complex process of political contention and collective action.

Personal interviews with Padre David Rodríguez and with 103 people who have known him provide the primary evidence for *Priest Under Fire*.[64] The interviews breathe life into the story and provide firsthand accounts for the analysis. Interviews, however, will always be problematic, particularly when examining an event that occurred decades in the past and when the key protagonist is a strong, charismatic leader. The goal of any scholar is to write a systematic, unbiased account of events. To be honest, it was quite difficult to spend two weeks with the revered "Padre David" and not be swayed by this man of principles who greatly loves and respects his fellow Salvadorans. Nevertheless, I felt confident that my scholarly neutrality would quickly return once I was out of his sphere of influence. After all, could this man really have done all of the things he had told me? How much was really true? How popular and ethical was he really? The controversy over the book *I Rigoberta Menchú* stemmed from the fact that the author did not verify some of Menchú's recollections.[65] If an author maintains too close an association with the subject, bias can undermine the objectivity of a book. While the reader will no doubt perceive that I present Padre David Rodríguez as nothing short of heroic, to a large extent this is how his followers viewed this priest who seemed to always be on their side. This is what made him such an effective leader, and thus to present him "objectively" is to reduce the power and mystique of his leadership abilities and personal appeal. To ensure that this book is not an unsubstantiated account of a key Salvadoran religious leader, however, I have verified all major events and actions in which Padre Rodríguez was involved. Fortunately, much has been written about El Salvador, and thus it is possible to verify and check facts. The interviews I conducted with Salvadorans who have known Rodríguez also helped me to verify specific events and activities. For example, Rodríguez talked with me about his actions in helping to win over workers at El Salvador's largest dam complex, Cerrón Grande, during the civil war. Another key event was Rodríguez's incorporation into an FPL cell composed of priests. When Rodríguez told me these stories it seemed to me almost incredible. However, I interviewed two priests who were in the same FPL cell, and they confirmed his story; and I interviewed a number of people who confirmed his actions at the Cerrón Grande Dam. Luckily, with these events, as with all of the key events that I describe in the book, other individuals or written accounts have verified his recollections.

The vast majority of the interviews I conducted in El Salvador were with people who supported liberationist and revolutionary actions during the 1970s and 1980s. Only a handful expressed some degree of disagreement with liberationism or with Padre Rodríguez. Everyone I interviewed expressed a high degree of respect for Rodríguez, his commitment to the people, his judgment, and his integrity. The people whom I interviewed, therefore, represent a biased, but judgmental, sample. I purposefully looked for people who had been "awakened" by Rodríguez, since the goal of my study was not to discover what percentage of Salvadorans disagreed with liberationist ideas but to discern how religious leaders inspired the people of El Salvador in the early 1970s to engage in contentious politics. I wanted to hear from his followers what compelled them to see Padre Rodríguez as a trusted and effective leader. I also wanted to establish proper timing in the rise of the Christian movement—to be able to confirm that ideas came first, the awakening of religious leaders came next, and then followed the training and awakening of lay leaders. Interviewing those who were moved to action by Rodríguez was the best way to accomplish this goal. The perspective of those who disagreed with or even despised Rodríguez is easily discovered simply by reading historical accounts of Salvadoran history during the 1970s and 1980s. This perspective is also evident in the book, in that the narrative recounts the steps the state and oligarchy took to capture and even kill religious leaders like Padre Rodríguez. No doubt plenty of Salvadorans hated the "red priests."

Perhaps the most satisfying part of conducting the interviews in El Salvador was discovering that my interviewees confirmed almost all of what Padre Rodríguez told me. Rodríguez had indeed led a remarkable life: he had functioned as a traditional priest, undergone a political awakening or conversion, challenged his bishop, defied the oligarchy and the state, trained and "awakened" many Catholic lay leaders, joined a revolutionary organization, carried out highly dangerous activities, and been elected as a member of the national legislature. What also impressed me when I was in El Salvador was that everyone seemed to light up when Rodríguez entered a room, his charisma still palpable in 2008 and 2013. Additionally, almost everyone seemed to mention his guitar playing and songs, as well as his soccer skills. Part of the importance of interviewing those who sympathize with a leader is to gauge his or her power of charisma, an essential quality for leadership.

No doubt there are some errors in this book, since re-creating history is a difficult task. However, as a scholar, I feel confident that I have captured the key outline of David Rodríguez's life as a priest, a liberationist, a revolutionary, and an elected official. His decisions, which included lying to his bishop, fathering two children, and justifying the use of violence, must be seen as part of a larger canvas. Just as George Washington justified violence and made other less-than-saintly decisions, we cannot dismiss the importance and convictions of a political leader simply because of the existence of several choices that some people may judge as unacceptable. Countless leaders have embraced violence and countless leaders have made questionable choices, yet many of those leaders are still revered for their desire to bring about a more just political or economic order. And, as we will see, what distinguished most religious leaders from leaders of political parties or politico-military organizations was that the former never intended to eventually acquire political power but simply wanted to help the poor and marginalized to become more effective at demanding their economic and political rights. After reading this story, the reader will be the ultimate judge.

2

The Training of a Traditional Priest

"I would like to be a pastor of souls"

The key events in David Rodríguez's early, and even adult, life take place in a small geographical region encompassing three of El Salvador's fourteen departments—Cabañas, San Vicente, and La Paz (see map 1). These three departments are in the center of El Salvador and east of San Salvador, the nation's capital. In the 1970s, their boundaries were also coterminous with the diocese of San Vicente, the domain of Bishop Pedro Aparicio y Quintanilla. The distance from the center of Cabañas, the northernmost of the three departments, and where Rodríguez's grandparents were born, to the center of La Paz, the southernmost department, where he currently lives and where Zacatecoluca is the capital, is a mere thirty-eight miles. Because he grew up, went to school, and practiced as a priest in such a relatively small geographical area, Padre Rodríguez became very well-known and respected throughout this region. In El Salvador, as in most Catholic countries, a priest is held in very high regard. Rodríguez remembers that his parishioners would never want to let him travel on foot, often offering him their horses or mules. Even his own mother addressed him as "Padre David" once he was ordained.

The Early Years

José David Rodríguez Rivera was born on April 11, 1940, to Lisandro Atilio Rodríguez and María Ana Rivera in a hacienda called Las Guayabillas, in the canton of Amatitán Abajo, municipality of San Esteban Catarina, department of San Vicente. He was delivered in the home of his uncle, José

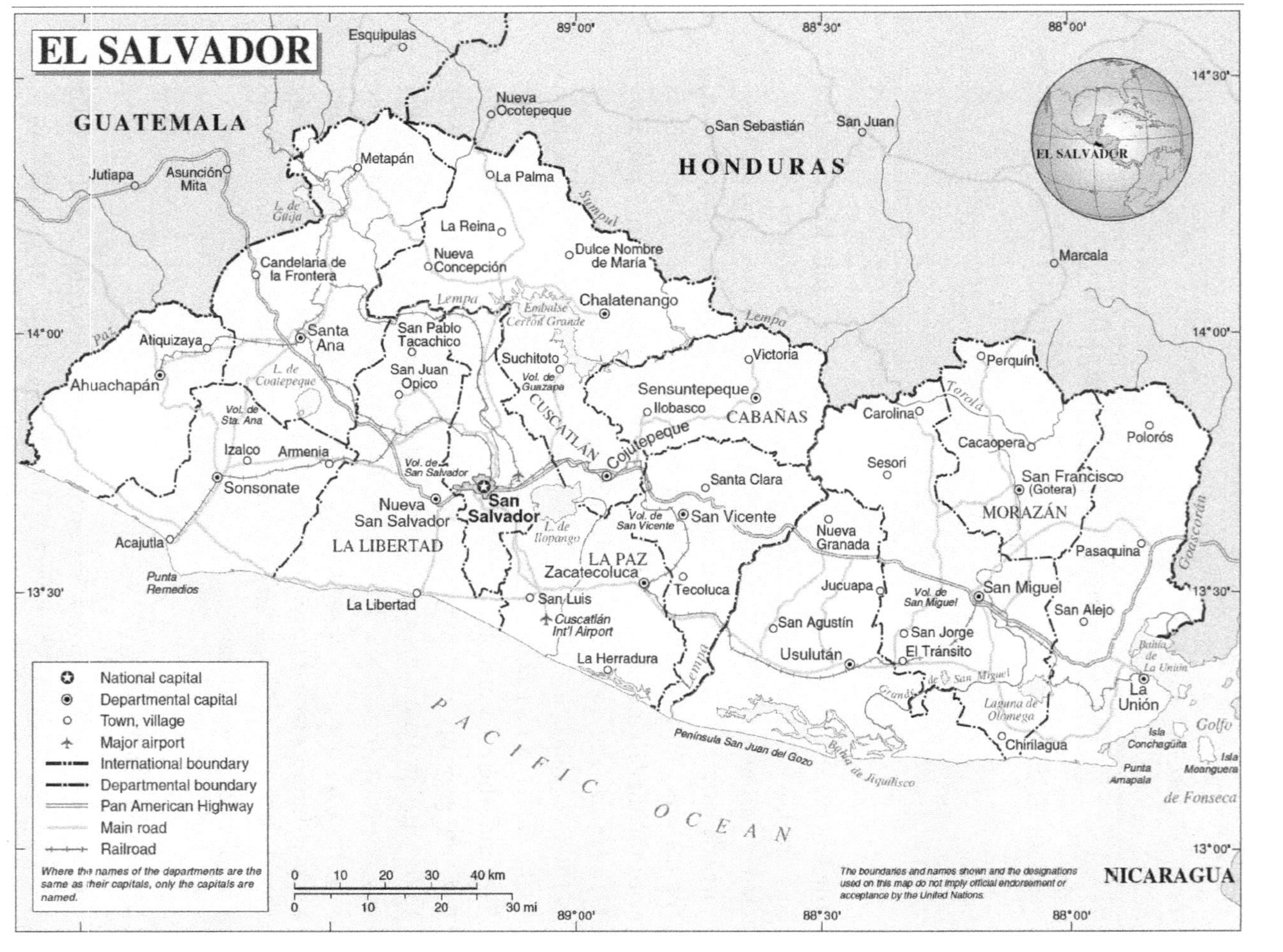

Map 1. El Salvador. Courtesy of United Nations Cartographic Section, Map #3903, May 2004.

Baires, called "Chepe"—a common nickname for "José"—who was married to Lisandro's sister. Although Rodríguez's first name is José, everyone eventually called him "David," perhaps presaging his eventual struggle against El Salvador's government and notorious security apparatus—a veritable Goliath. In fact, as we will see, Rodríguez would later write a song titled "David and Goliath."

Rodríguez's parents came from landowning families, meaning that he could be classified as belonging to a prominent rural family, or from the upper middle class. As one acquaintance put it, he was "from a favored family." His parents and grandparents were from northern El Salvador, the department of Cabañas, whose political center is the town of Sensuntepeque. Lisandro's father, a hacienda owner, came from a canton near Sensuntepeque called Santa Cruz, the place where Lisandro was born. Rodríguez's mother, whose family also owned a small hacienda, was from Cabañas as well, but from the town of Maquiligue, in the municipality of Ilobasco. Rodríguez characterizes his mother's and father's families as "small farmers," which in El Salvador means that you are quite fortunate, since you own a family farm. The vast majority of the Salvadoran population at this time, around 70 percent, either farmed very small plots of land—land that they owned, rented, or sharecropped—or had no land at all and labored in seasonal, low-paid agricultural jobs.

Rodríguez's parents met at a fiesta celebrating Saint Isidro Labrador, in a small town called San Isidro, which was "famous for its fiestas," and located between the larger towns of Ilobasco and Sensuntepeque. Once married, his parents set up their household in the town of Amatilan, in the department of San Vicente, not very far from where they had grown up. Lisandro was looking to follow in his father's footsteps as a farmer, however, so he moved his family to a hacienda, also in the department of San Vicente but near the municipality of San Esteban Catarina, about seven miles to the southwest. This hacienda was devoted to livestock and grains and is where Lisandro and María Ana had their first child, María Raquel ("Raquelita"), within a year after their marriage.

By the time David Rodríguez was born, Lisandro's father had purchased a new hacienda in the canton of Calderas in the municipality of Apastepeque, very close to San Esteban Catarina. The hacienda was known as either Los Huatales or La Laguna de Apastepeque, because there was a small volcanic lagoon in the canton.[1] Rodríguez's birth was registered in this municipality, because Lisandro had already decided to move his family to Los Huatales. Four more births followed: Benigno Antonio Rodríguez; Natividad de Jesús (who died at age four); Mérida Guadalupe ("Lupita"); and Ana María (who died at the age of two). Three of the surviving four children chose religious lives—David and Benigno as priests, Lupita as a nun—demonstrating Lisandro and María's influence as devout Catholics. Lupita, however, would eventually leave her calling, marry, and have two children.[2] Raquelita, although not choosing to become a nun, never married.

The hacienda Los Huatales was dedicated principally to the cultivation of sugarcane and the production of sugar. Rodríguez describes the life on a sugar hacienda as "very special" and a place where "there was great joy," particularly in the four months of harvest and milling (November through February). Lisandro would hire many workers for the seasonal production of sugar and its by-products, bringing music, celebrations, and frenzy to the hacienda. The work during this time was "very difficult," with the *trapiche* (mill) grinding the cane, and the cauldrons boiling the cane juice, often through the night. Rodríguez points out that, in contrast to the large sugar mills, at Los Huatales his father, the owner, would work as hard as, or even harder than, those whom he hired. He would also feed the workers the same food that his family would eat. When people arrived at Los Huatales, Rodríguez's mother would always immediately ask, "Have you eaten?" Indigenous people from Honduras would come with goods to trade in the city of San Vicente, and his father would allow them to spend the night on his property on their way to the departmental capital. Lisandro never charged them, and Rodríguez's mother would always feed them. The family would also celebrate the harvest jointly with the workers. Lisandro's children would work as well, the father saying, "off with your shoes and on with your sandals," meaning that they had to work like everyone else, from cutting sugarcane to helping produce the sugar. Rodríguez describes his father as hardworking and demanding: "My father was raised in the custom of the families of the north of El Salvador . . . whose children are . . . taught to work very hard. My father said that people should work from 6 a.m. to 6 p.m. He was very strict."

Although steeped with a strong work ethic, Lisandro was a kind, generous, and joyous man. After hard work, he was committed to providing entertainment—such as soccer, music, and fiestas—for his family, friends, and workers. Someone who worked at Los Huatales as a young man remembers that Lisandro would often say that "children deserve love, tenderness and understanding." Lisandro was motivated by the idea that people needed diversion from vices. Rodríguez recalls that his father would always say, "A soccer field that is open is a jail that is closed," reflecting a commitment to providing healthy outlets for young males. Lisandro also loved to sing and play the guitar and was often the center of attention because of his "good voice." Rodríguez and his brother, Benigno, inherited their father's love of music. Rodríguez recalls that his brother was more outgoing, like his father, and had a better singing voice, while he was more quiet, reserved, and shy, like his mother. Paradoxically, later in their lives, as El Salvador became gripped by conflict, Benigno would become more subdued, while David Rodríguez would emerge as a vocal, popular leader, almost always carrying his guitar.

Perhaps Lisandro's most important characteristic was his religious devotion. "He was very Catholic," recalls Rodríguez. Lisandro maintained close relationships with local priests, built a chapel on his hacienda, as most landowners did, and organized the annual procession and fiesta to the Virgin of Guadalupe, the patron saint of Calderas, the hamlet adjacent to Los Huatales. Religious fiestas, during the annual devotion to the local patron saint, represent one of the most important cultural and community events in Latin America. In Calderas the Rodríguez Rivera family was the financial patron of the annual fiesta and devotion to the Virgin of Guadalupe. Lisandro inculcated his Catholicism into his children at an early age. When the family would return from church on Sundays, Lisandro would use his two sons to get the message from the sermon to those on the hacienda who did not attend mass. Lisandro would get two chairs, have his young sons stand on them, and then instruct them: "Tell them, tell them what the priest said in church." Rodríguez recalls that he was very bashful at first, his brother being more outgoing; but after a while he became very comfortable explaining to the workers what the priest had said. At the service on Sundays, Benigno would sing, while Rodríguez would say the rosary. In effect, Lisandro was already encouraging his sons to become priests, or at minimum pious men, although he must have hoped that one of the two would carry on with the hacienda.

Lisandro was also a key leader in a lay Catholic organization called the Caballeros de Cristo Rey (Knights of Christ the Lord), founded by the bishop of the diocese of San Vicente, Pedro Aparicio. The general goal of the Caballeros was to promote Catholicism, but they also helped rid the region of vice, violence, and the "evils of communism." It was customary for peasants and people of the region to carry with them either a machete or a gun. While this made some sense owing to the need to use the machete for work, the carrying of weapons would often lead to violence at religious fiestas, such as the celebration of patron saints, when some of the men would drink too much. Obviously, priests and nuns found this violence at religious celebrations very disturbing. The Caballeros would promote the carrying of batons rather than weapons and would discourage drinking by finding illegal stills and fermentation equipment that produced *aguardiente* or *chicha,*[3] destroying the devices or reporting the illegal activity to the authorities. The government had established a Policía de Hacienda (Treasury Police) to a large extent to stop the illegal production and sale of spirits, so the Caballeros, even as a lay organization, were useful in this effort. Another role played by the Caballeros was to defame anti-Catholic ideologies, taking any opportunity to slander anyone or anything that seemed to promote "communism or the Protestant sects." The Caballeros were thus a traditional lay Catholic organization that helped to promote the conservative church as well as the power of the oligarchy. The Caballeros aided the "official party," the military-run Partido de Conciliación Nacional (PCN; National Conciliation Party), by discouraging people from participating in opposition parties that were deemed "communist," such as the Unión Democrática Nacionalista (UDN; Nationalist Democratic Union) and the Partido de Acción Renovadora (Renovating Action Party). In an election after the 1959 Cuban Revolution, when it was believed that an opposition party might win, Bishop Aparicio mobilized the Caballeros in the entire diocese and marched them to San Vicente to demonstrate against communism. Lisandro, being a well-known community leader, was a legionnaire in the Caballeros, meaning that he was in charge of one thousand Caballeros. In essence, the Caballeros had a political role, even if an indirect one.

As with all children who lived in rural areas in El Salvador during those times, schooling was either nonexistent, involved traveling long distances, or had to be provided by one's family. Since Rodríguez's parents valued education highly and were quite affluent by local standards, Lisandro decided to set up a school in a corridor of the family home so the children of Calderas could acquire basic education. David Rodríguez completed first and second grade under this arrangement. His teacher would travel from the small city of Apastepeque to Calderas to teach the children, and she recalls that "David was a very intelligent boy." Later, Rodríguez's father built a small school inside the hacienda walls, close to the main house, and eventually donated a small piece of property with a small structure that was turned into the regional school.[4] Lisandro's devotion to education, therefore, went beyond simply ensuring that his own children had access to schooling. Rodríguez recalls, "My father was very special, was very generous." These kinds of activities by men of means, however, were a double-edged sword in rural El Salvador. Some wealthy landowners believed that their generosity gave them the right to control local affairs and the local population. Some landowners, perhaps most of them, were not very generous, yet they believed that peasants should be grateful to them for providing them jobs.

The initial local arrangement, however, was not adequate to properly educate Lisandro's children, who, unlike the children of the local campesinos, would go on to higher levels of education. After several years of elementary education, Lisandro sent Rodríguez to school in Apastepeque's Urban Boy's School "Agustin Sánchez" so that he could complete his primary education. From very early on, the young Rodríguez exhibited a hunger for learning and a keen intellect. He performed so well in his first year at the school that they allowed him to skip fourth grade and go directly from third to fifth. Rodríguez believes that he "paid a price" for skipping a grade, since later in his education he felt less well prepared than the other boys. No doubt, Rodríguez also suffered by being in a rural school, normally less rigorous and well-equipped than schools in San Salvador or San Vicente. Since attending school in Apastepeque represented a tedious journey to and from Calderas, and Lisandro desired for his son to begin his religious education, an arrangement was made with the parish priest in Apastepeque for Rodríguez to live in the parish house during the week while he attended school. He would then go home to Calderas for the weekends and also when the sugarcane harvest required extra labor.

David Rodríguez lived in the Apastepeque parish house, known as "the convent," for three years. He recalls that he lived "under a strong discipline." Father Víctor Olivar was "very strict—he wouldn't let me go out; he wouldn't let me play; so I studied." Rodríguez also learned "all there was to being a good sacristan: tolling the bells, responding to the priest in Latin at Mass, sweeping the church, preparing the altar, saying the rosary, giving catechism, etc." Despite the honing of his religious skills, Rodríguez lamented that he could never toll the bells as well as the church's elderly sacristan. Rodríguez's apprenticeship as a sacristan earned him his stay in the parish house, but more importantly it reinforced the Catholic faith that his father had instilled.

Formal Religious Training

After finishing sixth grade, in 1951 Rodríguez went to study at the Minor Seminary "Pío XII" in the city of San Vicente, the political center of the department of San Vicente and home to the bishop of the diocese of San Vicente. Bishop Aparicio had recently founded the seminary, so Rodríguez was in the third graduating class, or "tanda." He remained at Pío XII until finishing secondary school at the Santo Tomás School and completing his preliminary religious studies, graduating in 1955. The Salesian religious order ran both the school and the seminary, where Rodríguez learned "Latin, religion, the Bible, liturgy, manners (*urbanidad*), and good customs." Rodríguez remembers that at the Santo Tomás School he was introduced to subjects that were new to him and that he had to "make a lot of effort . . . to put myself at the level of my peers." While at the seminary he met individuals whose lives would later intertwine with his, most notably Rafael Barahona, a fellow seminarian who would be a kindred spirit and share a parish with Rodríguez; Bishop Aparicio, who would be one of the bishops most opposed to liberation theology and who would suspend and attempt to excommunicate Rodríguez; and Óscar Barahona (no relation to Rafael), who entered the seminary at an older age, and would later become bishop of San Vicente, replacing Aparicio in 1983, and who would also attempt to excommunicate Rodríguez. Few of the students at Pío XII would continue their religious training, but Rodríguez, owing to his father's influence as well as his personal desires, persevered with the aim of becoming a priest.

When Rodríguez entered the Pío XII seminary, a conflict was under way between an organization formed by university students from San Vicente and Bishop Aparicio. The celebration of the patron saint of San Vicente had always been held in December, when students were in the capital on vacation. Aparicio, with the help of the Caballeros, decided to change the celebration to the proper date in March. This decision angered the university students, who had formed their organization precisely to carry out the patron saint celebration. Some of these students had known the bishop when he served as the chief of discipline at a well-known school run by the Salesian order in Santa Tecla (in San Salvador), called Saint Cecilia. The students at that school were the ones who had given Aparicio the nickname "Tamagás." When the students found out that Aparicio wanted to change the celebration to the month of March, they demanded that the bishop allow them to take out the image of San Vicente in December so they could continue to celebrate as always. Aparicio refused, so in protest the students broke into the cathedral and took the statue of San Vicente to the mayor's office. Aparicio became so enraged that he threatened to excommunicate the students responsible for the "sacrilege," and also for defying his decision. Nevertheless, after years of battling with the students, the bishop eventually allowed them to use the image of San Vicente in December while he celebrated the mass for the saint in March. Rodríguez says: "The church with all its power, with all of its Caballeros . . . could not end this tradition of the people."

In 1956, David Rodríguez entered the Major Seminary "San José de la Montaña," in San Salvador, the country's capital, "finally dressing in a cassock." The Jesuit order had established and led this "prestigious" seminary to provide religious training to men from all over Central America. The Jesuits exposed Rodríguez to a slightly more progressive version of Catholicism, as opposed to the conservative view of the Salesian order at the minor seminary. At the major seminary, Rodríguez developed friendships with seminarians from Guatemala, Honduras, Nicaragua, Costa Rica, and Panama, providing him with a broader, less provincial perspective. Nevertheless, Rodríguez attended the major seminary almost one decade before the Second Vatican Council ended, meaning that the church had not yet made its progressive shift toward the poor. At the major seminary, Rodríguez studied philosophy from Father Ignacio Ellacuría, a respected Spanish Jesuit, who would become a leading liberation theologian and would be murdered in 1989 by the Salvadoran military. Rodríguez also met Father Rutilio Grande, who offered classes on the Bible and would be killed by security forces in 1977 for his liberationist stance. The seminarians who were more "open" (progressive) would learn most from Father Ladislao Segura, who would urge the students to be close to the people and to know how the "word of God" related to the history of El Salvador. Nevertheless, Rodríguez states that at this time he was socially conservative, staying away from "politics." Although acquiring a global education and receiving training for a respected profession, so important for a potential leader, the liberationist outlook that would later make him a progressive "spiritual guide," as one individual called him, was yet to be developed.

Seminarians were expected to study most of the time, and social events, which had been common among the Salesians in San Vicente, were few and far between at the major seminary. Students were also expected to wear their cassock and a black, wide-brimmed hat whenever exiting the semi-

Figure 2.1. Rodríguez swinging a sledgehammer as a young seminarian at the Major Seminary "San José de la Montaña." The seminarians were putting up a large tent for an annual fundraising event. By permission of the Rodríguez Henríquez family.

nary grounds. The young seminarians loathed these cumbersome trappings and resisted wearing the traditional, Roman-inspired garb, which seemed foolhardy in a tropical climate. Rodríguez engaged in a "minor rebellion," as did other seminarians, by not wearing the hat and by wearing knee-length shorts when he played soccer—acts that would pale in comparison to those of future years. The church in El Salvador at this pre–Vatican II period was still excessively traditional despite the influence of the more cosmopolitan and intellectual Jesuits.

In 1959, Rodríguez went to study his first year of theology at the Major Seminary of Guadalajara, Mexico. At the time, Father José Salazar López, who eventually became the archbishop of Guadalajara and was named a cardinal, was the rector of the seminary. Bishop Aparicio had sent Rodríguez and the other seminarians—"about twelve to fifteen"—from the diocese of San Vicente to Guadalajara, because he was not pleased with the progressive influence of the Jesuits at the major seminary. Rodríguez believes that

Aparicio worked to acquire scholarships in Mexico for his seminarians so they would receive a more conservative perspective. Even before Vatican II, conservative prelates were suspicious of the Jesuits and their worldly ideas.

The situation for the church in Mexico was very different from that in El Salvador and most other Latin American countries. After the Mexican Revolution (1910–20), secularism prevailed and the church had to operate in a climate of suspicion and proscription. Rodríguez recalls that, since the Mexican Constitution was anticlerical, the seminarians studied there under pretense and religious life was a much more private affair than in El Salvador. The seminarians would wear civilian clothes, which made even Rodríguez, who had resisted wearing the black cassock, feel "a little strange." Religious processions, so common in every part of El Salvador, were absent in Mexico, except for ones in very small, rural towns. Foreign seminarians could not study legally in Mexico. To skirt the law, the church would create a false identity for the seminarians. Rodríguez was told, "You are going to say that you are a typographer." He was even taken to a printing press so he could see what a typographer did. If questioned by a government official, he could say that he was in Mexico working as a typographer and even be able to explain what his job entailed and where he worked. Because the seminarians did not have student visas, they were required to leave the country every time their short-term work visas expired, which Rodríguez did three times. The Salvadorans would travel from Guadalajara to Guatemala by bus. In Mexico City they would stay in the house of a family that helped the church, meaning that the bishops, priests, and nuns in Mexico had developed ties with many believers who wished to help the church operate effectively and in defiance of the government. The Salvadoran seminarians were so ill-funded that they had to do odd jobs in order to raise the money needed for the bus trip and for other necessities. Ironically, Rodríguez was already learning how to live a clandestine life, in defiance of a state, even as he was studying to be a priest. This "illegal" life was not only condoned but organized and encouraged by the church itself. When persecuted, the church would, like most institutions, promote its vital interests even if forced to break laws and operate underground.

The bishops of the Conferencia Episcopal de El Salvador (CEDES; Episcopal Conference of El Salvador) were eventually able to convince Bishop Aparicio and other bishops to bring back the seminarians they had sent abroad in order to "strengthen" the major seminary in San Salvador. When Rodríguez returned from Mexico he had several months to wait before the beginning of the second year in the major seminary, so to fill the time he taught classes in the Minor Seminary Pío XII, getting his first taste of teaching, an experience that would come in handy in the future. Rodríguez then returned to the major seminary, where he continued to study theology until graduating in 1963.

Prior to his ordination, Rodríguez decided to do the spiritual exercises of Saint Ignatius of Loyola, which took roughly four weeks to accomplish. Many priests and seminarians in El Salvador, including the future archbishop Óscar Romero, chose to perform these exercises, most likely because the Jesuits ran the major seminary. Most priests and seminarians completed the "normal exercises," which lasted one week, but Rodríguez opted for the longer period of spiritual reflection. He recalls that during his time in the seminaries and while he conducted the exercises, he "never had any doubts" about being a priest. He felt a true calling for the priesthood.

On December 29, 1963, José David Rodríguez Rivera was ordained as a priest, achieving his principal life's goal. He chose December 29 because it is the feast day of the prophet King David. Since he had not yet turned twenty-four, a requirement for ordination, the Jesuits at the seminary sought and obtained special dispensation from Rome so the ordination could take place. Soon after his ordination, Rodríguez celebrated his first mass, on January 6, 1964, in the parish house chapel in Apastepeque, where he had learned to be a sacristan. His mother and father were overjoyed and proud. Rodríguez had more good news for his family. Owing to his recognized potential, he was awarded a scholarship to study canon law at the renowned Pontifical University at Comillas, Spain, referred to simply as Comillas, which was also run by the Jesuit order. Consequently, from late January 1964 to June 1965, Rodríguez worked toward a degree in canon law at Comillas, where he took courses from the well-known theologian Eduardo Fernández Regatillo, whose books were used at the major seminary in San Salvador.[5]

While in Spain, Rodríguez met and became "good friends" with a priest from Argentina, Alejandro Mayol, who left a "good mark" in his life. Mayol belonged to the "worker priest" movement and was committed to the notion that priests should involve themselves in the lives of the poor. Worker priests would "leave their parishes and work" at a regular, usually menial, job.[6] Rodríguez points out that Mayol convinced him that priests "should not be supported by the people" but should instead work to support themselves. Rodríguez's relationship with Mayol was also musical, since both

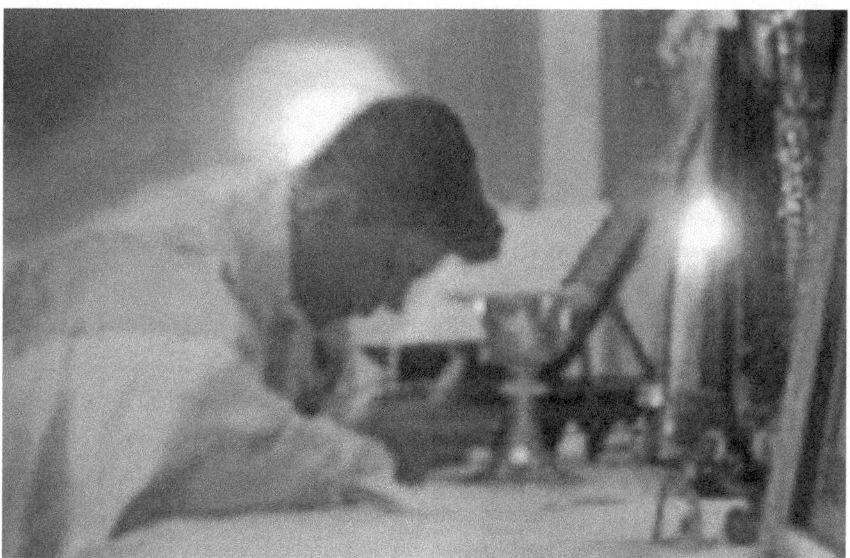

Figure 2.2. Rodríguez offering his first mass, in January 1964, in the parish house chapel in Apastepeque. By permission of the Rodríguez Henríquez family.

men liked to sing and play the guitar. While studying at Comillas, Rodríguez purchased a classical guitar, took lessons, and wrote the lyrics for three songs that Mayol recorded. One of these songs, titled "David and Goliath," would later become popular in El Salvador's Christian movement. Rodríguez points out that at the time he wrote the song his lyrics were conventional, so the battle between David and Goliath referred to the battle between the church and atheists. Father Mayol's songs, on the other hand, though inspired by the Bible, always had a strong social message. Later in his life, as we will see, Rodríguez changed the lyrics of "David and Goliath" to highlight the struggle between the peasants and the government of El Salvador.

While studying at Comillas, Rodríguez toured around Spain when he could, taking in the major sights. A dutiful son and sibling, he would send postcards and photos to his family in Calderas. In one photograph we see Rodríguez from behind, while he is facing a Spanish landscape of gentle, rolling hills, his black cassock flowing in the wind. Before him are many grazing sheep, though the shepherd is not visible. On the back of the photo, which he sent to his family, Rodríguez wrote, "The pastor with his sheep, something which I like very much, but I would like to be a pastor of souls."

Clearly, Rodríguez, like most priests at the time, was focused simply on the spiritual salvation of believers.

Upon completing his studies, Rodríguez was offered a scholarship to study international law at the Pontifical Ecclesiastical Academy in Rome, where priests receive training to enter the Vatican's diplomatic corps. A Spanish priest from Bilbao, whom Rodríguez had befriended while at Comillas, was offered two scholarships to the academy by his bishop, and he offered the second to Rodríguez. So, the two priests travelled to Rome in September 1965, ready to start their advanced and coveted training. Rodríguez recalls that he felt very uncomfortable at first, since the academy was "very formal and ceremonial," with dinners replete with gold silverware. After only three months at the academy, however, Bishop Aparicio saved him from his discomfort by recalling the young priest back to El Salvador. Upon reflection, Rodríguez considers that his educational experiences in Spain and Rome were "very conservative," despite the fact that Vatican II was already beginning to change the church during those years. If he had stayed in Rome, Rodríguez could very well have become a papal nuncio, and his life would have taken a very different path.

The New Church: Catholic Social Doctrine and Vatican II

While Rodríguez had been away from El Salvador, the Catholic Church underwent a doctrinal transformation, what one scholar describes as the creation of a "powerful and pervasive paradigm."[7] Pope John XXIII had called for a Second Vatican Council of all the world's bishops, which the pontiff inaugurated in fall 1962. The four-year-long council produced a number of documents that led to fundamental changes in Catholicism. These changes, however, at least their political and economic content, had started much earlier with the advent of what is known as Catholic social doctrine. In 1891, Pope Leo XIII issued the encyclical *Rerum Novarum* (Of Revolutionary Change), which is considered the wellspring of this doctrine. In his encyclical, the pope called for living wages and the right for workers to organize, and he urged governments to protect the weakest members of society. As workers associations were emerging in Europe, influenced by anarchist, Marxist, and socialist ideas, the Catholic Church worried that Christians would be seduced by these secular ideologies. Consequently, Leo XIII found it imperative to take a stance in support of the world's workers so they would have an alternative to the lure of "crafty agitators."[8]

In 1931, after the Great Depression shook the world's capitalist democracies, Pope Pius XI followed with a new social encyclical, *Quadragesimo Anno* (literally, In the Fortieth Year; also known as On Reconstruction of the Social Order). Building on the concerns of the earlier pope, Pius XI leveled a biting attack against capitalism, softened the critique of socialism, and discussed the need to involve lay leaders in the social work of the church. While defending the right to private property, the pontiff attempted to balance it with the needs of the "common good." Thus, prior to the 1960s, the Catholic Church had already become increasingly engaged with the world's most pressing *earthly* problems, seeing itself as having a say in economic and political affairs, albeit only tangentially. To a large extent, this move was precipitated by threats to the church's social standing coming first from atheistic Marxist ideology and then from savage capitalism, which seemed to worship profit rather than God.

Catholic social doctrine moved at a snail's pace between 1891 and 1960, but in the 1960s it accelerated too fast for many of the church's leaders and followers. That tumultuous decade brought a doctrinal paradigm shift that left many believers happy but also convinced conservatives in the church that even the Vatican had gone too far. Prior to the opening of Vatican II, in May 1961, Pope John XXIII, known as the "Good Pope," issued a powerful encyclical, *Mater et Magistra* (literally, Mother and Teacher; also known as On Christianity and Social Progress), and before the closing of Vatican II he issued yet another encyclical, *Pacem in Terris* (literally, Peace on Earth; also known as On Establishing Universal Peace in Truth, Justice, Charity, and Liberty), in April 1963, both of which continued to push the church's social doctrine into more progressive territory. Previous encyclicals had focused on the domestic problems of countries, but *Mater et Magistra* acknowledged the global North-South divide and asked the affluent nations to help the developing world. John XXIII also highlighted the plight of rural areas in the poor countries. About the rural poor, the pope wrote, "there is a manifest injustice in placing a whole group of people, namely, the farmers, in an inferior economic and social status, with less purchasing power than required for a decent livelihood."[9] In *Pacem in Terris*, John XXIII continued his assault on global inequality, but with an increasingly political bent. He called on Christians to "take an active part in government," guided by Christian ideals. He also discussed the notion of unjust laws: "If civil authorities pass laws or command anything opposed to the moral order and consequently contrary to the will of God, neither the laws made nor the authorizations granted can be binding on the consciences of the citizens."[10] Clearly, the Vatican was reaching out to the poor and calling on the wealthy to accept a more just economic system at both the national and the international level. Additionally, the pope suggested that God's laws were superior to secular laws and called on Christians to become active agents in promoting social justice.

We have already seen that *Gaudium et Spes* not only added to Catholic social doctrine but was also seen as an authoritative constitution of the church, since the vast majority of the world's bishops approved the document at Vatican II. While *Rerum Novarum* had suggested that states should side with the weakest members of society, the church was now committing itself to take on the role of champion of the poor. *Gaudium et Spes* continued to push this commitment by pointing out that while the church did not have a direct political or economic role, "when circumstances of time and place produce the need, she can and indeed should initiate activities on behalf of all men, especially those designed for the needy, such as the works of mercy and similar undertakings." Not only would the church promote the interests of the poor, but "she" would "initiate activities" on behalf of the weak. *Gaudium et Spes* also reinforced the idea of common or social property, stressing that the right to private property was legitimate only when used for just social ends. It thus supported the expropriation of private property when necessary. The document also promoted ideas that would resonate strongly in much of Latin America:

> In many underdeveloped regions there are large or even extensive rural estates which are only slightly cultivated or lie completely idle for the sake of profit, while the majority of the people either are without land or have only very small fields, and, on the other hand, it is evidently urgent to increase the productivity of the fields. Not infrequently those who are hired to work for the landowners or who till a portion of the land as tenants receive a wage or income unworthy of a human being, lack decent housing and are exploited by middlemen. Deprived of all security, they live under such personal servitude that almost every opportunity of acting on their own initiative and responsibility is denied to them and all advancement in human culture and all sharing in social and political life is forbidden to them.[11]

This statement accurately described the situation in which Salvadoran campesinos found themselves. In addition to not "sharing in social and political life," Salvadoran peasants were not even allowed to organize, and the political system shut out virtually all opposition. The document also emphasized citizens' right to political participation and captured the key problem with most Latin American political systems in the late 1960s: "It is inhuman for public authority to fall back on dictatorial systems or totalitarian methods which violate the rights of the person or social groups." This political critique was aimed at Cuba as well as at right-wing military dictatorships, but by the mid-1970s most of the people in Latin America would live under repressive right-wing regimes, rather than under communism.

Pope John XXIII lived only long enough to preside over the sessions in the first year of the Second Vatican Council. On June 21, 1963, Pope Paul VI was crowned as the new pontiff and very quickly expressed his full support for continuing Vatican II.[12] In 1967, less than two years after the closure of the council, Paul VI issued another powerful encyclical, *Populorum Progressio* (The Development of Peoples), making the church's social doctrine not only more progressive but, some believe, even revolutionary. In addition to supporting several of the points made by previous pontiffs and by *Gaudium et Spes*, Paul VI made two particularly important contributions, both of which again applied perfectly to Latin America. The encyclical states:

> Highly industrialized nations export their own manufactured products, for the most part. Less developed nations, on the other hand, have nothing to sell but raw materials and agricultural crops. As a result of technical progress, the price of manufactured products is rising rapidly and they find a ready market. But the basic crops and raw materials produced by the less developed countries are subject to sudden and wide-ranging shifts in market price; they do not share in the growing market value of industrial products.[13]

In effect, Paul VI was affirming one of the most widely accepted academic theories in Latin America: that the capitalist North exploited the developing South via an unfair, capitalist trade arrangement. The most radical description of this exploitative trade relationship was found in the highly influential "dependency theory," popular among many intellectuals in Latin America, the United States, and Europe. Dependency theory was derived from the work of Argentine economist Raul Prebisch as well as from Marxist and Leninist class analysis. Clearly, critical social theory was influencing the church and its theologians, who were the intellectual leaders in the development of the progressive doctrines that sprouted in the 1960s. Yet even those who eschewed this critical theory accepted the notion that the wealthy capitalist nations benefited unfairly from their trade relationship with the developing world.

The unjust state of affairs in Latin America begged for change. Paul VI wrote: "Changes must be made; present conditions must be improved." How would such change take place, though, via reform or via revolution? This was perhaps the most controversial question of the decade in Latin America, owing to the 1959 Cuban Revolution. Certainly the pontiff did not support or promote violence or a Marxist revolution. Nevertheless, one passage in *Populorum Progressio* would later be quoted extensively by liberationists to justify revolutionary change:

> We know, however, that a revolutionary uprising—*save where there is manifest, long-standing tyranny which would do great damage to fundamental personal rights and dangerous harm to the common good of the country*—produces new injustices, throws more elements out of balance and brings on new disasters.[14]

While the main intent of this passage was to point to the folly of revolution owing to its harsh, and particularly totalitarian, outcomes, the pope acknowledged that uprisings were acceptable in extreme cases of "manifest, longstanding tyranny." The Catholic liberationists would focus on the pope's exception clause because the situation in many Latin American countries, and certainly in El Salvador, included long-standing tyranny that trounced on personal rights and harmed most citizens. The natural conclusion for many church progressives was that, from a Christian perspective, rebellion was justified in Latin America given the unjust state of affairs.

The church's social doctrine, as it stood toward the end of the 1960s, promoted the following ideas:

- Both capitalism and socialism are destructive ideologies.
- Immediate and fundamental change is needed to bring about peace and justice.
- Rebellion is justified where long-standing tyranny exists.
- Catholics should take concrete steps to help the poor.

These Vatican-inspired, revolutionary ideas would move many religious leaders in Latin America to action, leading many priests and nuns to engage in contentious political activities.

The Still-Traditional Parish Priest

The doctrinal earthquake produced by Vatican II had yet to be felt in the small, traditional country of El Salvador when Padre Rodríguez returned to the San Vicente diocese in December 1965, prepared and eager to start his career as a parish priest. Bishop Aparicio gave the young priest a number of duties upon his return. First, and most important, Rodríguez was assigned his first parish in the town of Santo Domingo, a "small parish" with four cantons, only about seven miles west-northwest of his father's hacienda in Calderas. Aparicio also made him chaplain of the Divine Savior of the World School, located in Santo Domingo, which was administered by the sisters of a congregation founded by the bishop in 1956, the Daughters of the Divine Savior.[15] Bishop Aparicio also made him chaplain to the Fifth Infantry Brigade, headquartered near the city of San Vicente. The position came with the honorary rank of captain, technically making the newly minted priest a military man as well. Because Aparicio "spent most of his time in Santo Domingo, overseeing the order [of nuns] he had founded, rather than in San Vicente," he also turned Rodríguez into his informal, personal secretary. The new priest would answer the bishop's phone, "edit correspondence," communicate with other priests in the diocese, and do whatever "special missions" his bishop would assign to him. Finally, Aparicio put Rodríguez in charge of short courses on Christianity, called "cursillos de Cristianidad." While performing this task, Rodríguez first came in contact with the future archbishop Óscar Romero, who was in charge of these courses in the diocese of San Miguel. At the parish of Santo Domingo, Rodríguez's relationship with his bishop was excellent, since Aparicio saw him as an accomplished, well-formed young priest with great potential. The bishop was quite correct in his assessment; Rodríguez admits that in those years he held a relatively "conservative outlook," in the sense that he would "not get involved at all in politics."

In 1968, Aparicio transferred Rodríguez to the parish of the church of Nuestra Señora del Pilar in San Vicente, a more prestigious assignment since it was at the heart of the diocese, in the departmental capital. Aparicio's diocese, as stated above, comprised the departments of Cabañas to the north, San Vicente, and La Paz to the south, with a total population of just over 406,000 people, almost 99 percent of them at least nominally Catholic. Bishop Aparicio ministered to his See of thirty-one parishes with the aid of twenty-seven diocesan priests (priests trained to serve in a diocese rather

Figure 2.3. Rodríguez (*right*) with members of the Fifth Infantry Brigade soccer team. By permission of the Rodríguez Henríquez family.

than in a religious order), twelve priests from religious orders, and eighty-two nuns.[16] Because the diocese was unable to recruit and train sufficient numbers of priests, Aparicio had turned over most of the parishes in the department of Cabañas to the Pauline order and most of the parishes in the department of La Paz to Franciscans. Thus, most of Aparicio's priests who were Salvadoran and trained in the country, including Rodríguez, worked in the department of San Vicente.

In his new parish, Rodríguez continued with the additional duties that Aparicio had assigned to him in Santo Domingo, and his youthful rebelliousness was minor and nonpolitical. As chaplain for the Fifth Brigade, he taught courses on Christianity to both soldiers and officers. As he developed stronger links with the Fifth Brigade, Rodríguez organized a soccer team with the soldiers. One day, he said mass just prior to a game, so the team went to church wearing their shorts. Once the service was over, Rodríguez took off his garments, donned his shorts, and went to play in the game. This behavior was scandalous in the eyes of Bishop Aparicio and for many of the older people in the congregation. The bishop was so strict that he would send parents and godparents home if they were not properly dressed for a first communion or confirmation mass. He would then not start the service until the culprits were out of the church. The bishop would say to the adults, "To be a godfather you must set the example!" Although the Salvadoran church and the diocese of San Vicente at this time seemed to typify the traditional practice of Catholicism, the winds of change were already whirling throughout Latin America, and soon they would blow through the small country of El Salvador, shaking its church to the core.

Medellín, 1968, and Popular Catholicism

As Padre Rodríguez was finding his way as a priest in El Salvador, the bishops of Latin America were finding a Latin American response to Vatican II and the church's increasingly progressive social doctrine. In order to generate a Latin American stance, CELAM, founded in 1955, held its second general conference in Medellín, Colombia, from August 26 to September 6, 1968. We have already seen that this conference produced a powerful document with three sections, "Poverty of the Church," "Peace," and "Justice," that not only affirmed the progressive stance of the Vatican but emphasized the preferential option for the poor, a powerful set of ideas setting out how to the church should help the poor.

Ideas alone would not have resulted in the church's political and revolutionary engagement, however. It was the praxis of liberationist ideas by Catholic leaders that made the new pastoral that emerged from Vatican II and the Medellín Conference a potentially transformative force. The creation of communidades eclesiales de base (CEBs; Christian base communities) allowed religious leaders to both spread the liberationist ideas and to give the Salvadoran poor a clear understanding of why their lives were so difficult. These communities first appeared in Brazil in the 1950s and in Panama in the early 1960s, but soon after the Medellín Conference they spread throughout the region and acquired a liberationist dimension.[17] The CEBs represented the "most revolutionary element" of the new pastoral, since they led to the "emergence of popular organization," "grassroots leadership," and "participatory democracy," providing a vehicle for spreading liberationist ideas widely.[18] These base communities were composed of perhaps a dozen or more Catholics and led by Delegados de la Palabra (Delegates of the Word), who organized Bible study and reflection when priests were not present. *Catequistas* (catechists) were also important in that they trained new church members and helped to spread the new pastoral. Members of the community would of course worship and pray, but they would also examine their *realidad* (reality) by reading the Bible and discussing how a particular passage would relate to their lives and social condition. The term *realidad* became almost synonymous with the new pastoral and liberationist ideas. Essentially, learning about reality meant learning about the causes of injustice and exploitation. Priests, nuns, and Delegates would use a number of passages from the Bible to show the poor the injustice inherent in their reality and that God and Jesus wanted them to become liberated. One of the most used verses was from Exodus:

> I have indeed seen the misery of my people in Egypt. I have heard them crying out because of their slave drivers, and I am concerned about their suffering. So I have come down to rescue them from the hand of the Egyptians and to bring them up out of that land into a good and spacious land.[19]

For poor Salvadorans in the early 1970s, this passage demonstrated God's desire that his people both achieve liberation and receive land from an unjust government. Another popular passage legitimated the CEBs, suggested the superiority of socialism, and showed God's support for community, solidarity, and equality:

> All the believers were one in heart and mind. No one claimed that any of their possessions was their own, but they shared everything they had. With great power the apostles continued to testify to the resurrection of the Lord Jesus. And God's grace was so powerfully at work in them all that there were no needy persons among them. For from time to time those who owned land or houses sold them, brought the money from the sales and put it at the apostles' feet, and it was distributed to anyone who had need.[20]

Participation in the CEBs also demonstrated to the poor that the Bible proclaimed that Jesus was on their side:

> Blessed are you who are poor, for yours is the kingdom of God.[21]

And that Jesus disdained the rich:

> Truly I tell you, it is hard for someone who is rich to enter the kingdom of heaven. Again I tell you, it is easier for a camel to go through the eye of a needle than for someone who is rich to enter the kingdom of God.[22]

As religious leaders formed CEBs, the poor began to believe that God was on their side, that some of their priests and nuns were willing to help them, and that with the guidance of religious leaders they could and should fight for their political and economic emancipation. With the new liberationist ideas, the new pastoral, and the newly formed CEBs, the Latin American church opened a Pandora's Box by developing a highly palatable injustice frame, but the effects would not reach El Salvador until the convening of a watershed meeting of religious leaders in early 1970.

The Peaceful Parish of Tecoluca

Padre Rodríguez did not remain at the Pilar church in San Vicente for very long. In May 1969, Bishop Aparicio named him as parish priest of Tecoluca, a small town about seven miles directly south of San Vicente. The parish of Tecoluca, however, was physically large, compared to Rodríguez's previous two parishes. It encompassed a geographical area that included the eastern slope of the San Vicente volcano, the town of Tecoluca, and the area south of the volcano all the way down to the coast, including part of the department of La Paz. Rodríguez points out that his assignment to Tecoluca was a "sort of prize," owing to the wealth of the parish. The Tecoluca parish raised a sizable sum of money for the Salvadoran church and the San Vicente diocese, since it contained large cotton plantations and large cattle ranches in the plains south of Tecoluca, as well as coffee fincas along the skirt of the volcano. The landowners, who had close ties to the church, would regularly make substantial contributions to the parish priest. During harvest time the population of the parish would swell with the arrival of people from the "north"—the departments of Chalatenango, Cabañas, and Morazán—who would come to pick coffee beans and cotton and to cut sugarcane. These were precisely the type of migrant, landless peasants who suffered from low-paying seasonal work and were at the mercy of the large landowners and the almost feudal economic system. They were also some of the same seasonal migrants who would work at Lisandro's hacienda, where they would at least receive sufficient food and humane treatment.

Rodríguez's move to Tecoluca did not represent a normal rotation of priests, however. Bishop Aparicio decided to assign him to the parish in order to replace two priests, Rafael Palacios and Mamerto Sigarán, who had displeased the bishop. These clerics had studied abroad in Chile and Ecuador and were already trying to apply the new pastoral mission advocated by

Figure 2.4. Newspaper announcement, January 1969: "Padre José David Rodríguez, new parish priest of Tecoluca." By permission of the Rodríguez Henríquez family.

the Medellín Conference. The priests had not yet formed CEBs, but they had begun to train catechists in a manner that emphasized the ideas of the new pastoral. Bishop Aparicio had decided to reassign the two priests to another parish after only one year because their progressive efforts had generated complaints from the landowners. Father Sigarán had also tangled with Bishop Aparicio. Rodríguez remembers that Sigarán had looked for and acquired a position at a nearby hospital so "he could see how the people lived." One day at the diocese's meeting of the clergy, Aparicio, who questioned the priest's decision to work with the sick, barked at Sigarán: "How is it that you can be working with sick people and then hold the host at the altar?" Sigarán did not flinch, but rather carried on a "strong debate" with the bishop. At one point he asked Aparicio: "And the sick, are they not temples of the Holy Spirit?" Despite the bishop's concerns, Father Sigarán continued to work at the hospital. Aparicio, not able to accept a challenge by one of his priests, decided to remove both Sigarán and Palacios, replacing them with someone whom he found more to his taste. He had the perfect replacement—the trustworthy "Padre David."

The two priests in Tecoluca, however, had also butted heads with their parishioners. Rodríguez arrived at the parish at the heels of a conflict involving Father Palacios, who, in order to emphasize the centrality of Jesus to the church, had removed the statue of San Lorenzo, the patron saint of Tecoluca, from the center of the altar, placed a crucifix there instead, and moved the revered saint to the side of the altar. The parishioners complained to the bishop, so Aparicio ordered that Palacios return the saint to the center. Aparicio assumed that Rodríguez would set things right, bringing the parish back to a more traditional, less "political" orientation.

When he first arrived in Tecoluca, Rodríguez was a dynamic young priest who worked principally within the church's established groups. The Caballeros de Cristo Rey had a presence in Tecoluca, so Rodríguez worked quickly to "organize them better and multiply their numbers." As the parish priest, Rodríguez was the president of the Caballeros's local organiza-

Figure 2.5. The church in Tecoluca. Photo by author, January 2008.

tion. On several occasions, his father, Lisandro, well known in the region as a leader of the Caballeros, helped him to "give the lay organization greater dynamism." The bishop had also established a group for lay women, called the Parish Auxiliaries, and Rodríguez worked to strengthen that organization as well. These women served in traditional ways by visiting the sick, cooking for the parish priest, cleaning churches, and teaching catechism. Rodríguez, a lover of music, also established a band called Tiempo Nuevo (New Times) to play music at church events and in the fiestas for the patron saint. Although not yet awakened by the ideas of Medellín, Rodríguez was a very successful, popular priest because he would listen to the people of his parish and would introduce changes only after discussing them with the parishioners. Father Palacios had carried out changes without consulting the people, so even though he was trying to promote a new doctrine focused on the poor, the parishioners had resisted his efforts, showing that the peasants held conservative ideas themselves. Rodríguez eventually talked with the faithful and convinced them to move the saint to the side and place Jesus at the center of the altar.

While at Tecoluca, Rodríguez continued to serve as chaplain of the Fifth Brigade. Initially, while at Santo Domingo, he had experienced some problems with the military leadership, owing to the vast gulf between the soldiers and the officers. Rodríguez taught catechism to the soldiers and performed baptisms and marriages. He soon noticed, however, that the officers and sergeants treated the soldiers "very harshly." Officers and noncommissioned officers would sometimes "beat soldiers or put them in confinement for the slightest infractions." The soldiers would recount their treatment to Rodríguez and would at times "demonstrate a desire to rebel," but at this time the young priest had no desire to inspire insurrection. His relationship with the officers was good, even friendly, and with one officer he organized a soccer team composed of soldiers; the team joined the national soccer league and "did quite well."

War with Honduras

On July 14, 1969, El Salvador went to war with Honduras. Labeled the "Soccer War" and the "100 Hour War," this conflict had numerous important effects on El Salvador. Tensions between these neighboring countries centered on Salvadoran migration to Honduras at a time of economic problems in both countries and the fact that El Salvador was reaping the greatest benefits from the Mercado Común Centroamericano (Central American Common Market). Owing to high population density in El Salvador, many Salvadorans—around 300,000—had migrated to Honduras, where land was much more readily available. However, as the Honduran government began to carry out land reform, Salvadorans were evicted from lands they had been cultivating. Tensions reached a fever pitch at a series of World Cup qualifying round games when fans from both countries clashed, which resulted in the name "Soccer War."[23]

As the Fifth Brigade chaplain, Rodríguez traveled to the war front with the soldiers, reaching the Honduran town of Aramecina, which had been taken and occupied by the Salvadoran army. While his principal role as chaplain was to hold mass, hear confessions, and perform last rites, Rodríguez also provided food and cigarettes for the soldiers, who were "very poorly fed." Soon after the war, Rodríguez's position as chaplain to the Fifth Brigade was given to another priest, since his increased workload in Tecoluca did not allow him to continue to perform that task. Nevertheless, Rodríguez made friends in the armed forces that would help him in the future. His work ministering to soldiers and serving at a war front would also come in handy.

Although El Salvador "won" the war, the consequences of the conflict further aggravated the dire economic situation in rural areas. In a country where campesinos were already starved for land, the return of roughly 100,000 exiles from Honduras at war's end severely aggravated an already seriously flawed land-tenure and economic system. In addition to the large influx of people, the Common Market collapsed as a result of the conflict, and thus El Salvador's gains from that market quickly dissolved. These economic effects led to rising grievances among the Salvadoran poor, creating conditions conducive to political contention. The temperature in the already simmering economic cauldron became even hotter.

Within his first year in Tecoluca, Rodríguez began to experience some problems with his bishop and a few fellow priests, even though he had not yet turned toward liberationist ideas. One of the decisions at Vatican II and the Medellín Conference had been to eliminate the system of quotas for the services provided by priests. For example, in the parish of Tecoluca, as with most parishes throughout Latin America, priests charged for baptisms, marriages, first communions, special masses for the deceased, and so forth. Rodríguez recalls that he would be paid by the landowners when he celebrated masses for them, but he would feel a need to return to the same area and serve the campesinos as well. He began telling the campesinos that he would come back on a specific day to celebrate mass and talk with them. When he first did this they would express some concern, saying, "Padre, who is going to pay you?" Rodríguez would tell them not to worry about payment. Despite holding priests in high esteem, campesinos perceived their pastors as very concerned with money, hesitant to say mass or carry out religious rites unless being paid a specific, even listed, amount. In the Medellín document "Poverty of the Church," the bishops agreed to "overcome the system of fees, replacing it with other forms of financial cooperation not linked to the administration of the sacraments." In Tecoluca, Rodríguez began to do just that.

Rodríguez would visit the campesinos and serve their religious needs but ask only for voluntary donations rather than predetermined payments. One effect of the old quota system had been to keep church participation by the poor at a low level, owing to the costs of sacraments. In the past, when priests would say mass for the landowners, often at *ermitas* (small churches) on their haciendas, they would simply mention the names of the campesinos that had recently died. The campesinos were troubled by this practice, since they usually did not like the landowners, and correctly felt that they were not taken as seriously as the rich. The campesinos, of course, could not afford a special mass or even the baptism and first communion of their children. Rodríguez, however, began to say special masses, baptize, and offer first communion for the campesinos without asking for compensation. He also began to perform more marriages for campesinos, some of whom had not been married in the church because of the associated costs.[24] With these actions Rodríguez's work increased dramatically, since campesinos returned to the church in droves. However, although his work increased, the amount of money he received began to dwindle.

We can interpret his actions as the result of the greater concern for the poor as expressed by Vatican II as well as Medellín's call for ending payment for sacraments, but Rodríguez's humanitarianism also derived from the examples provided by the way his father treated his workers. For example, Rodríguez points out that when a worker was sick, Lisandro would either lend one of his vehicles or provide a horse so that the sick person could be taken to a doctor. Rodríguez, like his father, allowed his parish vehicle to be used to transport campesinos in need. He would also visit someone who was gravely ill to provide last rites. He learned from campesinos that at times some priests would say, "I will go tomorrow." Tomorrow would often turn out to be too late. Rodríguez recalls that he used to say often to his parishioners, "People will forget what you say and what you do, but will never forget how you treat them." For Rodríguez, the preferential option for the poor was simply the right thing to do. This may explain why some priests, like Rodríguez, would quickly and forcefully embrace the new pastoral, while others would reject the new doctrine.

Padre Rodríguez's reputation as a priest of the people thus began to grow; at the same time, however, the prized parish of Tecoluca experienced a decline in funds. Bishop Aparicio and some fellow priests began to criticize Rodríguez for "using his heart rather than his head" in running the parish. Church finances were of course an important concern for bishops, who needed funds to run their dioceses, schools, and seminaries. While the world's bishops at Vatican II saw a need to reject the old quota system, the church still needed money to maintain itself and its personnel. Bishops would soon discover that a church that opted for the poor and at the same time severely criticized the rich would find itself with a decimated treasury. The pressures from those concerned with the financial health of the institution would grow in the future as liberationists antagonized those who contributed the most funds to the church.

What Rodríguez did in his parish, however, tended to stay in his parish. Parishes in El Salvador, as in all of Latin America, were hierarchical and insular. Priests dealt almost exclusively with their bishops, often having little knowledge of what was occurring even in a contiguous parish. For example, if Rodríguez planned on staying overnight in another parish, he had to get his bishop's permission. Some of the foreign priests and priests from religious orders, such as the Jesuits, however, had already become familiar with the ideas associated with Vatican II and the Medellín Conference and were actively communicating across parishes. Rodríguez, for example, had gotten to know Padre Juan Macho, a Spanish priest of the Passionist order, who worked in the town of Jiquilisco, in a parish in the diocese of Santiago de María, located in the department of Usulután, adjacent to the eastern reaches of the parish of Tecoluca. The Lempa River divided the two parishes, with the town of San Nicolás Lempa in the Tecoluca parish on the western bank and the town of San Marcos Lempa in Padre Macho's parish on the eastern bank. Although the two towns were in different parishes, dioceses and departments, a lot of interaction occurred between them, since a bridge spanned the river. Rodríguez and Father Macho, who worked principally in the town of Jiquilisco, developed a very close relationship, and

Rodríguez would sometimes say mass in Macho's parish, since the parishioners liked his sermons. These interactions would soon grow much stronger and would have the effect of breaking down the walls between the parishes of El Salvador.

By the end of 1969, some signs emerged that the Salvadoran government was ready to consider limited changes to the unjust land-tenure system. The opposition parties, which had been able to gain representation in the Legislative Assembly after proportional representation was adopted in 1963, and even some members of the PCN had become convinced that land reform might be the best way to fend off a serious crisis or communist revolution in the country, as had occurred in Cuba. El Salvador, in fact, was perhaps the only country in Latin America that had not undergone some sort of land reform. Its neighbor Honduras, on the other hand, had recently carried out reforms. Consequently, President-Colonel Fidel Sánchez Hernández decided to convoke a national dialogue, called the Primer Congreso Nacional de Reforma Agraria (First National Congress on Agrarian Reform), held January 5–10, 1970.[25] The government asked the church to participate, so the country's archbishop, Luis Chávez y González, sent two representatives: Bishop Ricardo Urioste and Father José Inocencio Alas, from Suchitoto. Father "Chencho" Alas forcefully presented the church's position at the congress, which included a description of the plight of the campesinos. Immediately after his presentation, on January 8, several men kidnapped Father Alas as he was leaving the congress; he was abused as a captive, drugged, and then left alone in a remote mountain, completely naked.[26] Representatives of the oligarchy walked out of the proceedings early on, and the congress came to nothing. From this point on, the Salvadoran oligarchy was on the lookout for anything that smelled of reform, particularly any reform that had to do with land tenure, since land was the source of their wealth and power. For campesinos, the failed opportunity of the congress meant that their plight would continue for an indefinite period of time.

The Plight and Frustration of the Salvadoran Campesino

The economic condition of the Salvadoran peasant in the early 1970s was one of near enslavement and despair. Most campesinos led very difficult, short, unhealthy, poverty-stricken lives, during which they had little or no access to land, received very little pay for their work, had almost no support or protection from the government, and were often cheated and treated inhumanely. In short, they led lives that most concerned observers at the time would classify as unbearable. The preferential option for the poor promoted by the Medellín Conference would not have struck a resonant chord in any country in Latin America had there not been so many campesinos and workers who found themselves in abject poverty and conditions of excessive exploitation. While the ideas of Medellín certainly changed the ways in which the church in Latin American viewed the poor, the objective conditions of the campesino in El Salvador ensured that the new pastoral would find fertile soil in the stark reality of the Salvadoran peasant. Legitimate grievances abounded.

Rodríguez recalls that as campesinos gained greater confidence in him they began to express their problems. Those who worked on coffee fincas, for example, would say after mass, "Look, Padre, at the coffee finca they do not have a scale." Workers would be paid by the quintal (100 pounds), so to be paid fairly an accurate scale was essential. Rodríguez would ask them about this, and they would tell him that the coffee they picked would not be weighed but rather would be put into bins to determine the weight, and thus the payment to the campesino. The problem was that sometimes these bins would be too wide and thus the campesino would be cheated. A wide bin would hold perhaps 110 pounds, but the campesino would be paid for only 100 pounds. Additionally, the finca's *caporal* (chief administrator), would sometimes say, "You broke this number of branches," and fine the campesino for the damage, thus reducing wages. Consequently, in addition to low wages for long hours of backbreaking work, the campesino would be robbed in various ways. At some coffee fincas the situation was even more exploitative in that the caporal would pay workers in the form of credit, which meant that the campesinos could use their "pay" only at the finca's store. As a result, even the meager wages that they earned would eventually return to the landowner.

Conditions could be even worse in the cotton plantations of the coastal plains, where the bosses, according to Rodríguez, where downright "despotic." Often in the coffee plantations the campesinos would be given a place to live without having to pay rent, but on the cotton plantations the campesino would have to pay for dilapidated, crowded housing. Additionally, the campesinos always wanted to grow their own small patch of corn, called a *milpa*, for their own consumption. In many haciendas and ranches, the landowners would allow peasants to harvest a milpa in exchange for half of the harvest. Some campesinos would not even be allowed this arrangement, but would instead have to rent the land on which they grew their subsistence crops. At the cotton plantations, the owners would also have the fields sprayed with DDT or other insecticides, creating serious health problems for the campesinos. Rodríguez remembers that when small airplanes sprayed the fields with pesticides sometimes the chickens or pigs belonging to the campesinos would become sick and die. The fish in the rivers would die as well, making it more difficult for the campesinos to add protein to their diet. The loss of even one chicken had a strong, adverse effect on a campesino family.

Adding insult to injury, campesinos were treated inhumanely not only by landowners but more often by the caporales, who, ironically, were mostly campesinos themselves. The caporales would humiliate campesinos because they saw them as stupid, lazy, and gullible. The inhumane treatment would at times include public humiliation, beatings, rape, and false accusations that would result in incarceration.[27] The campesino always had to be very careful, submissive, and effusively deferential. Rodríguez points out that priests were not immune to perpetuating this dehumanizing treatment and would routinely accept submissive behavior from the campesinos, such as kissing the hands of priests, kissing a bishop's ring, and offering priests conveniences that campesinos themselves seldom enjoyed. Rodríguez recalls that it took a great deal of effort on his part to get campesinos to stop offering him gifts or giving him their best food. The campesinos would invariably offer a priest their horse or cart when traveling together.

In the face of these difficult living conditions, the campesino had no one to turn to. The hacienda or finca owners were usually not around, and even if they were, a campesino complaint would more likely result in job loss than in the resolution of the problem.[28] If campesinos complained to the local authorities, such as the mayor or the National Guard, they would be told something like, "Don't complain; be grateful to God that you have a job." If they tried to go outside their immediate locality, to their deputy (legislator) or to a government ministry, there would be either no response at all or an adverse response. Priests were also of little help. The most common response by priests to the campesinos' plight, according to Rodríguez, was, "Suffer here, suffer, God will repay you, He will bless you in heaven." Thus even priests condoned and at times participated in this unjust, inhumane, indifferent treatment of the campesino, representing the vast majority of the country's population.

Most campesinos, therefore, could see no way out of their dire predicament, particularly since no one with power defended their interests. In fact, the country's agrarian law did not allow campesinos to organize politically. When campesinos "voted," it would often involve a caporal taking their identification cards so that the caporal could vote for the PCN on behalf of all the campesinos in the finca or hacienda. Or, if the campesino went to the polling place, the bins in which they deposited their ballots were often made of transparent plastic, so the caporal or official standing by the table could easily see whether or not the campesino had voted for the PCN. Rodríguez points out that priests too were responsible for this disdain for the democratic process in that "they did not denounce" these practices. Even if the campesino knew full well the reasons for his plight, he would be foolhardy—indeed irrational—to attempt to rebel against the system. As far as all people of power were concerned, says Rodríguez, "the campesino was made to obey." And, as late as 1970, when the Salvadoran church began to express new concern for the plight of the campesino, no other powerful group or institution in El Salvador appeared to be committed to dramatically changing the status quo.[29]

The State and the Security Apparatus

Reforms were highly unlikely mostly because of the immense power of the state and its security apparatus, both of which were beholden to the oligarchy, whose principal goal was to maintain the status quo. At the end of the 1960s, El Salvador was saddled with a government and society that was dominated by the coffee-growing and coffee-exporting oligarchy that had consolidated its power at the end of the 1800s. We will not review Salvadoran history in detail, but to understand the historical context in which the liberationist cause emerged, and in which Padre Rodríguez toiled, it is necessary to understand the prevailing cultural, political, and economic milieu. In 1932 the country experienced a social upheaval and reactionary response that became known as La Matanza, the "mass killing."[30] This principally indigenous rebellion was organized by leaders of the Salvadoran Communist Party, including Agustín Farabundo Martí, one of the founders of the party. The state brutally repressed the rebellion, resulting in the killing of about 10,000 people, mostly peasants. As a consequence of this rebellion, the oligarchy turned over political power to the armed forces and became even more staunchly anti-communist. This meant that the state would accuse any attempt at bringing about economic justice as the work of external communist ideology. The oligarchs styled themselves as supporters of capitalism and democracy, yet the iron grip of the coffee-growing oligarchy represented neither economic nor political competition, but an airtight monopoly of economic and political power. The oligarchy also saw itself as devoutly Catholic, an easy choice as long as the church helped to preserve the status quo.

The oligarchy, the PCN, and the state created a number of institutions to preclude another rebellion like the one in 1932. The armed forces controlled the government through a political party that nominated military officers for the presidency. The civilians in the party would fill most of the government and legislative positions but were of course subservient to the armed forces, who in turn served the oligarchy. Elections were held, but their outcomes were preordained. However, in the 1960s, with pressures to liberalize the political system—some of this urging coming from the United States and its newly minted Alliance for Progress—a system of proportional representation was implemented so that opposition parties could gain some seats in the Legislative Assembly. A number of opposition parties, such as the newly formed PDC, gained seats in the Asamblea Legislativa (Legislative Assembly) and mayoralties in a number of towns, and eventually in the capital of San Salvador. The PCN, however, always won the presidency and a majority of seats in the assembly.[31]

Control of the population at the local level was accomplished by a number of institutions. The most notable was the National Guard, which operated mostly in the rural areas and was created soon after the 1932 uprising. In addition to the guard were the Treasury Police and the National Police. In the early 1960s the state also organized a paramilitary organization paradoxically called the Organización Democrática Nacionalista (ORDEN; Nationalist Democratic Organization), designed to keep the peasantry under control. *Orden* in Spanish, non-coincidentally, means "order," suggesting that the focus was on establishing control rather than on democracy. Colonel José Alberto Medrano, nicknamed "Chele" Medrano, founded ORDEN with U.S. assistance.[32] While the Kennedy administration may have hoped that democracy would spread in Latin America, the principal focus of U.S. policy was the containment of communist influence in the region. ORDEN, the eyes and ears of the Salvadoran government in the rural areas, offered a number of perks to peasants who would provide information to the government on activities deemed to be revolutionary. Once the liberationist movement began, ORDEN would serve as an essential intelligence apparatus for the government, undermining the organizational work of priests, nuns, and lay workers and putting all Christians at risk.

Aurelio, a former peasant whom I interviewed,[33] recalls how Medrano tried to organize peasants in the 1960s. Colonel Medrano himself visited Cinquera, a town in the diocese of San Vicente, a few times and lectured the men of the area, who ranged in age from eighteen to sixty. "Chele" Medrano would tell the peasants that the government was ready to develop the countryside, providing roads, clinics, and soccer fields, but that the men needed to first join ORDEN. Aurelio became the leader of one of the groups, each of which had about ten men. In 1969 another colonel came to Cinquera to talk with the leaders of the groups, most of whom, like Aurelio, were illiterate. The colonel said: "I've come to talk about a danger. The danger is communism." The peasants had no idea what the colonel was talking about—they knew nothing of La Matanza or Farabundo Martí, and even less of communism. When asked what communism was, the colonel "became animated" and said that it was what was happening in Cuba. A peasant then asked, "What is Cuba?" Aurelio, with humor in his eyes, narrated that even the colonel did not seem to know where Cuba was. However, the officer went on to say that Cuba was led by a terrible man named Castro who was "part human and part monkey" and "ate human flesh," particularly that of "children." The colonel finished by warning the peasants that under communism the people's land would be taken away. None of the peasants dared to tell the colonel that they had little or no land. Clearly, ideology played a strong role in the Salvadoran crisis.

ORDEN was first and foremost an anti-communist, anti-land-reform organization, since the Salvadoran oligarchy and military, and the United States, saw communism and the influence of the Cuban Revolution as the most clear and present dangers to their interests. Communism of course called for land reform, and the Cuban Revolution had carried out a land-reform program that had transformed the island's economy. As for the church, in the late 1960s, Catholic leaders and parishioners in El Salvador did not challenge the status quo in any substantial way. Aurelio recalls: "Until 1970 we were traditional Christians, a conservative church where religious practice was the only end." The centuries-long spiritual complacency, however, was about to come to an end.

Injustice, Grievances, and a Traditional Church

At the end of the 1960s, objective economic conditions, giving rise to legitimate grievances, were palpable in El Salvador. While these conditions had existed for decades, they worsened after the war with Honduras, when 100,000 landless peasants returned to El Salvador. In addition, the oligarchy, worried about the specter of land reform, began to treat peasants with even greater disdain, ignoring their calls for land and better treatment. These conditions led to the rise of serious grievances and some contention. No doubt, then, the existence of severe economic injustice is a necessary condition for the emergence of contentious politics. More is required, however, for those with extensive grievances to become involved in widespread social mobilization, so necessary for the rise of a social movement.

Until the mid-1960s, the Catholic Church still operated in a traditional manner, especially in conservative countries like El Salvador. We have seen, however, that beginning in the early 1960s, with Vatican II and two important papal encyclicals, Catholicism underwent revolutionary doctrinal changes that called for the church to be on the side of the poor. In 1968 the new ideas spread to Latin America, owing to the CELAM conference in Medellín. These doctrinal changes generated ideas that would help to create a powerful injustice frame. At the end of the 1960s, however, these revolutionary ideas had not reached a large number of Salvadoran religious leaders. No doubt some priests, mostly foreign ones, had already heard about the doctrinal changes in the church, and of course most of the Salvadoran bishops had attended Vatican II. Archbishop Chávez y González had also attended the 1968 Medellín Conference. The new, revolutionary pastoral, however, would not reach El Salvador until the archbishop decided to embrace it and encourage priests and nuns to apply it to their suffering country.

As the decade came to a close, Padre David Rodríguez was just one of many priests and nuns who carried on in traditional ways. Rodríguez received much of the same training that countless priests had received before him, and thus he acted in ways that were consistent with the traditional style of the church. Like many other would-be revolutionary leaders, Rodríguez was young, came from a relatively affluent family, and received a good, cosmopolitan education. When he began practicing as a priest, his parishioners viewed him positively because of his youth, enthusiasm, and humanitarian manner. Nevertheless, while poverty surrounded him, Rodríguez did not exhibit outrage and did not become engaged politically. Very soon, however, he would behave very differently: his parishioners would see him as a key leader in their struggle for liberation, while the government and his own bishop would peg him as a dangerous rebel and even a communist. What happened to cause such a dramatic change in a man who had a splendid, secure future before him?

3

The Awakening of a Priest

"You have ruined the parish!"

Upon entering the hacienda San Luis Las Posadas, Padre David Rodríguez was ready to shine. He had read up on San Isidro Labrador, the patron saint of the hacienda, and looked forward to providing a fresh view of the saint, highlighting his life and unique qualities. After he finished his sermon, Mercedes Tamayo de Rosales, who owned and ran the hacienda—a "strong woman" who rode horses "like a man"—approached the new, young priest gleefully to let him know that the clerics before him had never expounded so extensively and vividly on the saint's life. It was a stirring day for the landowner and the new priest. Not all was well at Doña Rosales's idyllic hacienda, however, suggested by its nickname, La Chenga Sola. Peasants called corn tortillas, their staple food, *chengas,* and because the workers would receive *only* tortillas—without cheese, beans, or meat—for lunch, Rosales's hacienda acquired the notorious name of La Chenga Sola, "Tortilla Only." Rodríguez, like the priests before him, knew about the nickname, but these were the sorts of things that priests would not discuss with the landowners, who were generous to the church, providing most of the funds for the parish and diocese. And, without the ermitas that landowners built on their properties, where would priests say mass and save the souls of campesinos?

The following year, 1970, in May, Rodríguez returned to the hacienda for the annual celebration of San Isidro Labrador. The young priest was still enthusiastic, but he had developed a more serious demeanor. By that year, liberationist ideas had already shaken him profoundly. After the mass, Doña Rosales approached Rodríguez and asked him to bless the watering troughs for her cattle, hoping that this gesture would keep her livestock healthy and strong. "How is that done?" Rodríguez asked, highly puzzled. "The priest from Zacatecoluca, when he came, would get on my jeep and bless the troughs from the back of my jeep," Rosales replied matter-of-factly. Rodríguez, who had already decided to help the campesinos, thinking on his feet, responded: "Fine, fine, I can do that. But let's make a deal. Why don't you give the campesinos something with the tortilla?" Rosales, who was well aware of the disparaging name given to her hacienda, became furious at his suggestion, retorting angrily, "In my hacienda no one comes to give orders; you [rule] in your church and me in my hacienda!" Rodríguez, somewhat taken aback but true to his commitment to assist the peasants, said, "Well, then, I'm not going to bless the troughs." Rodríguez never returned to the hacienda, but he heard people comment that Rosales was issuing strong warnings about him: "That priest is a communist!" Rodríguez recalls: "This was the first time I heard that people were calling me a communist." At the time he did not understand, and would ask people, "Why do they say I'm a communist?" From Rodríguez's perspective he was simply following the new pastoral as expressed by Vatican II and Medellín. In fact, Rodríguez, like any good priest, considered himself "solidly anti-communist." It may seem that Rodríguez was naive about being labeled a communist, but at the time he was such a committed priest, and Marxist ideas were so foreign and unappealing to him, that he could not imagine anyone considering him a communist. How did his outlook change so quickly, from serving as a traditional priest in one year to challenging landowners and being labeled a communist the next?

The First Week of Pastoral Reflection

Bruised by the failed land-reform congress in early 1970, the Salvadoran church was not going to wait for the government to take action. Archbishop Luis Chávez y González wanted to promote land reform and was also very receptive to a changing role for the church.[1] Consequently, the archbishop decided to sponsor a week of pastoral reflection to gather religious leaders for the purpose of considering how to implement the pronouncements of Vatican II and Medellín. By calling for a week of reflection, the archbishop was not acting as a rogue bishop but simply abiding by the wishes of Pope Paul VI, who advised the bishops of Latin America to hold conferences for the purpose of implementing the ideas of Vatican II.[2] At the 1968 Medellín Conference, the Latin American bishops had also urged the region's national episcopal conferences to take decisive action in promoting the new pastoral, in consciousness-raising, and in "implementing the organization of courses, meetings, etc., as a means of integrating those responsible for social activities related to pastoral plans."[3] The popular mobilization that began in El Salvador after 1970, therefore, was to a large extent precipitated by the ideational changes occurring in the Catholic Church and the church in Latin America; it was by no means simply the work of a few "radical" priests, as the Salvadoran government would later suggest. The actions that would follow the pastoral week were fully supported by the hierarchy—the pope, the Latin American bishops and the local archbishop.

El Salvador's bishops, however, were not all of the same opinion about the church's new posture and doctrine. Archbishop Chávez y González was able to get CEDES to sanction the pastoral week, but most of the bishops, including Bishop Aparicio, were not sympathetic toward the activist elements of Vatican II and Medellín. The conservative bishops had little interest in the week of reflection and refused to attend. Nevertheless, priests from every diocese received invitations to attend the gathering. In late 1969, Father Juan Macho invited Padre Rodríguez to participate in the pastoral week, since by then the Spaniard had gotten to know him well. Rodríguez in turn invited "thirteen priests" from his diocese who were the most sympathetic to the emerging changes.

The week of reflection took place from June 22 to June 26 in San Salvador and brought together those religious leaders who were most interested in the church's recent paradigmatic shift. At the time, only five dioceses existed in El Salvador, and representatives from all five attended the event. A total of 180 individuals participated in the meetings, including eighty-three priests (a few of them from the San Vicente diocese), thirty nuns, two seminarians, and thirty-three laypersons.[4] Rodríguez recalls that Pablo Richard, a well-known Chilean liberation theologian, spoke at the conference.[5] Priests in El Salvador were thus able to learn of the principal progressive ideas that were circulating all around Latin America from a key theologian.

The participants at the pastoral week, as Rodríguez recalls, agreed to make three principal recommendations for the Salvadoran church: to work toward the creation and consolidation of CEBs; to work at promoting and "forming" lay leaders; and to build and strengthen the cooperation among parish priests, which became known as the "joint pastoral." The CEBs would become the core ideational and organizational center of the movement's link to the people. The training of lay leaders would allow the liberationist leaders to spread their influence beyond their immediate orbit, since the lay leaders would eventually promote the new pastoral and organize believers well beyond the reach of priests and nuns. The joint pastoral led to the establishment of a group of progressive priests from the entire country who were committed to the new, progressive doctrine. This group began to meet monthly and initially called itself the "group of pastoral reflection," but eventually it became known as La Nacional, for "the national group of priests."[6] Owing to these new imperatives, the conference was a watershed event for the Salvadoran church. The bottom line was that the Salvadoran church's new pastoral mission would focus on liberating the poor of El Salvador by training and organizing them so they could fight for their political and economic rights. In short, from a biblical perspective, the liberationists became committed to taking the poor of El Salvador out of bondage and into the Promised Land.

For Rodríguez, the pastoral week represented his first real inauguration into the liberationist cause inspired by Vatican II and particularly Medellín. He recalls that this week of reflection gave him "the theological sense of what he was already doing." He now felt confident that the path he was on, which had already caused some problems, was indeed the right one. Most importantly, this experience motivated Rodríguez tremendously. As he recalls, "I came out charged up, very enthused!" Another important effect of the pastoral week was that the progressive priests in El Salvador began to meet regularly, both locally and at the national level. In addition to the meetings of La Nacional, Rodríguez attended meetings with the thirteen progressive priests of San Vicente. Backed by the pronouncements of Vatican II and Medellín, priests at these meetings "reaffirmed to ourselves that what we were doing was correct." Even with the existence of conservative priests and bishops, the liberationists would now have an organizational structure that would allow them to promote the new ideas and begin to train lay leaders. Rodríguez recalls that after the pastoral week, the progressives in the church became convinced that "the church had to help the peasants to liberate themselves from the oppression in which they found themselves." He points out that the revolutionaries who came later "reaped already fertilized lands"—referring to the work with the campesinos that liberationists began to carry out in 1970. The guerrilla organizations found a people "with a disciplined organization" as a result of the "new pastoral plan," which had been let loose by the archbishop and the pastoral week.

As noted above, within the church in Latin America, differing opinions existed over Vatican II, Medellín, and liberation theology, and the church in El Salvador was no exception. While most countries in Latin America had held episcopal conferences to apply Medellín's conclusions to that particular country, the CEDES-sanctioned pastoral week was late in coming and was pushed not by the bishop's conference but mostly by Archbishop Chávez y González, his auxiliary bishop, Arturo Rivera y Damas, and a handful of progressive priests, a number of whom were foreign. After the pastoral week's final document was presented to CEDES, the conservative bishops, including Bishop Aparicio, criticized the text and softened its progressive tone. The Jesuit priest Rodolfo Cardenal points out that it was "clear that the bishops did not want to commit themselves directly to the promotion of the campesino's liberation."[7] The pastoral week was therefore a key event in highlighting and intensifying the divisions within the church in El Salvador. In the coming years, as El Salvador entered a severe national crisis, this institutional division would become pronounced to the point of internal rupture.

After the pastoral week the die was cast. The priests who attended this watershed event, and later others, with the encouragement from two bishops, became increasingly committed to bringing socioeconomic changes to El Salvador by empowering the poor politically. Padre Rodríguez would be one of those liberationist priests committed to a new pastoral designed to free peasants from their earthly chains. And thus the young priest was destined to clash with Bishop Aparicio repeatedly. Just as the battle lines had been drawn in the secular world between proponents of land reform and the reactionary oligarchy, now the line was being drawn between the liberationist and the conservative sectors of the church. This battle would also become ideological, since the oligarchy in El Salvador would equate the liberationist cause with communism.

The Clash with Landowners

With the implementation of the new pastoral, many priests and nuns became the chief advocates for the Salvadoran campesino. Since campesinos had nowhere to turn, Rodríguez began to more actively promote their economic and political interests. His willingness to better serve the campesinos by offering masses, baptisms, and marriages at little or no cost was not necessarily seen as a bad thing by the landowners, although some were suspicious of his actions. However, once he began to serve as an advocate for the campesino, as happened at La Chenga Sola, his relationship with landowners deteriorated rapidly and irreparably. Rodríguez recalls: "All of the problems with the landowners occurred in [19]71 . . . yes it was '70 or '71." Thus, only after the Salvadoran church, led by Archbishop Chávez y González, decided to apply Vatican II and Medellín pronouncements to its pastoral work did Rodríguez and others begin to experience serious, irreconcilable conflict with the wealthy landowners of the country. In El Salvador, conflict with landowners meant conflict with the state and its security apparatus.

Rodríguez experienced perhaps his most significant clash at a large hacienda called Santa Teresa, owned by Rafael Carballo, who, ironically, had been minister of justice in the late 1950s. The hacienda was mainly a cattle ranch, but cotton and grains were also grown on its lands. The property contained a "large, beautiful" chapel, much as Lisandro's sugar plantation contained a small church. Typically, large haciendas and plantations would have both a small ermita and a National Guard or Treasury Police outpost at the *casco* (core) of the property. In essence, the landowner had at his property and at his disposal representatives of both church and state, institutions that helped to maintain order. Rodríguez points out that traditionally "the priest was very helpful to the landowners" and would say to the campesinos, "Suffer with patience, and God will give you the prize in the next life." Priests would normally develop good relationships with the landowners, since both the clergy and the diocese depended greatly upon the "charity" of the oligarchy. The Medellín Conference had criticized this long-standing collaboration between the church and those with power. In fact, this marriage to power had prompted the bishops of Latin America to advance the preferential option for the poor. In their new awakened state, the liberationists would start to undermine the traditions of the past.

Rodríguez believed he had developed an especially close relationship with Dr. Carballo, since both of them played the guitar. Carballo was an "excellent classical guitarist," while Rodríguez played mainly popular music, but he had taken classical guitar lessons when he studied in Spain. Eventually, via their love for music and the guitar, the two men had become "good friends." One day after mass, some campesinos anxiously told Rodríguez, "Look, Padre, Dr. Carballo has closed the river off to us." The campesinos, who lived in a *caserío* (a splay of houses) by a river near the hacienda and planted vegetables and corn, used the water from the river to irrigate their meager crops. They also used a road that went through the Santa Teresa hacienda as a shortcut to get to Tecoluca. Dr. Carballo had locked the gate at the road, meaning that the campesinos now had to take a much longer path to town. Rodríguez, confident in his friendship with Dr. Carballo, told the campesinos: "There is no problem. I will speak with him. We are friends."

When Padre Rodríguez conveyed the concerns of the campesinos to Carballo, he dismissed their grievances and spoke to Rodríguez "as if I were a child." Carballo lectured, "Enough. You are getting into problems. You are young. Learn to live." Upon finishing this unsolicited advice, Carballo wrote a check to Rodríguez for twice the amount of his usual donation. Recognizing that this "generosity" constituted a bribe, Rodríguez handed the check back to Carballo and expressed that he could not accept this atypical contribution, adding that what he wanted was for him to resolve the campesinos' problems by granting them access to water and to the barred road. Carballo then became "furious" and said to Rodríguez, "Don't come back to my hacienda." Rodríguez never returned. He had broken ties with yet one more powerful landowner. After he told the campesinos that Carballo was not going to help and that he would not be saying mass at the hacienda again, Rodríguez assured them that he would come back to celebrate mass just for them. When he returned two weeks later, Rodríguez said mass outdoors at the small hamlet near the hacienda, an act of defiance in the eyes of the former minister of justice. The local priest was now rejecting the landowner and favoring the local peasants, an act consistent with the church's new doctrine but an act of defiance in the eyes of El Salvador's elite.

As these conflicts between landowners and priests grew throughout El Salvador, the flawed manner in which the church had operated in rural areas became apparent, and new ways of operating emerged. Since many of the ermitas were on large fincas and haciendas, the church had been dependent upon the whims of the landowners. At first, when Rodríguez said mass for the peasants using the ermitas on private property, the landowners were suspicious but did not want to step in and prevent campesinos from hearing mass or being married or being baptized. However, once priests in El Salvador started to promote the new pastoral and to form CEBs, landowners reacted swiftly and denied the use of the ermitas on their fincas and haciendas. When Dr. Carballo told him not to return to his hacienda, Rodríguez had assumed the minister meant to his house on the hacienda. So, when Rodríguez had at first returned to his ranch to say mass for the campesinos on hacienda property, one of the administrators told him with regret, "Padre, the *patrón* [boss] said that you can't say mass here again." "Don't worry," Rodríguez replied. "You are simply abiding by your obligations."

With the loss of the ermitas inside the properties of the haciendas, Rodríguez decided to organize campesinos for the task of building new chapels in rural hamlets where he could say mass and begin to organize the people into CEBs. With the help of the peasants, he was eventually able to build adobe or brick ermitas that held as many as one hundred worshippers. He was used to this type of work, since at his first parish he had organized his parishioners for the purpose of adding two towers to the parish church. After just a short time the new chapels "multiplied," sprouting up throughout the parish. The process of moving from the chapels on the landowners' property to makeshift ermitas required an intermediary step of celebrating mass in the homes of peasants or even outdoors with a tarp to cover the provisional altar. These celebrations raised some eyebrows, since most priests and peasants believed that mass had to be celebrated in a "proper" church. Liberationist priests, however, often had to carry out sacraments and services for campesinos in unconventional ways and locations, "like the church of the catacombs."

The Forming and "Awakening" of Campesinos

The work of the liberationist priest (and nun) was not a lonely endeavor. After the pastoral week of 1970, progressive priests all over El Salvador began to meet to discuss how their new pastoral mission was proceeding. In this joint pastoral, priests would learn from and support each other, at times going into communities as a team.[8] Rodríguez remembers that he would explain to other priests his style of spreading the Gospel and of getting the campesinos more involved: "I would say mass, and then suggest, 'If anyone wants to stay to discuss in depth the Gospel that we live, please feel free to stay.'" At the beginning only a few would remain. For those who stayed, Rodríguez would discuss the Gospel but also talk about the changes proposed by Medellín and Vatican II. As time passed, more and more people remained after mass, eventually creating the "seeds for establishing Christian communities." Not only did increasing numbers of parishioners stay for discussions, but the initial period of thirty minutes of dialogue kept expanding to a point where they became "more like long seminars."

Part of the reason why more parishioners would stay to discuss the Bible after mass was that increasing numbers of people were attending Rodríguez's services. One former parishioner recalls:

> The church would fill up so much that at times there was no place to sit, no space to stand, many people were left outside the principal entrance, since there were so many people who would congregate. What was good and beautiful was that the vast majority of those present were there because they believed in and were convinced by Rodríguez's message, since it brought hope and life to these people.

Church attendance grew dramatically in many parishes, so Rodríguez was just one of many priests and nuns who were awakening the poor. The newly awakened priests were now transmitting the new pastoral to their parishioners, who picked up the enthusiasm of their pastors. Those parishioners with grievances, perhaps most, must have begun to wonder if their plight was soon to end, since priests were now engaged in seeking solutions to their earthly problems.

One vital change produced by the pastoral week that involved greater participation and community building was the emergence of courses for the "formation" of peasants.[9] Scholars have identified these courses, along with the creation of CEBs, as the vehicles through which religious leaders "awakened" the poor and equipped them with important organizational skills. At the first meeting of La Nacional, Rodríguez had met a French priest, Bernardo Boulang, who worked in El Salvador in an organization called Juventud Agraria Católica (Catholic Agrarian Youth). Father Boulang visited Rodríguez's parish in Tecoluca soon after the week of reflection and helped him to more effectively "relate the Bible to El Salvador's reality." He also helped Rodríguez with the "methodology of selecting the most committed lay leaders" and with establishing the first seminar for young lay leaders in Tecoluca. Very soon after the pastoral week, therefore, after he himself had been "awakened," Rodríguez began forming and "awakening" the peasants of his parish.

Interestingly enough, the first small course set up by Rodríguez was held in the house of a wealthy landowner in Tecoluca, who later became minister of agriculture.[10] Because he was seldom there, the landowner allowed Rodríguez to hold the course his house. Once it was fully developed, the short course would begin on a Friday afternoon and end on Sunday in the middle of the day, when a special mass was held for the trainees. The purpose of the course was to form young lay leaders by helping them to relate the Bible to the reality in Tecoluca "at a deeper level." The courses trained Delegates of the Word of God, who would be responsible for bringing people together in their communities for Bible discussion on at least a weekly basis. In general, lay leaders were either trained as catechists (those who taught catechism principally to children but also to adults) or as Delegates. Both of these types of lay leaders, however, would be "awakened" by learning that the plight of the poor was not inevitable or sanctioned by God. The students, Rodríguez recalls, "left the course very committed." Rodríguez continued with the courses and broadened them to include men of the Caballeros of Cristo Rey, women of the Parish Auxiliaries, and some peasants who would not necessarily become either catechists or Delegates. Rodríguez believes, however, that "the greatest dynamism was with the young Delegates of the Word," since they would serve as the acting priest when the priest was not available. In a country where one priest served roughly ten thousand believers, the Delegates took on substantial responsibility and "gained a great deal of local respect."

As he formed peasants, Rodríguez began to realize that he was starting to become involved in "political affairs," not only because he was raising the political and economic consciousness of the campesinos but also because he would often discuss with them the country's constitution, regularly identifying its deficits. He would point out that Article 101 of the constitution gave citizens the right to express their concerns to the government and required the government to respond. However, as most Salvadorans already knew, the government usually ignored or reacted negatively to citizen concerns, especially the concerns of the campesino. Rodríguez noted that the law which forbade campesinos to organize politically was inconsistent with the principles of the constitution. Rodríguez also highlighted the inconsistency that while the constitution guaranteed free and fair elections and a secret vote, campesinos were in many ways pressured to vote for the official party, the PCN. The campesinos, of course, already knew they were pressured to vote for the PCN, but they may not have known that their vote was supposed to be free and secret, since no one had explained the country's constitution to them, just as no one had discussed the Bible with them.

By pointing out the flaws of the land-tenure system and explaining the constitution and national laws to the poor, priests and nuns who advanced the new pastoral reinforced the ideas that the political and economic systems in El Salvador were corrupt, that the traditional church and oligarchy had helped to preserve these bankrupt systems, and that the only path toward liberation was for the poor to organize themselves and fight for fundamental changes. Perhaps most important, liberationist priests and nuns also told the people that the Catholic Church was on their side and would help them accomplish these goals. For the first time in Salvadoran history, priests and nuns were helping the poor to pursue their earthly rather than spiritual needs. Because the Catholic Church and its religious leaders had enormous status and respect, the poor began to feel that someone within the power structure was finally with them and that change might actually be possible. Rebellion was now a possibility, because a new, palatable way of seeing injustice could promote collective action on the part of the poor of El Salvador, and particularly the downtrodden campesino. An injustice frame was coalescing, just as the organization of the peasantry was beginning. These profound changes began soon after 1970, when the archbishop held the pastoral week of reflection, and reached full force in just a few years.

The landowners of the region were, of course, not happy with the new pastoral, particularly with the religious training of peasants. Consequently, Rodríguez's parish experienced a financial crisis. Even in estates where he had not experienced any problems, the owners stopped giving Rodríguez donations, since they had heard from other landowners that he was a "communist." The loss of donations from the landowners, combined with the fact that he was not charging the poor for his services, meant that Rodríguez was raising very little money for the diocese. The only money he brought in came from the collections at the end of mass—a paltry amount, since the vast majority of parishioners were in a state of abject poverty. At a certain point, Rodríguez stopped saying mass even in the haciendas in which he was still allowed because he did not feel comfortable or welcome. Once the revenue stream in the "wealthy" parish of Tecoluca dried up, Bishop Aparicio and the more conservative priests of the diocese began to say that Rodríguez had completely "ruined the parish." Several of the conservative priests, and those who were apolitical, told him that he had to use his "head more and his heart less." The preferential option for the poor had a number of effects, as we will see, but a very practical effect was that the church lost a great deal of financial support from the wealthy. This was only natural, since the church was now not only asking the rich to provide more for the poor but also depicting the rich as social sinners, responsible for the prevailing poverty.

Rodríguez was by no means the only priest to raise the ire of the oligarchy. On November 28, 1970, Father Nicolás Rodríguez Aguilar (no relation to Rodríguez) was murdered in a hamlet in the department of Chalatenango.[11] At the time, most people accepted the government's explanation that the crime had been the result of a botched robbery, but it is now clear that the murder was most likely the first killing of a member of the progressive church by conservative sectors in El Salvador. Father Rodríguez Aguilar had denounced injustice and had butted heads with local landowners. Despite the incipient tensions between the oligarchy and the church, Rodríguez remembers that "no one imagined that a priest would be killed" for promoting the new pastoral.

Clearly, the year 1970, a full ten years prior to the start of the civil war and the assassination of Archbishop Romero, marks the start of the conflict between the oligarchy and the progressive church, with the strong reaction by the oligarchy to the land-reform congress, the subsequent kidnapping of Father Alas, quarrels with progressive priests after the first pastoral week, and the murder of Father Rodríguez Aguilar. Most narrations of the Salvadoran state's attack against the church have focused on 1977, after Father Rutilio Grande was murdered and the Salvadoran archdiocese issued its "Study Concerning the Persecution of the Salvadoran Church."[12] No doubt, in 1977 the oligarchy and the state unleashed its full fury against the church, but it was in 1970 that the liberationist pastoral emerged and the oligarchy commenced its crusade against progressive religious leaders. In that year, liberationists began to highlight the plight of the poor, called for land reform, embraced a new pastoral that would train scores of lay leaders, and helped to mobilize the poor, as we will see.

These actions placed even the conservative prelates in the crosshairs of the reactionary sectors. The oligarchy early on accused Bishop Aparicio of being a "communist," since at first the bishop used the terminology of Vatican II and Medellín in his sermons. In February 1972, after landowners charged him with being a progressive, Aparicio uttered these strong words: "If defending the poor . . . if defending those who are naked, if defending justice, is being a communist, here I am, I'm a communist! Take me to jail. If speaking of social justice is to be a communist, then, yes, I am a communist!"[13] Soon, however, the Salvadoran church would experience an internal crisis, with some priests and bishops maintaining their faith in the new pastoral and others becoming convinced that the progressive stance of the church was a grave mistake. Bishop Aparicio would adopt the latter stance, and as a result, he and Padre Rodríguez would have a serious falling out.

Elections of 1972: The Demise of the Democratic Option

Despite rising tensions in El Salvador and the lack of true political competition, the opposition political parties still held on to some hope that the elections of February 1972 would be free and fair and would finally bring to power leaders who would be more responsive to the needs of most Salvadorans. The leading contenders were Colonel Arturo Armando Molina, who had been President Fidel Sánchez's personal secretary, representing the PCN; and José Napoleón Duarte, leader of the PDC, who led the Unión Nacional Opositora (UNO; National Opposition Union). With the opposition united, victory would be assured as long as the vote counting was relatively fair. Early in the vote count it became clear that UNO was going to win, so the government halted the tally and found ways to alter the results. Officially, Colonel Molina won the election by a small margin, fewer than ten thousand votes, but objective observers knew that the victory was the result of fraud, low turnout, and the usual manipulation and intimidation. The PCN's disregard for the will of the voters convinced many Salvadorans that elections were not the best way to achieve the changes that were so desperately needed to make El Salvador a more modern, just, and democratic country. Although opportunity for the political opposition had increased somewhat in the 1960s, in 1972 the state abruptly shut down that opportunity, fearing that reformists would come to power.

In Tecoluca, a young man named Antonio "Toño" Navarro had run for mayor as a Christian Democrat in the elections. Navarro had spent some time in San Salvador and had belonged to a leftist union. As a Christian Democrat, Navarro was well versed in the church's social doctrine. During the political campaign, many parishioners asked Padre Rodríguez about Navarro, and he told them that the young candidate was interpreting the social doctrine accurately. Navarro, as one of the first group of young people trained by the PDC, had attended courses run by the Comité de Organización Política Electoral Independiente (Committee for Independent Electoral Political Organization, or Venezuela's social-Christian political party). As campesinos saw that Navarro represented their interests, learned more about their constitutional rights, and saw that "Padre David" respected him, the young candidate's popularity had soared. Consequently, little doubt existed that Navarro had won the election, but "trucks with national guardsmen arrived in the night, took over the mayor's office, and installed" Atilio Cañas, the PCN candidate, as mayor. Navarro tried to contest the decision but to no avail. Rodríguez recalls that by the time of this election he was already aware of a pamphlet that circulated in Tecoluca titled *El Rebelde* (The Rebel), published by the FPL, which said that elections did not provide the proper road to opposition.[14] When Navarro's victory was taken from him, many people who sided with the opposition, including Rodríguez, began to accept the fact that elections were meaningless in El Salvador. Real change might require extralegal methods.

Soon after the fraudulent elections, Father Boulang invited Rodríguez to attend another gathering that would solidify his commitment to the new pastoral and to bringing about socialist change to El Salvador. Since he was pleased with what Rodríguez was doing in Tecoluca, Boulang said to him: "Look, I have the possibility of four paid tickets with all expenses paid to go to Chile. . . . We have thought that you could go." Rodríguez accepted the invitation and attended the Primer Encuentro Latinoamericano de Cristianos por el Socialismo (First Latin American Encounter of Christians for Socialism), held in Santiago. The term *liberation theology* had already emerged, since in the previous year the Peruvian priest and theologian Gustavo Gutiérrez had published his influential book *Teología de la liberación* (*A Theology of Liberation*, translated into English in 1988).[15] Rodríguez flew to Santiago along with Father Boulang, a nun, and a young lay leader who represented Acción Católica Universitaria Salvadoreña (ACUS; Salvadoran Catholic University Action). Rodríguez recalls that with some remorse he asked Bishop Aparicio permission to go to a meeting in Brazil organized by the liberationist bishop Hélder Câmara, since Aparicio would never have given him permission to attend the controversial meeting in Chile. Rodríguez indeed went to Brazil, from where he sent Bishop Aparicio a telegram, but the principal reason for his trip was to participate in the Christians for Socialism gathering. At this point, Rodríguez's actions as a liberationist priest placed him in the uncomfortable position of lying to his bishop.

More than four hundred priests, nuns, and lay workers attended the April 1972 meeting, which was designed to bring together Christian leaders—including some Protestants—who were convinced that socialism, not capitalism, was the best way to achieve economic justice and development in Latin America.[16] The meeting also served to demonstrate support for Salvador Allende's socialist government, elected in 1970. At this unique encounter, a quote from Ernesto "Che" Guevara, the Argentine revolutionary leader who fought with Castro's insurgent movement in Cuba, was prominently displayed: "When Christians dare to give full-fledged revolutionary witness, then the Latin American revolution will be invincible."[17] Rodríguez met a number of progressive church leaders and theologians, such as Father Gustavo Gutiérrez, Bishop Sergio Méndez Arceo from Cuernavaca, Mexico, and Father Gonzalo Arroyo from Argentina. He came across Father Pablo Richard once more, eventually becoming "good friends" with the theologian. The election of Allende in Chile was a beacon of hope for liberationist Christians, who hoped that his socialist government would lead to fundamental changes in Chile and beyond. Some of the delegates to the meeting met with President Allende during a gathering at the presidential palace. The meeting room was so crowded that many of the attendees, including Rodríguez, had to sit on the floor. During the high-profile encounter, as Rodríguez remembers, excursions were organized so that attendees could "know the experience of Christian communities . . . and of pastoral work" in the region and could see how cooperatives worked. Rodríguez traveled to Brazil, Peru, and Colombia and saw firsthand how progressive religious leaders in those countries implemented the preferential option for the poor.

The meeting received criticism from many quarters, but Rodríguez claims that the "pros and cons" of socialism were presented and that it was not an exercise in "blind allegiance to a particular economic system." Nevertheless, those who attended the meeting were highly critical of capitalism and the ills that economic exploitation had wrought in Latin America. While in Chile, Rodríguez participated in a political demonstration for the first time, in support of the Allende government and organized by the Movimiento de Acción Popular Unitario (Unitary Popular Action Movement). Rodríguez points out that before this meeting he had not studied socialism or Marxism seriously. At the meeting he realized that socialist ideas were "consistent with" Vatican II and Medellín and with the new pastoral that the Salvadoran week of reflection had embraced. While the Catholic Church was not sympathetic to Marxism or the call for armed revolution, it was undeniable that recent encyclicals and Vatican II had heavily criticized capitalism, had denounced the exploitative international economic system, and had called for substantial transformations throughout the world.

When just over a year later, on September 11, 1973, President Allende took his own life when sectors of his government violently assaulted the presidential palace in a military coup with the cooperation of the U.S. government, many Catholic progressives lost all hope that democratic elections could lead to fundamental changes in Latin America. Thus, many groups and individuals—from Marxists to Christian liberationists—who wanted progressive transformations to take place moved toward the conclusion that revolution, rather than the ballot box, was the only viable way to achieve justice. In fact, the 1972 elections in El Salvador had already started to produce this frustration with the democratic road to reform. Ironically, while the liberationists and other opposition groups in El Salvador had given up on elections, most political parties, including the PCS, were still trying to achieve influence in the Salvadoran political system via the ballot box. After the military coup in Chile, the family that lodged Rodríguez while he was at the Christians for Socialism meeting left the country hurriedly, stayed with Rodríguez in Tecoluca, and eventually moved on to Cuernavaca, Mexico.

Owing to Rodríguez's increasingly progressive ideas and activities, an exasperated Bishop Aparicio attempted to transfer him to the town of Olocuilta, about twenty-three miles west of Tecoluca, where the bishop hoped the rebellious priest would be isolated in a less contentious parish. Although Rodríguez had already experienced numerous run-ins with landowners and had attended the progressive gatherings mentioned above, the tipping point for the bishop had been Rodríguez's refusal to welcome the new president of El Salvador at his parish in Tecoluca, the fraudulently elected Coronel Armando Molina. In an effort to gain some legitimacy, Molina was visiting towns all over the country in what he termed a "mobile government." Molina had made plans to visit Tecoluca in December 1972. The mayor of Tecoluca, Atilio Cañas, himself fraudulently elected, was thrilled that the president was visiting his town; so he wrote a letter to Rodríguez and informed him that he should welcome the president by saying a few words and seeing that the Tecoluca church bells were tolled in his honor. Additionally, Cañas let Rodríguez know that since the president had family in the region, Molina would be giving a sizable donation to the parish.

Rodríguez discussed the mayor's letter with lay leaders in Tecoluca only a few days after receiving it, something a priest would not have done in the past. Those who discussed the matter were in "unanimous agreement" that Rodríguez should not receive the new president. Rodríguez then wrote a blunt response to Mayor Cañas. In the letter, dated December 15, 1972, Rodríguez states that he will not participate in the ceremony for Molina and points out that, since his arrival in Tecoluca, he had tried to work with the government but the government had acted "hypocritically" and criticized his actions to help the poor, unjustly defaming him as an "agitator" and a "communist." Toward the end of the letter, Rodríguez writes: "I will not be present at such an act."[18] It is clear from this letter that Rodríguez was now willing to take a confrontational stance toward the authorities, using words such as "hypocrisy," "insincerity," and "injustice." This kind of rebellious attitude toward authorities by a clergyman had been virtually unheard of in El Salvador but was now becoming increasingly common as the liberationist pastoral continued to grow in popularity and influence.

A few weeks after this event, on January 6, 1973, Bishop Aparicio wrote a letter to Rodríguez letting him know that, owing to his "posture toward the authorities which will bring negative effects," he was transferring him to Olocuilta in early February.[19] Rodríguez asserts that, after the electoral fraud, Aparicio himself had stated that priests should not lend legitimacy to the newly installed government. However, as some priests would express later, the bishop's words would often be different from his deeds. The move to Olocuilta would take Rodríguez away from his parishioners, who were just beginning to assert themselves. Aparicio noted in the letter that Father Rafael Barahona would be taking over the Tecoluca parish. Father Barahona, however, was also sympathetic to the liberationist cause and did not want to be forced to replace Rodríguez. The two priests, unhappy with the prospect of being transferred, tried to discuss the matter with the bishop, but Aparicio ignored them.

In the last two years, the parish of Tecoluca had changed dramatically: the parishioners were now much more assertive and active, Rodríguez was becoming a local legend, and the new pastoral was spreading like wildfire. When the parishioners found out that Bishop Aparicio was going to transfer their priest to another parish, some of the lay leaders decided to stop the transfer. One of the key leaders was Toño Navarro, who had told Rodríguez soon after hearing of Aparicio's decision, "No, you are not going, you are not going!" Having already lost his bid to become mayor, Navarro was not about to lose the priest who had been so active in calling for political and economic change. He was not alone. Víctor Hernández, another key leader in the parish, was also outraged by the bishop's desire to remove Rodríguez from the parish. Hernández was the president of a peasant cooperative in Tecoluca that Rodríguez had helped to establish in 1971 with the assistance of the Caballeros. Hernández had also become the first "legionnaire" of the Caballeros in Tecoluca, responsible for one thousand members. He also served as a Delegate of the Word and had been a key organizer of his small community called La Cayetana, a nearby caserío that would soon be at the heart of a storm.

Navarro and Hernández, along with other parishioners, organized a march from Tecoluca to Bishop Aparicio's cathedral in San Vicente. The marchers left Tecoluca early in the morning carrying the image of San Lorenzo. Once they arrived in San Vicente, the protesters sought an audience with the bishop. Aparicio refused to speak with what he considered a group of uppity malcontents. On the third day of their vigil, the demonstrators entered the cathedral through an open door and then brazenly used the church's public address system to publicly denounce Bishop Aparicio. This effort to keep Rodríguez in Tecoluca received national press coverage and attracted the attention of the government, the oligarchs, and also the nascent guerrilla organizations. The bishop was convinced that Rodríguez was behind the parishioners' defiance, but Rodríguez asserts that at the outset he had asked Navarro and Hernández to accept the bishop's decision. A young woman who participated in the march recalls that she and some members of her family did so because "of the love they had for their parish priest." Rodríguez was no longer just a well-liked priest but a popular local leader as well. Moreover, the recently trained lay leaders had become community organizers willing to challenge the local bishop.

Bishop Aparicio had already made up his mind to place Father Barahona in Tecoluca and would not budge. Barahona, in a strong letter to Aparicio, stated that the bishop's actions were inconsistent with the spirit of Vatican II, which called upon bishops to treat their priests as "friends" and to "consult" with them on all matters concerning their dioceses.[20] Proposing a compromise, Barahona urged Aparicio to allow Rodríguez to stay in the parish of Tecoluca, but at another church within the parish. Eventually, Aparicio agreed to divide the parish in two, appointing Barahona as parish priest of Tecoluca, while assigning Rodríguez to the southeastern, coastal area of the parish at the hamlet of San Carlos Lempa. The small community was ten miles away, almost directly south of Tecoluca. This compromise came only after a delegation of priests from the diocese of San Vicente, appointed by Aparicio, negotiated with Rodríguez, Barahona, the Caballeros, and lay leaders in Tecoluca. The move to San Carlos was certainly a step down for Rodríguez, and a strong rebuke, but organized Christians and progressive priests had challenged their bishop and prevented Rodríguez's transfer to Olocuilta. In effect, Rodríguez was still on his home turf.

The Sub-Parish of San Carlos Lempa

Although the town of San Carlos Lempa had "a nice little ermita," there was no parish house, so Rodríguez continued living in Tecoluca with Father Barahona. Nevertheless, Rodríguez began to spend considerably more time in the coastal areas. His duties became much more difficult, in that living conditions were poor, the small communities near the coast were infested with malarial mosquitoes, and vices—drinking, gambling, and prostitution—were much more prevalent than in the communities around Tecoluca. The parishioners in Tecoluca were mostly traditional campesinos, tied to the land, who had a strong sense of community and obligation, whereas the people in the coastal areas tended to be more transient. The population in the area would swell during the cotton harvest owing to the onslaught of seasonal workers coming from the northern parts of the country. Rodríguez compares it to "the wild west" in the United States (as he had seen in movies). Nevertheless, the new priest had some help: Cirilo "was an old man who kept the church clean, tolled the bell, and acquired what was

Figure 3.1. Small church at San Carlos Lempa, the sub-parish of Tecoluca. Photo by author, January 2008.

needed" for the new sub-parish. He would say, "Don't worry Padre, we will get along, from hunger we will not die."

A Protestant evangelical church existed in San Nicolás Lempa, a larger town just over four miles northeast from San Carlos Lempa and alongside the large Lempa River. When the minister heard that a Catholic priest had come to serve in San Carlos, he challenged "Padre David" to "debate the Bible." Animosity between Catholics and the "sects" of Protestantism still reigned in El Salvador, even though Vatican II had called for greater Christian unity. Rodríguez did not answer the challenge, but one day he decided to visit the minister. Upon seeing Rodríguez, the minister said with passion, "The devil has entered my house!" Armed with the unifying spirit of Vatican II, Rodríguez proposed that they work together, saying, "The Bible is not something we should use to argue but to bring us together." Rodríguez recalls that in the past priests would urge catechists to harass Protestant pastors. In fact, one of the missions of the Caballeros had been to drive evangelicals out of San Vicente. Part of the reason for holding Vatican II had been the concerns over declining numbers of Catholics in the world. The great fear in the Vatican was that Catholics would turn either to Protestant "sects" or, even worse, to Marxism. The new pastoral called for the preferential option for the poor partly so that the poor would not turn to other religions or to secular organizations.[21]

Despite the difficulties, Rodríguez began to construct a sub-parish at San Carlos. He started soccer teams, established a chorus, and organized *pastorelas* (Bible stories expressed theatrically). As he had done in Tecoluca, Rodríguez also began to identify natural leaders to develop into catechists and Delegates of the Word who would in turn help form CEBs and Bible circles, small groups of peoplewho would read and reflect on key liberationist passages from the Bible. He proceeded as before by asking people to stay after church to discuss the Bible, and from there he identified the leaders who would organize the campesinos into base communities. Rodríguez recalls that peasants were not used to expressing their opinions, so the task of getting them to assert themselves was difficult. Campesinos articulated their concerns mostly with each other and seldom to authorities, such as government officials, priests, or security forces. Such reticence was perfectly rational given that authorities seldom helped campesinos. Slowly but surely, however, Rodríguez gained their confidence, and once the campesinos realized that he would not betray them, they began to voice their problems and to express how the Bible, and particularly the Gospels, related to their reality as repressed and exploited peasants. Rodríguez recalls that some of the participants who could read would find verses in the Bible that he himself had never connected to the life of the Salvadoran peasant. Rodríguez would say that campesinos demonstrated a "beautiful wisdom,"[22] and would assert, "I am learning more about the Bible here than I learned in the seminary." Eventually, Bishop Aparicio heard what Rodríguez was telling the campesinos and admonished him, saying angrily, "How can you say that!"

When Rodríguez had been parish priest of Tecoluca his visits to San Carlos Lempa were few and brief, and he had hardly ever stayed overnight. Now that he was the priest of the sub-parish, however, he was able to better organize the people there, so his popularity in the entire parish of Tecoluca continued to grow. Remembering those days, Rodríguez says, "I had a great deal of credibility." The liberationists developed strong, personal ties as never before with the people, which helps to explain their newfound ability to mobilize the poor.

At one small community, called La Pita, near the mouth of the Lempa River and at the southernmost tip of the parish of Tecoluca, Rodríguez met a family that would change his life. The Henríquez family had a fifteen-year-old daughter, Mercedes ("Merci"), who was away at school in San Juan Nonualco, a mere two miles west of Zacatecoluca. One Sunday, Merci happened to be in La Pita, so she attended Sunday mass, finally meeting the "Padre David" whom everyone was talking about. She remembers that he looked at her and she became nervous, thinking, "Why is he looking at me?" One of her aunts told her to confess with the new priest and, though hesitant, she relented. At confession, Rodríguez asked her why she had not been at mass before. (Rodríguez, like all priests, wanted everyone to attend mass, at least on Sundays.) She explained that she had been away at school and that she was from the Henríquez family. She saw Rodríguez a number of times after that first meeting and "felt that there was a mutual attraction." Merci could not imagine any future with a priest, thinking to herself, "I live on an island with animals!" No one as respected, popular, and educated as "Padre David," she thought, could be interested in her. Merci Henríquez, however, was a highly intelligent girl, and she was studying in San Juan Nonualco because her talents had attracted attention in her small town. Like Padre Rodríguez, her potential had been apparent at a very early age. Even though he was at a higher social status, Rodríguez enjoyed talking with her and often turned up when she least expected it. Henríquez confided, "I began to fall in love with him."[23] "But then the suffering began," she recalls. "I finished middle school, and did not see him again." A year or so later, she remembers that people were telling her that Rodríguez "was hiding because they [the government] wanted to kill him." Henríquez then attended high school in San Salvador and became involved in the student organization Movimiento Estudiantil Revolucionario de Secundaria (MERS; Revolutionary Secondary Student Movement). In a few short years, however, she and Padre Rodríguez would again cross paths.

At San Carlos, Rodríguez organized pastoral missions to the small coastal communities of the parish to teach catechism to children, visit homes, and promote biblical reflection. At first he would go with a few young Delegates and catechists, staying in one community for a few days. Eventually, Rodríguez and Barahona would organize joint pastoral missions throughout the entire parish, much as Father Rutilio Grande's pastoral teams were doing in the parish of Aguilares, in the archdiocese of San Salvador.[24] These pastoral missions allowed Rodríguez to gain the trust of people in coastal areas who for the most part had become estranged from the church. Additionally, the joint missions enabled Rodríguez to continue to visit the communities around the town of Tecoluca, making it possible for him to preserve his links to the people whom he had first organized while he had been the sole parish priest. Rodríguez remembers that, even though the parish had been technically divided in two, it was really "one parish with two priests." In addition to working with the Passionist priests in the diocese of Santiago de María, Rodríguez worked closely with the progressive priests from his own diocese, including Porfirio Martínez from San Isidro Labrador, Miguel Flores in Cinquera, Ramiro in Verapaz, Benigno Rodríguez (his brother) in Villa Dolores, Alirio Macías in San Esteban Catarina (who would later be murdered), and Vicente Sibrián in Victoria (who eventually joined the guerrillas).[25] These were some of the most progressive priests, and they tended to cooperate with each other as much as possible and to participate in joint pastorals. These networks of progressive priests and nuns were developing throughout El Salvador, not just in the diocese of San Vicente. In fact, the most extensive networks operated in the archdiocese, where many priests worked and where most Salvadorans lived.

Barahona and Rodríguez also began to develop a formal pastoral plan for their parish. Although they had already created a number of courses and formed Bible circles and CEBs, they felt that the parish needed a "well defined" plan to enrich and expand their pastoral work. In January 1974, the two of them, along with thirty-three lay leaders from seventeen com-

Figure 3.2. Rodríguez at a church service, with his guitar and a young boy singing, circa 1974. By permission of the Rodríguez Henríquez family.

munities in the parish, met to develop a plan for their parish. The group identified some of the reasons why the pastoral mission of the parish was not progressing adequately, including "fear," "pessimism," "lack of organization," and "egoism on the part of some."[26] Despite these problems, they determined that parishioners had acquired a higher level of social consciousness and that church attendance had increased significantly. The participants decided that at minimum they would fashion a plan that would help the parish's organizational strength. The new plan divided the parish in two: the central zone, centered at Tecoluca and led by Father Barahona; and the coastal zone, centered at San Carlos Lempa and led by Rodríguez. Each zone was then subdivided into five areas. Every month, the CEBs in the ten areas would meet to discuss the progress of the pastoral plan. Every two months, four representatives from each zone would meet at the sub-parish level (Tecoluca and San Carlos). The plan also called for the parish to establish contacts with CEBs in the other parishes in the diocese. The general goal of the plan was "to make decisions as Christians based on reality as it is illuminated by the light of the faith."[27] In addition to understanding the causes of poverty, concerted action was an imperative of the plan.

Within a year, the pastoral plan included a parish council composed of two delegates from each area (a total of ten) and the two priests of the parish. The purpose of the council was to evaluate the plan and ensure that it proceeded smoothly. After one year, in January 1975, in a council meeting for the purpose of evaluating the parish's strategy, the participants identified a number of problems and difficulties that had arisen. Several delegates reported that some members of the communities expressed fear of being labeled a "communist" and "fear of repression." They also discussed the reactionary attitudes of some of the people in the communities in which they operated. It is clear that the increasing polarization in the country was beginning to have a direct effect on the CEBs and the pastoral work of the parish. The conflict that had emerged between the church and the state was now being manifested within the communities in the parish. This was to be expected, since the work of the liberationist priests and the CEBs was the reason why the oligarchy and the state were furious with the church. What is clear is that before the emergence of state repression, the Catholic Church, via progressive priests and nuns, provided political opportunities and substantial vehicles for developing the organizational strength of Christians with grievances.

Campesino University: "The University of Life"

Rodríguez had already attained a national reputation as a liberationist, or "red," priest, but in terms of training lay leaders his influence at this point had mostly been felt in the parish of Tecoluca. Bishop Aparicio had moved him to San Carlos Lempa in an attempt to minimize his activities and influence, but Rodríguez's new assignment placed him in a perfect position to train lay leaders from all over El Salvador, since Father Juan Macho's parish of Jiquilisco was right across the Lempa River, in the diocese of Santiago de María. Padre Macho had founded a training center for campesino formation at a small place called Los Naranjos, near the town of Jiquilisco. Emulating what a U.S. Maryknoll priest had done in the parish of Santa Ana, Macho had written to his Passionist order in Spain and acquired funds to create the training center for peasants. He set up the Centro Naranjos in an abandoned school that was owned by an order of nuns, who donated the buildings to him. The purpose of Centro Naranjos was to offer practical education and training to peasants, such as first aid, farming techniques, and animal care, as well as Bible study with a focus on examining the people's realidad.

Once it was ready to operate, Father Macho invited Rodríguez to offer classes at Centro Naranjos. Rodríguez was delighted and agreed to teach Salvadoran history. He used popular, and often revolutionary, songs to inspire discussion. For example, Rodríguez would sing the song "I Am Latin American," which included the following lines: "If we have to fight, let's fight, if that is the way to triumph." Once the song was over, Rodríguez would ask the students, mostly campesinos, "What do you think of this song?" His goal was to get students to realize that a struggle was essential for producing necessary changes. The discussions inspired by the songs would invariably lead the campesinos to "criticisms of the country's land-tenure system." Rodríguez also used a common method of training with cassette tapes, called "Juror #13." The cassettes contained debates on a number of community problems. Different characters in the program—the landowner, the mayor, the campesino, the priest—would state their opinion concerning the problem under consideration. After listening to the entire program, the students in the course would discuss the issue, the various opinions, and finally decide, as a juror would, whose stance had the greatest merit. Rodríguez remembers that most of the students would enjoy this program, since "it was almost like a soap opera." The programs, which "came from South America," were designed to raise people's "social conscience."[28] Rodríguez points out that, at the start, the students had little in-depth knowledge of Salvadoran history. When he spoke of the rebellion of Anastasio Aquino (an indigenous leader), La Matanza, or the taking of property from the indigenous people by the oligarchy in the late 1800s, the response would often be an incredulous, "I did not know that."

The teachers at Centro Naranjos offered courses principally to lay leaders (Delegates of the Word and catechists) who had been identified by their priests as "natural leaders." The individuals selected showed themselves to have not only leadership potential but also a commitment to the new pastoral mission. The priests who ran the center would send letters to various parishes letting them know that a course was going to start on a specific day, and then the parish priests would let the center know how many campesinos had the proper qualifications to attend that specific course. Once they had enough students, twenty to thirty, the center would enroll them and prepare everything to commence the course, which would last up to four weeks. The Passionist order financed most of the cost, meaning that neither the campesinos nor their home parishes had to pay tuition, food, or lodging. Students who attended the courses gained a "great deal of local prestige," to a large extent because of the practical skills that they acquired, which they could then use to help the campesinos in their local area in very direct, useful ways. For example, the graduates would help people in the countryside with first aid, organic farming, preserving the fertility of the land, and literacy. The Catholic Church's radio station, YSAX, started broadcasting literacy courses that the lay leaders would use to help teach people in their communities to read. These literacy courses also served as a consciousness-raising vehicle, since the content was replete with the liberationist message. In effect, poor campesinos were able to take courses that enhanced their practical skills and raised their political consciousness because of the resources available to the church and the liberationist commitment of Catholic religious leaders.

Centro Naranjos eventually offered courses at four levels, the fourth level being reserved for the "most committed" catechists and Delegates. As the students progressed, the courses grew more political and emphasized organizational skills. Rodríguez remembers that at the fourth level the discussions covered such themes as political parties, ways to organize people, and the untenable land-tenure system. The liberationists managed to establish six important training centers in the early 1970s, a veritable "network of campesino training centers." After the first center was set up in the parish of Santa Ana, in Chinalinga, called Centro Castaño, a French priest established another one, Centro San Lucas, in San Miguel, that focused on health training. Father Walter Guerra created a center called Divine Providence in Santa Ana. The archdiocese started a center in Chalatenango in Chacalcollo. Father "Chencho" Alas created a center in Bermuda. Eventually, the directors tied together the work of the centers and created an educational network they referred to as "Campesino University." Rodríguez points out that his involvement with these centers and Campesino University was a "good experience" because his commitment grew and he was able to visit many parishes and meet lay leaders in many parts of the country, giving him a broader, national perspective. Rodríguez says, with great satisfaction, that to this date he will come across someone who will say to him, "Because of you I became committed [to the cause]."[29] Rodríguez recalls: "These were intense times of much reflection, commitment, and much sincerity." He adds that the network of centers and the joint pastoral promoted by the week of reflection generated "much solidarity" among communities and "broke the borders between our parishes." The Christian movement by the mid-1970s was gathering tremendous strength and organization. Not only did the church facilitate the training of peasant leaders, but the liberationist pastoral facilitated the flowering of a network of religious leaders throughout El Salvador.

Francisco Castro y Ramírez was the bishop of the diocese of Santiago de María when Centro Naranjos opened its doors. Although conservative, Bishop Castro y Ramírez allowed his priests a reasonable amount of leeway, more so than Bishop Aparicio. After the death of Castro y Ramírez, Father Óscar Romero was named bishop of Santiago de María, in October 1974. Soon after arriving at his new post, Bishop Romero began to hear pernicious rumors about the courses at the center. The mother superior of the Salesian order in Jiquilisco complained to Romero that some priests who taught there, Rodríguez in particular, were teaching politics and communism and were "brainwashing" the campesinos, instead of teaching religion. Bishop Aparicio likewise complained to Bishop Romero, since the bishop of San Vicente was bothered by the fact that his wayward priest was teaching courses in another diocese. Bishop Romero decided to see for himself if the rumors were true. One day, Romero visited the center and stood outside Rodríguez's classroom, behind the open door, to listen to his lectures and discussions. After listening to Rodríguez's class, Bishop Romero reportedly told Padre Macho, "If Rodríguez is a communist, I am more of a communist than he."[30] In fact, after listening to Rodríguez's class three times, the future archbishop told one priest: "Rodríguez opened my eyes and evangelized me from behind that door."[31] After Romero's reassurance, Centro Naranjos continued to offer courses, Rodríguez continued teaching there, and many lay leaders from parishes all over the country continued to receive training. Rodríguez was now forming dozens of Salvadoran peasants at a time.

Rodríguez recalls that within himself and within these lay leaders there seemed to be four stages of commitment and political awakening. The first stage involved understanding that there were great injustices in El Salvador, without necessarily identifying the causes. Rodríguez would tell students that this is like having a "fever but not knowing its source." The second phase involved identifying the sources of the injustice, which involved gaining social "consciousness." The third phase required the individual to make a commitment to work to promote social justice by eliminating the sources of that injustice. In the final phase the individual became "incorporated into the struggle" and gave selflessly for the common good. For many who embraced the liberationist cause, incorporation would come later, after the repression, when thousands of peasants incorporated themselves into the politico-military organizations. Rodríguez's depiction of what happened to many priests and peasants demonstrates the awakening that occurred in the early 1970s owing to the new injustice frame developed by liberationist ideas and the transmission of those ideas, first by priests and nuns and then by lay leaders.

The Salvadoran campesinos finally gained the political insight and organizational and practical skills necessary for becoming active, empowered citizens. The lay leaders trained at Centro Naranjos and other centers would bring the Bible to rural areas and help campesinos to interpret the Gospel in ways that were meaningful to their reality.[32] Essentially this meant that campesinos began to see their plight not as the will of God but as the result of an exploitative socioeconomic system, replete with social sin, and maintained by the government on behalf of selfish and greedy landowners, who were at the service of international capitalism. Although most campesinos were most likely well aware of the unjust conditions in which they lived, the liberationist perspective gave them a Christian-based injustice frame that provided a clear explanation for their plight, a clear enemy to combat, and a realization that they had a strong ally—the Catholic Church—if they decided to fight for their rights. In essence, the new interpretation of El Salvador's putrid economic and political systems employed dependency theory, class analysis, but mostly the Gospel—a combination that was much more palatable to the campesino than a purely theoretical, atheistic Marxist analysis. In any case, while El Salvador's political parties were still hoping to gain political office via the ballot box, and the politico-military organizations were still at a fledgling state, the Catholic Church's liberationist priests and nuns were already working for the earthly liberation of the poor.

For campesinos, as for priests and nuns, embracing the liberationist perspective generated some ethical problems. Rodríguez notes that campesinos are "inherently honest people." The activities at the training centers often required that the student lie to authorities. Some of the lay leaders training at Centro Naranjos, for example, attended courses without the knowledge of their parish priest or bishop (principally those who came from conservative parishes). If the parish priest asked the campesino, who had been gone a couple of weeks to take a course, "Where have you been?" the campesino would have to make up a lie or the priest might become angry. Also, once campesinos started becoming involved in peasant organizations that operated clandestinely, they would often have to lie to authorities. Rodríguez admits that he had that same "crisis of conscience," since he often found himself obfuscating the truth when communicating with Bishop Aparicio. To deal with this internal crisis, the progressive priests in Tecoluca agreed that rules and laws could be broken if one was involved in fighting for a more just society, which was after all "God's plan." A peccadillo was irrelevant when working toward the liberation of an oppressed people.

All in all, according to Rodríguez, the liberationists in El Salvador, priests and nuns alike, "contributed greatly to waking up the people." He adds that "the methodology of popular participation was implemented by the church," suggesting that it was the church rather than the politico-military organizations that initiated the process of political mobilization. The lay leaders who were formed by the centers and parishes "developed a great deal of credibility with the people." At first they were simply Christian lay leaders, but over time they became key community leaders, owing to the leadership, practical, and organizational skills they gained in the courses they had taken. Rodríguez says that these leaders had "a good perception of what was happening in the country even if they couldn't read and write." "We would say," Rodríguez remembers, the campesinos "have studied in the University of life." In the 1970s, liberationists trained "approximately 15,000 lay leaders" at these centers.[33] The church in effect created an army of Christians who were committed to making El Salvador a more just country, knew the causes of the existing injustice, had acquired leadership and organizational skills, and could count on a powerful and respected ally—the progressive church. It is truly remarkable that liberationists accomplished this in a non-democratic country in just about four years of intense effort.

A Splintering Church

The correspondence from this early period that is preserved in files from the parish of Tecoluca reveals that the liberationist priests were becoming more combative not only with the authorities but also with their bishops and with those within the church who resisted the new pastoral mission.[34] The best example of this attitude is an undated flyer titled "The Church Is a Family or It Is Nothing," signed and distributed by a "group of priests" and addressed to the "people of God—hierarchy and faithful."[35] The flyer is found between two other documents in chronological order, suggesting that it was written and issued between January 1973 and July 1974. In the document, the group of priests, which includes Rodríguez, Barahona, Rafael Palacios (who would be killed in 1977), Vicente Sibrián (who would join the guerrillas), Marcial Serrano (who would be killed in 1980), and seven others, openly criticized Bishop Aparicio, saying that he was not supporting his priests, was authoritarian, was excessively involved in the order of nuns he founded in Santo Domingo, had no commitment to the new pastoral, transferred priests with great frequency for political reasons, was not open to dialogue, and discriminated against the liberationist priests. The statement concluded by saying that the priests were not in accord with the way the diocese was being governed, not in accord with the recent reassignments, and that "all future repression is no solution to the problem." One section of the document states that the priests are living in a condition of "fear." The flyer also indirectly suggests that the bishop should resign. Despite the changes inspired by Vatican II, these were harsh, personal criticisms—the use of the words "repression" and "fear"—for an institution that historically had been highly hierarchical and deferential to authority. Without doubt, Bishop Aparicio, upon reading this flyer, must have become livid and even more convinced that some of his priests were too radical and insubordinate. Additionally, the reaction of the Christian base communities in Tecoluca to Aparicio's attempt to reassign Rodríguez shows a rising level of assertiveness on the part of newly organized Christians. In the past, bishops could act unilaterally without having to worry about repercussions from parishioners or clergy. Now both priests and parishioners were challenging the decisions of bishops! These rebellious, more democratic actions, however, were spawned by some of the ideas promulgated by Vatican II and Medellín, which called for new, more democratic ways of governing dioceses.

In the diocese of San Vicente, and specifically the parish of Tecoluca, the emerging conflict within the church and between the liberationist church and the government was already evident. In an anonymous, undated document titled "Reflections Concerning the Ecclesiastical Problem of San Vicente," these words set the stage quite accurately:

> If a priest in the line of biblical prophesying takes the side of the poorest, of the exploited and oppressed masses, and clamors for their justice, then he is considered a "political priest." On the other hand, if the ecclesiastical authorities participate in official acts of the government . . . that is not considered political. Christ was not a politician, neither should the clergy be. But the actions of Christ had political consequences. Christ was judged and tortured by political tribunals . . . and was condemned to death. . . . In the times in which we live neutrality is impossible.[36]

Here we see the base of the problem. Liberationist priests were challenging the church's historically close relationship with the government, since they had taken to heart the changes generated by Vatican II and the preferential option for the poor promoted by Medellín. The government and some priests and bishops within the church, however, were critical of that stance and thus resisted the efforts made by those priests who promoted the new pastoral. These differences would not have spiraled out of control were it not for the specter of communism, meaning that the ideological polarization of the time—capitalism versus communism—raised what should have been simply a reconcilable difference of focus into fundamental and destructive clashes.

Despite this polarization, a large group of priests remained in the middle. They were mostly sympathetic to the needs of the poor and were critical of the government, but at the same time they argued that the liberationists' commitment to socioeconomic and political change was "too exaggerated" and would "pull the whole church" into conflict. Rodríguez and other liberationists would argue that "the Mother Church had to worry about its children's souls *and* bodies." Once the oligarchy, the government, and security forces decided that the church was politically involved and promoting socialism, they attacked the liberationists as they would any other enemy, forgetting their religiosity or conveniently interpreting the church's new pastoral as heresy. For the oligarchs, if Catholic doctrine questioned their economic interests—justified by capitalist ideology—then priests and nuns would become their enemies.

Figure 3.3. Rodríguez making his priestly rounds on horseback, mid-1970s. By permission of the Rodríguez Henríquez family.

Soon this division would devolve into a horrible conflict between the progressive segment of the church and the government, and into an ugly tension between the liberationists and their detractors within the church. Rodríguez would ask some of the more conservative priests later on, "How is it possible that when I was chaplain of the army no one said anything, but now that I am a chaplain for the guerrillas, I am questioned?" In San Vicente in 1970 there were thirty-six priests, and thirteen of them were inspired by the new pastoral, including "three older priests." Three of these thirteen priests would eventually be murdered by the government—Alirio Macías,

Rafael Palacios, and Marcial Serrano, one of the older priests. Two of the priests would join the FPL, including Rodríguez. Bishop Aparicio would become one of the key bishops in the conservative faction of the church. At one point, he would forbid the distribution and reading of *Orientación*, the archdiocese's weekly paper, because he considered it subversive. To justify his decision, Aparicio would say, "I am the bishop here [in San Vicente], not the archbishop [Romero]." Rodríguez remembers, however, that *Orientación* would be consumed "like hot bread," just like the radio broadcasts of YSAX, the Salvadoran church's radio station.[37] Adding fuel to this already hot fire was that those who resisted the new pastoral viewed it as nothing more than communism and the priests who promoted it as either communists or their dupes. Just as some priests, like Rodríguez, joined or supported the FPL and other politico-military organizations, others joined or supported the government and oligarchy, and even ORDEN, the repressive intelligence-gathering paramilitary organization.

The Infamous Link with Marxism

In the early 1970s, two revolutionary, or "politico-military," organizations emerged that advocated armed struggle as the only route to deposing the unjust state and oligarchy and bringing justice and socialism to El Salvador. The first to emerge was the FPL, which grew out of a dispute within the PCS. The secretary-general of the PCS, Cayetano Carpio, disagreed with the party's support of the government during the war with Honduras and its participation in elections. Carpio believed that the PCS was too wedded to nationalism and to Soviet tutelage. He argued that the party should embrace its revolutionary heritage and fight against the military dictatorship, as was occurring in Vietnam. He lost the argument, however, with most of the party leadership wanting to participate in elections and believing that revolution in El Salvador was not yet possible. Carpio resigned from the party and, along with about half a dozen others, founded the FPL on April 1, 1970. The other clandestine group to emerge was the Ejército Revolucionario del Pueblo (ERP; People's Revolutionary Army). This organization began with a nucleus, called "el grupo" (the group), composed of young leaders from the PDC and Catholic Agrarian Youth who had become convinced that El Salvador would change only through the barrel of a gun. Prior to the founding of these two organizations, the leaders of each group met in an effort to forge one organization, but their attempt failed, principally because

Carpio, the most intransigent and orthodox revolutionary leader, did not want to include Christians in his Marxist organization.[38] In just a few years, however, Carpio would realize that organized Christians and their religious leaders were too valuable to ignore.

In 1973 and 1974, Rodríguez's popularity, progressiveness, and willingness to challenge authority, as he recalls, "awakened an interest in the different revolutionary organizations that existed." Rodríguez remembers that, soon after being transferred to San Carlos Lempa, he was approached first by Shafik Handal, who had become the leader of the PCS after Carpio's departure. Rodríguez, who by this point felt a need to develop ties with popular organizations, assigned a group of Delegates to develop a relationship with the PCS. It is important to keep in mind that one of the ideas of liberationism was that the church should be more attuned to the world and work with progressive groups to accomplish the liberation of the poor. Handal put Rodríguez in contact with the PCS organization Asociacion de Trabajadores Agropecuarios y Campesinos de El Salvador (Association of Agricultural Workers and Peasants of El Salvador), but after only a few meetings Rodríguez and his Delegates decided to break off ties because they did not sympathize with the ideas of the PCS. In particular, Rodríguez remembers that his Delegates and catechists operated in a very democratic manner, while the PCS was exceedingly authoritarian. Additionally, despite his sympathies with the ideas of liberation theology, Rodríguez was leery of Marxism and its associated organizations.

Rodríguez's second contact with a leader of a revolutionary organization was with Rafael Arce Zablah, a young university student who was a co-founder of the ERP. Rodríguez recalls that Father Boulang facilitated the contact with Zablah because the French priest "had many relations with them [the ERP]." Arce Zablah, however, was soon transferred to the eastern part of the country, in the department of Morazán, where the ERP established the bulk of its guerrilla army, and was killed in battle some years later. As a result, Rodríguez lost contact with him and the ERP. Although it attempted to recruit people from all over the country, the ERP early on decided to move its operations to the more remote, mountainous department of Morazán, where its leaders believed a guerrilla army could be more successful.

Felipe Peña, another university student, was the third revolutionary who worked to develop ties with Padre Rodríguez. Peña, a founding member of the FPL, was an active member of ACUS, was associated with the PDC, and had been a catechist himself. From 1970 to 1974, to become a member of the FPL, one had to be a Marxist, and thus an atheist—or at least its members did not demonstrate their belief in Catholicism, especially since Cayetano Carpio was an orthodox Marxist-Leninist. However, the nascent organization eventually decided to welcome Christians. In 1974 the FPL issued a communiqué to progressive priests and Christians in general inviting them to join the organization. As one FPL leader recalls, the letter stated that "between Christians and revolution there was no contradiction, since they were two tributaries of the same river."[39] One priest, Benito Tobar, has suggested that the letter was written at least in part by a liberationist priest, which would indicate that the link between some of the liberationists and the FPL may have commenced even before 1974.[40]

The FPL decision to accept Christians was astute. Rodríguez points out that for most campesinos, if an FPL leader said, "I am an atheist," no matter how well prepared that leader was, the campesino would reject the message. Many of the rural people of El Salvador were Christians first and revolutionaries second. Certainly some of the campesinos who later "incorporated" themselves into the FPL eventually embraced Marxist ideology, and some even gave up their faith, but for most of them Christianity was ingrained in their being. The overwhelming majority of the country was Catholic, so for a revolutionary movement to grow and triumph in El Salvador, as "Che" Guevara had surmised, it had to be at least partly Catholic. It is clear that the emerging politico-military organizations, which promoted socialism, needed the liberationist Christian movement. No record exists of whether or not Cayetano Carpio supported this move or was convinced by others to support the opening to Christians, but because Carpio dominated the FPL, he must have agreed to this practical alliance.

Peña was more acceptable than the other leaders who approached Rodríguez, because he was active in a Catholic organization and came to Tecoluca to stay, thus showing greater commitment to Catholicism and to Rodríguez's followers. According to Rodríguez, Peña instantly won over the peasants because of his "conceptions, attitudes and work methods." Rodríguez remembers a day when Peña, unable to attend a meeting in Tecoluca, sent another student to represent him. The campesinos were shocked by his replacement. Rodríguez had been discussing the Bible and how it related to their reality, and when he was done the young man put Rodríguez's Bible aside and said, "Well, we're done talking of this *babosada* [drivel], let's talk about politics!" All of the peasants left before the student finished his talk.

Outside, one campesino, infuriated by the student's attitude, said to Rodríguez, "The next time this bastard comes, I'm going to comb his hair with my machete!" Rodríguez, other priests, and lay workers had already worked for a few years with the campesinos at examining how the Bible related to their problems, and this upstart had disparaged what they had taken very seriously. Moreover, the university student had also disrespected their revered priest. The vast majority of campesinos valued or at least respected Catholicism, priests, and the Bible. These sentiments explain why liberationism became such a strong, ideational force in developing El Salvador's popular Christian movement of the 1970s, and why priests and nuns became such powerful, popular leaders at the same time that the politico-military organizations where just getting off the ground.

Rodríguez recalls that Peña was very intelligent in that he developed ties with all the key leaders of the parish, but did it so "discreetly and compartmentalized" that only later did he realize what Peña had done. Rodríguez describes him as someone who "handled the Bible and the Christian faith well and [possessed] the [necessary] political commitment." Peña, as an FPL leader who hoped to inspire a popular insurrection, certainly saw the potential of the campesino mobilization that had been occurring in Tecoluca and realized that Christian leaders like Rodríguez needed to be incorporated into the popular movement. Since Peña and other opposition leaders went to Tecoluca to meet and recruit Rodríguez, they must have understood that this young priest had become a strong, popular figure in that area. At the time he met Peña, however, Rodríguez still had many doubts about which road to take as a priest. One of the things that bothered him the most was that being involved in the liberationist movement required him to lie frequently to people like his bishop, his family, and others. Peña would quote the Bible to Rodríguez and say, "Padre, don't feed pearls to swine," suggesting that the truth was like a pearl and giving the truth to malicious people would potentially lead to greater harm. Rodríguez recalls: "[Peña] helped me greatly" in dissolving his doubts. Not long after meeting and working with Rodríguez, however, Peña was killed in an urban guerrilla operation, in 1975.

By early 1974, Rodríguez suspected that a number of his catechists and Delegates were involved with the FPL. He realized that they were having meetings and were acting in a secretive manner. In fact, some of the peasants would ask Rodríguez if they could use the sacristy in the Tecoluca church to hold meetings. Rodríguez would sometimes listen and realize that they were involved in "serious work." Although concerned, he was also very impressed that these campesinos had become politically active. How could he chide them if he had been the one who trained them to become active in demanding their rights? Some of the most active lay leaders had become somewhat frustrated with the peaceful tactics of the liberationist arm of the church, which denounced injustice and trained and organize the poor but did not take combative action. Many of the leaders were young and impatient. They wanted more than the liberationists could offer. Consequently, it was only natural that some of them would find the politico-military organizations appealing. In this initial period, a number of catechists and Delegates joined the FPL or another clandestine revolutionary group.

Unlike the church, the FPL used strong, forceful methods. For example, caporales were often the individuals who most directly mistreated campesinos. The FPL would decide to capture a particularly distasteful caporal and "give him a *suggestion*." They would say to the caporal, "Look, you are . . . hurting the campesinos . . . you have to put yourself on their side, not on the side of the patrón." The FPL also started to carry out propaganda efforts by issuing communiqués denouncing a particular hacienda or a landowner for unjust actions. It was only natural that the lay leaders would at some point yearn to take bolder political action. Rodríguez recalls that some catechists in meetings would start saying, "Well, here in the parish we talk a lot but we don't do anything!" These lay leaders began to discuss forming a popular organization, their militancy being influenced by the association some of them already had with the "revolutionary organizations." It was clear that the FPL, which was becoming the largest clandestine revolutionary organization in the area, was interested in recruiting both priests and lay leaders into its ranks.

The Fraudulent Elections of 1974

The 1974 legislative and mayoral elections, held on March 10, saw more fraud and one of the first violent acts against the population that opposition groups would later use as an example of government "massacres." In the town of San Francisco Chinameca (known by its diminutive Chinamequita), in the diocese of San Vicente (the department of La Paz), the UNO coalition candidate for mayor, Sixto González, won by a margin of only 144 votes. The local electoral commission quickly confirmed González as the victor over the PCN candidate, Ezequiel Martínez Cardona. The electoral junta in the department, however, refused to recognize the victory, and the PCN decided to take the mayor's office the day prior to the installment of the new mayor. Those who supported González and UNO initiated a protest in the town plaza. Then at 1:00 a.m., on May 1, a military jeep appeared with ten guardsmen and Martínez Cardona. The guardsmen dispersed the crowd by beating the people who had gathered there. Three more trucks arrived filled with about sixty guardsmen and the outgoing PCN mayor. The guardsmen then began to sack the homes of suspected UNO supporters and also broke into the town's church, arresting the sacristan, Bernardino Martínez, and taking his keys. At the end, 150 people were arrested, and one person, Alberto Vásquez, was killed.[41] Bishop Aparicio denounced the state repression at a church service in Chinamequita the following month. He said that no mass would be offered until the keys and the sacristan were returned, emphasized that the church was not interested in political parties but only in "charity and justice," and called for the government to "respect the will of the people." The bishop continued forcefully: "To promote human rights, to teach peasants to read and write . . . explain to them what a minimum wage is . . . to teach them . . . to unite them to help themselves mutually, is not, Misters Exploiters . . . indoctrinating communism. It is solely to liberate our peasants from exploitation."[42] At this point, mid-1974, Bishop Aparicio, though concerned about the political posture of the liberationists, still denounced the government when it acted brutally, particularly when it did so against the church.

In July 1974, Víctor Hernández, who had helped to keep Rodríguez in the parish of Tecoluca, was killed in an FPL operation designed to convince a coffee finca caporal to treat workers with respect. Hernández and three other FPL members stopped the caporal on a dirt road to urge him to change his ways. The caporal took out a gun immediately and shot Hernández in the forehead. The three other FPL members then killed the caporal. Rodríguez, deeply saddened by the death of the young leader, at first was led to believe that Hernández had died mysteriously of "a headache." At the funeral, however, Hernández's family told Rodríguez the truth about Victor's involvement in the FPL. Rodríguez recalls that Hernández would admonish him when he would criticize Fidel Castro and the Cuban government. Rodríguez, very wary of communism as a blueprint for change and development, had no intention of joining forces with Marxists. Victor, one of Rodríguez's catechists and "natural leaders," however, had been one of the first campesino leaders to be groomed by the FPL to "carry out recruitment for the politico-military organization" in the region of Tecoluca.

With Hernández gone, the activities of the FPL and the organization of peasants in general began to be attributed increasingly to Padres Rodríguez and Barahona. A communiqué from the Caballeros of Tecoluca dated July 20, 1974, states, "We deny totally that the priests of the parish are agitating the campesinos" or "forming guerrilla groups." At the end of this communiqué, the Caballeros ask that the campaign of "calumny" against their priests stop, that the president of the country not accept rumors spread by "unscrupulous persons," that the constitution, the UN's Universal Declaration on Human Rights, and minimum-wage laws be respected, that salaries be increased and the price of staple items controlled, that unjust practices in the haciendas be corrected, and, finally, that laws be passed to allow campesinos to have land to till to meet their basic needs. It is clear that in the mid-1970s, even though small armed groups had already emerged, the church and organized campesinos simply desired political and economic reforms rather than revolutionary change. Rodríguez remembers that the liberationists called only for a better life for the poor and minor "redemptive demands." This reformist emphasis would quickly change owing to the introduction of much more violent repression on the part of the Salvadoran state.

Political "Awakening," Leadership, and Social Mobilization

The revolutionary ideas that emerged from Vatican II and the 1968 Medellín Conference did not have major repercussions in El Salvador until Archbishop Chávez y González called for a pastoral week of reflection in 1970. This gathering brought together the most progressive religious leaders in the country and set a course for the establishment of a new pastoral mission that transformed the Salvadoran church. Perhaps most important was that the leading bishop in the country, along with his auxiliary bishop, sanctioned the new pastoral and encouraged priests, nuns, and lay leaders to promulgate it widely. The new pastoral promoted the preferential option for the poor, which explained that the poor were in a state of injustice not because of their sins but because of the social sins of the wealthy. The new ideas also suggested that dramatic change was both necessary and possible and that the poor should work together in Christian communities to demand their rights. While religious leaders became the key transmission belts in promulgating this new pastoral and in "awakening" the poor, they did not embrace these ideational changes until they themselves were convinced of the need for change and the need to mobilize the poor—until they themselves were "awakened."

These revolutionary ideas were a necessary beginning, but they would not have made an impact unless religious leaders promulgated them, helped to convince the poor of their relevance and importance, and then applied them in a way that would help the poor to become politically organized. The CEBs, the training courses offered at parishes, the Bible circles, and the development of Campesino University all helped both to spread the new pastoral widely and to train lay leaders who would then become community and even political leaders themselves. While Padre Rodríguez was one of the most active priests in El Salvador, these activities were carried out in almost all parishes in El Salvador, raising the political consciousness, organizational capacity, and political ambitions of the poor, all of which were necessary conditions for the emergence of a strong social movement.

The Salvadoran church had a tremendous advantage over all other opposition groups—political parties, unions, and the politico-military organizations—in mobilizing the poor. First, most Salvadorans were Catholic. The average Salvadoran had little notion of socialism or Marxism. Second, priests and nuns were highly respected. Third, the Salvadoran church, though not wealthy like the oligarchy, had tremendous resources. Thus, the Christian movement flowered almost immediately after the pastoral week. We have seen that Padre Rodríguez carried out training and mobilizing activities with great success soon after the week of reflection and continued to do so for several years, forming base communities and Bible circles, training lay leaders in the parish of Tecoluca, and training lay leaders at Centro Naranjos. Many other priests and nuns did the same, eventually training an army of Christian leaders who were bent on pushing for reforms in their country. The Salvadoran church provided unparalleled opportunities for the poor of El Salvador to organize and mobilize for political action. It also facilitated the nascent Christian movement's attaining a tremendous amount of organizational strength. While the Christian movement mushroomed in the early 1970s, the political-military organizations remained small, under-resourced, and continually at risk of being detected by the security forces. In fact, at the same time that the Christian movement was expanding, half a dozen people "without a cent or a pistol" formed the first politico-military organization, the FPL.[43] Religious leaders, therefore, were way out in front of the FPL and the ERP in mobilizing the poor in the early 1970s.

In fact, the FPL and the ERP began to develop links to Christians not just because many of the two groups' leaders had been influenced by Catholic thought, but also because they realized that the religious movement was gathering tremendous strength and legitimacy.[44] The FPL and the ERP began to recruit peasants in Tecoluca in the early 1970s; but, while these organizations incorporated a handful of people, the church trained and awakened hundreds if not thousands. The FPL and the ERP also began to seek an alliance with progressive church leaders, evidenced by the efforts they made to recruit Padre Rodríguez and the FPL letter to religious leaders. What the FPL had in its favor was that they were willing to use force, which would become a preferred option for many of the young campesino leaders once the repression began. In the early to mid-1970s, however, the poor of El Salvador looked to the church rather than the politico-military organizations for guidance. A Christian message of hope and change was much more appealing than an atheistic, Marxist theory of class conflict.

As the new pastoral spread and the mobilization of the poor progressed, conflicts quickly emerged. The preferential option for the poor elicited a harsh response from the oligarchs, who saw reform as a slippery slope toward revolutionary change. In order to challenge the calls for reforms, especially land reform, the oligarchy chose to focus on anti-communism.[45] Just as the liberationist church relied on new ideas to organize the poor, the oligarchy embraced capitalist ideology and vilified socialism and Marxism. Consequently, Padre Rodríguez, like other priests and nuns, was labeled a communist almost as soon as he began asking landowners to treat their workers better. The liberationist pastoral also began to create divisions within the Salvadoran church itself, between those who embraced the preferential option for the poor and those who feared that the new pastoral was too political. No doubt, some of the conservative clergy simply did not agree with the progressive turn the church had taken as a result of Vatican II and the Medellín Conference. In the early 1970s, however, the conflict with the oligarchy and the conservative sectors of the Salvadoran church had not yet reached a fever pitch.

4

The Radicalization of a Priest

"You are now 'Joaquín'"

On December 29, 1974, a number of lay Catholic leaders from the parish of Tecoluca hiked quietly along a rough, steep path in the direction of the Cave of Tacuazín. This cavern once served as the headquarters of Anastasio Aquino, the indigenous leader of the Nonualco people, who led a peasant-Indian rebellion against the Salvadoran government in 1833. It is thus popularly known as the Cave of Anastasio Aquino. The Nonualcos resided in parts of the current departments of La Paz and San Vicente before the Spanish conquered Central America in the early 1500s. The Spanish, in classic colonial fashion, transformed the area's economy to fit their needs. The colonists took Nonualco lands and eventually planted indigo, greatly desired by "civilized" nations to make blue dyes. When independence from Spanish rule came in 1822, El Salvador, with the rest of Central America, became part of Mexico in the next year. By the following year, however, the countries of the isthmus formed the United Provinces of Central America. Aquino worked in an indigo plantation and raised an army in late 1833 to resist policies that put peasants at economic risk. Aquino and his small army boldly took the city of Zacatecoluca and then marched into the city of San Vicente, meeting no resistance. Arriving at the church of Pilar, where many years later David Rodríguez would serve as parish priest, the indigenous leader proclaimed himself king of the Nonualcos. Eventually, the flustered government in San Salvador was able to raise an army and put down the rebellion. The Spaniards captured Aquino, condemned him to death, and executed him by firing squad. He has served as an icon of a revolutionary, insurgent spirit ever since.

Once they reached the summit of Tacuazín Hill, the lay Catholic leaders who were headed to the clandestine meeting could see the dramatic panorama of the departments of La Paz and San Vicente. The Chinchontepec volcano was off to the northeast, while the Pacific Ocean spread out before them to the south. From here, Anastasio Aquino would have spied the region that he was attempting to reconquer. The group could see the entrance to the cave, about eighty feet high, only when they reached the very end of the steep climb. The participants entered the cave and began their stealthy encounter. Padre Rodríguez was among them, since lay leaders had invited him to say mass at the gathering. Some of these leaders were already members of the FPL, so Rodríguez's participation at this secret gathering signifies his first direct participation with that group. It was to be a solemn and significant ceremony, precipitated by the government's recent slaughter of several campesinos. Rodríguez recalls that someone implored at the meeting, "The best way to avenge the death of the campesinos is to organize the people, to *fight* for changes in this country." The Spanish verb *luchar* can mean an actual fight or more generally a struggle. However, at this point the word *fight*, without doubt, implied the use of violence. The group committed itself to unifying peasants in the Tecoluca parish under an organization that would be called the Unión de Trabajadores del Campo Vincentina (UTC-V; Union of Agricultural Workers of San Vicente), a group that would expand nationally, later be known simply as the UTC, and become closely linked with the FPL. In fact, from its inception the UTC-V was the creation of both religious leaders and FPL leaders.

Padre Rodríguez's participation in this gathering gave the occasion a strong religious dimension. In the ceremony, Rodríguez pointed out that the killing of campesinos was a violation against human rights and "against the image of God that was in them, the temple of the Holy Spirit." One of the liberationist ideas that Rodríguez had internalized fully and promulgated forcefully was the notion that since God had made man in his image, any aggression or abuse against a human being was an affront to God. Thus, the killing of peasants represented a heinous and mortal sin. Rodríguez added that there was a need to "fight for liberation and for the unity of our communities." He recalls: "It was a very important mass; very important for me; a commitment." At this point the young priest was undoubtedly becoming involved in founding a popular, peasant organization, the UTC, with incipient ties to a politico-military organization, the FPL. This meeting also constituted a revolutionary and "illegal" assembly, since Salvadoran labor law prohibited peasants from forming political organizations. Nevertheless, Rodríguez states, "One of the most beautiful memories that I have in my life is the founding of the UTC in the Cave of Anastasio Aquino, in the Hills of Tacuazín."[1]

In less than five years, Padre David Rodríguez experienced an awakening that transformed him from a traditional priest, who worked closely with his bishop, to a liberationist priest, who constantly butted heads with his bishop and tried to promote the interests of the poor. Now, however, he had rapidly radicalized and moved toward rebellion. He was by no means the first priest to join a rebel organization, since this is exactly what the famous Colombian priest Camilo Torres had done. Torres had uttered the phrase, "If Jesus were alive today, he would be a guerrilla."[2] How did Padre Rodríguez transform from a liberationist priest into a radical priest in such a short span of time?

Massacre at La Cayetana: The Introduction of Outrage

One day in November 1974, Bishop Aparicio received a brief communiqué from "informants"—most likely from the Fifth Brigade in San Vicente, the National Guard, or ORDEN—suggesting that Padre Rodríguez was involved in instigating rebellion and arming the campesinos. In this anonymous "report," titled "Information from Tecoluca" and dated November 22, 1974, "informants" are said to report that Rodríguez was involved in "political meetings" in various towns, that in the canton of La Cayetana he had "formed a group of armed men to which he was providing guerrilla training," and that he often traveled to the University of San Miguel along with a "number of men" in his brother's vehicle. The government and oligarchy considered the country's national university system a breeding ground of Marxism and radicalism. The report details the number of meetings that Rodríguez allegedly attended, noting when and in whose homes they took place, but nowhere does it identify what Rodríguez is actually doing, and the reference to an armed group simply says that it is "suspected that he has organized a group."[3] It is clear that this anonymous report sent to the bishop was meant to serve as a justification for the terrible event that was about to take place. Just one week later, on November 29, 1974, government soldiers killed six peasants at the small, isolated hamlet called La Cayetana, in the canton of León de Piedra, which lies at the eastern skirt of the San Vicente volcano.[4] The anonymous report had charged that

Rodríguez was radicalizing the peasants in that hamlet. Rodríguez points out that this massacre was a "very important event" both for the parish of Tecoluca and for the nation, since it was "the first massacre of peasants" perpetrated as a reprisal for their political organization. He adds that the caserío of La Cayetana was "one of the first communities where the people became fully organized."

For years, the residents of La Cayetana had rented small plots of land within a coffee finca owned by the Angulo family to plant beans and corn. In 1972 the Angulo family decided to rent the finca to a military officer who wanted to plant cotton on the land. The campesinos in the first two years were not organized, so they accepted their fate. However, to plant cotton many trees were cut, cotton plants were sprayed with insecticides, and in 1973 the new owner brought in his own laborers—soldiers—to do work that campesinos had been hired to do in the past. Owing to these changes, the campesinos lost access to land, their environment was made toxic, and they lost the paid work they were accustomed to having.

The plight of the people of La Cayetana demonstrates how the campesino suffered in El Salvador, even at a time when some economic indicators suggested that the country was doing quite well. In sum, their already difficult life was reaching a point of desperation. So, in 1974, the campesinos, initially led by Víctor Hernández, asserted themselves by trying to rent the land once more so they could plant their beans and corn. The campesinos decided to mark off some plots of land within the former coffee finca. They consulted Rodríguez, who suggested to them that they pay rent for the land as they had done in the past. The campesinos decided to establish a small commission, and in April 1974 the members went to the administrator to pay the rent. The administrator, however, refused to accept the money, so the campesinos kept the funds but said they would put it aside in reserves. They then decided to plant corn, which meant they took the bold step of removing the cotton plants in the areas they had demarcated.

In November, six National Guardsmen arrived at La Cayetana to arrest Leoncio Hernández, Víctor Hernández's brother. Some of the residents deflated the tires of their jeep, forcing the guardsmen to leave on foot without Leoncio. The guardsmen blurted angrily, "We will return." A few days later, on November 29, three trucks with about sixty guardsmen and policemen and nine members of ORDEN, armed with rifles, grenades, tear gas, and a cannon, surrounded and entered La Cayetana. They proceeded to ransack houses, accuse people of rebellion, and steal money. They then captured a number of men, forced them to take off their clothes, humiliated them, and said, "Let Padre David save you today. You are subversives, listening to that priest." As the guardsmen tried to leave with the men they had arrested, the women of the town surrounded and hung on to the trucks. A few minutes later several men from the canton of León de Piedra arrived to confront the guardsmen. The men stood in front of the trucks to bar their progress. The guardsmen then fired, killing three campesinos. The remaining townspeople tried to hide in a nearby house, but the guardsmen hunted them down and killed three more men. They took the bodies of the deceased and also took the men they had arrested earlier.

Padre Rodríguez, who was at the parish house in Tecoluca, received a frantic call letting him know what had transpired. He immediately contacted the local authorities to determine where the captured men could be found. Rodríguez learned nothing from the authorities, and no one admitted to having the arrested men in their custody. The captured men were eventually released, naked, and little by little they returned to their community. The bodies of the six dead men were eventually found in a state of decomposition on a small crest of a hill, near a dirt road. The men were buried there in a mass grave.

The massacre at La Cayetana was a watershed event in which several parties crossed the line: the government embraced repression, some campesinos embraced rebellion, and Rodríguez and other liberationist leaders began to radicalize as they began to seriously consider how to deal with a government that killed Christians when they demanded their constitutional and economic rights. Rodríguez remembers that after the massacre, "the situation became tense and demonstrations occurred in Tecoluca and other communities . . . denouncing the government, denouncing the Guard." The massacre received extensive national attention. The Legislative Assembly debated the horrible incident, with the PDC calling for an investigation. Even Bishop Aparicio issued a protest, writing a short, telegram-style note to the assembly that stated: "bloody, barbarous events Tecoluca, with unequivocal signs religious persecution iron curtain style . . . profound bitterness . . . energetic protest."[5] The MNR issued a prescient statement on December 6, saying that "the governmental violence could provoke a bloodbath in El Salvador."[6] Rodríguez points out that instead of putting out the fire by terrifying the people of the region, the massacre created intense "indignation" and generated "greater opportunity to organize people." The popular mobilization that the liberationists and other groups had already accomplished allowed for a strong response to the repression, rather than capitulation.

This massacre had a radicalizing effect on Rodríguez, since the government, the security apparatus, the unjust system, and the landowners had all been directly or indirectly responsible for the death of six campesinos who had simply tried to promote their economic and political interests.[7] La Cayetana was a community in Rodríguez's parish and had been organized by his friend Víctor Hernández, a lay leader. The shock and outrage of this government repression moved Rodríguez toward taking a more combative path. His participation in the meeting at the Cave of Anastasio Aquino was a direct result of the massacre. Padre Rodríguez would most likely never have embraced the revolutionary option had the state not decided to brutally repress campesinos who had just started to organize politically. Any doubts he may have had about whether or not to support campesinos who wanted to fight for their rights evaporated as a result of the massacre at La Cayetana.

Rodríguez remembers that little by little he had developed respect for the manner in which the FPL operated. For some time he had been given copies of the FPL newspaper *El Rebelde* (The Rebel), which he would read. Father Barahona, who was a bit more cautious, would say to him, "Be careful; do not get involved with that." Rodríguez's assessment was that the newspaper was "serious and presented well the unjust conditions of the country." The FPL would also ensure that campesinos could attend the church-sponsored courses, particularly the longer ones, by organizing other campesinos to help with the crops and duties of the students who attended the courses. In effect, the FPL had already been indirectly assisting the liberationists in forming campesinos.

Rodríguez recalls one individual's experience. Nando was an illiterate campesino who eventually became the secretary-general of the UTC in the San Vicente zone. Nando had a reputation as a violent drunk in the town of Tecoluca, but once he became "organized"—incorporated into the FPL—he stopped drinking, gained a desire to learn, and worked toward the common good. Rodríguez observed that the FPL was sometimes able to convert people more effectively than the liberationists. The catechists and Delegates of the Word who were already incorporated would sometimes use the sacristy of the church in Tecoluca for their meetings, since they wanted to include their religiosity in the clandestine organization. Once, Rodríguez decided to do as Bishop Romero had done with him and watched how the lay leaders conducted a meeting. He recalls that their "method of criticism and auto-criticism was very much like a heartfelt confession." Those members of the FPL who engaged in questionable behavior or in risky acts that could jeopardize the organization, such as getting drunk, would agree to do "penance" by helping out a community member. Rather than saying prayers as penance, the "sinner" would perform "good acts," such as helping to repair a house or helping people with their crops. The focus was to promote community solidarity and behavior that was conducive to that solidarity. According to Rodríguez, the FPL, like the liberationist church, was attempting to form "new" men and women with a spirit of Christian fraternity.

By the end of 1974, the liberationist religious leaders had reached a difficult crossroads—a point where their new pastoral had a political dimension that was in conflict with the state's interests. They had helped to raise the consciousness of campesinos, had trained them to understand better their needs and interests, and had helped them to become organized to fight for their rights. Now, however, some of the campesino leaders who were catechists and Delegates were becoming involved in secular, popular organizations, some with links to armed Marxist groups, and thus they became targets of the state. Rodríguez points out that it was difficult for him to simply disassociate himself from the people he had "awakened" and helped to "open their eyes." The majority of liberationist priests and nuns kept the politico-military organizations at arm's length. Some of them, however, took the "qualitative jump" and decided to accompany the peasants and workers on their struggle for justice. They did this, however, mostly because the state refused to reform and instead chose to repress.

The Incorporation of "Joaquín"

Not long after the meeting at the Cave of Anastasio Aquino, Padre Rodríguez took the bold step of becoming fully incorporated into the FPL. Before making this choice he had to resolve in his mind the thorniest question: Should he join an organization that employed lethal force to achieve its political aims? Rodríguez was able to resolve his doubts to his satisfaction. He points out that "the Catholic Church has long supported the right to self-defense," derived from Saint Thomas Aquinas's ideas of just war. He argues that El Salvador's armed, popular movement "was like a people defending themselves," and thus represented a "just cause," one of the key conditions for a just war. Another condition for a just war is that all alternate avenues have been exhausted. As far as Rodríguez was concerned, the popular movement and the church had employed all avenues to promote democracy and peaceful change, but the government's response was rejection and then knee-jerk repression. Also, Pope Paul VI had stated that rebellion was justified in cases of long-standing tyranny, which fit El Salvador perfectly, a country that had been ruled by the oligarchy and armed forces since 1932.

According to Rodríguez, in the FPL's incorporation process each aspirant was asked three questions. First, are you disposed to give your life for the secrets of the organization? Second, are you willing to adhere to the statutes and principles of the organization? Finally, and most critical, are you willing to kill for the interests of the people? These questions did not come as a complete surprise, since Rodríguez had already discussed them with Felipe Peña. Additionally, liberationist priests knew that under certain conditions violence might be the only option for a people to become liberated. Rodríguez was also well aware of a case in which the FPL had killed a peasant who was a threat to the organization. The case concerned a young man whom Rodríguez had "formed" and had developed a close bond with while in San Carlos. Rodríguez had taught him to drive, and the young man had at times served as his driver. At one point, before the massacre at La Cayetana, as death squads and the National Guard began to kill or disappear several leaders of the FPL and Christian lay workers, some campesinos had noticed Rodríguez's driver with soldiers after several people were taken from a bus and identified as subversives by a hooded person. The FPL began to trail the young man and discovered that he was the one who was pointing people out to the security forces, perhaps as a member of ORDEN. So, the FPL carried out what they termed an *ajusticiamiento,* a death penalty. Rodríguez believes that his driver had identified to the authorities as many as sixty individuals who were eventually killed or disappeared.

Personal considerations also convinced Rodríguez to become involved with the FPL. In general, he realized that the liberationist cause, devoted to creating a better life for the poor of El Salvador, could only go so far given the violent reaction by the government. Peaceful Christians calling for change in El Salvador would simply be fed to the proverbial lions. Consequently, those Christians who embraced the need for change had to seek protection and had to fight back. Second, Rodríguez himself was experiencing outrage at the violence directed against Christians he had helped to train and with whom he worked. Could he in good conscience be a true pastor if he re-

Figure 4.1. Rodríguez speaking at a gathering, mid-1970s. By permission of the Rodríguez Henríquez family.

mained on the sidelines as the young men and women whom he had "awakened" were gunned down? The answer was obvious for Padre Rodríguez: he had to "accompany" his parishioners no matter the personal consequences. Finally, Rodríguez realized that if he was to continue working with the oppressed in an increasingly repressive environment, he would have to find a way to protect himself. The FPL, an organization that he now respected, was the best form of protection. By the end of 1974 Rodríguez was fully aware that he needed protection, since he had already been identified by the oligarchy and state as a dangerous "third world" or "red priest" and as the priest who had "incited the peasants at La Cayetana to violence."

The FPL was a clandestine, armed group and thus worked in cells, known as *colectivos,* in a compartmented manner. The cells were composed of about five or six individuals, and each person would be brought into the group by a *responsable*—the person responsible for incorporating that person and also that person's principal contact. The members of a cell did not know anyone else in the FPL, so Rodríguez, for example, would not know if any other priest or nun was in the organization. Certainly there would be some suspicions, but the strict discipline of the FPL ensured that members did not reveal their involvement in the group to anyone. This "created a sense of mystique," since all FPL members knew of the general struggle and the organization's existence, but for each member the politico-military organization at this time was but a small group of committed members. No doubt a mysterious sense of a grand purpose and engagement in collective action must have motivated some campesinos who had suffered for decades at the bottom of the socioeconomic ladder.

Not long after the meeting at the cave, Rodríguez was incorporated into a "special collective" of priests who were working with the FPL. His responsable said to him, "You are now 'Joaquín,'" which from then on was Rodríguez's nom de guerre. In addition to his pseudonym, Rodríguez became a *compañero* (comrade; literally, companion or colleague). In the politico-military organizations, as well as in the popular organizations, the members were always fraternally known as *compañeros* or *campañeras, compas* for short. Rodríguez's collective was led by a young man with close links to the Catholic Church.[8] This collective did not last long, however, since the various priests were soon incorporated into other collectives because they were very valuable leaders. Rodríguez remembers that it was challenging to direct a group of priests who were not used to taking orders. "It was very difficult for us," he laughs. Although he was now Joaquín, Rodríguez comments that very few people would call him by his pseudonym. Since he had been such a popular priest for several years, people still preferred to call him "Padre David."

The FPL then placed Rodríguez in a more active, operational collective. The cell was located in Zacatecoluca, the departmental capital of La Paz. He recalls that his responsable was a young man—a *cipote,* or kid—to whom he had given first communion. The young man said with an air of authority to Rodríguez, "Look, Padre, tomorrow we are going to carry out a distribution of propaganda in the market in Zacatecoluca." Rodríguez responded in disbelief, "Everyone knows me, how am I going to distribute propaganda!" The young man parried with, "We are going to do it at 4:00 a.m." Rodríguez remembers that he was sure he was being "used as cannon fodder." They arrived at 4:00 a.m., quickly distributed the propaganda in the market, and then left on a bus that passed through the town very early. The operation went off without a hitch. Rodríguez remembers that his decision to become an FPL member came quickly to a point of crisis. He points out humorously that priests were not well suited for a political organization, because, "we think we know everything," are "very individualistic," and are "not very disciplined." Additionally priests were "very public men," recognizable by many people. But the most difficult pill to swallow was that priests were key leaders in their parishes and were not used to taking orders, especially from their own parishioners. Rodríguez's initial experience in an operational cell was most likely a test of his willingness to engage in actions for, and take orders from, the organization, since he was soon moved to another cell. The FPL leadership was probably still cautious about priests and wanted to test their commitment prior to fully accepting them into the organization.

The FPL was organized into three divisions—military, political, and the popular militia. Rodríguez's next assignment was in a cell within the political division. The goal of this division was to organize and educate people politically, as Rodríguez had been doing all along by using the Bible to make people aware of their reality. It made no sense to have priests carrying out *pintas* (painting slogans on walls), distributing propaganda, or doing other mundane yet dangerous tasks when they had a good education and were capable of organizing and motivating people. Rodríguez's principal responsibility at first was to organize the CEBs that were aligned with the FPL or that had "developed a revolutionary spirit." Rodríguez recalls, however, that as he began to accompany a newly organized people, he felt that it was "the pastor who was following the sheep." Nevertheless, he was now literally a soldier of Christ—a priest fighting for the teachings of the Gospels, albeit in an organization that also espoused Marxist ideas.

Although nominally Marxist in orientation, most of the FPL leadership shared Christian roots. Even FPL leader Cayetano Carpio, the former secretary-general of the PCS and an orthodox communist, had been a seminarian as a young man.[9] Rodríguez recalls that he always felt welcome and appreciated by everyone within the FPL. By the time he became incorporated, the FPL had already decided that communism and Christianity were compatible. Rodríguez estimates that "the majority" of FPL recruits at first "were catechists [and Delegates], who were the most committed," and who no longer found in their church's "pastoral plan a clear response to the problems of injustice." Rodríguez remembers, however, that some FPL leaders would jokingly refer to him as "el brujo" (the warlock). According to Rodríguez, the PCS was more suspicious of Christians than was the FPL. He recalls that one FPL leader would say to him, "We are with you, brujo, until death! After death we'll see whether we go to heaven or hell." Rodríguez estimates that "95 to 99 percent of the organization [FPL] was composed of Christians," mostly Catholics, mostly campesinos. He points out that the Marxists and atheists were in the minority and would usually "remain silent" on issues of faith. In fact, some members of the organization would at times be criticized in public, during auto-criticism time, for making fun of someone who was saying the rosary. The conclusion during these times of critical reflection was that "everyone must be respected," and as Rodríguez points out, the FPL leaders "knew perfectly well that Christianity was what motivated most" of their followers. Some of the atheistic leaders would say, the "revolutionary mystique motivated people because they knew that they were fighting for a greater purpose." Rodríguez remembers that the Christians would add that people were motivated when they "knew that Jesus was with them and that God was with them."

The Torture of Father Barahona and Rising Repression

The state and oligarchy loathed the liberationist work and mass mobilization that Padres Rodríguez and Barahona had accomplished in their parish. On May 7, 1975, three National Guardsmen arrested Father Barahona at 10:00 p.m. as he was driving three of his parishioners in his car toward Tecoluca. Mayor Atilio Cañas drove the guardsmen in his truck. The guardsmen searched Father Barahona's car and immediately accused him of carrying "subversive propaganda." They took Barahona and his three passengers to the National Guard headquarters in San Vicente and then to their headquarters in San Salvador. In a letter to Bishop Aparicio, Father Barahona said that his possessions were again examined in San Salvador and that a copy of *El Rebelde* had been added, "probably in San Vicente."[10] Padre Barahona was then "tortured" by three plainclothes agents for about half an hour.[11] During his ordeal, Barahona relates, one of the agents yelled mockingly at him, "I am excommunicated, I am excommunicated!" After his suffering, Barahona was admonished by the National Guard sub-commander, Colonel Flores, and released at 10:00 a.m. Bishop Aparicio, despite his conservative stance, did not take kindly to the capture and torture of one of his priests. After Barahona informed him of what happened to him at the hands of the authorities, the bishop wrote a letter to Colonel-President Molina, the Legislative Assembly, the Supreme Court, and chiefs of the security apparatus. In the letter, Aparicio asks for the "free exercise of the Catholic religion," questions whether the National Guard is a security force or a force for the persecution of citizens, and wonders if the constitution has two interpretations, one for the authorities and one for citizens. He concludes by issuing an "excommunication decree" for those involved in the crime against Padre Barahona.[12] It is important to note that even a very conservative prelate was well aware of the extant injustice in El Salvador at the time.

It is clear that the oligarchy and government, rather than yielding some ground to swelling popular demands, decided to step up the repression. The next assault against campesinos came on June 21, 1975. At 1:00 a.m., forty to sixty National Guardsmen, accompanied by two "orejas" (literally, ears; members of ORDEN), drove into the community of Tres Calles, in the department of Usulután, adjacent to and east of the department of San Vicente. The guardsmen went in through a window of the house of José Alberto Ostorga, fifty-eight years old, "searching for weapons." They shot and slashed with machetes Ostorga and three of his sons, Jorge, José, and Héctor. Another son, thirteen-year-old Juan, was badly beaten. At the same time, other guardsmen invaded the house of Santos Morales, whom they also shot and slashed with machetes. The guardsmen left without finding any weapons. In addition to the murders and violence, government security agents robbed their victims.[13] The small town of Tres Calles was next to the parish of Jiquilisco, in Bishop Romero's diocese, where Padre Juan Macho worked and where Rodríguez had taught at Centro Naranjos. After going to Tres Calles to pray and console the people, Bishop Romero sent a confidential letter to his friend Colonel-President Molina. In the letter, Romero provided the details of what had occurred and expressed deep concern. Remarkably enough, however, the letter was very respectful and in no way exhibited outrage, as Aparicio had done when peasants were murdered at La Cayetana.[14]

Romero then sent a letter to his fellow bishops to inform them of what had happened at Tres Calles. In the letter he writes that on his second visit to Tres Calles, nine days after the massacre, he was "surprised at the number of Christians who came from Tecoluca" and at the presence of priests from the diocese of San Vicente (one of whom was Rodríguez). He goes on to say that while their conduct was "correct" he wished that the songs they had chosen to sing were not the protest songs that the peasants had learned at the training centers.[15] Romero ends his letter by asking his fellow bishops for advice, although it seems that the principal reason for writing the letter was to express his surprise at the level of rebelliousness on the part of the attendees.

The wave of government violence soon hit the capital of San Salvador, and the reaction by progressive priests would escalate the conflict between the church and the oligarchy-controlled state. On July 30, 1975, government security forces massacred protesting university students as they marched by the social security building in San Salvador. The students had decided to protest the violation of university autonomy in the city of Santa Ana, the departmental capital to the northwest of San Salvador. The students in that city had demonstrated to denounce the government's expenditure of large sums of money to host the Miss Universe Pageant. As they marched down a major avenue in San Salvador, the students found the road blocked by tanks and soldiers, who then opened fired on the marchers and left at "least thirty-seven dead and several more dozens disappeared."[16]

On the day of the massacre, Rodríguez was participating in a workshop retreat of progressive priests, sponsored by La Nacional, on the banks of Lake Ilopango, just east of the capital. Upon hearing the news, the priests agreed to take forceful action to protest the government repression. First, the priests would issue a public statement denouncing the massacre. Second, they would send a letter to all bishops highlighting their concerns about the continued repression. Finally, in a bold move, they committed themselves to occupying the Metropolitan Cathedral in San Salvador to protest the escalating violence.[17] The priests representing La Nacional took the proposal to a general meeting of priests who also concurred with taking action. At the same time, Rodríguez and other incorporated priests informed the FPL about La Nacional's decision to occupy the cathedral. Rodríguez points out that "the FPL moved all its pieces to be present at the cathedral."

The Occupation of the Metropolitan Cathedral

On August 1, 1975, at the Metropolitan Cathedral in San Salvador, forty priests, led by Archbishop Luís Chávez y González and Bishop Arturo Rivera y Damas, concelebrated a mass for the slain students. After the mass a number of progressive priests, along with some nuns and lay workers—"about forty" individuals, as Rodríguez recalls—took control of the cathedral. "We shut the cathedral doors, put up loudspeakers, and started making denunciations," remembers Rodríguez, adding, "we also played revolutionary music." The date was of particular importance, since it coincided with the celebrations, from August 1–6, for El Salvador's patron saint, the "Divine Savior of the World." This occupation would be replete with symbolism and meaning.

Upon taking over the cathedral, the liberationists issued a communiqué in which they described themselves as a "group of Christians formed by priests, religious men and women, and lay persons." The document condemns the recent repression, mentioning the massacres at La Cayetana and Tres Calles and the July 30 student massacre, and calls on the government to free all students who have been taken into custody, return the bodies of all students who have been killed to their families, dismiss all of those in the government who are responsible for the repression, compensate the families of those who have been killed, and guarantee safe exit to those who have occupied the cathedral.[18] A standoff was in play between liberationists and the state.

Most noteworthy politically was that the occupation of the cathedral led to the founding of the Bloque Popular Revolucionario (BPR; Popular Revolutionary Bloc), composed of a broad array of popular organizations associated with the FPL. The existing politico-military organizations had already realized that to defeat the Salvadoran state they would need strong popular support, as the Vietnamese rebels had accomplished in their struggle against their government. Since El Salvador was densely populated and devoid of large mountains or truly isolated regions, Salvadoran revolutionaries, but mainly the FPL, assumed that a Cuban-style revolution was unlikely to succeed in their small country.[19] The politico-military organizations were convinced that they would be able to defeat the state only if they aligned themselves with large, well-organized popular movements such as the Christian movement that the liberationists had created. The founding of the BPR at the cathedral occupation did just that—brought together a large amalgamation of popular forces, namely, secondary school teachers, university students, secondary school students, a regional peasant group, artists, and the Federación de Trabajadores del Campo (FTC; Federation of Rural Workers). The FTC brought together the Federación Cristiana de

Campesinos Salvadoreños (FECCAS; Christian Federation of Salvadoran Peasants) and the UTC that Rodríguez had helped to found but that had now spread to Chalatenango. At the time of its founding and later, the BPR represented by far the largest consolidation of popular organizations in the country.

Rodríguez remembers that within the cathedral an ideological conflict quickly emerged. Some of those inside the church, mainly from the youth wing of the PDC, although in agreement with denouncing the government, were not in accord with linking the occupation of the cathedral with the birth of the revolutionary bloc. They began to feel resentful and said to the progressives, "You have manipulated us." Indeed, most of those who had taken over the cathedral were already "organized" and sympathetic to the FPL and its goal of creating a large popular bloc to fight against the regime. A small group of nuns, who prayed but did not join the more rebellious group, was also inside the church. Father "Chencho" Alas was associated with the Frente de Acción Popular Unificada (FAPU; United Popular Action Front), a recently created popular bloc that was linked with the Resistencia Nacional (RN; National Resistance, another politico-military organization that had sprouted from the ERP, after the latter organization experienced serious internal problems). Rodríguez recalls that FAPU did not have the extensive organization that the FPL had developed. At one point Father Alas decided that he wanted to leave the cathedral, but he was prevented from leaving "for his own safety," since he would most likely be arrested. Father Benito Tovar also wanted to leave. A number of priests had decided to join forces with the politico-military organizations, but some had joined the FPL, some the ERP, and some the RN. These politico-military organizations, though fighting for the same things—to overthrow the repressive state and bring economic justice and socialism to El Salvador—engaged in competition rather than unity of action.

After six days, with little food or water but with a reasonable amount of support from people outside the cathedral, the occupying group issued another communiqué. In this statement the group explained the religious origins of the occupation. The new announcement stated that the group had taken over the cathedral because "it was a symbol of Jesus Christ," who was "on the side of the oppressed," and it was thus the proper place to "renounce injustice and announce the reign of God." The group also announced that it would end the occupation of the cathedral because they did not want more repression to take place, they had now helped to form the BPR, and they had raised the consciousness of the people about the repression in the country. The communiqué also rejected the government's assertion that the groups involved in the occupation were "communist."[20]

The occupiers had been carrying on negotiations with the government with the help of Archbishop Chávez y González. Consequently, on August 8 the occupation came to an end, and for the first time ever the likeness of Jesus Christ, "The Savior," was not brought to the cathedral in a long religious procession to commemorate the country's patron saint. The killing of the students, the cathedral occupation, and the general political unease undermined the traditional religious celebration. The government had refused to accept any of the demands from those inside the cathedral, other than to give them safe exit. Nevertheless, as the communiqué stated, those inside the cathedral had made the nation and the government take notice of the strength of the liberationist movement and the popular organizations.

The year 1975 was also a personally a tragic one for Rodríguez: his father, Lisandro, died at the age of sixty-two, on November 14. Lisandro had suffered from diabetes, and by the time of his death he had lost his eyesight. Padre Rodríguez was able to see his father the day before his death and say good-bye. He remembers his father with great affection and respect. Lisandro instilled in him a love for life and humanity, qualities that undoubtedly made Rodríguez more likely to embrace the liberationist pastoral. Although a conservative man, Lisandro was kind and fair. One former peasant who worked at the Rodríguez sugar plantation said that Lisandro "was like a father" to him. Others who worked at the Rodríguez plantation remembered Lisandro fondly and recall those earlier years in Calderas as an idyllic time. Those whom I interviewed who knew Lisandro remembered him very fondly, and some were moved to tears when discussing him. A family member remembers that "David took after his father, Lisandro, while Benigno took after their mother." Although this statement contradicts an earlier statement by Rodríguez referring to their youth, "Padre David" was now a without doubt a more bold figure than was his brother. Lisandro was buried in a tomb next to the chapel that he had built on his property in Calderas, where he still remains.

Figure 4.2. Rodríguez Rivera family burial plot in Calderas. Photo by author, January 2008.

The Drawing of National Battle Lines

The national stage was now set for dangerous confrontation. The radical opposition—popular organizations, liberationists, and politico-military organizations—was coalescing, becoming more powerful, and determined to promote revolutionary change in El Salvador. The government, the security apparatus, and the oligarchy, on the other hand, were bent on preserving the status quo, particularly to block any changes inspired by what they saw as socialist or communist ideas. The moderate opposition—mostly the left-of-center political parties and professionals but also much of the Catholic Church—only desired reform, but it was for the most part ignored by those who held power, a major mistake on their part. The fact that many of those who were calling for reforms were Christians, rather than radicals, fell on deaf ears. Those who challenged the state and the status quo were now deemed to be communists or their fellow travelers.

The following years would witness increasingly virulent conflicts. Peasants affiliated with revolutionary organizations carried out a number of land seizures in fincas and haciendas near the towns of Chalatenango, Cinquera, Tecoluca, and Zacatecaluca. Rodríguez was often named as an instigator in these peasant "redemptive actions." In fact, within the FPL, Rodríguez had now been moved from his responsibilities of organizing CEBs to a broader role of organizing campesinos in general. His role in the FTC increased greatly, since the peasant federation was one of the largest and most powerful organizations within the BPR. These peasant organizations were also overflowing with Christian lay leaders who had been formed by the liberationists. In the next two years, Rodríguez acted as a liberationist priest principally behind the scenes, coming and going from a number of parishes, for the purpose of helping peasants to organize politically and demand their rights.

On March 14, 1976, elections were held for deputies in the Legislative Assembly, as well as mayors throughout the country. The opposition, under the UNO banner, having had enough of fraudulent elections, boycotted the polling. Consequently, the PCN and small right-wing parties won all the seats in the Legislative Assembly and all mayoral offices. Now that the centrist opposition was no longer part of the political system, the likelihood of alienation and radicalization would increase. Soon after the election, a May Day rally was held in Tecoluca. When the parade went by the house of a member of ORDEN, Rubén Sánchez, some peasants tried to spray-paint a slogan on his property. Sánchez, who had a pistol, tried to stop them, fired his weapon, and wounded four peasants, one of them seriously. Two days later, the newspaper *El Diario de Hoy* published a story stating that the problems were caused by the parish priests of Tecoluca, who had organized the May Day celebration, and that the demonstration was directed against the PCN mayor of Tecoluca, making it a partisan event. These accusations implied that Padres Rodríguez and Barahona were involved in the political opposition. The two priests then sent a letter to the newspaper, defending themselves, but the conservative daily refused to publish their version of the events.[21] In the letter Rodríguez and Barahona asserted that they did not organize the May Day event, were not even in Tecoluca on that date, and were not involved in any political party.[22]

President Molina, though conservative, found himself leading a country that was on the verge of a violent eruption. His own institution, the armed forces, had at times become convinced that some reforms were needed, especially to stop the influence of radical ideas. As a result, toward the end of his administration, Molina attempted to carry out some limited land reform, calling it "agrarian transformation," since the oligarchy equated the term "land reform" with communism. Molina and his minister of agriculture and livestock, Enrique Álvarez Córdoba, a progressive member of the oligarchy, had introduced a land-reform program in 1973, but the proposal never made it past the president's cabinet. Álvarez Córdoba and two other ministers then resigned in protest.[23] Nevertheless, in June 1975, Molina had established the Instituto Salvadoreño de Transformación Agraria (ISTA; Salvadoran Institute of Agrarian Transformation) and enacted the Law of Agrarian Transformation in preparation for making some changes to the land-tenure system. Then, on June 29, 1976, after the assembly had passed the law, Molina made his gambit and initiated the First Agrarian Transformation Project. Land would be expropriated, but the government would compensate the landowners. The initial project took place in the departments of Usulután and San Miguel and involved almost 146,000 acres, affecting 250 landowners.[24] The oligarchy responded quickly. The Asociación Nacional de la Empresa Privada (ANEP; National Association of Private Enterprise), the oligarchy's most important association, and the newly formed Frente Agrario de la Región Oriental (FARO; Eastern Region Agrarian Front) lashed out at the government and all others who supported the new program. By October, Molina had abandoned his meager attempt at reform. The government's about-face resulted in Father Ignacio Ellacuría's famous editorial titled "At Your Orders, My Capital!" In Latin America, superior officers are often addressed as "My captain," "My colonel," and so forth. Ellacuría applied this military form of address, but instead of saying "My captain," he substituted "My capital," suggesting that the officer corps in El Salvador took its orders from the economic elite rather than their own military hierarchy. It was a scathing but completely accurate attack on the dominant officers within the armed forces as well as the oligarchy. Ellacuría, a Jesuit theologian and liberationist, would later pay with his life for this article and other efforts at opposing the government and oligarchy. Molina's lackluster attempt at land reform also turned the church into a scapegoat for the oligarchy, since they saw liberationist ideas as the cause of peasant rebelliousness. ANEP and FARO began a defamation campaign against the church soon after the attempted land-reform program failed.[25] Land reform had been stymied once more, and tensions continued to rise.

National polarization reached a fever pitch by the end of 1976. On November 26, a group of peasants made a number of basic demands—fair wages, humane treatment, access to small loans—at the finca La Paz Opico, located in the parish of Tecoluca. A clash ensued and a watchman was killed. Immediately, a number of newspapers and advertisements by private groups such as FARO charged that the parish priests of Tecoluca had organized the "hordes" that led to the death of the watchman.[26] FARO stated that the communists in the region "obey the Parish Priest of Tecoluca, David Rodríguez."[27] Padre Barahona wrote a letter to Bishop Aparicio in which he roundly rejected the notion, perpetrated in the press, that he or Rodríguez had organized any demonstration in Tecoluca that eventually led to the clash at La Paz Opico and the death of the watchman. Barahona wrote that no demonstration took place in Tecoluca, and added: "The problem at the finca has nothing to do with the parish and is strictly a labor problem, related to pay anomalies, inadequate food, etc."[28] This event in Tecoluca, however, was overshadowed by what occurred soon thereafter in the archdiocese of San Salvador.

The hacienda Colima was located near Suchitoto in the parish of Aguilares, whose priest, Rutilio Grande, had already been accused of organizing peasants and turning them into rebels. The hacienda was owned by two brothers, Eduardo and Francisco Orellana, who were members of El Salvador's powerful oligarchy. The Colima farm had been affected by the government's Cerrón Grande construction program to dam the Lempa River at a point just north of Suchitoto. Some of the peasants who lived on the land of the Colima farm were supposed to be relocated and felt that the Orellana family had not done enough to support their cause. On December 5 about two hundred peasants, with the help of FECCAS, came to see the two brothers to push for their demands. While there is no satisfactory record of what happened, Eduardo Orellana was shot dead during the ensuing clash. The peasants say that his own brother, Francisco, killed him with a stray shot. Francisco, on the other hand, insisted that the peasants had killed his brother.[29]

The death of Eduardo Orellana further infuriated the oligarchy, which quickly charged the church with inciting the "hordes." Both Rutilio Grande *and* David Rodríguez were fingered as the principal instigators.[30] A number of groups funded by the oligarchy purchased advertisements in the leading newspapers to denounce the church and its activities.[31] Reacting to the accusations, the priests of La Nacional issued a communiqué in which they stated that although they were "accused of being communists . . . of violating the fundamental principles of Christianity, of instigating violence," they were only taking on "the cause of the poor and the struggle against injustice."[32] They could certainly have added that their actions were consistent with church doctrine. The Molina government, pressured by FARO and ANEP, then began a systematic repression of the church in January 1977, knowing that Archbishop Chávez y González was about to retire.[33] The hope within the oligarchy was that the Vatican would not choose Bishop Rivera y Damas as archbishop, and would instead choose a more conservative prelate to head the divided and radical Salvadoran church.

Archbishop Romero and President Romero

On February 3, 1977, Pope Paul VI appointed Óscar Arnulfo Romero y Galdámez as archbishop of El Salvador, making him the bishop of the diocese of San Salvador. The conservative forces in El Salvador breathed a sigh of relief. As bishop of Santiago de María, Romero had shown himself to be a critic of the liberationists. Romero was close to the Molina government, had rubbed elbows with the oligarchy, and was associated with Opus Dei, an exceptionally conservative Catholic group. In fact, not long after being appointed archbishop, but after he had himself undergone a conversion, Romero told a group of progressive priests that his "job was to finish you off," rein in the "Marxist priests and base communities," and "improve relations with the government."[34]

On February 14, only days before the upcoming national elections, the FPL killed former Tecoluca mayor Atilio Cañas. As narrated in chapter 1, this event put Padre Rodríguez at great risk, forcing him to go into hiding. Since he had a solid alibi and Bishop Aparicio was convinced of his innocence, the government eventually ceased its efforts to apprehend and prosecute him for Cañas's death. Rodríguez was nonetheless a marked man and the authorities would use any misstep on his part to order his arrest. Rodríguez explains that the security forces and the government worked under the assumption that "killing a dog ends the rabies." For the right wing in El Salvador, communism was like a virus that could be eliminated only by destroying those who were infected. In the daily *La Prensa Grafica*, a ghost organization, "Committee of Free Salvadorans," issued a paid advertisement that said "the enemy is at the gates" and suggested that "incendiary and revolutionary slogans . . . with the blessing of priests" were leading the country into another communist uprising like the one in 1932.[35] The allusion to 1932 was inflammatory, since everyone knew that the outcome in that year was a large massacre, La Matanza.

The state and its security forces soon realized that the popular movement, rather than shrinking, was gaining strength. The oligarchy and its associates then decided to install a more forceful president, one who would target the leadership of the liberationist, revolutionary, and popular movements. Priests, nuns, catechists, Delegates, and lay leaders were the easiest targets to identify, since they worked much more openly than did the leaders of the clandestine organizations. The oligarchy, together with the most conservative military officers, put forth General Carlos Humberto Romero as the PCN's next presidential candidate. Younger military officers, on the other hand, had viewed Colonel Molina as too conservative, so they viewed General Romero not only as a reactionary but also as the right-hand man of the most recalcitrant segment of the oligarchy.[36] As minister of defense from 1972 to 1976, Romero had "gained a reputation as a hardline anti-communist, a determined opponent of even a limited agrarian reform, and a believer in the ruthless use of force to stamp out popular opposition to the military government."[37]

The opposition, again under the UNO banner, decided to participate in this election, but instead of the usual Duarte candidacy the coalition decided upon a safer candidate: retired colonel Ernesto Claramount.[38] Their vice-presidential candidate was José Morales Erlich, a PDC leader who had been mayor of San Salvador. The elections took place on February 20, 1977, but fraud was once again extensive and blatant.[39] In protest, UNO decided to occupy Plaza Libertad, just one block away from the Metropolitan Cathedral and adjacent to El Rosario church, to denounce the vote fraud. Roughly fifty thousand people, including the presidential and vice-presidential candidates, crowded the plaza and the surrounding area. Late on February 27, the government sent in the National Police, resulting in "at least four dozen people killed," while Claramount with fifteen hundred supporters sought refuge in El Rosario.[40] Claramount and Erlich had no recourse but to go into exile. Elections were once again proven to be a pointless effort at capturing even limited political power.

In the midst of the electoral fiasco, on February 21, Padre Rafael Barahona was once again detained and abused. Perhaps his arrest was a "punishment" for the death of Atilio Cañas, since he was also seen as a rebel priest, and Rodríguez had evaded the government's grasp. Bishop Romero had been officially installed as archbishop the day before Barahona's detention, so the new prelate went to see President Molina immediately to secure the release of the priest. Molina released Barahona but reportedly told the new archbishop, "These priests of yours have become politicians, and I hold you responsible for their behavior."[41]

Government repression against the popular organizations and the liberationists had now increased to such a degree that CEDES issued a letter on March 5 listing the things that concerned the bishops and making some "just demands." Bishop Aparicio (president of CEDES at the time), Archbishop Romero, Bishop Marco René Revelo, and Father Freddy Delgado (secretary-general of CEDES) all signed the letter. Romero had yet to undergo his conversion, and the others, though highly conservative, were nevertheless concerned about the increasing violence and attacks against their institution. The letter demanded that all types of violence cease and identified the armed forces, security forces, and paramilitary organizations as the key perpetrators of the violence. The bishops also demanded an end to the intimidation of priests, both foreign and national. They charged that FARO and ANEP, with the aid of the national press, were carrying out a defamation campaign against the church. At this point the bishops seemed united in their concerns about government repression, the lack of human rights, and the incessant, unwarranted attacks against the church, even though they were also worried about the politicization and radicalization of some religious leaders.[42] The oligarchy and state, however, would not consider the urgent pleas of even the conservative bishops. The reactionaries had instead already decided to viciously attack liberationist leaders within the Salvadoran church.

On March 12, 1977, National Guardsmen murdered Father Rutilio Grande, a Salvadoran Jesuit priest who had pioneered the joint pastorals and established many CEBs in Aguilares, a town about eighteen miles directly north of San Salvador, in an area that would eventually become a stronghold of the guerrilla movement. Father Grande was well known to the people of El Salvador and within the church hierarchy, so his murder not only reverberated throughout the country but also demonstrated the government's complicity with the brutal tactics of the security forces. Rodríguez points out, as many people have, that Grande's murder had a strong impact on the archbishop, because Romero knew that the Jesuit priest was in no way a "communist or Marxist, but a humanitarian." On the same day that Grande was killed, Manuel Barahona, Father Rafael Barahona's brother, was murdered as he was driving Rafael's car. It is clear that this was a case of mistaken identity and that on that ill-fated day at least two priests were to be murdered—Rutilio Grande and Rafael Barahona.[43] According to a former military officer, Francisco Mena Sandoval, Grande's murder was masterminded by Major Roberto D'Aubuisson, an ultraconservative officer, and General Ramón Alvarenga, the director of the National Guard. After Grande's death, D'Aubuisson stated: "It is very urgent that various priests be terminated; it has to be done well and rapidly."[44] As the nation reeled from Grande's murder, little mention was made of the fact that Padre Barahona had also been targeted for death.

The murder of a priest rocked the Catholic Church to an extent that all bishops, both conservative and progressive, united to defend their harried institution. Archbishop Romero, however, took a bold and unusual stance that angered the conservatives within the church. The new archbishop decided to shut down all churches in the country and have one single mass that he would offer in the Metropolitan Cathedral. On that day the archbishop would tell the entire nation exactly what happened to Father Grande and about the state's persecution of the church. Romero also ordered all parochial schools closed for three days so that families throughout the country could reflect upon the repression taking place.[45] Rather than silence the church, the murder of Father Grande turned Archbishop Romero into a national loudspeaker, becoming known to this day as the "voice of the voiceless." The conservative papal nuncio, Bishop Emanuele Gerada, argued with Romero about his decision, insisting that a single mass violated canon law. Romero, nevertheless, went on with his plan and held the single service on March 20, and closed down the schools. The procession for Father Grande's funeral saw roughly fifty thousand people take to the streets, both in mourning and in protest of the government's repression of the church.[46]

By early April, Padre Rodríguez was once again in the line of fire. Bishop Aparicio "punished the parish" of Tecoluca by leaving it without a priest, since the bishop decided to temporarily suspend both Rodríguez and Rafael Barahona. In defiance of his bishop, Rodríguez returned to the parish house in Tecoluca in disguise and organized a small, select group of catechists to celebrate Easter Mass. Rodríguez offered the mass at a land occupation carried out by peasants in a nearby community. At the service, the local population saw Rodríguez for the first time after he was accused of killing Mayor Cañas. As soon as the mass ended, Rodríguez quickly disappeared again. Another land occupation took place on May 9 in the hacienda San Francisco in the canton of Platanares, jurisdiction of the town of Zacatecoluca. In May 1977, the CEBs of Tecoluca issued a six-page assessment of the situation in the parish. The document states: "the only way to get out of this quagmire (*fango*) is to organize ourselves in consequential organizations that will bring us to the path of liberation, defending us from all those who want to suck even our last drop of blood." It warns about the conservative Protestant sects that are being financed by the United States, as well as the defamation being carried out by ANEP, FARO, and the government. The document also urges people to keep practicing their faith and says "the times of the catacombs of the first Christians are about to be repeated in our country." The text ends with this line: "Fight for the prompt return of our priests!!!"[47]

The land occupations that were being legitimated by the presence of priests raised the ire of the landed oligarchy. In a paid advertisement in the newspaper *Diario de Hoy,* the departmental junta of the "Cattlemen of Peace" (a fictitious organization) railed against Padres Rodríguez, Barahona, and Alejandro Vantin. The advertisement asserted that these priests have "an appetite for blood," and that the area of Tecoluca "has been the victim of a meticulous subversive effort that commenced at the pulpits of priests, in student classrooms and in the countryside, bent on bringing about a class struggle."[48]

As Rodríguez continued to come and go in disguises to say mass, accompany peasants involved in land occupations, and participate in demonstrations, the parishioners of Tecoluca and beyond developed a sort of mystical impression of him as someone who could appear and disappear at will, perhaps with the help of God. Rodríguez indeed had help, but his ability to move about undetected came principally from being in a clandestine FPL cell that had safe houses in various locations in the area, but mostly in the city of Zacatecoluca. His clandestine life was also made possible by the help of many priests, nuns, and lay workers who gave him shelter. Rodríguez explains that he often disguised himself as an old man, an old woman, or a Protestant minister. Bishop Aparicio eventually replaced Padres Rodríguez and Barahona with Father Julio Mejía, who took over the parish of Tecoluca.

Attempt at Conciliation

In an effort to decrease tensions between the government and the church, the country's bishops met with President Molina and other government officials on April 20.[49] President-elect Carlos Romero and the papal nuncio, Bishop Gerada, were present. What went on at this meeting serves to show how each side saw the situation in which the country foundered. At the outset, Molina stated that some priests, mostly foreign, had become politically active and were accusing the state of wanting to destroy Christian communities. Molina then argued that it was "international communism" that was responsible for the violence against the state, the kidnapping of Foreign Minister Mauricio Borgonovo Pohl (recently taken by the FPL), and perhaps even the death of Father Grande.[50] Clearly, even Molina, who did not represent the most conservative sectors in the country, believed that communism was the only threat to the nation and responsible for the existing crisis. Archbishop Romero then asserted that he was sorry about the violence being perpetrated against the state by the armed groups, but that the church's evangelization along the lines promoted by Vatican II and Medellín should not be confused with Marxism-Leninism. Bishop Aparicio, as president of CEDES, then said that he agreed with the archbishop and added that the church had not become involved in party politics, that it was simply promoting the human rights of campesinos, and that recent land occupations by campesinos had occurred in cases where clear injustices existed. Regrettably, this meeting did little to resolve the polarization that existed in El Salvador. We can see, however, that even as late as 1977 the conservative bishops saw the situation clearly: the real problems were injustice and repression, not communism or the politico-military organizations.

Less than a month later, another priest was murdered. A death squad killed Padre Alfonso Navarro on May 11, soon after a clash with landowners. As early as 1971, oligarchs had accused Navarro of being involved in subversion.[51] The Unión Guerrera Blanca (White Warrior Union, also known as "White Hand") claimed responsibility and said that his killing was in revenge for the death of Foreign Minister Borgonovo Pohl, whom the FPL had killed the previous day. The FPL had wanted to trade the minister for thirty-seven political prisoners, but the government did not negotiate.[52] During this time, many paid advertisements appeared in the press condemning the church and specific priests, including Rodríguez. Also, flyers began to appear that read "Be a Patriot; Kill a priest!" and "Rebel Priests to the Wall [i.e., firing squad]."[53] One cartoon shows two overweight men from behind, riding motorcycles. At the top it reads "God makes them . . . and . . . the Devil makes them walk together." The man on the left is a priest, a cross on his back; and at his waist is written "traitor priests." The man on the right is a communist, with a hammer and sickle on his back; and at his waist is written "communists." The message was clear: those priest who were the fellow travelers of communists were traitors both to their country and to their church.

CEDES once again issued a statement, signed by Bishop Aparicio, denouncing the repression against the church. In the letter, the bishops said: "We unite with our archbishop of San Salvador and with him condemn the wave of violence" taking place in the country; "the church condemns Marxism-communism . . . but with the same intensity condemns . . . the liberal-capitalist system" and calls for unity and dialogue so that the country can

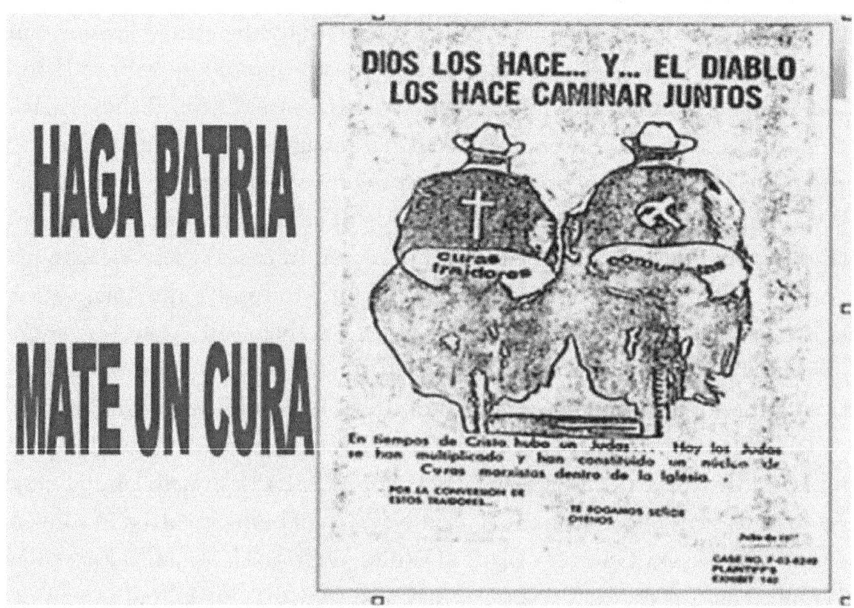

Figure 4.3. Death squad flyer targeting priests. "Be a patriot, kill a priest." Origin unknown.

find a way toward social justice as the only way to keep the country from falling "toward violence and totalitarianism of any type."[54] The document ended by calling for an end to the campaign against the church. Once more the conservative bishops demonstrated their rhetorical support for the doctrines promoted by Vatican II and Medellín, as well as their abhorrence of the violence being perpetrated against their institution.

As the date for Carlos Romero's ascent to the presidency approached, the liberationists hoped that Archbishop Romero would not attend the ceremony, since it would show allegiance to a fraudulently elected executive and a repressive government. The coordinator of the Círculos Biblicos (Bible Circles) of Tecoluca sent a letter to the archbishop on the members' behalf expressing support for the archbishop and urging that he not participate in the transfer of power of a "regime that has persecuted so much a humble people, and the church, for having placed itself on the side of the humble people." The letter also informed the archbishop that Padres Rodríguez and Barahona had been "threatened not to return to their parish."[55]

In late June, the archdiocese issued a booklet titled "A Study on the Persecution of the Church in El Salvador," which detailed acts of repression against the church as well as the general repression under which the country was living. Although the document begins its detailed listing of acts of repression and persecution in 1976, it also lists the initial cases of repression: San Francisco Chinamequita and La Cayetana, both occurring in 1974, and Tres Calles, in 1975. These three "massacres" were becoming the Christian movement's key examples of state repression, since many communiqués and leaflets issued by CEBs highlighted these incidents. No doubt a key motivating factor for the publication of the booklet was the recent murder of two priests. The booklet lists literally hundreds of cases of physical and verbal attacks against the church, priests, nuns and lay workers. From February 21 until May 14, 1977, for example, eighteen priests had been exiled or forced out of the country, the majority (thirteen) being foreign. Two of the Salvadoran priests who left the country because of ongoing death threats were "Chencho" and Higinio Alas, who had pioneered CEBs as well as built a training center in the parish of Suchitoto. The archdiocese's publication also noted that the persecution was being carried out by the government, the mass media, and the oligarchy's private enterprise organizations, such as FARO and ANEP.[56]

The fraudulently elected General Carlos Romero received the presidential sash on July 1. After consulting with various priests, Archbishop Romero decided to boycott the ceremony. Upon taking power, President Romero stated: "I am fully conscious that it is necessary to attack at its origin the causes that engender discontent."[57] Like Molina, President Romero spoke of the need for reforms but instead focused on repression, in an attempt to destroy anyone who opposed the government and the status quo, thus ignoring the church's report on repression and persecution. By November 25, owing to increased conflict, his government passed the Defense and Guarantee of Public Order Law, which criminalized the diffusion of information that disrupted the "tranquility of the country." Such vague language gave the government carte blanche to arrest anyone it wanted. According to political historian Tommie Sue Montgomery, from the day of President Romero's inauguration until October 15, 1979, when he was ousted from power, "El Salvador was buffeted by a rising spiral of mass demonstrations and protests, government repression, left-wing kidnappings, occupations of public buildings, labor strikes and death-squad murders."[58] By the end of 1977, the Salvadoran bishops issued a statement that said, "We are crossing the darkest period of our history."[59] The statement came soon after the liberationist priest Miguel Ventura was taken from his church during mass, "strung up by his wrists, and beaten." Ventura survived, but three of his catechists were kidnapped and "were never seen again."[60]

Romero's government would attack the church with greater precision and intensity than Molina's government. El Salvador's right-wing was particularly interested in stopping the pastoral activities of the church in the countryside. Although the oligarchy and the state were rightly worried about the violent acts of the politico-military organizations that operated principally in San Salvador, they were mostly worried about the organization of the peasantry and the land occupations that had been taking place. These actions were attributed directly to the work of religious leaders like Padre Rodríguez, who called for the liberation of the campesinos. In the first year of the Romero government, "the chief form of persecution against the church was the constant impeding of its pastoral activity in rural areas" by repression and intimidation, committed principally by the National Guard and ORDEN.[61] The new president, however, slowed down both the attacks against the church in the cities and the high-profile cases because of hearings in the U.S. Congress on human rights violations in El Salvador and the international furor over the claim by Unión Guerrera Blanca that it would kill all Jesuits in the country.[62] According to the Latin America Bureau, General Romero's government chose to focus on the department of

Chalatenango in its strategy of repression because it would "complete the repression begun under the previous regime in the departments of San Salvador and San Vicente," since these departments accounted for "the greater part of the peasant organizations' local branches."[63] The oligarchy and its government were concerned more about the popular organizations than the armed guerrillas since they were able to put "50,000 to 100,000 people on the streets."[64] The historical record shows that while the politico-military organizations were still carrying out sporadic acts of violence, the chief targets of the government's repressive apparatus were liberationist priests and nuns, as well as lay leaders, who represented the backbone of the popular organizations. The state was convinced that liberation theology was the same as, or even more dangerous than, Marxism, since both challenged the status quo, but liberationists had a much larger following.

A Clandestine Life

For Padre Rodríguez a clandestine life (*clandestinidad*) was the best way to remain alive, since it was now clear that the military government had no qualms about killing priests and would have killed him had he not been in hiding. Rodríguez recalls that from March 1977 to October 1978 he worked mostly covertly to organize peasants and to develop the "pastoral of accompaniment" or "pastoral of the catacombs." At this point his activities were not solely in the parish of Tecoluca, but also in parishes and locations in several parts of the country, and often in San Salvador. Rodríguez would stay in a number of places, almost always moving regularly from place to place and receiving sanctuary in churches, schools, and homes of friends and sometimes relatives. He was also, of course, carrying out activities on behalf of the FPL. The government was trying to crush the CEBs, so one of Rodríguez's responsibilities was to create a network of base communities to increase communication between them and to help them with ways to continue to organize. As the government increased its repression against the church, Rodríguez saw his work with the Christian communities and the FPL as being one in the same thing.

El Hospitalito, "the little hospital," was the diminutive name given to the Hospital of the Divine Providence in San Salvador, where advanced cancer patients who had no family were treated. When he was in San Salvador, Archbishop Romero spent most evenings there, since he had no official residence.[65] The Carmelite nuns who ran the hospital would allow Rodríguez to stay there as well, but they did not inform the archbishop, since they were well aware of the tensions within the church. Eventually, the nuns told Rodríguez that they did not want to keep lying to Romero, saying to him, "We want to tell the archbishop that you are passing through here, what do you think, Padre?" Rodríguez worried that Romero would not approve and insist that he find another safe place to stay, a difficult task in such a dangerous environment. Nevertheless, he wanted to respect the wishes of the nuns who had treated him so well. When the nuns told Romero that "Padre David" sometimes stayed at the Hospitalito, the archbishop said, "No, it's not a problem, but have him come, have him come, I want to talk with him." The next time he went to the Hospitalito, Rodríguez met with Romero, who asked him all sorts of questions about what he was doing and how he was moving about the country. Rodríguez told him "everything," which was "practically a confession." Romero then said to him: "I understand you and you have my support. And, I will tell the sisters here . . . to prepare a place for you." Rodríguez, having received the blessing of the archbishop, decided to stay more often at the Hospitalito, rather than place his relatives or friends in San Salvador in danger. Naturally, he was delighted that the archbishop did not reprimand or shun him. On another occasion at the hospital, Rodríguez saw the archbishop walking, seemingly troubled and deep in thought. Rodríguez said to him, "Good morning, Monsignor Romero. Are you worried?" "Yes," he responded, "I am wondering if I should go to the meeting of bishops or not; they are always questioning me." Rodríguez recalls that he thought to himself with wonder, "An archbishop asking a mere priest" for advice! Rodríguez told him that he should go, since "it will be of value," their questioning of him represented a "questioning of their own behavior," and that "one day they will realize that they are wrong." The archbishop thanked him and went to the meeting. The Hospitalito was such a safe place that Rodríguez brought many of his private family mementos there. Unfortunately, at some point they were destroyed or taken, since it was dangerous to have the possessions of a wanted priest.

Despite the show of unity toward the start of 1977 and even later, the church, like the country as a whole, finally divided into two irreconcilable camps. Archbishop Romero, his auxiliary bishop, Rivera y Damas, and many priests and nuns continued to embrace and promote the liberationist pastoral, which now also included the condemnation of state repression. No doubt, many priests and nuns stood in the middle, those who accepted the new pastoral but did not actively promote the political mobilization of the people. On the conservative side stood those who accepted the changes endorsed by Vatican II but not necessarily the proactive conclusions of Medellín. This group was opposed to the church taking any concerted action that could be perceived as "political." This conservative group, a part of which actually loathed the changes promulgated by Vatican II, was also staunchly anti-communist and believed that communist ideas had influenced some members of the church, like Fathers Alas, Barahona, Grande, and others, including of course Rodríguez. By the end of 1977, Bishop Aparicio was firmly in the most conservative group and would soon speak ill of Padre Rodríguez, his once loyal assistant. Archbishop Romero began to issue harsh criticisms against the government and security forces after Father Grande's murder, meaning that church-state relations spiraled downward precipitously. The Vatican, concerned about its relationship with the Salvadoran government, appointed Bishop Rivera y Damas to the diocese of Santiago de María in late 1977 and named the conservative bishop Marco Revelo as Archbishop Romero's auxiliary. The goal was to separate the two liberationist bishops, especially since they were in the country's largest diocese, and place a conservative prelate next to the increasingly progressive Romero as a check on the archbishop.

As the church continued to splinter, intense conflicts emerged within the institution. The church issued a condemnation of President Romero's Defense and Guarantee of Public Order Law on January 1, 1978, but only three bishops signed the document.[66] In March 1978, Rodríguez and more than three hundred priests and nuns signed a letter denouncing the papal nuncio. The principal point of the letter was to bring attention to Nuncio Gerada's cozy relationship with a government that was repressing the church and its own people. Rodríguez recalls that in a "very strong denunciation," the letter said: "How can the Nuncio, a representative of the Pope, offer toasts with cognac in receptions while the people are being massacred?" The signatories also said that Gerada was operating at the "margins of the faith."[67] The national press printed the letter immediately, causing an "earthquake," according to Rodríguez. Infuriated by the rebelliousness of his priests, Bishop Aparicio issued a letter of excommunication listing the ten priests from his diocese who had signed the missive, including Rodríguez and his brother, Benigno, for "disrespecting papal authority." The suspension and excommunication process meant that these ten priests could not continue serving as priests. The priests from other dioceses who also signed the letter, however, were not punished by their bishops. The San Vicente priests decided to remain in their parishes and "attend to the people, but not say mass." Rodríguez remembers that Father Antonio Martínez, an older priest from the nearby parish of San Isidro Cabañas, would celebrate mass, and Rodríguez would sing in the choir. However, the older priest, who was against the suspension, eventually said to Rodríguez when he would arrive on Sunday, "I'm tired, you go ahead and say mass." Rodríguez remembered, with a chuckle, "It was a small, remote town, who would find out?" Bishop Rivera y Damas, who had a doctorate in canon law, represented the ten priests before the Vatican and was able to prevent their expulsion from the church. Although concerned about liberationists and church-state relations, the Vatican was not willing to excommunicate priests even when they criticized the pope's nuncio in San Salvador.

As he became more aware of the precarious state of his liberationist priests, including the Jesuits, Archbishop Romero became a more forceful proponent of the new pastoral and a more vocal critic of the government. On August 6 he promulgated his much-awaited third pastoral letter, coauthored with Bishop Rivera y Damas, and titled "The Church and the Popular Organizations." As he had in his previous two letters, Romero referred to Vatican II and Medellín documents extensively, demonstrating to all Salvadorans that his ideas were not revolutionary but rather the expression of the new Vatican doctrine and the beliefs of many of the bishops in Latin America. He also voiced his aversion to communist ideology, writing in his second letter that Marxism was "incompatible with the Christian faith."[68] The third letter elaborated on the critical issue of the popular organizations that had sprouted in the country, such as the BPR and its associated popular groups. Romero forcefully supported and justified the right of the people to organize politically, citing the UN's Universal Declaration on Human Rights, as well as *Pacem in Terris* and the "Justice" document of the Medellín Conference. Romero denounced "terrorist" violence, alluding to the actions of the politico-military organizations, but also condemned the evils of "institutionalized violence" and the "repressive violence of the state." The archbishop, however, saw the popular organizations not as violent groups, as the government suggested, but as legitimate expressions of a people under the yoke of an unjust economic and political system. And, he boldly cited Pope Paul VI's justification of insurrection, found in *Populorum Progressio,* which stated that rebellion was necessary under conditions of "long-standing tyranny."[69] In the eyes of the oligarchy, the state, and the security apparatus, the archbishop had now placed himself squarely on the side of the popular organizations which the conservative forces saw as Marxist-inspired and promoters of revolutionary violence.

The Capture of a Rebel Priest

Clandestine life came to an abrupt end for Padre Rodríguez in the early morning of October 5, 1978, when the National Police captured him and Guillermo Cuéllar, commonly known as Piquín, a lay leader and singer. Rodríguez had participated in an evening celebration of the patron saint San Francisco in the parish of San Francisco Mejicanos, and he needed to go to Zacatecoluca to attend an FPL meeting. Piquín offered him a ride, since he was on his way to "Zacate" himself. At a red light, Rodríguez urged Piquín to drive on since it was four in the morning, but when they ran the light a police car stopped them. One of the policemen recognized Rodríguez, so the officers instructed the two men to sit by the road while they searched the automobile. All they found in the car where documents from Piquín's radio show, "What's Happening in the World," in which he would talk about contemporary events and relate them to the Bible. Within a few minutes, more policemen arrived in a car and a truck. Eventually, the two men were taken to the police station.

Because Rodríguez was already living a clandestine life, his absence was not quickly noticed, but Piquín was missed almost immediately. Rodríguez comments that he was "lucky" because the first detective who came to interrogate him was someone he had catechized as a child in San Vicente. The detective gave Rodríguez soap so he could bathe and a room with a bathroom where he could sleep. The other detective, whom Rodríguez assumed would be the "bad cop," also recognized him, because he was related to Bishop Modesto López and was thus privy to some of the affairs of the church. The second detective told Rodríguez, "Don't worry, Padre, we'll just make a report, the formalities." Piquín was not treated as well—he had to sleep on the floor of a prison cell—but he was not mistreated.

After a few days, Rodríguez was taken to the regional police chief. He was summoned to an office and came face-to-face with the commander of the Fifth Brigade, Colonel José Guillermo García, as well as with Bishop Aparicio. Colonel García, whom Rodríguez had known when he served as chaplain to the brigade, bluntly told him, "Look, this is the last time that you will be saved; you have to change [your ways]." Once they were out of the police headquarters, Aparicio said to Rodríguez, "You cannot do this again," obviously suggesting that things would not go well if he were to be captured once more. On October 6, the day the police released Rodríguez, Monsignor Romero noted in his diary that the archdiocese was informed that Padre Rodríguez was treated "with great respect because they wanted to leave the impression" that they were not repressing the church or mistreating priests, but only going after communist infiltration. Romero also notes that Aparicio was present upon his release, but that unfortunately the bishop did not support the church's just charge that the government was carrying out repression against the church.[70] It is ironic that Rodríguez's gentle treatment at the hands of the National Police and the military was very likely the result of his being one of Aparicio's priests, yet the bishop considered him to be a rogue cleric. Most likely, Aparicio's connections helped to save Rodríguez from almost certain death.

After the arrest, Bishop Aparicio was even more hesitant to give Rodríguez a parish, saying to him, "Wait, let us see, let us see." Eventually, the bishop agreed to let him work with his brother, Benigno, in the parish of Villa Dolores, hoping that this move would keep his rebellious cleric out of trouble. Benigno's parish was located in the department of Cabañas, about seventeen miles northeast of the city of San Vicente. Like his brother, Benigno sympathized with the new pastoral and was also critical of the government; however, he was a much more cautious priest, "timid," and would often say to his brother, "You must think of your . . . family." Benigno was well aware that relatives of liberationists were often targeted by the security forces and death squads. The FPL, knowing that Benigno was Rodríguez's brother, made overtures to him, inviting him to meetings, but "he never became involved."

During the time Padre Rodríguez worked with his brother, on November 28, security forces killed Father Ernesto Barrera when the army attacked an FPL safe house in San Salvador. As far as the government was concerned Father Barrera was vivid proof that some priests had crossed the line by becoming armed Marxists. According to Rodríguez, Barrera was not a combatant but just happened to be at the safe house when the ambush occurred. Rodríguez points out that he could have met the same fate had the security forces found a safe house in which he was staying. After Barrera's death, the link between radical priests and armed guerrillas became crystal clear in the eyes of the government and oligarchs. Archbishop Romero made the difficult decision, after meeting with his clergy, to attend Father Barrera's funeral, so the conservative forces began to also see him as allied with the politico-military organizations. Romero had asked at the meeting of priests, "What would his mother do?" The answer was obvious to him, and so Óscar Romero, along with sixty priests, participated in the funeral, despite criticism from the government.[71]

Rodríguez maintained his ties to the FPL while he was at Villa Dolores, since "it helped me greatly with my security and with my work with campesinos." At this point his brother did not know of his incorporation into the FPL, and Rodríguez knew that, although generally sympathetic to the liberationist cause, his brother did not approve of clergy having connections with the politico-military organizations. Rodríguez decided to use more caution while working alongside his brother. He remembers that one day he entered the church at Villa Dolores and saw a number of young men with cans of paint who were getting ready to carry out some pintas. Rodríguez said to them, "Are you sure you are prepared to do this?" Some of them then challenged him, saying, "Whose side are you on?" Rodríguez realized that what they wanted was support, not questioning. By then, many Christians were committed to the popular movement or the politico-military organizations and were done taking orders or following the advice of established authority figures, including the liberationist priests who may have "awakened" them in the first place. Although the liberationists may have been the ones to mobilize the poor to fight for their rights, as the conflict moved from contention to rebellion the politico-military organizations would begin to take center stage.

A Happy Reunion

One day in 1978, Padre Rodríguez was in San Salvador and found himself face-to-face with Mercedes Henríquez, from La Pita, who was now a young woman. Henríquez relates that she had met and befriended a priest, Father Jacinto,[72] while she was attending school in San Salvador. Since she had become a catechist after meeting "Padre David" in La Pita, she would go with Father Jacinto "teaching catechism in the marginal areas of San Salvador." As she got to know the priest better, and realized that he was sympathetic to the popular organizations, Henríquez started asking Father Jacinto, "Have you seen or heard anything about Padre David?" Father Jacinto would ask her with interest, "Why do you want to know?" She would usually respond, "Oh, I used to know him." After a while, Father Jacinto became suspicious that Henríquez was more than just curious about the liberationist priest.

Father Jacinto, who was also involved in the popular movement, would indeed see Rodríguez now and then, and started telling Henríquez, "Padre David sends his greetings." She recalls that she thought that he was "lying," just to keep her from pining away for Rodríguez.

One day, Henríquez was about to go to a class when Father Jacinto said to her, "Are you leaving? Look, I bet you won't guess who I am bringing." "Who?" she asked. Father Jacinto then said with humor, "The one you are always asking about, your divine tormentor!" David Rodríguez was now a rebel priest who had defied his bishop and believed that the hierarchical church had gone astray. Merci Henríquez was now a young woman and also involved in the "struggle." Their initial attraction was now complemented by a greater mission—the liberation of the people of El Salvador. Henríquez confided, with a conspiratorial hush, "We established a relationship."

Soon after that reunion, Henríquez became pregnant, but she hesitated to tell Rodríguez or anyone else. "I would shut myself into my room," she recalls. "I tried to pretend I was not pregnant." Rodríguez said to her one day, still unaware of her pregnancy, "Why don't we leave the country?" At the time, she remembers, he was very "persecuted, and we didn't know what was coming." Once it was impossible for her to hide her pregnancy, Henríquez returned to La Pita, and "there I had the baby," on November 29, 1979. She told her mother and father that Padre Rodríguez was the father, but she was too scared to tell him she had given birth to their child. She remembers that her father went to Villa Dolores with a letter from her explaining that she had given birth to their child and recounting "all that I had gone through." She recalls being "very anxious, waiting for my father to return. I thought that David would not believe me." When her father returned, she asked with great anticipation, "Well, how did it go?" Her father replied solemnly, "He said that, if he had known, you would not have suffered. He also said that he wants to see the child." Henríquez became very "emotional, overjoyed, and relieved at David's reaction." Too many priests had fathered children and never acknowledged them or their relationships. In fact, Rodríguez remembers one well-known conservative priest who had two children yet never acknowledged them. Rodríguez also points out that a "good percentage of priests" eventually left the priesthood to marry. He acknowledges that there is a "great deal of hypocrisy in this matter" and that often "priests lead a double life." Rodríguez wanted to remain a priest but would at the same time accept his responsibility to his *compañera* and their child. Not long after finding out he was a father, Rodríguez met with Henríquez and their child, Roberto ("Tito") Carlos. Henríquez remembers that it was a wonderful reunion. When Rodríguez finally met his son, he "asked me for forgiveness for what I went through." He also told her that "they would be together"—he would not abandon her or Tito. Henríquez then incorporated herself into the FPL, acquired the pseudonym "Flor," and was assigned to the urban commandos in Salvador.

The 1979 Conference of Bishops at Puebla

The profound division in the Salvadoran church was symptomatic of the rift being experienced in the church throughout Latin America. The bishops who were not sympathetic to the pastoral line established by the 1968 Medellín Conference had not been idle since that historic CELAM encounter. In the ensuing ten years, conservative bishops had mobilized and taken action to moderate the rebellious tone of the new pastoral. In fact, as early as 1972 the conservative bishop Alfonso López Trujillo had been elected secretary-general of CELAM. Bishop López Trujillo was prepared to bridle the liberationists at CELAM's third plenary conference of bishops, held at Puebla, Mexico, from January 28 to February 13, 1979. Additionally, the new pope, John Paul II, elected on October 16, 1978, was much less sympathetic toward the liberationist line than was Pope Paul VI. Conservatives took steps to minimize the participation of liberationist bishops, and especially the theologians who had developed liberation theology. The liberationists went to Puebla anyway and did their best to influence the outcome.[73]

El Salvador's episcopal conference, CEDES, in an effort to present a united front, chose three conservative bishops to attend the Puebla meeting—Pedro Aparicio, Marco Revelo, and Freddy Delgado. Nevertheless, because Archbishop Romero was a member of the Vatican's Pontifical Commission for Latin America, he was able to attend as a representative of that group.[74] At the Puebla conference, Bishop Aparicio paradoxically demonstrated both his support for liberationist ideas and his staunch anticommunism. At one point he stated that in El Salvador there had been an "infiltration of Marxist priests."[75] On another occasion he spoke about how the wealthy in Latin America enriched themselves at the expense of the peasantry, and asserted that in El Salvador "horses and dogs are being treated better than the campesino."[76] As the bishops deliberated at Puebla, an article appeared in the Salvadoran newspaper *El Heraldo* and also in a Mexican newspaper, quoting Bishop Aparicio, who said that the Salvadoran government had "the right to defend itself against priests who became engaged in political subversion," adding that the first priest who was killed (referring to Rutilio Grande) was a Marxist. Aparicio also stated that he had presented a detailed report to the Vatican concerning the activities of Marxist priests that included recordings and documents.[77] Aparicio's comments were particularly bitter for progressive Christians, since he was justifying the repressive actions of the state directed against the liberationists. The dirty linen of the Salvadoran church was out there for all to see, but this was in fact the same sort of conflict that the entire Catholic Church faced after the bombshells that were Vatican II and Medellín.

Bishop Aparicio's comments also hit home when, on January 20, Father Octavio Ortíz Luna was murdered, along with four lay youths. Father Ortíz was part of a group of five priests—the other four were from Belgium—working in San Salvador. When he was murdered, forty others, including two nuns, were detained for being suspected of taking part in "guerrilla training." The government eventually released the nuns for lack of proof.[78] It seemed to the liberationists that Bishop Aparicio was justifying the killing of priests who were suspected of rebellious activity or of being "Marxists." The church was shaken again on June 20 when four armed men killed Father Rafael Palacios as he was approaching his car.[79] Recall that, in 1969, Bishop Aparicio had removed Palacios as parish priest in Tecoluca, replacing him with Rodríguez, because the bishop thought Palacios was too progressive. Father Palacios was transferred to the archdiocese and was serving as parish priest in the parish of San Francisco, in the Mejicanos neighborhood of San Salvador, when he was murdered.

Owing to the intense repression, Archbishop Romero continued to denounce the government's actions against the church and the popular organizations. The security forces directed much of their repression against the BPR, since it was the largest grouping of popular organizations. No doubt many people saw the government attacks against the politico-military organizations as legitimate owing to the FPL's kidnappings and killings of government officials as well as private citizens. For Romero, however, popular organizations like the BPR represented the people and their struggle for justice and human rights. He made a clear distinction between the acts of the FPL and the ERP, on one hand, and the peaceful actions of the popular organizations, on the other. The strategies of the BPR included the occupation of churches, government ministries, and embassies. When the government attacked BPR members who participated in these protest actions, often resulting in deaths, Romero would denounce and publicize these actions, which were often ignored or misrepresented by the conservative mass media. After the government killed nineteen BPR members who had occupied a church, the archbishop condemned the action and begged the government to accept the BPR's "just demands."[80] Although radicalization was progressing, the popular organizations still made relatively moderate demands via peaceful demonstrations.

The Sandinista Victory and the Onset of Civil War

Perhaps the only event that could have further intensified El Salvador's crisis, and more quickly radicalized and unified the opposition, was a revolutionary victory in a neighboring country, which is exactly what happened on July 19, 1979, in Nicaragua, when the Frente Sandinista de Liberación Nacional (Sandinista National Liberation Front) guerrillas overthrew the hated, dictatorial Somoza regime. For the opposition in El Salvador, the Sandinista victory was a motivational shot in the arm. A group of guerrillas, supported by a popular front, had been able to defeat a right-wing dictator backed by the United States. Consequently, a great sense of enthusiasm and optimism permeated the opposition groups, including of course the politico-military organizations. Quickly, pintas appeared on walls stating "Somoza today—Romero tomorrow."[81] Salvadoran liberationists were also motivated by the fact that progressive church leaders had been influential in bringing down the Somoza regime in Nicaragua.

The Sandinista triumph also had a tremendous effect on the Salvadoran security forces, state, and oligarchy, as well as on the United States. Naturally, the oligarchy was concerned that unless they acted quickly and boldly, the opposition in El Salvador would emulate the Sandinistas, take over the government, and carry out extensive land, political, and economic reforms. Unlike in Nicaragua, however, where much of the economic elite had abandoned Somoza, the oligarchy in El Salvador was mostly unified and ready to back a repressive counterinsurgency state.[82] The armed forces saw themselves as "defenders" of the state and feared a revolution that might also destroy their institution, as had happened in Cuba and was now happening in Nicaragua. The armed forces, however, unlike the oligarchy, were soon to show that they were not united. The United States, which had established a "no second Cuba" policy after the Castro regime came to power in 1959, was now forced to deal with the "second Cuba" it had dreaded, in Nicaragua. U.S. concerns centered on not "losing" another government that was friendly toward Washington and preventing communist inroads in Latin America. Washington now looked at tiny El Salvador as the place where it had to draw the proverbial line in the sand to prevent further communist advances. Future president and PDC leader José Napoleón Duarte wrote in his memoir: "It was not until after the Sandinista guerrillas marched victoriously into Managua in July 1979 that any U.S. government official tried to reach me to discuss the problems in El Salvador."[83] The U.S. embassy in San Salvador sent an ominous warning to Washington: "If confronted with a Nicaragua-type situation the El Salvadoran military establishment could easily collapse in four to six weeks."[84]

About two weeks after the Sandinista victory, Salvadoran security forces killed another Salvadoran priest. On August 4, three men with machine guns entered the church in the town of San Esteban Catarina, in the diocese of San Vicente, and gunned down Father Alirio Macías.[85] Macías had been a member of La Nacional and had embraced the new pastoral and come into conflict with landowners. One peasant who worked with Rodríguez and Macías remembers: "We had news that they were going to kill Macías and came to him with it two days before he was killed. He didn't believe it and said he would think about it."

Despite the violence and polarization, some middle ground still existed in El Salvador. A number of military officers were neither supporters of the Romero regime nor sympathetic toward the revolutionary opposition. These officers, like the opposition political parties, wanted reforms rather than revolution. Already a group of young military officers who called themselves the Movimiento de Juventud Militar (Movement of Military Youth), composed principally of captains and lieutenants, had been plotting to oust President Romero, not just to bring about reforms but to end the rampant corruption in the armed forces.[86] The young officers, with support from some more senior officers, moved to oust General Romero on October 15. They did so while President Romero and his family "unexpectedly" visited the United States, suggesting that Washington was at least aware of the impending coup.[87] The two military officers who comprised a provisional junta were Colonel Adolfo Majano, representing the progressives, and Colonel Jaime Abdul Gutiérrez, who represented the more conservative wing of the armed forces tied to the PCN and close to the United States.[88] The most reactionary officers, including Major Roberto D'Aubuisson, were left out of the enterprise, since the plan was to, at minimum, purge them from the security apparatus.

The provisional junta took control of the country and issued a remarkable proclamation that made a number of promises: to end violence and corruption; to guarantee human rights; to promote an equitable distribution of resources (including a land reform program); and to pursue "positive international relations."[89] The intentions of the original coup plotters were extensive and daring. They promised to take the following actions: purge the armed forces of corrupt officers by even putting some of them on trial; eliminate the PCN, ORDEN, and the Agencia Nacional de Seguridad de El Salvador (National Agency for Salvadoran Security, equivalent to the CIA); and begin a dialogue with the popular organizations.[90] The provisional junta quickly announced that civilians would participate in the government. Leading opposition figures joined the junta, including Guillermo Ungo of the MNR. The cabinet included Salvador Samayoa, a philosophy professor; Héctor Dada and Rubén Zamora, both Christian Democrats; and the progressive oligarch Enrique Álvarez Córdova, who had pushed for land reform in 1976. Overall, the military-civilian junta was probably "the most broadly representative government the country had ever experienced."[91] Archbishop Romero also backed the coup, the plotters having consulted with him on numerous occasions prior to taking action.[92] If the young officers and their more senior supporters had been able to control the aftermath of the coup, the crisis in El Salvador could very well have been diffused, preventing the bloodshed of the 1980s, since at the time only the armed forces had the power to force the oligarchy to carry out reforms.

To make the coup more broadly based, however, the young officers had brought into their conspiracy some conservative officers who were able to infiltrate the reformist group and eventually outmaneuver them. These right-wing officers, led by now-general José Guillermo García, who was given the defense ministry and was backed by Washington, slowly but surely gained control of the situation and left the civilians out of the loop, particularly when it came to "security" matters, which really meant the repression of the popular organizations and liberationists. Remarkably enough, what started out as a "revolutionary"—but more accurately a modernizing, anticommunist—military government, similar to those in Peru and Panama in 1968, turned out to be a military-dominated, repressive, and reactionary regime that received the blessing and backing of the United States, and carried out the worst repression the country would ever experience.

The more radicalized left was skeptical of the new government, although the PCS was initially supportive. Obviously, the politico-military groups were opposed to carrying out reforms under the tutelage of the armed forces. Likewise the popular organizations did not support the coup. Consequently, those priests who supported the popular organizations, like Rodríguez, were also skeptical or noncommittal. Since the new government was promising reforms, the popular organizations decided to become even more assertive in their demands. In late October, in a concerted effort, the three largest popular fronts—BPR, FAPU, and the Ligas Populares (Popular Leagues, linked to the ERP)—occupied the Metropolitan Cathedral, two government ministries, forty radio stations, and a number of coffee fincas. In these occupations, the popular fronts "demanded higher wages, lower prices for consumer goods, land reform, public trials of . . . [some military] officers, and an answer to the whereabouts of the 'disappeared.'"[93] While the civilians and some officers in the junta wanted to start making reforms and were amenable to a dialogue with the popular organizations, the "conservative officers unleashed a brutal assault on the popular movement."[94] The increased death toll and disappearances, along with the conservative officers' unwillingness to commence reforms, led the majority of the civilians on the junta to resign. Then Samayoa made the surprising announcement that he was joining the FPL, and he immediately went into hiding. The lukewarm hope that existed turned to ice. The military officers were now governing alone, but they had already been working, with pressure from Washington, to bring in new, more conservative civilians in hopes that the government would be more palatable to the citizenry.

The military junta leaders now turned to the only party that would join their cause that was not on the extreme right—the PDC. The leaders of the PDC, fearful that continued association with the armed forces would tarnish their image, decided to save their principal leader, Duarte, for an anticipated future election. Consequently, Héctor Dada, foreign minister in the first junta, and José Morales Erlich, the PDC president, joined a new junta, announced on January 10, 1980.[95] José Ávalos, a doctor not affiliated with any political party, was the third civilian on the junta. The PDC had made a deal with the military prior to joining the new junta: their participation depended upon the new regime carrying out land reform, ending the repression, nationalizing the banks, beginning a dialogue with the popular organizations and purging a few conservative military officers.[96] Overall, the PDC was only asking the military to carry out the key elements of the original "revolutionary" proclamation. The conservative elements within the armed forces, however, had already increased their presence, so the reform efforts would be stymied and the repression would reach alarming rates.

Opposition Unity

On January 11, 1980, at the University of El Salvador, in San Salvador, the three principal popular blocs—the BPR, FAPU, and the Popular Leagues—along with the Communist Party front, the UDN, established the Coordinadora Revolucionaria de Masas (CRM; Revolutionary Coordination of the Masses). The popular organizations would now try to act in concert, a most alarming turn of events for the oligarchy and the conservative elements within the armed forces, as well as for the United States. On January 20, CRM affiliates occupied 330 churches throughout the country while the FTC organized the occupation of twenty-four rural plantations, demanding higher wages.[97] Then on January 22, the CRM organized the largest demonstration in El Salvador's history, called the "March of Unity," demanding that the government carry out the reforms it had promised after the October 15 coup. Estimates vary on the size of the crowd, but as many as 250,000 people may have taken part in the mass demonstration.[98] The military, ignoring the new civilian junta, responded as it had all along—with unrestrained repression. Forty-nine protesters were killed and hundreds injured.[99] By the end of the month, Colonel Majano was saying that civil war was "almost inevitable."[100]

The repression would now also include political leaders from opposition parties. On television, the recently retired Major Roberto D'Aubuisson accused PDC leader Mario Zamora of being linked with the FPL. A few days later, three armed men entered Zamora's house and shot him to death. Héctor Dada quickly resigned from the junta, and four days later ten more PDC members resigned from the government, including Rubén Zamora, Mario's brother. The PDC was now at a crossroads, since most of the party members wanted to disassociate themselves from the repressive, military-dominated government. The result was that Héctor Dada and Rubén Zamora formed a new political party, the Movimiento Popular

Social Cristiano (MPSC; Popular Social Christian Movement), and took most of the PDC members with them.[101] With the members who represented the progressive wing of the party gone, the PDC was now a right-of-center party.

As the PDC crisis unfolded, on March 6, the junta finally announced its land-reform program, called the Basic Agrarian Reform Law. What the Salvadoran church had called for in 1970 was finally being announced, but only after a decade of escalating crisis. Ironically, the government decreed a state of siege the following day, arguing that order was required for the program's implementation. The reformist elements in the armed forces, the PDC, and Washington saw land reform as a necessary condition for preventing revolution or anarchy. However, the popular organizations, opposition parties, and the politico-military organizations were skeptical of the government's sincerity, while the hardline officers and the oligarchy were convinced that land reform was tantamount to instituting socialism and caving in to the opposition. Rather than ameliorating tensions, the much awaited reform simply further divided the two extremes. The program was literally too little, too late. The reform called for all estates larger than 500 hectares (1,236 acres) to be purchased by the government and turned over to peasants to be held collectively. The reform was not only late in coming but its implementation was a complete disaster. An ISTA worker gave a chilling account of one incident:

> The troops came and told the workers the land was theirs now. They could elect their own leaders and run the co-ops. The peasants couldn't believe their ears, but held elections that very night. The next morning the troops came back and I watched as they shot every one of the elected leaders.[102]

In addition to the repression, much of the land that was purchased by the government was given to members of ORDEN or cantonal civil patrols, organizations closely associated with the security apparatus.[103]

On March 9, the greatly reduced PDC membership voted almost unanimously to allow Duarte to become a member of the junta,[104] possible only since the progressive PDC members had deserted and started their own political party. The next day the MPSC announced that "a program of reforms with repression runs contrary to the fundamentals of the Christian Democrats."[105] In effect, they were saying that the mantle of Christian democracy was no longer represented by the PDC. The PDC had started out in the

1960s as a political party that promoted the church's social doctrine, which stood for land reform, economic justice, and respect for human rights. The party, however, also had a staunchly anti-communist streak. Clearly, Duarte and his followers represented the anti-communist line more strongly than the Catholic social doctrine line.

The Murder of Archbishop Romero

The conflict between the government and church reached a sad, horrific climax on March 24, 1980. On that day a lone sniper entered the chapel at the Hospitalito and shot Archbishop Romero through the heart while he said mass. The nation was stunned. Archbishop Romero had been an advocate of peaceful change. Although the people of El Salvador had become almost accustomed to the fact that the government would not hesitate to kill a priest (they would soon kill nuns), no one ever expected that they would have the audacity to kill the country's highly popular, internationally renowned archbishop. For Rodríguez, Romero had become a "disciple of Jesus, just, honest, and austere . . . a true prophet willing to offer his life." Rodríguez remembers that the national press in El Salvador, controlled by the oligarchy, had done its best to disparage Romero, at times showing him "with fangs" in caricatures.

Because he sided with the liberationists and popular organizations, Archbishop Romero had become a danger to the interests of the oligarchy and the reactionary officers in the security forces—those with almost absolute power in El Salvador. Romero not only helped to strengthen the Christian movement from 1977 until his death but had become "the voice of the voiceless." One study suggested that 75 percent of people in the rural areas and 47 percent of those in urban areas listened to Romero's Sunday homilies.[106] In these homilies the archbishop condemned the ongoing repression and highlighted the need for economic justice. When the CRM emerged earlier in the year, Romero had praised this step toward unity on the part of the popular organizations, saying, "I am pleased that they are finally breaking away from sectarian and partisan interests and managing to find a broader unity. I will always encourage this."[107] In February the archbishop had written a letter to President Jimmy Carter, as a fellow Christian, urging him not to send military advisers or military aid to El Salvador.[108] In his Sunday homily on the day before his death, Romero included these strong words that terrified and angered the security apparatus:

> I want to make a special appeal to soldiers, national guardsmen, and policemen: Brothers, each one of you is one of us. We are the same people. The peasants you kill are your own brothers and sisters. When you hear the words of a man telling you to kill, remember instead the words of God, "thou shall not kill." God's law must prevail. No soldier is obliged to obey an order contrary to the law of God.[109]

Instead of stopping the repression, as the archbishop urged, the reactionaries silenced the revered Óscar Romero.

With the archbishop gone from the scene, the Vatican was forced to make a difficult decision: Who would replace the martyred Romero? Rather than choosing a conservative bishop, which could have alienated more Christians, or allowing another liberationist archbishop to rise, Pope John Paul II appointed Bishop Rivera y Damas as the apostolic administrator of the archdiocese. Monsignor Rivera y Damas would simply manage the archdiocese for the pontiff. According to Rodríguez, Rivera y Damas "could not make any significant decision" as administrator "without consulting" with Rome. Despite the pope's effort to tone down the Christian movement, neither the Vatican, nor the state, nor the oligarchy, nor the security apparatus, nor the United States would be able to stop the popular and revolutionary movement that was growing in strength and rebelliousness. These groups were populated by Christians who had now become outraged at the loss of their oracle, the voice of the voiceless, Óscar Romero.

Repression, Radicalization, and Rebellion

In 1970, when the Salvadoran church called for land reform and held the pastoral week of reflection, most progressive religious leaders envisioned reforms that would yield a more just economic environment for the country's poor, particularly the campesinos. Liberationist priests and nuns also called for political rights and the sanctity of the electoral process. Padre Rodríguez pushed not just for better wages and working conditions for peasants but also for the government to respect the constitution. Had the oligarchy and state carried out reforms as the liberationists demanded, the Christian movement would most likely have remained reformist and redemptive. Even if the politico-military organizations had continued to grow, it is doubtful that Christians would have embraced them as they ended up doing, particularly since many religious leaders would have been satisfied with economic reforms and the government's respect for the constitution.

The state and oligarchy, as often happens when confronted with demands for reforms, however, decided to repress, both because they saw the calls for reform as manageable and because the oligarchy saw land reform as an affront to their wealth and way of life. As the state, with the encouragement of the oligarchs, began to repress, organized Christians became outraged and more belligerent. Demands grew, and resentment toward the state and the oligarchy grew. Likewise, as the oligarchy perceived a growing religious movement that pushed for greater change, it began to impugn the liberationist religious leaders. Soon a spiral of violence and recrimination ensued. Priests and nuns became targets and in turn they became more intransigent. The Christians these leaders had formed and organized also became more radicalized. The tragic events of the mid- to late 1970s lend credence to the notion that social movements radicalize principally as a result of state repression.

Although he is not representative of the majority of priests, in that he joined one of the politico-military organizations, Padre Rodríguez's radicalization is instructive. For several years after the 1970 pastoral week, Rodríguez operated as a priest devoted to the new pastoral mission that focused on the preferential option for the poor. He called for reforms that would both raise the standard of living of campesinos as well as allow them to organize politically. What he wanted was completely in line with the pronouncement of the Catholic Church. His actions, while not traditional, were not socialist, radical, or revolutionary. As the state carried out vote fraud and repression, this reformist priest transformed into a rebel priest. The 1972 vote fraud that led to the election of Colonel Molina resulted in a clash between Rodríguez and both the mayor of Tecoluca and his own bishop. Soon thereafter, numerous events increased his outrage, including the death of Víctor Hernández, the events at Chinamequita, and the torture of Father Barahona. The key incident that prompted him to become a rebel, however, was the massacre at La Cayetana. The mounting repression, the calumny against him and his fellow liberationists, and the need for safety all conspired to convince him to incorporate himself into the FPL. Only a handful of priests joined a politico-military organization, but as the repression mounted against the church and against the Salvadoran people, many religious leaders became convinced that the only way out of the crisis was for the Salvadoran people to unite and fight for their rights. Archbishop Romero's acceptance of the popular organizations lent credence to this conclusion, since his conservatism was challenged by the killing of his priests and the constant attacks against him and his church. As for the lay leaders whom the liberationists had trained, their decision was easier: the repression led them to join forces with the popular and politico-military organizations.

Rodríguez could have joined any politico-military organization, so why did he join the FPL? One of his boyhood friends joined the ERP, and other priests also joined or worked with the ERP. However, the FPL was particularly strong in Tecoluca, and thus several of the leaders he had trained ended up joining the FPL, such as Víctor Hernández and Toño Navarro. Rodríguez also had great respect for Felipe Peña, a leading FPL leader. It was also the FPL that issued a letter that invited progressive priests to join the organization. Rodríguez points out that he developed "great respect" for the organization because it had been able to transform campesinos into people with a strong sense of solidarity. As the repression increased and he considered his options, he decided to say mass at the Cave of Anastasio Aquino and thus became intimately linked with the FPL and the BPR.

The late 1970s also saw the Salvadoran church divide into two camps. The increasing repression, even the murder of Romero, no longer unified them. This massive rift would have important ramifications, since after Romero's murder organized Christians would no longer be able to look to any bishop for succor. Additionally, as the Salvadoran church pulled back its support for the popular organizations, the political opportunities—resources, safe meeting places—that had been available in the 1970s quickly evaporated. No doubt this dramatic change not only convinced many Christians to ally themselves with other organized groups but also made them bitter toward the "hierarchical" church and more open to a people's church. The religious leaders who accompanied the rebellious Christians into this new arena of conflict would likewise eschew the bishops and turn to the Bible to construct a new church of the catacombs.

5

A Revolutionary Priest

"The 'Che' of the Bible"

Not long after Archbishop Romero's murder, a group of priests converged at the parish of San Sebastián, a small town in the municipality of Cojutepeque, located just east of Rodríguez's first parish in the town of Santo Domingo. The clerics were grief-stricken. They greeted each other warmly but were burdened with the knowledge that their ten-year struggle to liberate the Salvadoran poor would now take a different, more problematic path. Padre Rodríguez participated in this last meeting of La Nacional, a hurriedly planned encounter to deliberate on the proper course of action in the light of the archbishop's assassination. The attendees soon realized that only three options were available to them. One was to leave the country, as Benigno Rodríguez and Rafael Barahona would choose to do.[1] Another option was to remain in the country but cut ties to the popular movement and serve in a more traditional manner. The third path was to either join or accompany the popular movement and lead a clandestine life, as Rodríguez had already been doing. Rodríguez recalls that he said at the meeting, "I respect the decision of those who leave the country and of those who decide to stop getting involved, and I hope that you will also respect my decision." He explained to those in attendance that he felt responsible for "getting many people involved in the process and that now he felt he could not abandon them." It was a "very difficult time for the priests, who had been meeting for a long time," he recalls. Of the roughly thirty progressive priests who attended the meeting, about ten chose each path.[2] Rodríguez, of course, chose what could be considered the most difficult, dangerous path. All of the priests, however, pledged to respect each other's choice without judgment or resentment. They all knew that each path was difficult in its own way, and that each path came with its own price. This was an "intense and sad meeting," since it would be their last and it came at the heels of the murder of the revered archbishop.

While Romero's murder was only one of thousands that were linked to the church's demands for social justice, beginning with the killing of Father Nicolás Rodríguez in 1970, the assassination of the archbishop showed clearly that reason was useless and that only strong, armed opposition to the regime had any prospect for bringing about a new society. Numerous instances of state repression had occurred over the last ten years when calls for justice and democracy had been uttered. The peaceful opposition, including the church, had been patient despite the obstinacy of the security apparatus and the oligarchy. Romero's death finally pulled El Salvador into a state of civil war. The Christian movement would now build its own "church of the catacombs." Some of the liberationists and the people they had mobilized would take the path of rebellion, joining or accompanying the revolutionary movement that would quickly begin to coalesce into the strongest armed opposition the country had ever seen. For Padre David Rodríguez the impending insurgency would yield a new phase in his activities as a leader. He would no longer be a nearly autonomous liberationist priest, but rather a mid-level leader in a sizable revolutionary movement.

The Galvanization of the Revolutionary Opposition

Immediately after the murder of the archbishop, Rodríguez decided to become more active politically, so the last meeting of La Nacional was not a decision point for him. He and about a dozen other liberationist priests decided to go on a hunger strike inside the Metropolitan Cathedral to denounce Romero's assassination. Loudspeakers were set up outside the cathedral, and the hunger strikers would periodically make denunciations against the government and armed forces. On March 30, 1980, the day of Romero's funeral, Rodríguez and the other priests on the hunger strike moved to the towers of the cathedral so they would not interfere with the ceremonies on the main floor of the church. During the funeral procession, unknown individuals (most likely from the army or National Guard) detonated bombs and then fired into the large crowd. Rodríguez witnessed the unfolding scene from one of the towers. He remembers that the men firing into the crowds were on the roof of the National Palace as well as on the Civic Plaza, both adjacent to the cathedral. The large crowd in attendance panicked, and most people were hurt or killed because of "trampling and asphyxiation, [rather] than from bullets." Rodríguez recalls that he was struck by how many shoes were left on the plaza, obviously because many people had been killed, wounded, or fled the scene hastily. People rushed into the cathedral to find safe haven, and some of the bodies struck down by bullets were also taken there. The conservative bishops of El Salvador had not been welcome at the funeral. Bishop Rivera y Damas, along with a number of bishops from Latin America and Europe who were present, witnessed the macabre scene. The prelates issued a statement that said: "Bishop Óscar Arnulfo Romero is a martyr of the liberation called for in the Gospel."[3] The only Salvadoran bishop to sign the statement was Arturo Rivera y Damas. The country's archbishop had been murdered, and most of the bishops remained eerily silent. The Vatican would remain oddly quiet as well.

Five days after Romero's murder, on April 4, the MNR, the MPSC, and ten unions and professional organizations not affiliated with the popular blocs formed the Frente Democrático Salvadoreño (FDS; Salvadoran Democratic Front). This would merely be a preliminary step toward a stronger unity on the part of the opposition. Two weeks later, a mass rally of 100,000 people led to the founding of the Frente Democrático Revolucionario (FDR; Democratic Revolutionary Front), which brought together the FDS and CRM and coalesced all the popular organizations.[4] This union represented the most extensive opposition possible in El Salvador at this time and could legitimately claim to represent the majority of the people in the country. The suggestion that in El Salvador the Duarte government was pitted against two extremes—the ultra-right and the communists—was simply not true. Duarte represented the reformist right, especially once the left wing of his party deserted him, and was thus besieged by the reactionaries, led by some military officers in the government, who were supported by the oligarchs. While there was indeed an extreme left, in the politico-military organizations, most people who opposed the regime, including professionals and political parties, now represented by the FDR, were either progressive reformists or social democrats. If they were now aligning themselves with the politico-military organizations, it was principally because the regime, through its repression, had given those centrist and left-of-center groups no other possible choice. Many individuals had now chosen to align themselves with the armed opposition, even if it was Marxist, because they felt that they needed to protect themselves from the repressive security forces and paramilitary organizations. This was indeed the case for the popular Christian movement that the liberationist religious leaders had created and mobilized starting in 1970. Rodríguez's association with the FPL had transpired precisely because of government repression and the need for self-defense, since his "heart was always with the church" rather than with the FPL.

After the bloodshed at Romero's funeral, Rodríguez rushed to Villa Dolores, but he and Benigno then quickly left the parish after getting several warnings that they were going to be killed. Rodríguez relates that "someone very close to us" told them that "the military in Sensuntepeque," about seven miles north-northwest of Villa Dolores, "was planning an operation against us." He then sat down with his brother and said, "We have to leave right away." They abandoned the parish that very day, leaving everything behind. The two brothers took different routes for their own safety. Rodríguez left on a horse with just his guitar—the one he bought in Spain in 1964—and rode to a parish house in the small town of Guacotecti, just outside of Sensuntepeque. The priests at this parish then went to Villa Dolores to see if they could recover some of the brothers' belongings. Upon returning, they informed Rodríguez that soldiers had arrived at Villa Dolores early in the morning, the day after their departure, and had ransacked the parish house and church.

Compounding the danger to his family, the minister of defense, General José Guillermo García—who had been the commander of the Fifth Brigade when Rodríguez was captured—charged that David Rodríguez had put many haciendas at risk and dispatched soldiers to Calderas, where they looted and burned his family hacienda and took his mother, María, into custody. García had been protecting the farms of the wealthy landowners in San Vicente, who had practically abandoned them after the land seizures. According to Rodríguez, García stated that most of the landholdings were in turmoil and that Padre David had been responsible for their demise. The soldiers, according to one relative, "dismantled everything . . . they took the livestock, the mill (*trapiche*), the motor [of the mill], everything, everything of value . . . even the roof tiles." The operation was led by a captain who was the leader of the civil patrols in the area and was reputed to have killed a number of people, including those who had worked for Rodríguez's father. Luckily, the local people challenged the army, and Rodríguez's mother was released and whisked away to San Vicente. Not long after the destruction of their house, Benigno, along with his sister Raquelita and their mother María, fled to Mexico, and later immigrated to the United States.[5]

Figure 5.1. Rodríguez with his mother, María Ana, early 1980s. By permission of the Rodríguez Henríquez family.

Once again, Padre Rodríguez returned to a clandestine life, along with other priests who embraced the "pastoral of the catacombs," reminiscent of the hidden lives of the early Christians. His conversion and route to rebellion had been a difficult one, just as it had been for Romero. He reminisces: "I was very conservative . . . many crises had to pass, many repressions in my life [had to occur], to start understanding the situation." In a sense, it is remarkable not that traditional people became radicalized but that they did so only after repression had reached such a high level and after so many people had been murdered. The opposition could not rightfully be classified as one of knee-jerk rebellion, but rather as one that pushed its cause slowly and peacefully until given no other option but to arm themselves.

The politico-military organizations had called for violent revolution in the early 1970s while the liberationists worked toward peaceful reforms, but the Christian movement turned to the armed rebels only when it was the only available choice. Ten years of pressing for reforms had now led to violent confrontation.

The violence directed against the church and the political opposition escalated dramatically after Romero's murder. In 1980 about six hundred people were killed and almost a thousand were disappeared monthly by the various state security organizations or private death squads.[6] For a small country like El Salvador these numbers are frighteningly high. Also, they do not adequately convey the horrific nature of the repression that took place in El Salvador. People were not simply murdered or disappeared but were often raped, tortured, mutilated, and at times left in public places in hideous conditions for others to see, in an effort to terrorize people into inaction. Incredibly enough, despite this extensive, horribly sadistic repression, people were still willing to challenge the government, taking the path of risk-steeped behavior in order to accomplish a common goal of greater justice. Granted, part of the rationale for joining the guerrillas was also self-defense, but survival could also be achieved by either moving away from the conflict zones or leaving the country. Many chose instead to fight the government.

The Popular Church Emerges

With Archbishop Romero gone, the Salvadoran church hierarchy veered toward a more conservative, or more timid, position. The conservative bishops, and Bishop Rivera y Damas, became committed to focusing on institutional unity. The liberationists in the church, however, had gone too far down the path of contention to return to a church dominated by conservatism and a need for institutional preservation. In June 1980, liberationist priests, nuns, and lay leaders met to take stock of the situation. The result was the creation of the Coordinadora Nacional de la Iglesia Popular (CONIP; National Coordination of the Popular Church). Rodríguez remembers that at a meeting held in Europe the liberationists argued about what to call the new organization. Some of the priests were concerned about starting what could be seen as a rebel church. Rodríguez recalls that when the name was debated, particularly the use of the word *popular*, one priest said: "No! That popular church [name] . . . sounds too much like China." Nevertheless, those who wanted to focus on the catacomb and popular nature of the new organization won the debate. On August 3, CONIP issued a statement saying that "the recent escalation of military repression, the lack of understanding in some segments of the clergy and hierarchy, and the lack of communication between the base communities have shown us that we need to evaluate and benefit from the shared results of our experiences."[7] Rather than yielding unity, the savage murder of Archbishop Romero had finally split the Salvadoran church into two camps. Those who wanted to actively continue to support the liberationist line would join or sympathize with CONIP and work with the popular organizations, either directly by "accompanying the people" or by collaborating with the revolutionary effort. The hierarchical and more conservative side of the church, which now included all of the bishops, returned to a Catholicism whose principal function was spiritual, rather than earthly liberation. As a result, the organizational and moral strength that the Christian movement had derived from the support of Archbishop Romero and Bishop Rivera y Damas had now evaporated.

The escalation of the repression in 1980 continued to target religious leaders as well as the growing number of opposition leaders. On October 7, Father Manuel Reyes, another Salvadoran diocesan priest, was murdered. On November 27, twenty people were abducted at the end of an FDR conference held at the church in the Jesuit high school in San Salvador, called the Externado San José. Six FDR leaders who had been seized were soon found murdered, including the oligarch and president of the FDR, Enrique Álvarez Córdova;[8] Juan Chacón of the BPR; Enrique Barrera of the MPSC; Manuel Franco of the UDN; Humberto Mendoza of the Movimiento de Liberación Popular (People's Liberation Movement); and Doroteo Hernández, a labor leader. The government claimed that it had nothing to do with the murders, but numerous witnesses testified that they had seen soldiers at the scene of the kidnappings. It was clear to informed observers that the government was behind the assault, as was later confirmed. On the following day, November 28, Father Marcial Serrano, parish priest of Olocuilta, diocese of San Vicente, disappeared and was never found. On December 2, three American Catholic nuns—Dorothy Kazel, Ita Ford, and Maura Clarke—and one female lay worker—Jean Donovan—were reported missing after arriving in the country. Their bodies were found a few days later buried close to San Salvador's international airport and showed signs of having been raped and tortured. This atrocious act received world attention and raised the ire of the United States, since in this case U.S. citizens had been killed. Washington suspended aid after the death of the four Americans, but quickly resumed its assistance after some soldiers were rushed to trial. Clearly, preventing another Nicaraguan revolution was Washington's principal goal.

Rodríguez came out of hiding to attend the funeral mass of the four women at the cathedral in San Salvador, as well as the burial of one of the nuns, Ita Ford, in the department of Chalatenango, north of San Salvador. Rodríguez entered the church in the city of Chalatenango clandestinely and, at the time of the offering, began to sing the song "La Misionera" (The Female Missionary), which he had originally written while in Spain. Rodríguez had written two new verses in honor of the four slain women. Soon after starting to sing, and as others joined in, Rodríguez noticed that Bishop Rivera y Damas, who had celebrated the mass, had turned and looked at him, obviously having recognized his voice. At the end of the mass, someone told Rodríguez that the bishop wanted to have a word with him, so he walked over to the prelate. "What are you doing here?" the bishop asked with surprise, but not in an accusing manner. "Well, this is an event in which I wanted to participate," Rodríguez responded. The bishop then told him, "Come with me to the burial." Rodríguez had planned to leave the church at the end of the service, but he decided to change plans and attended the burial with the bishop. After the burial, Rivera y Damas gave Rodríguez a ride in his car to his prearranged pickup point, at a rural intersection, and did not leave until a car arrived for the rebel priest. Rodríguez then left for the coalescing guerrilla front in the department of Chalatenango. Recalling this event, Rodríguez says: "It made me very happy because one is always thinking that the bishops are furious." Remarkably enough, Rivera y Damas wanted to talk with Rodríguez and even offered him safe conduct to his destination. Most likely, although he knew that Rodríguez was involved with the FPL, the bishop saw him first and foremost as a fellow priest in need of protection. Also, Rivera y Damas had not long ago been one of the principal promoters of the liberationist pastoral.

In December 1980, a service was held at the Metropolitan Cathedral for the six murdered FDR leaders, and Padre Rodríguez boldly offered the homily. A *Time* article pointed out that only two thousand people attended owing to fear and also reported: "Shouted the Rev. David Rodríguez, a Salvadoran priest: 'We know that in the blood of the martyrs who lie here is the spirit of liberty.'"[9] A photo taken at the mass by Alain Keler shows Rodríguez at far left, microphone in hand, a piece of paper in his left hand, his head raised, and emotionally charged, speaking to the crowd.[10] To his right stands Father Rogelio Ponceele, who would soon minister to the people in the guerrilla-controlled areas in the department of Morazán and was one of the Belgian priests who had worked with the murdered Father Octavio Ortíz.[11] Five priests are visible in the photo and above and behind them is a large banner with the letters FDR. Ten priests concelebrated the mass for the killed opposition leaders. In his homily, Rodríguez is quoted as saying that "every day there are more brethren in this nation who prefer to have their bodies killed rather than have their spirits die."[12] After the funeral, an FDR spokesman warned that the murder of the opposition leaders "leaves the people of this country no way out of the present situation except insurrection."[13] Rodríguez, the only priest present who agreed to be identified by name, told reporters after the funeral, "I've already been burned. I can't get burned any more than I am."[14]

Rodríguez points out that he agreed to speak and say the homily at these funerals because he had the protection of being in the FPL, while some of

Figure 5.2. Rodríguez (with microphone) at the funeral for the six slain FDR leaders. Photograph by Alain Keler, December 1980. By permission of Corbis Corporation.

the other priests who had decided to stay in El Salvador were vulnerable. A video taken by a German journalist shows Rodríguez at the front of the cathedral harshly condemning the murders. It is clear from the video that he is highly politicized, but by now it is also clear that there were very few options at the time for anyone who was concerned with the interests of the poor. Rodríguez points out that while liberationist priests were constantly accused of being "political" because of their progressive stance, conservative priests and bishops who were supportive of, and cozy with, the government never suffered any criticism. Some priests attended government banquets while the state was killing people on the streets; one photo taken while the war was already under way shows a bishop "blessing helicopters."[15] Early in the year, when Archbishop Romero had received an honorary degree from Louvain University, in Belgium, the monsignor said: "The course taken by the church has always had political repercussions. The problem is how to direct that influence so that it will be in accordance with the faith."[16] Clearly, both church factions were linked with, and supported, groups that employed violence for political ends in the war to come, but the reactionaries were responsible for most of the deaths during the 1970s and through the end of the civil war.[17]

The Civil War Begins

As we have seen, conflict between the oligarchy-controlled state and the opposition—both reformist and revolutionary—started in 1970. By the end of 1980, however, the civil war between the state and the guerrilla forces began in earnest. The five politico-military organizations in El Salvador decided to combine forces to create a united front, as the Sandinista front had done in Nicaragua. The five groups—the FPL, the ERP, the RN, the PCS's Fuerzas Armadas de Liberación (FAL; Armed Forces of Liberation), and the Partido Revolucionario de Trabajadores Centroamericanos (PRTC; Revolutionary Party of Central American Workers)[18]—formed the FMLN. Owing to the increasing repression, the continued support from many opposition groups, and the recent Sandinista victory, the FMLN hastily planned a "final offensive" for early 1981. The country certainly seemed at the brink of chaos and possible popular uprising, since opposition groups, including the liberationists, for ten years had tried in vain but peacefully to convince the state to carry out reforms.

Just prior to the offensive, the FPL provided Rodríguez with a "contact" so he could "incorporate himself into a [guerrilla] front" (an area controlled by the insurgents). Some FMLN leaders were optimistic about their chances of toppling the government, so the plan was to incorporate as many supporters as possible into the assault. Rodríguez's contact failed to arrive, however, and other members of his "cell" had already joined the mobilization for the offensive, leaving him "uncoordinated." Eager to participate, Rodríguez traveled to San Salvador, to a neighborhood called San José Cortez, in the suburb of Ciudad Delgado, to search for an FPL contact. He knew a woman fruit vendor there who was reliable and was also involved in a CEB. She quickly found him a contact, and this enabled Rodríguez to integrate himself into an FPL collective that was tasked with carrying out "popular militia" operations in the capital. The militias were part of the popular organizations; they provided security for demonstrations and marches and helped to protect communities that were loyal to the popular movement. The militias, however, were now going to become part of the final offensive and would thus serve as a support element for the FMLN's military offensive.

The military assault on San Salvador and other cities and towns commenced on January 10, 1981. The FMLN wanted to carry out their campaign before Ronald Reagan assumed the presidency in the United States, because the insurgent leaders knew that the new administration would shower the Salvadoran government with military and economic aid. President Carter supported the Salvadoran government and had even increased aid, but Reagan promised to provide even more funding to prevent a possible communist revolution.

Owing to the trust he had within the FPL leadership, Rodríguez was soon made chief of the popular militia of Ciudad Delgado, "commanding three columns." At this time, he began to carry a pistol regularly when on a mission. In the future he would also carry a rifle in the guerrilla-controlled areas. "I never had a problem carrying a rifle," he says. Rodríguez, however, also points out: "Thank God, I was never in an armed confrontation." The only time he fired a weapon was during "training and target practice." For several years, Rodríguez had faithfully served as the chaplain to the Fifth Brigade in San Vicente, had been friendly with the military, and even served as a chaplain in the war with Honduras. Working with a military organization was not foreign to him. When he worked with the armed forces, the church and government praised his efforts as patriotic, but now that he worked with the insurgents he was deemed a terrorist.

The popular militias were responsible for organizing support for the FPL, distributing propaganda, carrying out pintas, and facilitating the flow of goods to the front in Guazapa, the remnant of a volcano where the FMLN had set up a major camp. The militia units under Rodríguez's command carried out operations to hinder troop movements by erecting barricades, stopping a train, and harassing military posts. His units also served as guides for the guerrilla columns that attacked military barracks in or near Ciudad Delgado. At one point, Rodríguez was informed that an entire column of an RN militia had been left leaderless since their commander had been killed. He conveyed this information to the FMLN command and was instructed to take temporary control of the unit. Rodríguez recalls that although his unit was outnumbered and out-resourced, the Salvadoran military tended to be somewhat "stupid, like a bull that you could easily fool." Some of the information he received came from within the security forces themselves, from informants such as cooks, carpenters, and cleaning crews who worked for the military or the police but who were supporters of the FPL or another rebel group. Ciudad Delgado was a particularly difficult place to carry out subversive operations, because the headquarters of both the Treasury Police and the National Guard were located there, and thus the neighborhood was swarming with security personnel. Rodríguez and the members of his militia would joke that if you walked down the street in Ciudad Delgado, "either the man in front of you or the man behind you was a policeman; and, if not, then *you* were the policeman!"

Although demonstrating that it could carry out a national, well-organized offensive involving thousands of armed guerrillas and even more supporters, the FMLN did not achieve its principal goal of taking over the capital and bringing down the government. From this perspective, the final offensive was a failure. Although the leaders of the five politico-military organizations that comprised the FMLN agreed to carry out the January offensive, the FPL did not enthusiastically support the attack, since Cayetano Carpio, also known as "Marcial," had embraced a "prolonged popular war strategy." Carpio was convinced that El Salvador's conflict would be similar to the one in Vietnam, where French and then U.S. military forces had been forced to withdraw, but only after a long struggle involving a large popular movement. Carpio thought that the 1981 offensive, which depended upon the insurrection of the population, was doomed to fail, since it was a naive strategy promoted by the ERP. The FMLN guerrillas were also not very well equipped for a decisive military operation. One former guerrilla points out that in 1980 only about one-fifth of FPL combatants were armed and that the FMLN forces did not possess mortars or artillery, essential for assaulting military installations.[19] If the FMLN had truly been the creation of a well-organized communist conspiracy, they would have been well armed by the time of the offensive. Nevertheless, the government of El Salvador was in such a weak position in early 1981 that Duarte commented that it was "a miracle the guerrillas did not defeat the army."[20]

The offensive left behind many wounded combatants, and one of Rodríguez's responsibilities as leader of the militia unit in Ciudad Delgado was to "requisition" (borrow or steal) vehicles to transport the wounded. The FPL maintained contacts with sympathetic doctors, nurses, priests, and nuns who would help treat wounded guerrillas. Rodríguez points out that a militia unit would approach someone in a parking lot who had just parked his or her vehicle and say, "Look, we are from the FPL, and we need your vehicle. Don't worry, we'll use it and then return it to you." People would be "frightened" and thus would hand over the keys. Over time, the population could easily tell whether the people asking for their car were common thieves or guerrillas, principally by the way they comported themselves. The FPL militia would always be respectful, usually return the car, and even leave a thank-you note. Rodríguez points out that on several occasions when he asked for someone's car, the person would recognize him. Naturally, the news spread that Rodríguez had not left the country, as a number of priests had done after Romero's death, but was in fact actively participating in the rebellion. Some of those whom I interviewed pointed out that while they never saw him during the civil war, they heard stories about "Padre David" working for the guerrillas.

The second anniversary of Archbishop Romero's murder was quickly approaching, and Rodríguez took charge of providing security for the somber event that, without the repressive environment, would have drawn literally hundreds of thousands of participants. Owing to the start of the civil war, and the fear of a repetition of the repression at the archbishop's funeral, no celebratory mass had been held at the first anniversary. The mass for the second anniversary took place on March 24, 1982, at the church of the Calvary in San Salvador, a beautiful Gothic structure that was finished in 1950. The parish priest had no idea that the celebration was going to be managed by the FPL. Upon seeing Padre Rodríguez, the parish priest became very nervous and asked him, "What are you doing here? Are you going to celebrate mass?" Rodríguez told him no, but later, when the priest who was to perform the mass failed to show up, he took over and carried out the ceremony. The parish priest "became furious" with him. Rodríguez recalls that "much fear [existed] in the Christian communities," so the turnout at the anniversary was paltry. Many Christian lay leaders had also by then incorporated themselves into the FMLN and thus were not available to help organize or mobilize people for the event. Nevertheless, Christians throughout the country remembered the archbishop with vigils and prayers, and the FMLN announced a twenty-four-hour truce in memory of the venerated martyr.

Revitalizing the Christian Base Communities

After the 1981 offensive, Rodríguez reported to the FPL that the Christian sector needed to be reconstituted, so he was then incorporated into the Comisión Nacional de Masas (National Commission of the Masses) and given responsibility for revitalizing the CEBs. He spent the remainder of 1982 and the beginning of 1983 in that capacity. At this point Rodríguez worked mainly with CONIP and with the CEBs that still existed. In addition to organizing and reviving the communities, he worked with parishes in the guerrilla-controlled areas to ensure that the church officially registered the baptisms, marriages, and deaths that occurred in these areas. Toward the end of 1982 he traveled throughout the country in the various "liberated zones," working to organize and serve the CEBs that were still active. Most of the support that the armed insurgents received, in terms of food, clothing, medicines, and information about movements of the armed forces, came from the people of El Salvador, who were mostly Catholic. The remobilization of Christians was therefore essential for the long-term survival of the armed rebellion. Owing partly to Rodríguez's efforts, the Primer Congreso de las Comunidades Cristianas (First Congress of Christian Communities) was held in Guazapa in March 1983. The congress had to be terminated early because the armed forces carried out a major military assault in the region, during which several FPL *comandantes* (commanders; the highest rank in a guerrilla army) were killed. Those who were attending the congress were rushed out of the "front," so Rodríguez returned to San Salvador briefly.

With the loss of some of the FPL leadership, Rodríguez was then transferred back to the Guazapa area in May and given the responsibility of organizing and supervising the FPL's *poderes populares locales* (PPLs; local popular powers). He remained there until the end of 1984.[21] Another reason for his transfer was that his presence as a priest in areas not controlled by the FMLN was beginning to put people at grave risk. On one occasion in late 1982, after Rodríguez had performed marriages in towns around Tecoluca, government forces killed a Protestant pastor and some of his parishioners in the nearby canton of El Campanario. As the facilitator of the PPLs, Rodríguez was responsible for the way in which people governed and defended themselves in the guerrilla-controlled areas. What the FMLN called "the front," or guerrilla-controlled zones, were areas where the armed rebels and their supporters operated with relative freedom, although government forces could always carry out attacks.[22] In these zones, the Salvadoran government was virtually absent. Consequently, the FMLN took on the responsibility of organizing the population in these areas, both to establish an alternative to the government and to gain the much-needed cooperation of the local people. These zones represented what scholars have termed "multiple sovereignty," a condition that often precedes the success of an insurgency, since it signifies the government's loss of control of a significant number of its citizens and sizable parts of its territory.[23]

One critical role of the PPLs was the organization of communities in case there was an attack by government troops. In such an event, which occurred often during the war, entire communities would leave their towns and go into the hills or mountains on what was referred to as a *guinda*. When the military would attack and encircle a community, the operations were performed so slowly that the popular militias could evacuate the civilians to safe territory in time. The Salvadoran military, as Rodríguez points out, was often referred to as a "9-to-5 army"—even by the U.S. government—because they would operate only during normal work hours. At times, however, the army caught communities unprepared or tracked them down, and the end result was often a massacre. Rodríguez says: "Massacres were not rare; there were many of them," since the military used a "scorched earth" campaign.[24] Early in the war only men and older boys were evacuated, but once the military began to kill women and children who stayed behind, the guindas included entire communities. Rodríguez points out: "We never thought they would kill old women and pregnant women," but the armed forces considered "women and children as guerrillas, so they [were] eliminated." As the war progressed, however, the Salvadoran armed forces, under pressure from the United States, began to adopt U.S. counterinsurgency strategies that called for winning the hearts and minds of the local population, reminiscent of the same efforts during the recent Vietnam War. The armed forces were still quite repressive, but they began to commit fewer massacres and to provide some token assistance to the campesinos.[25]

Rodríguez recalls that when he first witnessed a guinda he was taken aback by how well the campesino leaders reacted to government attacks, relying on their knowledge of the territory to evade capture. One of the successes of the FPL, as a guerrilla army, was that they did not leave communities at the mercy of the armed forces. Nevertheless, most of the organization of these communities and the actual leadership in the guindas was carried out by local campesino leaders who were not guerrilla combatants but belonged to the PPLs or to the popular militias. These campesinos, with help from the PPL leadership, would also organize defense tactics using land mines and sharpshooters to delay the attacking government forces. Rodríguez recalls that the security forces, often assisted by members of ORDEN, would continually destroy the crops planted by the people of the communities in and near the controlled areas. When they lost their milpas, the campesinos would rely upon tubers (*malanga* and *yucca*) and the fruit *ujuste* as alternative crops. The areas around El Paisnal, where Father Rutilio Grande had ministered, and Cinquera, in the department of Cabañas, where Rodríguez was well known, were particularly conflictual. Because these were "contested zones," military operations, despite the efforts of local leaders, would often leave the population, and consequently the guerrillas, without food.[26]

The war effort required a continued source of comestibles, and the PPLs were responsible for ensuring that food was available for the guerrilla army as well as for the people in the controlled regions. Since the areas around the Guazapa volcano were rife with abandoned sugar plantations, Rodríguez, in his PPLs role, was responsible for ensuring that all the equipment used for sugar production was safely stored, often buried, when the government carried out a military operation. The goal was to ensure that the military did not discover that the FMLN and the local population had put the sugar mills to work. Rodríguez would also organize the distribution of food to Cinquera, a more dangerous area for the rebels. He recalls that long canoes would be used to transport livestock and food down the Lempa River to the beleaguered town. On one occasion, they transferred a comandante, as well as his bodyguards and assistants, from Cinquera to Guazapa. One of the bodyguards had a cat that all of the sudden knocked over a radio which then turned on at a very high volume, creating a brief panic in the group. Fearing that they would be discovered by the armed forces, someone quickly threw the cat overboard. Long after this incident, the compas would often say, "Remember that cat?" Then they would all laugh.

Music was an important medium for maintaining morale, and Padre Rodríguez always included music in his religious services and in daily life at the front. Rodríguez would say, "My role is to instrumentalize the people," suggesting that they would become more instrumental in the popular movement, but would then jokingly say, "So, I have to bring more musical instruments to the front." Some of the nuns in the local schools would say to him in jest, "Padre, have you instrumentalized the people?" At the front, big fiestas would periodically be held, with bands playing loud music and compas dancing. The journalists who were present would scratch their heads, saying, "How is this possible, so close to the capital?" A local musical group called Los Farabundos would often play at functions organized by the PPLs.

Another of Rodríguez's responsibilities was to establish links with the workers at the Cerrón Grande dam. Recall that CEBs organized by Father "Chencho" Alas had challenged this massive government project. Consequently, the workers at the dam were sympathetic to the popular organizations and now to the armed guerrillas, often referred to as *los muchachos*, the young men. The effort to reach out to these workers required extensive planning and entailed a great deal of risk. Rodríguez and his group would walk at night to Cerrón Grande so they could arrive before sunrise. They would then remain hidden the entire next day. In the evening they would enter the dam complex and meet with the workers. As Rodríguez recalls, "Soldiers were everywhere [in the area]," so it was "a difficult effort." After the meetings, they would walk back to Guazapa in the middle of the night. Rodríguez carried out this operation five or six times, and points out that the armed forces "never found out that we had this relationship with the workers." Through this effort, the FMLN was able to expand its organization in the region, conduct some operations with the help of the workers, and collect very important intelligence, such as the size and activities of government forces.

By this time, the area around the Guazapa volcano was the largest and most important FMLN "frente" in the country, with the presence of all five guerrilla organizations. From the upper parts of the volcano and from some mountain areas, the guerrillas could see San Salvador clearly. At night it seemed that the capital, aglow in lights, was even closer. Rodríguez remembers a German journalist who traveled to the front in Guazapa and marveled at the fact that the guerrillas could operate almost at will so close to the capital of a government that was receiving massive amounts of U.S. military and economic assistance. It was a dangerous area, however, because the FMLN would install many land mines in the outer perimeter to keep government troops out. A number of compas and soldiers were killed and even more maimed by these anti-personnel mines.

A Guerrilla Priest?

As it became stronger, the FMLN would occasionally take over towns in an effort to expand its area of control or simply to demonstrate its strength. The front was like an amoeba that would grow, contract, and change shape. The government seldom penetrated some areas, but on the fringes of the controlled zones the government would vie with the FMLN for control. Usually, the FMLN would take over a town for a day, or at most two, and then the government would dispatch forces to recapture the town. At first, FMLN efforts to take over small towns did not go very well. When the FPL first took over the town of Tenancingo, close to Guazapa, some of the guerrillas had not been in a town for perhaps as long as two years, so they essentially plundered it, taking everything from utensils to livestock. Since medicines were essential in the front, the town's pharmacy was cleaned out. Identity cards were also very useful for the FMLN, so the mayor's office was broken into and ransacked. The FMLN quickly realized that, when taking over a town, the political leadership had to coordinate matters with the comandantes to ensure that the guerrillas acted properly. It was essential that the local population not develop resentment toward the FMLN.

When the FPL entered Cinquera in 1983, Rodríguez coordinated the political element of the takeover. His role was to meet with the mayor, the local priest, and any other local leader. With a loudspeaker, Rodríguez announced that there would be no vengeance on the part of the FMLN and asked people to voluntarily donate what they could to the war effort. While he was making this announcement, someone came to Rodríguez saying that there were some compañeros about to kill members of a family that was hiding behind the town's church. It is important to note that many of the guerrillas had lost family members to the armed forces and also to members of ORDEN. Some of the ORDEN members would still be living in the towns that were temporarily occupied by the FMLN, and thus it

Figure 5.3. Rodríguez in guerrilla-controlled territory, circa 1984. By permission of the Rodríguez Henríquez family.

was very tempting for some of the guerrillas to exact vengeance. Rodríguez rushed to the church and told the compañeros that the FPL's policy was that no revenge would take place. The compa who was leading the small group of guerrillas told Rodríguez that the men in the family had been in the civil defense and added angrily: "This guy killed my father, my whole family . . . if you want to stop this you are going to die too." Rodríguez responded calmly, "You can kill me if you want, but the agreement that we have is to respect people's lives." The young rebel ended up backing off, and Rodríguez took the family to the town's plaza so that the leadership could decide what should be done. We have to wonder what this guerrilla may have done had he not faced the well-known "Padre David."

Over time, the FMLN combatants increasingly acknowledged the political dimension of the war, giving "greater respect to the political authority." When some time later the FPL captured Tejutepeque, less than five miles southeast of Cinquera, things went much better in terms of the coordination between the guerrilla army and the political authority. Rodríguez had created small political commissions to visit the mayor, the clinic, and the priest to ask for cooperation. One of the members of the commission that went to talk with the priest rushed back to Rodríguez and said that when he had told the local priest that "Padre David" was the political coordinator, the priest had said with great enthusiasm, "I want to see him!" When Rodríguez saw Father Jesús González Valle, who was somewhat conservative, walking briskly toward him, he cautiously walked toward the approaching priest, while several journalists who were present at the takeover turned on their tape recorders. Rodríguez recalls, "He embraced me and said, 'hello, colleague, it's been so long since I've seen you!'" Rodríguez was perplexed since he was expecting a confrontation. Father González Valle then went on to give an impromptu speech at the town plaza lauding "Padre David," an event that was later reported in the national press. Rodríguez remembers with humor that when González Valle ended his soliloquy, he whispered to him, "Take care of my jeep because the guerrillas want to take it!" In a short article covering the government's recapture of Tejutepeque, the *New York Times* reported: "The Rev. José David Rodríguez, a priest from the eastern province of San Vicente, led the guerrilla attack, according to the Rev. Jesús González Valle." The article then quotes González Valle as saying, "Since he's a colleague, it was a great pleasure to see him."[27] This event is interesting since, although Father González Valle showed warmth toward Rodríguez, his assertion that "Padre David" had led the fifteen hundred guerrillas who assaulted Tejutepeque gave credit to the notion that some priests were intimately involved in the armed guerrilla movement. Now that "evidence" existed that Rodríguez was a guerrilla commander, he would certainly be executed summarily if captured by the security or military forces. Rodríguez's image as a "guerrilla priest," however, was promoted even within the liberationist church. A fellow liberationist, Astor Ruiz, is reputed to have called him "the 'Che' of the Bible" in the early 1980s. As a result of these political efforts, the guerrillas were not only getting stronger militarily but were also winning the most important struggle: gaining the support and trust of the population. At every takeover of a town in a contested zone the FPL would gain a few recruits.[28]

Although the military and political effort on the ground was improving, a serious crisis soon erupted within the FPL leadership. Cayetano Carpio, the founder and leader of the FPL, had been losing his appeal owing to his orthodoxy. Mélida Anaya Montes, the FPL's second in command, with the pseudonym of "Ana María," on the other hand, was growing in popularity. Rodríguez points out that Ana María was more open to developing unity with the other armed and popular organizations, while Carpio's view of unity was that the other organizations should accept the FPL as the revolutionary vanguard. Rodríguez notes that Carpio was so dogmatic that he even classified the other revolutionary organizations as the enemy, saying, "You don't negotiate with the enemy." Ana María also wanted to welcome new, younger leadership into the FPL, while Carpio tended to say, "We veterans have to guarantee the revolutionary process."

As more FPL members began to agree with Ana María's line of thinking, some FPL leaders began to question a number of decisions that Carpio had made. On one occasion, a Mexican newspaper published a photo of him manning an anti-aircraft gun, with a caption saying that this was the first such gun in Chalatenango. The photo had actually been taken in Lebanon during one of Carpio's trips abroad. Some members of the political leadership urged Carpio to publicly refute the caption, since it was a lie and because they believed that the power in El Salvador resided in the organization of the people and not in weaponry. Carpio refused to make a correction. Rodríguez, as others have suggested, believes that Carpio promoted a "cult of personality." Carpio began to accuse Ana María of having sold out the FPL.

In April 1983, the dispute erupted into violence and a leadership scandal that Rodríguez describes as an "earthquake within the FPL." Ana María was murdered in Managua, Nicaragua, where the FMLN leadership operated in safety. To the great shock of the FPL membership, the leadership, after a quick investigation, accused Cayetano Carpio of the murder at an emergency meeting a few days later. Carpio committed suicide almost immediately, suggesting that he was in fact guilty (although his suicide note denied it). The murder and suicide generated a serious split within the FPL, pitting those who were followers of Ana María against those who remained loyal to the more orthodox Marcial.

Cayetano Carpio was probably the most radical Marxist ideologue in the FMLN. With his passing, the remaining FMLN leaders were to a large extent led by the desire to bring democracy and economic justice to El Salvador. No doubt some of them were still Marxists, but many had originally become involved in the movement influenced by the ideas of the church's social doctrine. Additionally, many of the lower leaders and the vast majority within the popular and revolutionary movement had virtually no knowledge of Marxism.[29] In fact, there is an oft repeated story about one guerrilla who was reading something by Marx and said to another compa, "Hey we need to have this old guy come talk to us."

As a result of this FPL rift, culminating in Ana María's murder and Carpio's suicide, the FPL experienced problems with its international networks of support, since the "internationalists"—organizations in foreign countries that supported the FMLN—feared, correctly, that the guerrilla organization was in disarray. Carpio's followers started a new group called the Movimiento Obrero Revolucionario (MOR; Revolutionary Worker Movement), which tried to keep control of the FPL's revolutionary networks and facilities, both national and international. Since Carpio had been the face of the FPL, and the full story of what had happened in Managua was not widely known, many foreign groups decided to provide assistance to MOR rather than the FPL. Every year, a "congress" of all the "Óscar Romero" Christian solidarity committees worldwide would take place in Mexico. The FPL had established these committees abroad to raise financial support for the war effort and to get the word out about El Salvador's political and economic "reality." In 1984 the annual meeting was to be held in Nicaragua, and as Rodríguez recalls, "the meeting was very difficult" owing to the split within the FPL. Delegates from the Netherlands, for example, decided to stop their assistance to El Salvador since they were uncomfortable with the crisis stemming from the murder/suicide within the FPL leadership and simply did not know which group to support. Rodríguez recalls that the committee from Italy, however, became convinced that it should continue to support the FPL. It became clear that the FPL now had to work tirelessly to regain the confidence of its supporters abroad. The relationship with members of MOR was very strained, and Rodríguez recalls that their view of the FPL was that it had become "rightist, selling out to imperialism, and serving as agents of the CIA." Nevertheless, with the help of Italian solidarity organizations, the FPL was eventually able to reestablish many of its international networks. Additionally, the vast majority of the FPL members had sided—and now continued to side—with the position of Ana María, who was not an orthodox Marxist. As a result, MOR very quickly became a rump organization with few followers.

Demonstration Elections: 1982 and 1984

As the strength of the FMLN grew, the Salvadoran state, armed forces, and oligarchy, under great pressure from the United States, began to accept the need to make changes both in the armed forces and in the political system.[30] It was clear that the military-led government, despite its civilian facade, had scant legitimacy, and that an elected civilian government was sorely needed. A new constitution and new elections might convince Salvadorans in the political middle—those who had little allegiance to the government but who also did not support the guerrillas—that real changes were taking place in the country. Consequently, in March 1982 the government held elections for a sixty-member Constituent Assembly that would elect an interim president and write a new magna carta. The elections were marred by the fact that only the parties of the right participated. The PDC did not even occupy the political center, since those party members who had been on the left of the political spectrum, the majority, had left the party in 1980. The key left-of-center parties, the MNR and the MPSC, were convinced that campaigning for the assembly would be a highly dangerous endeavor. Prior to the election, the most reactionary Salvadorans organized a new political party, the Alianza Republicana Nacionalista (ARENA; Nationalist Republican Alliance), in an effort to prevent the PDC from running the country. The new party was led by Roberto D'Aubuisson, who had been responsible for planning the murders of Archbishop Romero and Father Rutilio Grande and had also attempted to carry out a counter-coup not long after the October 15 coup that ousted President Romero. Naturally, ARENA had a great deal of financial backing, since it gained support from the most conservative oligarchs, who wrongly saw Duarte and the PDC as leftists.

Although the PDC won a plurality of the vote, gaining just over 40 percent, ARENA and the PCN together were able to command a majority in the assembly with a combined total of thirty-three seats versus the PDC's twenty-four. Other, smaller parties held the remaining three seats.[31] Fearing that D'Aubuisson would become the country's provisional president, Washington jumped to action and succeeded in getting the assembly to elect Álvaro Magaña, a banker with close ties to the armed forces. Clearly, the Reagan administration did not want the elections to hamper the flow of U.S. military aid, and D'Aubuisson's election would have risked controversy in the U.S. Congress. Nevertheless, the new legislators elected D'Aubuisson as president of the Constituent Assembly. ARENA and the PCN then proceeded to undermine the already feeble land-reform effort.[32]

Another attempt at increasing the legitimacy of the Salvadoran state came on March 24, 1984, when a presidential election was held under the new constitution, approved late in the previous year. Since none of the PDC, PCN, or ARENA candidates won a majority in the first round, a runoff election pitted the PDC's Duarte against ARENA's D'Aubuisson. Duarte won the vote count, garnering 53.6 percent, and was inaugurated on June 1, making him the first civilian to hold that office in fifty-three years. The installment of an elected, civilian government allowed the Salvadoran armed forces and oligarchy, as well as Washington, to accuse the FMLN and the FDR of being anti-democratic and claim that the government was the true representative of the Salvadoran people. The FDR and the FMLN had indeed opposed the electoral process, but free and fair elections were really impossible in El Salvador at a time of civil war. Few pointed out that one key political party, ARENA, was the construct of a highly repressive oligarchy and of an individual who had planned the murder of the archbishop and at least one priest.

Now that a civilian government was in power in El Salvador, Washington was able to more easily supply military and economic aid to the Salvadoran armed forces with the hopes that they could be "professionalized." The key goal was to defeat the FMLN, which had been able to mount large-scale military operations, while the armed forces seemed to operate in a timid, lackluster manner. Total U.S. military aid to El Salvador in 1983 had been $81.3 million, but in 1984 and 1985 the amount of aid jumped to $196.6 and $136.3 million, respectively.[33] Nonetheless, the U.S. government's largesse "made little headway in professionalizing the Salvadoran armed forces, let alone fostering democratic professionalism."[34] The massive amounts of U.S. assistance to the Salvadoran economy and the armed forces did nevertheless allow the government of El Salvador to continue to fight the FMLN and maintain itself in power.

A Family Tragedy

Families who lived in the guerrilla-controlled zones and contested areas not only had to endure military attacks and privations but also suffered from the lack of good medical services. Padre Rodríguez's and Merci Henríquez's son, Tito, contracted hepatitis while living in the front in Guazapa during 1981, when he was only two years old, and owing to lack of proper treatment his liver became severely damaged. At first they believed that Tito had been cured, since he did receive some initial medical care. However, some months after the treatment, Rodríguez and a doctor visited a safe house in San Salvador where Henríquez and Tito were staying. The doctor did not know her, and even less that she was Rodríguez's compañera, or that the small boy was their son. Tito was running around without a shirt, and the doctor noticed something suspicious in his abdomen. The doctor went up to him, took a look at his stomach, and then said to Henríquez, "Come, come look at your boy." He then pressed on Tito's abdomen around the liver and said, "No, this boy is not well." Henríquez rushed Tito to a hospital, where he was diagnosed with "severe hepatitis." Henríquez had been working in Nicaragua in communications, translating secret messages from code and being responsible for changing codes. It was a demanding, stressful job. This important assignment in Managua, however, offered her the opportunity to take Tito to Cuba to be examined by specialists. The doctors in Havana told her that he "would have a short life." She arranged to have Tito's "clinical history" sent to the United States, but "treatment would cost too much." Henríquez had to make a difficult decision and recalls: "I decided that people in the front needed the money."

In 1983 and 1984, Rodríguez traveled to Cuba to visit his gravely ill son. He remembers that Tito received "very good treatment and care." The FPL allowed him to return to Cuba several times to see his son, but always with a formal reason—usually to receive some training. The first time he went to Cuba, Rodríguez was also sent to learn marksmanship and karate. Tito was put on a waiting list, since the doctors wanted to perform a liver transplant, but he died in 1984 at the age of five, while Rodríguez was at the front. An FPL comandante whom he had known since the mid-1970s went up to him and said, "Look, we have received a communication for you." Rodríguez recalls with sadness, "I started to read a letter from my compañera from Cuba, saying that our son had died, and asking me what we should do." He told her to have Tito buried in Cuba and to return to Nicaragua to her work. It was a very difficult decision, but returning Tito to El Salvador would have been costly and dangerous. Rodríguez remembers that his son loved to play with Legos at the hospital in Cuba. He was emotional when recalling this sad event in his life, but nevertheless stoic when recounting what happened to little Tito. By this time, and at least partly owing to his son's experience in Cuba, Rodríguez had gained "respect" for Cuba's socialist system, particularly its focus on health care, education, and land reform, benefits that Salvadoran peasants had gone without for too many years.

Toward the end of 1984 the FPL's political commission called Rodríguez to Chalatenango to ask him to travel abroad to repair the links with the Óscar Romero Christian solidarity committees. Rodríguez attached himself to an FPL unit in Chalatenango while he awaited the proper time to exit the front. This was a normal procedure, since leaving guerrilla-controlled areas required traversing a specific zone with the cooperation of an FPL contact. The safest way to reach that contact was with the support of a guerrilla unit. One day, the unit he was traveling with moved through the town of Vainilla on its way toward La Montañona, a guerrilla stronghold about forty-seven miles north of San Salvador, close to the Honduran border.[35] As it exited the small hamlet, the guerrilla unit saw the lights of an approaching car, so Rodríguez and the guerrillas melted into the foliage along the road, leaving one operative behind to see who was approaching. It turned out that a well-known priest was in the car[36] on his way to celebrate Christmas in Vainilla. The cleric asked for Rodríguez, perhaps thinking that it would help him to show he knew the rebel priest, so the operative went to ask the commander whether or not "Padre David" could go speak with the priest. The approval given, Rodríguez went to talk with the priest, who was "very happy" to see him. In fact, the priest told Rodríguez to go to a certain finca where someone would give the guerrillas two pigs. After this fortuitous meeting, the guerrilla group picked up the pigs and tamales and had a big feast. No doubt a great deal of sympathy and support still existed within the church for the liberationist cause and the revolutionary movement among many of the priests who had decided to stay in the country but remain silent about the need for social justice.

Before Rodríguez was able to leave the front, however, the guerrillas "concentrated their units" and attacked the Fourth Brigade garrison at El Paraiso, in the department of Chalatenango, whose construction the United States had financed and overseen. The garrison was supposed to be "impenetrable," Rodríguez recalls, but the FMLN successfully raided the installation and took many prisoners. Rodríguez was called back to help with the interrogation of some of the captives, who had been transported to the small town of Plan del Horno, near the Honduran border. Because the FPL had assaulted the garrison in the middle of the night, many of the prisoners were in their underclothes and they did not know who was a cook, a soldier, or an officer. After about two or three days of trying to figure out who was who, several of the prisoners came to Rodríguez to tell him that they had known his father, Lisandro. They also said they were nervous because the army had told them that if they were captured the guerrillas would "put out their eyes and cut off their ears and noses." Rodríguez told them "those are lies" and that the "captured soldiers would be released [to the Red Cross]." Rodríguez was thus able to identify the officers, who were eventually released in "prisoner exchanges." For the most part, military personnel who were captured by the FPL were treated well, and sometimes soldiers would end up joining the guerrillas. As the news of this humane treatment spread, soldiers would often surrender with little or no resistance, which of course helped the guerrillas greatly in their war effort, especially in capturing weapons.

An Internationalist Priest

When he finally left the front, Rodríguez became a member of the FPL's Comisión Nacional de Finanzas (CONAFIN; National Finance Commission), which was responsible for all FPL finances. He was also named as the FPL's representative to the FMLN's Comisión Financiera (COFIN; Finance Commission), headquartered in Mexico City. COFIN was somewhat artificial, since finances were handled principally by each of the five guerrilla organizations—the FPL, the ERP, the RN, FAL (Communist Party), and the PRTC. COFIN was established to a large extent because some international organizations would provide assistance only to the FMLN and not to the individual organizations. While working for COFIN, Rodríguez learned firsthand of the conflict inherent in an organization composed of several groups. The five guerrilla organizations had to find ways to distribute their financial resources. Naturally, the smaller groups wanted an equal distribution of funds, while the larger ones, particularly the FPL (the largest), sought a distribution of money proportionate to the size of each organization. At the start, little coordination existed between the different groups in the international fund-raising ventures. Often, Rodríguez would be arriving at a country and discover that someone from one of the other groups had just been there raising money. Over time some cooperation developed, but overall the FMLN was really a grouping of five different organizations, each with its own leadership, goals, and operations. As Rodríguez points out, "Each one prayed to its own saint." The unity of the FMLN in 1980, therefore, had been a bit of a chimera.

In Mexico, Rodríguez, now more often called "Joaquín," was also in charge of a tiny office that oversaw the financing of the PPLs. The office consisted of "a small, round table, a typewriter, and two secretaries." The FPL wanted the PPLs to raise their own funds independently from the funds raised for the war effort. Rodríguez's office eventually produced a brochure that provided information on the PPLs to potential supporters. A number of projects—"to raise chickens, to grow corn, to help organize [people], to capacitate people"—were approved by COFIN and received some financial support. In fact, when sympathizers visited the COFIN/CONAFIN offices in Mexico City they would want to visit Rodríguez's PPLs office and would comment, "You people in this little office make a lot of noise!" Only the FPL sought to raise funds strictly for the PPLs. Also, the FPL's financial office, CONAFIN, was quite small compared to some of the other organizations' offices. Rodríguez is convinced that the FPL received more support from international groups because those groups sensed that the FPL was using fewer funds for overhead costs.

Naturally, the war effort needed money if the guerrilla organizations were to have any chance at overthrowing the U.S.-supported Salvadoran government. Much of the international support came from "solidarity groups—churches, workers, and syndicates." Before Rodríguez arrived at CONAFIN, the FPL had already developed many international networks of support. Rodríguez's job, therefore, was to help "rescue" some of the groups that had been lost as a result of the Cayetano Carpio debacle, to continue working with the groups that had been maintained, and to develop and strengthen ties to churches and to other religious groups. Rodríguez recalls that the groups in Italy were essential in regaining many of the groups in Europe, although one very important group in Europe was "never rescued." In addition to churches, nongovernmental organizations that provided aid to the third world, such as Bread for the World and Land for People, also collaborated with CONAFIN. Of course, Rodríguez, as a former priest, worked extremely well with the Óscar Romero solidarity committees worldwide, which were normally led by priests and principally worked through churches.

Rodríguez believes that the FPL selected him for these financial responsibilities because funds from abroad came mostly from Christian organizations, and thus hearing a priest discuss the people's plight in El Salvador would generate more donations. Another reason for being selected was that as a priest he was able to move around the country much more easily than others. His popularity within the liberationist and even moderate sectors of the church meant that he could always stay at a parish house, a Catholic school, or a convent and not be afraid of being turned over to the authorities. Another likely reason, which Rodríguez did not express, was that he had a high degree of integrity and was thus trusted implicitly.

He was also a risk taker. Rodríguez confesses that part of his job entailed depositing large sums of money in bank accounts in Panama, a country sometimes referred to as the Switzerland of Central America because its banking laws protected the identity of its depositors. During the years he raised money for the FPL and the FMLN, Rodríguez would at times travel to Panama and deposit as much as $300,000 into an anonymous account. This action would be quite risky since the United States maintained a large military and intelligence presence in Panama. Rodríguez would always travel with a false passport, reminiscent of the time he was a seminarian in Mexico. He recalls that it was a "superhuman" effort to repeatedly carry out these nerve-wracking operations. On one occasion, a compañero who was going to deposit money in an account in Panama became too nervous at the last moment and did not enter the bank. Even more menacing was returning to El Salvador with money or with FMLN documents, resulting in almost certain torture and death if captured. These jobs required nerves of steel, perhaps even more so than being an armed guerrilla in the front. Rodríguez remembers what happened to a close friend who was carrying an FMLN "communication" (a small piece of paper) while traveling in a bus. A number of policemen entered the bus to search the passengers, and his friend ate the piece of paper. One of the policemen saw him do it, so they took him off the bus and he was "disappeared," never to be seen again.

External Assistance

The aid that the FMLN received from Cuba and Nicaragua, even though paling in comparison to the assistance that Washington showered on the Salvadoran state, was important for their continued existence and programs. Just as important, however, was the aid provided by nongovernmental organizations and church networks devoted to either helping the war effort directly or to assisting the Salvadoran people in general, as described above. Consequently, the FPL and other guerrilla organizations developed links with numerous international groups, some of which did not wish to be identified as cooperating with the FMLN.[37] Rodríguez points out that the humanitarian assistance provided by some of these groups was very important to the FMLN, since it meant that more of their limited funds could be used for the war effort. One of the methods the FPL used to raise funds was to invite selected members of international donor groups to the front so that they would develop a personal connection to the people and to the projects they were funding.

The mayor of Berkeley, California, Eugene G. Newport, for example, visited the guerrilla front in Chalatenango in the mid-1980s. Berkeley was a sister city to the town of San Antonio Los Ranchos, located in a guerrilla-controlled zone, about twenty-seven miles northeast of San Salvador.[38] Mayor Newport and the City of Berkeley had also been instrumental in financing a network of small guerrilla "hospitals" named after Martin Luther King Jr., and the mayor wanted to visit them. Rodríguez organized Newport's visit and recalls that he was a "black, tall, strong man that no horse could support," so they commissioned a few of their lanky horses to allow the mayor to travel through the countryside. Rodríguez recalls that while Newport was visiting the hospitals the Salvadoran Air Force conducted an air strike "right on top" of the visitor and his hosts. Rodríguez says: "We all hit the ground and, after the bombing was over, got up and found Newport asleep, snoring," probably exhausted from the arduous trip. They all had a hearty laugh at the end of the incident.

Although much of the financial work was designed to provide assistance to people living in guerrilla-controlled territory, as well as boots, clothing, and food for the combatants, the acquisition of weapons was also vital for the war effort. Rodríguez points out that most of the weapons used by the FMLN were those taken from the Salvadoran armed forces.[39] Some of the weapons were brought in from outside the country, principally through Honduras and Nicaragua. At one point, an FMLN leader who had learned to fly an airplane would bring weapons into El Salvador whenever possible. On one occasion, he could not spot a signal on the ground that showed him where to land, and "as he was circling to find the signal, his plane was detected by the Salvadoran Air Force." The Salvadoran military quickly dispatched airplanes, helicopters, and ground troops to intercept him. The guerrilla pilot tried to land quickly, but his plane got tangled in some wires and crashed. He exited the plane safely, but the weapons were lost. Although weapons and training from abroad helped the guerrilla effort, this foreign assistance was not the decisive element in determining the FMLN's strength. In fact, with proper assistance and greater unity it is very likely that the FMLN would have defeated the Salvadoran armed forces in the early 1980s.[40]

During the first few years Rodríguez worked at CONAFIN/COFIN, the dynamics of the war changed significantly. From its formation in 1980 to about 1983, the FMLN enhanced greatly its war-fighting capabilities, reaching a point where it formed battalions, with as many as a thousand combatants. The 1981 offensive and the subsequent attack on the El Paraiso garrison were relatively large-scale, conventional military attacks. The FMLN had transitioned from small, hit-and-run, often urban guerrilla tactics to nearly conventional military assaults, despite the fact that they had no air force, heavy weapons, or large transport vehicles. As the United States increased its control of the Salvadoran government's war effort, however, U.S. doctrine, training, and material support began to change the military balance and landscape. The result was the creation of rapid-response battalions and the augmentation of Salvadoran airpower. The United States formed the Atlacatl, Belloso, and Atonal Batallions soon after the 1981 FMLN offensive.[41] Consequently, after 1983, and with the increased capabilities of the Salvadoran military, the FMLN was forced to dissolve its battalions and revert to more traditional hit-and-run guerrilla tactics.

Salvadoran officers who were sympathetic to U.S. counterinsurgency, "low-intensity conflict," strategy prevailed over those officers who had employed less sophisticated and brutal tactics. In effect, as Rodríguez points out, the ultimate goal of the U.S. counterinsurgency campaign was, as Mao had formulated, to "take the water away from the fish"—the water being the people and the fish being the guerrillas. Although the strategy called for winning over the hearts and minds of Salvadorans, the civilians in FMLN-controlled zones were viewed as the enemy. The strategy, according to Rodríguez, included "capturing people, destroying fields, closing down stores" for the purpose of "terrorizing people and isolating them" from the guerrillas. As a result, the civilian population suffered greatly in the guerrilla-controlled areas and only those who were most loyal to the war effort remained, most people leaving their towns for San Salvador or other parts of the country, or even abandoning the country all together. Refugee camps in San Salvador and in Honduras were filled with people. Naturally, the FMLN and its five component groups felt that it was essential to assist the people who stayed in the fronts. It also felt that it was necessary to repopulate the abandoned towns as soon as possible.

In 1986, the FMLN, with the cooperation of groups in various countries that opposed the Salvadoran government, established the Sister City project in the United States, Canada, and Europe. The idea was that, while hesitant to support a guerrilla army, some people would be willing to help a community, particularly the returning refugees. At roughly the same time, a repopulation program led by the Salvadoran Catholic church was under way to repatriate refugees who had fled to Honduras and parts of El Salvador to escape the destruction of the war and the repression of the state. Rodríguez argues that the Sister Cities program was the work principally of the FPL and that the repatriation work "was excellent," both in helping the people directly but also because the assistance provided through the program freed up funds that the FMLN had been using to pay for these resettlement efforts. The Sister Cities program not only raised funds for the refugees and their communities but also provided safety, since people from the United States, Canada, and Europe would accompany the refugees when they returned to their communities.

Rodríguez points out that the people who had left their communities were miserable in the refugee camps in San Salvador and Honduras. He recalls that one day when he was at the refugee center at the San José de la Montaña major seminary in San Salvador a man told him with sadness: "When I smell the moist soil in the soccer field [where Rodríguez had played as a seminarian] I want to return [to my land] and plant my milpa." Rodríguez is convinced that even though the refugee centers would provide basic needs, even education, people would get "sick" and suffer from "trauma" simply because they were away from their hometowns. One person said to him: "I am in a golden cage, but caged." The suffering was particularly intense for those who were in Honduras, since they were not even in their own country. One of the great tragedies of the war was the displacement of over one million people from their homes, their families, and, for many, from their country.[42]

For much of the civil war, from 1985 to 1991, Rodríguez's paramount role was to raise money for the FPL/FMLN and to return the funds to El Salvador to help finance the armed rebellion and the communities at the front. His travels took him to Latin America (Nicaragua, Mexico, and Panama), Europe (France, Spain, Italy, Switzerland, the Netherlands, Germany, Austria, Sweden, Norway, and Finland), and the United States (Boston, Philadelphia, Los Angeles, Washington, D.C., Seattle, Chicago, Austin, San Francisco, New York, San Antonio, and Portland). Many countries did not support the U.S.-backed Salvadoran government, and France and Mexico even formally recognized the FDR as a representative political organization in late 1981, much to Washington's displeasure. While traveling in Europe, Rodríguez would ride in a first-class compartment, since the FPL believed it would be better for his security. However, he would have very little money and would often be the only first-class passenger "eating fruit and cheese in my seat." Rodríguez's role in the FMLN and the FPL was crucial, since he was able to regain the trust of international supporters after the FPL crisis and was thus able to keep financial support flowing. After collecting funds, Rodríguez would often have the responsibility of bringing some of the money back to the fronts in Chalatenango, Guazapa, San Vicente, and Usulután, meaning that for several years he entered and exited El Salvador numerous times. During the time he worked in the FPL/FMLN finance offices in Mexico City, Rodríguez continued to serve as the FPL's representative to the PPLs as well as to CONIP.

Still a Dangerous Affair

Although he was now in an administrative position focused on helping to finance the war effort, Rodríguez continued to be exposed to dangerous situations. On one occasion the FMLN political leadership summoned the financial commissions to the front so the FMLN comandantes could get a briefing on the fiscal situation. During the meeting, a "large military invasion" occurred and the entire leadership had to be moved out of the area quickly. Rodríguez was with the leadership when they were ambushed by a Treasury Police unit. In the chaos, he found himself alone and lost in the department of Chalatenango. Rodríguez walked for an entire afternoon and remembers picking up abandoned packages of cigarettes and sugar, thinking "they will either be useful to me or to someone else." In the early evening he heard distant voices and someone talking on a radio. Although he could usually distinguish between a compa and a soldier, and he sensed that they were compas, for some reason he was hesitant to approach the group. He waited until dark, slowly approached the group, and discerned that they were a commando guerrilla unit, but not from the FPL. In the morning Rodríguez decided to approach them but with "hands raised, holding a white handkerchief," to be sure they did not shoot him. The commando leader was able to confirm via radio that the FPL had been able to regroup everyone who attended the leadership meeting, except for "Joaquín." This commando unit was one of several "special forces" units and was commanded by a well-known guerrilla leader known as "El Diablo."

Before they could reunite Rodríguez with the other FPL leaders, however, the commando unit had to accomplish an important mission: cross the border in order to ascertain whether the Honduran military was going to participate in an anticipated military operation with the Salvadoran army. Rodríguez recalls that he was coming from Mexico and was thus "well fed," while these guerrillas were "young men" in excellent shape. They walked the entire next day, and Rodríguez ran out of water. These young guerrillas were trained to carry and drink their own water, each one responsible for his own survival. Luckily, Rodríguez was able to trade the cigarettes he had picked up for some water. At one point, when they were climbing a steep hill, called Mataras, Rodríguez needed both hands to raise himself and said to one of the compas, "Look, can you grab my rifle?" The young rebel said to him with a sneer, "You give your rifle to no one!" Rodríguez arrived at the summit utterly exhausted. He recalls with admiration that, instead of resting from their cross-country trek, the commandos found a deflated soccer ball and began playing! After a few more reconnaissance missions, a total of three days, the squad was able to return the spent Rodríguez to the FPL. Upon their return, they joked: "Joaquín, the *brujo*, met *el diablo* at Mataras, and they are going to write a novel about it."

On another occasion, Rodríguez entered El Salvador and stayed in a nondescript hotel in San Salvador. The routine was to then "make a contact" using a prearranged "sign and countersign." For example, Rodríguez might be holding a shoestring or a tube of toothpaste in his hand. The contact, who knew what he was supposed to be holding, would then approach him and say something prearranged, such as "How is your son doing in the hospital?" The countersign might be, "The doctor has already operated on

Figure 5.4. Rodríguez in guerrilla-controlled territory dressed for a videotape interview with a foreign journalist, circa 1988. He laughed at this photo, because guerrillas would never dress in this manner at the front. By permission of the Rodríguez Henríquez family.

him." With this sign and prearranged dialogue, an unknown contact would be able to ensure that he had met the right person. Once the contact was properly made, the person would let Rodríguez know at which safe house he could overnight while he was in the capital. Rodríguez would then take a taxi to a location close to the safe house and walk the rest of the way. On this occasion, however, the taxi driver recognized the rebel priest since the man was from Tecoluca. Because of this coincidence, Rodríguez told him to take him to the School of Divine Providence instead, where he waited for some days for further instructions, since he had missed his one chance to stay at the specified safe house. Eventually, Rodríguez was taken by car to La Jeca, one of the training schools under the banner of Campesino University, because a military operation prevented passage to the front. However, several people recognized him there, and thus Rodríguez stayed in his room and the kitchen staff was asked to take food to him so he would not be seen. One of the workers at the facility started to complain, saying, "If that student is sick then he should go home," which was the school's policy. Then things turned even more dangerous, since a military unit was approaching the school. Those who were in the FMLN began to quickly bury what they had. Rodríguez was carrying some materials for Radio Farabundo Marti, the FPL's clandestine radio station.[43] Eventually, Rodríguez made it out of the school but still had to wait several days to enter the front in Chalatenango.

Rodríguez and others waited to enter the front near the town of Metapan, close to where the borders of Guatemala, Honduras, and El Salvador meet. The densely wooded area, a forest preserve, was called El Trifinio. This general location, in the department of Santa Ana, in the western, more tranquil part of the country, allowed for the safest entry into the guerrilla front. While the group waited, however, a compañero who was going to get tortillas for everyone asked Rodríguez to watch his rifle and backpack for him (they were, after all, not commandos). Rodríguez took off his shoes, grabbed a book, and began to relax. All of a sudden an army squad began to fire at the group. Everyone picked up their things frantically and ran for cover. Rodríguez grabbed both rifles, but in the rush he did not close his compañero's backpack and had to run with his shoes untied. Eventually the army patrol was unable to follow them, since the guerrillas were relatively well armed and were very familiar with the terrain. In the process, however, Rodríguez had lost most of the contents of his friend's backpack and the materials he was bringing to Radio Farabundo Martí.

The 1989 Election and the End to the Civil War

As the war raged on, a number of attempts had been made by the FMLN and both the Magaña and Duarte governments to negotiate a peaceful settlement to the conflict. As early as 1983, each side had expressed some desire to end the war, and meetings were held beginning in 1984 at the town of La Palma, but the Salvadoran government insisted that the FMLN lay down its weapons before any real negotiations could take place. Given the excessive government repression of the 1970s and early 1980s, unilateral disarmament was not a reasonable option for the FMLN. Additionally, in 1983 the FMLN was ascendant, and thus victory seemed like a reasonable possibility. Consequently, no real progress was made during the Magaña or Duarte administrations.

The situation had changed dramatically by 1989, however. In the mayoral and legislative elections of the previous year, ARENA increased its share of the vote significantly, having formed a coalition with the PCN and winning thirty-one out of sixty seats in the Legislative Assembly.[44] The party had jettisoned its caustic death-squad leader D'Aubuisson for a more moderate candidate, Alfredo Cristiani. The new ARENA leader was a member of the oligarchy and had close ties to the United States, having studied at Georgetown University, and was thus a rightist but without the murderous affiliation of the former ARENA firebrand. In the March 19 presidential election, Cristiani defeated the PDC candidate by getting 53.8 percent of the vote.[45] Although the left did not participate in the election, Cristiani had made negotiations with the FMLN-FDR one of his campaign promises. The church, led by Archbishop Rivera y Damas, had initiated a Debate Nacional por la Paz (National Debate for Peace) in the previous year that attracted more than sixty organizations, although the right declined to participate.[46] Days after his inauguration, Cristiani called for peace talks. The United States, owing to the changes taking place in the USSR and in Eastern Europe, was no longer as worried about communism as it had been in the past. When the FMLN organized in 1980, after the Nicaraguan revolution, the United States was on Cold War footing, and thus support of the anti-communist Salvadoran regime, no matter how brutal, was of paramount importance. Now that the Cold War seemed to be ending, the U.S. security imperative was fading, especially since aid to El Salvador was costly and still controversial. As for the armed opposition, the FMLN was tired of the conflict and realized that political participation, one of the key motivations for the conflict, was a real possibility. FMLN leaders had also experienced ideological changes as the Soviet Union itself was changing. Support for Soviet, Vietnamese, or Cuban Marxism was fading in favor of social democracy. It is important to point out, though, that despite the existence of some hardcore Marxists like Cayetano Carpio, most of the leftist opposition in the 1970s, including the liberationists, would have been completely satisfied with social democracy. It was state repression that radicalized most of the people who ended up supporting the FMLN. In any case, by the late 1980s and early 1990s the political climate was propitious for compromise and negotiations, owing to the diminished ideological polarization.

The FMLN, however, decided to demonstrate its power by carrying out another major military offensive. This decision stemmed from two motivations: first, the FMLN wanted to show its continued vitality, an imperative for carrying out successful talks; second, the negotiations had made little progress in the immediate months after Cristiani's election. After two meetings, one in Mexico and one in Costa Rica, the "headquarters of the National Federation of Salvadoran workers was bombed, killing ten union leaders," so the FMLN canceled the third meeting.[47] Perhaps another large offensive would convince the government to press on with the talks.

Rodríguez was not in El Salvador on November 11, 1989, when the largest FMLN assault of the civil war took place, since he was still working internationally to raise money for this second, major guerrilla offensive that would include coordinated attacks against several cities, including the capital. Nevertheless, being in Mexico City, Rodríguez was privy to discussions within the FMLN and the FPL concerning this final effort to topple the government. He points out that the FMLN made some bad calculations, since the leaders never considered that El Salvador's military command would use its air force to bomb poor neighborhoods in San Salvador. At the time of the offensive the FMLN actually had acquired some handheld anti-aircraft missiles, but no one was trained to use them. Had they been able to use them, this offensive and thus the war might have gone a different way. As the assault began and FMLN forces entered San Salvador, the military high command decided to bomb the poor neighborhoods in and near San Salvador—Mejicanos, Soyapango, and Ciudad Delgado—where the FMLN had the greatest presence and support. Rodríguez remembers hearing that after a few days of the offensive, some people, mostly affluent Salvadorans, "were already planning their retreat [out of the country]." The offensive shocked both the Salvadoran and U.S. governments, since the rebels demonstrated that they were still strong militarily.

On November 16, while the offensive was ongoing, one of the most heinous attacks against the church took place. Six Jesuit priests, along with their housekeeper and her daughter, were murdered in cold blood on the campus of the Universidad Centroamericana "José Simeón Cañas," the Jesuit-run university in San Salvador. The Jesuits in El Salvador had always been a target of the state, since they supported the liberationist movement, called for land reform, and, after Romero's murder, became the principal and only intellectual critics of the right-wing governments that ruled the country. The Salvadoran government claimed that the Jesuits were supporting the FMLN and justified the assault by announcing that weapons were being stockpiled on the university's campus. No weapons were found. Owing to tremendous international criticism, President Cristiani ordered a government investigation; it led to some arrests, but justice was never carried out.[48]

Similar to the first offensive in 1981, the FMLN guerrillas were unable to defeat the Salvadoran state, which by then had a military that was much larger, more "professional," and better equipped than the FMLN, thanks to U.S. largesse. After the offensive in San Salvador, the war continued as a stalemate, with neither side able to defeat the other. As the pressure to end the conflict continued, the two sides, tired and seeing negotiation as the best way to end the fighting and achieve some goals, finally signed a comprehensive peace accord in January 1992, in Chapultepec Park in Mexico City. Rodríguez was not involved in the peace accord negotiations, but he points out that one Jesuit priest, Father Rafael Moreno, "played a very important role." The Salvadoran church, of course, through the efforts of Archbishop Rivera y Damas, had served as the principal force in calling for and fostering the talks.[49] Peace had finally come to El Salvador, and Padre David Rodríguez was already thinking about returning to his beloved Catholic Church.

A Family Once More

As the peace talks progressed and optimism was in the air, Rodríguez and Merci Henríquez were able to spend more time together and began to look forward to a brighter future. Henríquez recalls that she and Rodríguez "had not been able to see each other very often during the war." She had spent

Figure 5.5. Rodríguez with his daughter, Ana Ruth, circa 1991. By permission of the Rodríguez Henríquez family.

most of the war serving in communications, a job that was "tremendously stressful, since it required a great deal of concentration, and mistakes were not allowed." The FPL made some effort to keep couples together, or at least to provide opportunities for them to see each other as much as possible. However, the imperatives of the war and the need for tight security precautions made these sorts of accommodations difficult. They did manage to spend some time together, though, and on October 30, 1990, Rodríguez and Henríquez had a daughter, Ana Ruth, whom they called "Anita." Henríquez believes that she became pregnant while visiting Rodríguez in Mexico at the CONAFIN offices. She remembers that after becoming pregnant, people would jokingly ask her, "How are things with the Father?" She would always laugh with them.

At the end of the conflict, all Salvadorans rejoiced at the beginning of a new dawn. For many Salvadorans, however, the conflict had been horrendously costly. Estimates suggest that as a result of the war approximately seventy-five thousand people lost their lives or were disappeared, yet this number does not include the loss of life in the 1970s. The war and state repression also displaced, internally and abroad, "at least one-fifth" of the population.[50] Countless families were separated, many never to be reunited. Tens of thousands of individuals were arrested, tortured, abused, and raped. The psychological effect of this prolonged, bloody, and terror-filled assault on Salvadorans is unimaginable and will never really be assessed. Not one of the people whom I interviewed for this book was untouched by the conflict. The vast majority told me that they had lost at least one family member, and most had suffered some familial separation during the full length of the conflict, between 1970 and 1992. A number of informants told me they had lost a large portion of their family. My intent had not been to ask interviewees about their loss or suffering during the war, as I simply wanted to know about Rodríguez's actions; but once I broached the topic of the war, most people would end up discussing their experiences with utmost frankness. With the peace accords, Salvadorans looked forward to a day when they could, if not forget the conflict, at least look back on it as part of history.

State Strength, External Actors, and Revolutionary Failure

The Salvadoran civil war is instructive in several ways in our quest to understand the likelihood that a social and revolutionary movement can be successful. El Salvador represents a case where a combination of an exceptionally strong, armed revolutionary movement, a powerful popular movement, and a group of opposition political parties were unable to bring down a repressive, authoritarian government. Despite the efforts of leaders like Padre Rodríguez to create a more just government, the Salvadoran state was able to fend off revolutionary change by preventing the FMLN from winning the war. It seems clear that several reasons conspired to prevent the political, popular, and armed opposition from taking control of the country, despite the existence of a patently unjust political and economic context, a highly palatable injustice frame, many committed leaders, and strong popular and then revolutionary movements.

In early 1980, the popular movement had reached its zenith of power. In March of that year, Archbishop Romero became a martyr, and the politico-military organizations had started to develop stronger guerrilla armies in the countryside. If the FMLN had been ready to begin large-scale operations soon after the death of Óscar Romero, there is little doubt that the Salvadoran regime would have passed into history in the same manner as the Batista (Cuba, 1959) and Somoza (Nicaragua, 1979) regimes, and the FMLN would have taken control of the country. This failure to seize the moment, owing to a lack of unity and organization on the part of the armed resistance, is a prime reason for the lack of success at the early stages of the conflict. By the time the FMLN attempted its "Final Offensive" in early 1981, the time for popular rebellion had passed, to a large extent owing to extensive state repression in 1980. Also, during the 1981 offensive the FMLN simply did not have the unity and weapons to carry out a successful military operation, despite claims that the rebels were receiving extensive military assistance from Cuba and Nicaragua.

A second important factor is the strength and unity of the Salvadoran state. In both the Cuban and Nicaraguan revolutions, armed guerrillas joined forces with other aggrieved sectors, including members of the oligarchy, to bring down a despised dictatorship. In El Salvador, the state was continuously backed by the oligarchy, and that state was not led by a hated, brutal dictator, as in Cuba and Nicaragua, but by the armed forces, at least as late as the first three years of the civil war.[51] The fact that the oligarchy never failed to support the military-controlled state made it much more difficult for the FMLN and its allies to win the war. And, once General Romero was removed from power by his own armed forces, a despised dictator no longer provided a focal point for the opposition.

The Salvadoran state was also able to achieve some degree of legitimacy in the early to mid-1980s by carrying out a limited land-reform program and holding elections. While these efforts did little to diffuse the committed opposition, they must have convinced many Salvadorans that the state was taking steps to implement economic and political reforms. The left did not participate in the elections, but many Salvadorans did participate, an act that must have given them some satisfaction in comparison to the patently fraudulent elections of the 1970s. Had some land reform and free elections taken place in the early 1970s, the civil war most likely would have been averted. Nevertheless, the limited reforms and the "demonstration elections" of the 1980s made it more difficult for the opposition to paint the state as reactionary and repressive.[52]

Despite the state's ability to gain some much needed legitimacy, in the first three years of the civil war the FMLN grew in size and power, eventually mounting large-scale military operations that threatened to bring down the government. The FMLN's rising power, however, was checked by increasing U.S. military aid and U.S. tutelage in fighting the civil war. While the FMLN had limited external assistance, the Salvadoran government enjoyed the largesse of a superpower. Washington showered tremendous symbolic, logistical, intelligence, military, and economic support on the tiny country of El Salvador, forcing the FMLN to go back to small-scale guerrilla operations by 1984. In both Cuba and Nicaragua, Washington cut off military aid to the Batista and Somoza regimes months prior to the rebel victories. In El Salvador, however, the United States sustained its support to the Salvadoran government until the end of the civil war. And, in fact, part of the reason why the ARENA government eventually pushed for a negotiated end to the war was because Washington was showing signs of reducing its aid, owing to the end of the Cold War. The extensive amount of U.S. aid to the Salvadoran government, then, also helps to explain why the FMLN and its allies did not succeed in bringing down the Salvadoran government.[53] One succinct comment from General Juan Rafael Bustillo, chief of staff of the Salvadoran Air Force, sums it up: "If it weren't for the support we've received from the United States, this country would probably be just another domino."[54] U.S. aid helped to strengthen the Salvadoran state vis-à-vis the power of the less generously supported and only partially unified FMLN. Padre Rodríguez and others in the FMLN and FDR did their best to raise funds for the guerrilla war effort, but their successes paled in comparison to the enormous amounts of funds that Washington delivered to the Salvadoran state. And, as Rodríguez, pointed out, the FMLN was always a five-headed organization, at times working at cross-purposes.

The Christian dimension of the struggle received a tremendous blow after Archbishop Romero was murdered. Eager to mend the rift that had developed in the institution and appease the Vatican, the bishops of El Salvador focused on spiritual liberation and the unity of the institution, though Archbishop Rivera y Damas certainly worked hard to bring about a peace accord. By the mid-1980s the Vatican began to criticize liberation theology, and thus many Salvadoran Catholics began to see the popular church and liberationism as indeed too political. With Romero's death and the focus on mending fences, the opportunities for religious organizing that existed in the early 1970s were greatly diminished by the early 1980s.

In summation, the strength of the Salvadoran state, shored up by the unified oligarchy and U.S. support, made it virtually impossible for the FMLN and its allies to overthrow the Salvadoran government, especially since the limited FMLN unity came after the peak of popular mobilization and resentment. No doubt some divisions existed in both the armed forces and the oligarchy, but these divisions were not sufficient to result in defeat.[55] In hindsight, reforms could have prevented the civil war if the progressive officers who carried out the 1979 coup had kept the hardliners from taking control of the military and state. However, the most reactionary oligarchs were able to control the situation, the reactionary officers got the upper hand, and, with U.S. generosity, those more reactionary economic elites and officers were able to forge sufficient unity and carry out some limited changes to keep the FMLN from winning the war.

6

A Democratic Priest

"Padre David has the word"

On a sunny day in February 1997, in the heat of the campaign for the Legislative Assembly, David Rodríguez Rivera and a compañero drove to a bank in San Salvador to withdraw a loan for his political campaign. As they drove away from the bank, on Roosevelt Avenue, Rodríguez noticed a man on a motorcycle in his rearview mirror. Over the years, he had become adept at spotting those who were in the government's security forces, simply by the way they carried themselves or were dressed. He purposefully ran a traffic light that had just turned red. When he noticed that the motorcycle behind him did the same, Rodríguez knew the man was after him. He then decided to drive to a nearby FMLN office, but noticed a second motorcycle with two men approaching. He said to his compa with certainty, "they are assassins." Before they reached the FMLN office, Rodríguez entered heavy traffic and had to slow to a stop. One of the men got off his motorcycle and walked toward Rodríguez's car. Upon reaching the vehicle, the man pulled out a gun and said to Rodríguez menacingly, "Get out of the car!" Used to dangerous situations, he floored the gas pedal, but the man quickly emptied his pistol into the car. Luckily, the bullets struck Rodríguez only in his left wrist and right knee, not producing serious wounds. Injured but not flustered, he then drove his car into the motorcycle that was in front of him, knocking the driver and passenger off the vehicle. Rodríguez and his companion then pulled out the pistols they had in their car and fired at the assailants, who got nervous, mounted their motorcycles, and sped away. When Rodríguez drove his car into the motorcycle, he also crashed into a large, concrete flowerpot. He and his companion tried to get a motorist to stop so they could get some assistance, but no one stopped to help them. Rodríguez realized that passersby probably thought he and his companion were criminals. The two of them then got back into their damaged car and drove off toward the FMLN office. Rodríguez became very tired, owing to loss of blood, so he stopped the automobile and told his compa to get help. Eventually, some compañeros arrived and took Rodríguez to a hospital, where he spent fourteen days and underwent operations on his wrist and knee.

Ironically, after spending years hiding from a repressive government, years carrying out clandestine operations, and years traveling in and out of El Salvador during a civil war, Rodríguez suffered his first violent attack during an electoral campaign five years after the war had ended. An investigation uncovered that the assailants were National Guardsmen, but it was never clear whether this was a premeditated political assassination or simply a robbery attempt, since at the time crime was rampant in El Salvador, particularly in the capital, and many former security personnel were in desperate financial straits. No one was ever charged with the assault. But why was Rodríguez engaged in a political campaign if his principal goal was to return to the church? And now that the FMLN was a legal political party, would the Christian and revolutionary movements achieve their principal goals?

The Church Beckons

Immediately after the two sides signed the accords, the FMLN still needed funds and international support. Consequently, for the first four months of 1992, Rodríguez retained his duties in CONAFIN and COFIN. Once the demobilization of the armed forces and the FMLN began, however, Rodríguez went to Las Pampas, a community near Tecoluca, designated as a demobilization site for FMLN ex-combatants. He did not remain idle. Linking up with a Spanish priest, Rodríguez built a small meeting hall to offer courses for the reinsertion of combatants into normal, as well as Christian, lives. As in the past, he wanted to form leaders who would carry out pastoral missions and help the community in Las Pampas. Additionally, he became involved in the many and difficult postwar tasks of reinsertion into society, land distribution, and the struggles for the rights of those who were disabled, as well as assisting women who had lost husbands and children in the war.

The church, however, was still Rodríguez's principal calling. Now that the war was over, and despite the conflict he had experienced with his bishop,

Rodríguez's greatest hope was to return to the church. To test the waters, he decided to approach the current bishop of the San Vicente diocese, José Óscar Barahona Castillo, who had been his classmate in the Minor Seminary "Pío XII." Bishop Barahona had replaced Pedro Aparicio upon the latter's retirement in 1983 and shared Tamagás's conservative perspective.[1] When Rodríguez raised the possibility of his return to the church, the bishop was dismissive and noncommittal at first, saying, "Let's think about it."

After numerous requests, Bishop Barahona finally agreed to allow the rebel priest to return to the diocese, but under a number of conditions that, Rodríguez laments, were "for my conscience impossible to accept." The bishop insisted that Rodríguez leave the country for three years ("for my own safety"), work under a priest in a probationary period for one year upon his return, and issue a formal apology stating that his course of action during the civil war had been a mistake. Rodríguez was willing to accept the first two conditions, although leaving the country would be a great sacrifice, since he felt that El Salvador was going through a key historical moment that he had helped to shape. The third condition, however, was "unacceptable," since Rodríguez had no remorse about his course of action and felt that he had taken the correct path, both morally and spiritually. Interestingly enough, however, Rodríguez was surprised that the Cooperative for Diocesan Priests welcomed him back, although he had made no contributions to the cooperative for many years.[2] After he rejected the bishop's terms, Rodríguez, who still wanted to serve the poor, returned to his work with the FPL and the FMLN.

Some readers may find it remarkable that a bishop would allow a priest who had become involved in an armed insurgency to return to the pulpit. However, once a seminarian is ordained a priest, he remains a priest unless excommunicated, and Rodríguez was never excommunicated. What had happened to Rodríguez was that Bishop Aparicio had suspended him, meaning that he could not serve as a parish priest or offer sacraments. However, while he was working for the FPL in the late 1970s and for the FMLN and FPL throughout the civil war, Rodríguez performed many sacraments that the church recognized, because canon law allows suspended priests to perform sacraments if people do not have access to a practicing priest. For Padre David Rodríguez, however, his hopes of returning to the altar had now turned into an impossible dream.

By the end of 1992, FPL leaders began to work assiduously to incorporate the organization as part of the newly formed political party, the FMLN.

The five politico-military organizations, and their umbrella front—the FMLN—had done a remarkable job in challenging a powerful state, backed by a superpower, but now they had to completely transform themselves from a five-headed guerrilla organization into a unified political organization. To accomplish this task in the country's central region, the FPL formed a committee to direct the work in the departments of Cabañas, San Vicente, and La Paz. This was the area encompassed by the diocese of San Vicente, in which Rodríguez had served as a priest and where he was best known.[3] Consequently, Rodríguez was assigned to work in this collective, which had its headquarters in the town of Zacatecoluca. Putting aside his hopes of returning to the church, he put all his energies into helping to form the new political party.

By the first months of 1993, the FPL decided to decentralize the work of forging a political party, and the leaders named Rodríguez as regional coordinator of the organizing work in the department of San Vicente, with headquarters in the city of San Vicente. No one would rent the FMLN office space in that city, so they had to work out of the offices of an already legal party, the MNR. The hesitance to rent space to the FMLN stemmed from residual fear of the Fifth Infantry Brigade and, as Rodríguez recalls, the large "conservative population in San Vicente." The key task at the time was to acquire sufficient signatures to legalize the FMLN. Rodríguez's office was successful in this endeavor, and the party became eligible to participate in the elections scheduled for 1994.

As it prepared for elections, the FMLN organized a general assembly, a sort of primary convention, to determine its presidential, legislative, and mayoral candidates. Rodríguez was elected unanimously to become the candidate for a legislative seat representing the department of San Vicente. Those elected to the Legislative Assembly were called deputies (*diputados*), and two candidates would run for each seat, the titular deputy and the alternate (*suplente*). This meant that the Legislative Assembly really had twice as many elected representatives as there were seats. Rodríguez points out that at this early phase of party formation, becoming a candidate was a selection rather than an election, since very few people participated in these initial political conventions. Despite his obvious popularity, the political commission of the FPL approached him to let him know that the PRTC had absolutely no candidates at the national level. María Valladares, also known as "Nidia Díaz," a well-known PRTC comandante, for example, was not a candidate, so the FPL leadership proposed to Rodríguez that he cede his candidacy to her. Rodríguez, who understood the need for unity, agreed willingly. The salary of a deputy was quite high, so giving up the possibility of attaining such a position was a true sacrifice.

When Rodríguez told the party members in San Vicente that he would be giving up his candidacy, they were upset and said to him, "Why did you cede to her?" Rodríguez explained that "what was important in the election was not who won but that the FMLN become stronger." Another convention took place, and although some FPL members from San Vicente argued that Rodríguez should be the candidate, he took the floor and spoke glowingly of Valladares, proposing that she should be the candidate. He eventually convinced the delegates, and while Valladares became the candidate for the legislature, Rodríguez was selected by the party as its candidate for the mayoralty of San Vicente.[4] He knew, however, that his chance of being elected mayor of San Vicente was miniscule, owing to the city's conservative streak.

Rodríguez's renewed direct involvement in politics as an official mayoral candidate raised the ire of the bishop of San Vicente. Bishop Barahona interpreted his action as an affront, especially since the prelate had agreed to bring Rodríguez back into the diocese. The bishop issued a letter of excommunication against Rodríguez, and it was "read in all the parishes of the diocese of San Vicente." Barahona charged Rodríguez with having "taken up arms and being directly involved politically." The bishop also took up the charge, leveled against the rebel priest by Bishop Aparicio years earlier, that Rodríguez had repeatedly stated that he had "learned more from peasants [about Christianity] than in the seminary." Additionally, Barahona brought up an old, erroneous accusation that Rodríguez had "prohibited the rosary" while he served with the FPL. In fact, Rodríguez had always provided sacraments and religious services while working for the FPL and the FMLN. The Tribunal Supremo Electoral de El Salvador (Salvadoran Supreme Electoral Tribunal), which oversees the country's elections, was unsure itself as to whether Rodríguez, a priest, should be a candidate for office, and at least one political party sought to bar him from running for office. The constitution stated clearly that priests were forbidden from holding public office, but FMLN lawyers argued that because Rodríguez did not have a parish and there was a current excommunication letter against him, he could be a candidate. Eventually other bishops interceded, and the excommunication was dropped. Rodríguez had now survived two attempts to have him excommunicated.

The Democratic Transition

The March 1994 elections represent a watershed political event, since the FMLN put forth candidates for the very first time. ARENA came out victorious, winning the presidency and the largest bloc of seats in the Legislative Assembly. Nevertheless, the FMLN established itself as the country's most important opposition party, winning the second-largest number of seats in the assembly. For a first election, soon after the end of the civil war, this was an auspicious democratic beginning—free elections with a meaningful opposition.

As expected, Rodríguez lost the race for mayor of San Vicente. He points out that "no one wanted to monitor the voting, so ARENA could carry out all the fraud they wanted." Of the thirteen mayoral races in the department of San Vicente, the FMLN won only two—in Tecoluca and San Esteban Catarina. After losing the race, Rodríguez continued to be in charge of the FMLN's political organization in the department of San Vicente. He threw himself into the task of enhancing the FMLN's organization in the thirteen municipalities of the department, forming municipal committees to ensure that the two FMLN mayors did not function as mayors had in the past but rather in ways that would follow the key goals of the FMLN—democracy and social justice.

Rodríguez also looked for a paying job. In May he was hired by the Fundación para la Promoción de Cooperativas (Foundation for the Promotion of Cooperatives), an organization founded by Archbishop Chávez y González in the late 1960s. The foundation assigned him the task of revitalizing the six weakest cooperatives. Rodríguez points out that this was a "special job" since they were "cooperatives that no one wanted to visit." In fact, one representative from the foundation had recently been "robbed and stripped down to his underpants by bandits" when visiting one of the cooperatives near the Pan-American Highway. Another cooperative that was experiencing difficulties was in an area called La Montañona, which, owing to its high elevation, had been a guerrilla stronghold during the war. This cooperative was located within a nature preserve that former FMLN combatants had been awarded as part of the "land to combatants" program. A conflict ensued between the ex-combatants and "about sixteen families" that lived at the top of the mountain. These families had been cutting down trees to sell as firewood. Rodríguez realized that to solve the problem he would have to remain in the area for a few days, rather than going for a few hours and then returning to San Salvador, as other officials had done. A Peace Corps volunteer, Tony Gasbarro, worked there and had conducted a study of the forests in the area. Using Gasbarro's analysis, Rodríguez was able to facilitate the development of a forest management plan, which the Ministry of Agriculture approved. The project allocated the participants a salary for taking part in preserving the forest. The cooperatives he worked with received assistance from numerous groups, but Rodríguez points out that his principal objective was political—to organize the members of the cooperatives and assist them in developing unity and consensus. As a priest, Rodríguez had focused on helping the poor to organize themselves, and now he was helping citizens (mostly poor) do the same.

Disenchantment: The Move to Marranitos

The peace accords included a program for the reinsertion of ex-combatants into society. As mentioned above, part of the program included the distribution of land to soldiers and guerrillas. One of Rodríguez's efforts was to acquire land titles for parcels of land that peasants had occupied during the war. This was a difficult process, since simply being a peasant in a guerrilla-controlled, or contested, zone did not carry automatic designation as an "ex-combatant." The government reinsertion program had some dedicated funds for the purchase of lands and for providing education and training for ex-combatants. Some of the landowners, however, did not want to sell their lands. Rodríguez remembers that he "put himself fully" into this task, since land reform had been a principal motive for the Christian, popular, and revolutionary movements.

In fact, Rodríguez himself had been left landless as a result of the war. One of his sisters had returned to El Salvador in 1988 to sell the family farm in Calderas. Naturally, because of the war, the land sold at a very low price. A small parcel of land still belonged to the family, and both Rodríguez's mother and father are now buried there. As with other ex-combatants, Rodríguez had inscribed his name on the master rosters to apply for some land, but he had neglected to sign a separate document that was required to get his request authorized. The bureaucratic steps to apply for land were complicated, even for those in the know like Rodríguez. Most importantly, if ex-combatants did not inscribe themselves on the master rosters it was almost impossible for them to get land. Rodríguez was living in Las Pampas, however, an area that had been formally designated to be parceled out to former guerrillas. For the moment, he at least had a place to live and thus continued to work organizing people in the community.

While Rodríguez was living in Las Pampas, a friend of his with the common nickname of "Chepe" encouraged him to accept credit to buy livestock, a program for the middle ranks of the FMLN. Chepe, who lived in Marranitos, in the municipality of Zacatecoluca, told him, "I will take care of them [the cattle]." Chepe was typical of those individuals who had remained in contested zones during the war. He recounts that he had cooperated with the guerrillas extensively, as his heart was with the rebels, but he would also feed government soldiers if left with no other choice. The FMLN combatants who wanted to live in Marranitos were experiencing a common problem in getting some land: the landowner did not want to sell his land to former guerrillas. The ex-guerrillas had formed a cooperative called Islas Malvinas, and Chepe, as their representative, asked Rodríguez to help them to get the land. Rodríguez recommended they go to ISTA, since that agency had property to distribute. However, because they were already negotiating with a landowner, they had essentially given up their right to acquire land from ISTA. Complicating matters, the individual who had started negotiations with the landowner had acted on his own initiative, not really knowing what the ramifications would be by opening up negotiations to get land for the cooperative. ISTA ended up selling the land to the military, at a high price, for parceling out to ex-soldiers. The people in the area wanted to prevent the soldiers from resettling in the land, but Rodríguez told them, "We can't do that. We have a peace accord. We have to negotiate." He then proposed that the cooperative of Islas Malvinas buy some of the land from the military. They agreed, and then Rodríguez, as well as others, signed up as ex-soldiers in order to purchase the land. After they acquired the land, Rodríguez donated a part of his property and gave another parcel to an old compañero who had returned from Nicaragua. As Rodríguez explained this Kafkaesque process of getting land, it became clear that poor peasants, even if they had collaborated extensively with the FMLN, had a very difficult time acquiring land after the peace accords. The key combatants had a much easier time, since they were on the rosters early on, but even then bureaucratic hurdles presented formidable barriers for most peasants.

In early 1995, during Easter, Rodríguez made the difficult and painful decision to move from Las Pampas to the canton of Marranitos, where he now had almost eight acres of land, along with some cattle.[5] He made the move because he had become disheartened by the way many of the demobilized FMLN ex-combatants were carrying out their lives in Las Pampas. After many years of struggle against the government for a more just society, the former compas seemed to have lost all sense of solidarity and become "individualistic and selfish," often "ignoring the needs of their community." Many of Rodríguez's personal belongings had even been stolen from his small house at Las Pampas. One day, a compañera died in the small local clinic while giving birth. The baby and the father were left alone. Rodríguez returned to the community one night and found the husband and the baby with no one providing them any assistance. Rodríguez became upset when he found out that only two women at Las Pampas had assisted the father and newborn. He set up the available sound system and began to admonish the community, reminding them how much solidarity there had been in the front. "I renounce Las Pampas!" he said emotionally into the microphone. Rodríguez realized that he had found much more solidarity in Marranitos. After the burial of the compañera, he left Las Pampas and settled in Marranitos. He asked the FMLN leadership to transfer his duties as a party organizer to the department of La Paz, which they did.

In 1996 the FMLN leadership organized congresses and conventions to transform their party into one, unified organization rather than an amalgam of the five groups that had constituted the guerrilla fronts. The goal was to form a more powerful FMLN that would compete effectively in the 1997 elections, since only by acquiring political power could more substantial reforms be carried out in Salvadoran society. The party needed money, and the FPL asked Rodríguez to travel abroad to sell the organization's belongings, principally office equipment, in Panama and Nicaragua. Rodríguez also became involved in the development of a unified party organization in the department of La Paz, now that his permanent residence was there. As the March 1997 elections approached, Rodríguez was nominated at a party convention to run as the alternate deputy for the department of La Paz. Before his nomination, party leaders from La Paz had come to see him in Marranitos and said, "You have to propose yourself as a candidate!" Rodríguez pointed out to them that he was not really from La Paz, had important duties working to revitalize cooperatives, and was enjoying his organizing work with his community in Marranitos. Additionally, he had loaned the party some money for the 1994 election, had not been paid back, and was thus broke and in debt. Rodríguez also recalls that at the time he was disappointed with the way the party was operating. The competition for candidacies for elected office had become contentious and "very infantile, with accusations" and with much "immaturity." He points out that by this time, Joaquín Villalobos, the influential leader of the ERP, "with seven compañeros," had left the party. Villalobos had started a new party and now cooperated with ARENA on neoliberal economic reforms. In the eyes of the FMLN faithful, Villalobos had sold out once he acquired political power, his talk of social justice turning into nothing but rhetoric.

Despite his financial precariousness, Rodríguez was convinced that the FMLN was in great need of leaders who were still committed to the social justice platform that had inspired the rebellion in the first place. He thus agreed to run as the alternate to the titular deputy, who was well known in the area. Since La Paz is a large department, with twenty-three municipalities and covering a large geographic area (for El Salvador), the campaign would be physically demanding. As the campaign wore on, however, the principal candidate, who had collaborated in the war but had only recently joined the FMLN, told Rodríguez that he could not deal with the contentious FMLN internal politics—"I can't take this," he said. Candidate David Rodríguez then ended up doing most of the campaigning and eventually became the titular candidate for the Legislative Assembly.

Campaigning as an FMLN candidate in the early postwar period was a delicate and sometimes dangerous endeavor, as we saw at the beginning of this chapter. Although the war had ended, many Salvadorans still feared being associated with the left, since some people resented or even hated those who were in the FMLN. Rodríguez remembers that the campaign was most difficult in places where the ARENA party had developed a strong following. He recalls that, when campaigning in the canton of Veracruz, a crowd of people did not allow him to stay in the community. Rodríguez's car, with loudspeakers blaring (a typical campaigning style), came across a number of men walking up the only road that led to the community, carrying ARENA flags and armed with machetes. Some of the men started yelling, "We don't want guerrillas here; out with the cow killers."[6] The compañero who was with Rodríguez became nervous and said, "Let's leave, let's leave!" Rodríguez, however, decided to proceed slowly through the crowd, not wanting to miss an opportunity to perhaps get a few votes. After a while, Rodríguez admits, "We could do nothing in that canton [to win over potential voters]." The political work that the FMLN faced was daunting. The PDC and ARENA had dominated the political scene for the last decade, and they tried to portray the FMLN as the party responsible for the war and the economic crisis. Moreover, people vividly remembered the repression of the recent past, and anyone with FMLN sympathies must have felt some degree of fear.

In the March 1997 elections, the voters of La Paz chose Rodríguez as their FMLN deputy in the Legislative Assembly. In this national election, only the second in which the FMLN participated, the party made substantial progress in the polls, winning 33 percent of the vote, less than 3 percent behind ARENA, which again garnered the largest vote percentage. In the 1994 elections ARENA had received 45 percent of the vote, while the FMLN had trailed well behind with just 21.4 percent. From May 1, 1997, until April 30, 2003, Deputy David Rodríguez served as an elected FMLN legislator (he was reelected for a second three-year term in 2000). In 2000 the FMLN continued to improve its electoral standing in legislative elections, earning 35.22 percent of the vote, trailing ARENA by less than one percentage point.[7]

Diputado David Rodríguez Rivera

Rodríguez was now embarking upon a more ordinary life, even though he was a national legislator. Gone were the days of the liberationist struggles, of clandestine activities, of the difficulties of fighting a civil war. He would now use his elected office to improve in a legal and safe manner the life of his constituents, who for the most part were still the same poor, rural campesinos he had always helped. Interestingly enough, owing to his reputation as a priest, Rodríguez would often be introduced on the assembly floor as "Padre David," and even the members of ARENA would say "Padre David has the word" when it was his turn to speak! When he first entered the legislature in May 1997, Rodríguez was still using a crutch, owing to the attempt against his life during the campaign.

The FMLN party leadership in the Legislative Assembly put Deputy Rodríguez on several legislative commissions (committees): Public Works, Economy and Agriculture, and Justice and Human Rights. Rodríguez points out that he was lucky to have been elected in 1997, because the FMLN deputies during the first assembly (1994–97) were new to the electoral process and thus had to learn the ropes as well as get the assembly, particularly ARENA, used to having an opposition. Since the 1984 election, the PDC and ARENA had monopolized the political process, having reduced the PCN to a rump party. However, by the 1997 election ARENA had be-

Figure 6.1. Rodríguez in the Legislative Assembly, late 1990s. By permission of the Rodríguez Henríquez family.

come the dominant party, and both the PDC and the PCN had become inconsequential parties. Rodríguez points out that before the FMLN entered the electoral process, the assembly would approve national budgets very quickly, since "legislators never read them" and almost no one disagreed. With the FMLN in the opposition, some debate and questioning of expenditures took place when the budget came up for a vote, but owing to the FMLN's inexperience, budgets continued to pass relatively quickly. The FMLN was still new as a party and had too few seats in the assembly to act as an effective opposition. During the first assembly in which the FMLN acted as an opposition, the party was further weakened by the departure of the popular ex-comandante Joaquín Villalobos. Rodríguez points out that Villalobos made a cynical pact with ARENA: the former guerrilla and his followers in the assembly (seven of them) would "vote for a value added tax, called IVA, and ARENA would help their group with reintegration," as well as with "posts in commissions." This political accord between two former enemies became known as the Pact of San Andres.

By the second election, in 1997, when Rodríguez was elected, the party had gained invaluable experience, and FMLN deputies worked with a well-defined "legislative platform," while FMLN mayors had a "program of government" for their municipalities. The FMLN had successfully waged a guerrilla war for twelve years against a government armed to the teeth. Within four years of reaching a peace accord with the government, the party was now less than three percentage points away from winning a plurality of the Salvadoran vote. Despite setbacks, this was a remarkable accomplishment. As for Rodríguez, he had transitioned from being a priest, to working for a guerrilla front, to being a legislator. This constituted a remarkable shift in leadership roles, all of which seemed to fit him like a glove.

The work schedule for a deputy was very hectic. From Monday to Thursday, Rodríguez's days were filled with meetings. The various commissions met on the first three days of the week, and on Thursdays the plenary sessions and debates took place. On Wednesday afternoons the political parties would have their own meetings. Rodríguez points out that "it was the FMLN that started this tradition [of party meetings]." Rather than going into legislative debates without a plan, the FMLN decided to meet as a party, sometimes with other, like-minded parties and deputies, to be more effective at the plenary sessions. Other parties then began doing the same thing. During the week, Rodríguez would also welcome people from La Paz or anyone who knew him. Salvadorans would show up at the Legislative Assembly and say, "I want to talk with Padre David." Some legislators would joke that Rodríguez was "running a confessional" in the assembly, most likely because other legislators seldom saw their constituents. Rodríguez would help the people who came to see him connect with the commission that dealt with the issues that concerned them. Then on the weekends, starting on Friday, Rodríguez would travel to La Paz to serve his constituents there. His life as a legislator was just as busy as it had been as a priest, as a liberationist, and as a revolutionary. Rest was fleeting, but according to many informants, Rodríguez thrived when helping either his parishioners or his constituents.

Working on the Justice and Human Rights Commission was frustrating, Rodríguez recalls, because some of the most conservative, "recalcitrant" deputies from ARENA and the PCN were members. One PDC deputy called one particular ARENA legislator "the Doberman," owing to his aggressiveness and tenacity. Rodríguez recalls that this ARENA deputy would "let nothing go by" in the assembly. The PDC deputy would say: "When they have no arguments left, they sic the Doberman on us!" The ARENA deputy would always say to the FMLN deputies, "You were the ones who violated human rights . . . you left the economy shattered . . . you were the cow killers, the bridge cutters!" The right, of course, feared that the commission would find a way to investigate war crimes, and Rodríguez points out that "there were still violations going on." As in other countries in Latin America that transitioned to democracy in the 1980s and 1990s, the armed forces and the political right, which had been guilty of the vast majority of human rights violations, made sure to discourage any investigations that would uncover, but particularly prosecute, past crimes.

Although the Comisión de la Verdad para El Salvador (Truth Commission for El Salvador), established by the peace accords to investigate human rights violations during the civil war, determined that the vast majority of human-rights violations had been perpetrated by the state and paramilitary groups, the FMLN had also committed human-rights violations, such as forced recruitment, the summary execution of infiltrators, the use of children as soldiers and collaborators,[8] the mistreatment of female guerrillas, and the murder of a number of mayors in the department of Morazán.[9] One particularly egregious case, not included in the commission's report, involved an FPL regional commander, Mayo Sibrián, who was responsible for the FPL's para-central region, incorporating the departments of San Vicente, La Paz, and parts of Usulután. By the time the problems started, in 1986, Rodríguez was already away from the area, but he eventually heard about the horrible ajusticiamientos in what had been part of his parish and diocese. Comandante Sibrián had ordered the summary execution, often after brutal interrogation, of hundreds of FPL combatants between 1986 and 1989 (when he was demoted), accusing his victims of being government infiltrators. Eventually, and much too slowly, the FMLN high command dealt with the actions of Sibrián by carrying out a summary trial and having him executed by firing squad in 1991.[10] When asked about these violations, Rodríguez offers that Sibrián "became psychotic" and "began to suspect even his own shadow," similar to "what happened in the Soviet Union."[11] In effect, some high-level leaders within the FMLN may be happy that an amnesty law exists.[12]

By the late 1990s the problem of street gangs had raised its head, and the right argued that the ombudsman for the Justice and Human Rights Commission "was protecting criminals." The FMLN, on the other hand, suggested that political killings were still taking place and that the ombudsman was essential for the protection of the political opposition. The right would counter that it was the gangs that were responsible for the killings and that stronger law enforcement was needed. Rodríguez points out that gangs were "certainly a problem" but that even though they "were criminals they were also human beings and thus their rights had to be protected." He also suggests that ARENA used the gang problem to weaken the state's efforts to prosecute human-rights violations. So, more often than not, the Justice and Human Rights Commission would lack a quorum, since the right, not wanting human-rights violations brought before the legislature, would simply boycott the meetings. When the right would not show up, the FMLN deputies would decide that it was a waste of time for them to attend the meetings. Rodríguez laments: "I suffered much; it was a very difficult commission."

Rodríguez recalls that the Economy and Agriculture Commission was the one he "liked the most." He felt that the FMLN deputies on that commission were excellent, "very well prepared and with good capacity for debate." In this commission, the deputies were exposed to "all the problems of the economy." In a sense, the key issues that had given rise to the civil war could now be discussed openly in the commission and the assembly, as had briefly occurred twenty-seven years earlier at the First Congress on Agrarian Reform. As we would expect, Rodríguez became intimately involved in the issues of forgiving the agrarian debt of ex-combatants and the revitalization of the agrarian sector. In order to accomplish these tasks, the FMLN initially brought forth a proposal to strengthen ISTA. ARENA, having controlled politics since 1989, had infiltrated ISTA, and thus the institute had become a vehicle for political patronage and electioneering for the party. A new proposal was made to disband ISTA and replace it with a new organization, but the proposal was never taken up, since ARENA still controlled the assembly and wanted to keep the institute as it was.

Serving Constituents

While serving as a deputy, Rodríguez continued to work in the FMLN's regional office in Zacatecoluca. Consequently, on the weekends he would spend a great deal of time with the communities in the department of La Paz. Even though his participation in the church was now almost "nil," Christian communities continued to invite him to functions, and most people still referred to him fondly as "Padre David." Rodríguez asserts, "I believe there is no canton that I did not visit, no community that I did not visit, when I was a deputy." While I was with Rodríguez in El Salvador in January 2008, I was amazed at how his presence would affect people when they saw him, even though he had been practically absent from the area during the war. Almost always, individuals would light up and greet him fondly as "Padre David" or "Chele David." Only once, when we entered a small group of dwellings near the town of Tecoluca, did a few young men treat him with disrespect, saying, "Here comes Padre David the revolutionary," and "Padre, how is 'Che' Guevara?" The men, however, were quite drunk and appeared to be social outcasts, though perhaps politically active. This was the only time I felt uncomfortable or threatened while I was with Rodríguez on my two visits to El Salvador for this project.

One piece of legislation that Rodríguez is very proud of helped to open up the Legislative Assembly to the people and media of El Salvador. In 1994 the FMLN had begun to fight for this right, but nothing had come of it.

Figure 6.2. Rodríguez with his constituents, circa 2001. By permission of the Rodríguez Henríquez family.

Once elected, Rodríguez "threw himself fully" into this bill. In the past, members of the assembly had worked behind closed doors, making it impossible for citizens to know what their deputies were doing, not unlike many legislatures. One of the FMLN's goals was to make government more transparent and accountable. Rodríguez recalls, "We fought to open up the Legislative Assembly," not only so that people could watch the plenary debates but so they could "listen to the debates in the commissions." Nevertheless, even after the bill was passed the presidents of the commissions could push a button that cut off the sound to anyone observing the debate from behind the glass partition. At times the debates in the commissions would be heated and the president would say that the sound should be cut off. "We would fight over the button," says Rodríguez, laughing. He believes that this "sunshine" legislation, which he co-sponsored, went a long way to put a check on what legislators did, forcing them to be somewhat more accountable to citizens.

For example, if a commission was debating an issue and concerned citizens were present, Rodríguez would say, "Why don't we allow a delegation of those present to tell us what the problem is from their perspective?" The commission would then have to vote on his proposal, and since the people could see how the legislators voted, the deputies would often approve the motion. Rodríguez asserts that campesinos would usually explain the problem "better than us," since they were living the problem rather than debating it from afar. As when he was a priest, Rodríguez delighted in the wisdom and honesty of the Salvadoran campesino.

Although the assembly eventually became much more open to citizens, problems arose because of security. Security personnel were distrustful of average citizens, so they would carry out extensive searches and often treat people rudely or disdainfully. Rodríguez became concerned that people would be hesitant to visit the assembly simply because of security "searches" and harsh treatment. One day Rodríguez saw the chief of security at the assembly, with whom he had clashed, searching an old woman. Rodríguez said to him, "Let her pass. What, she's going to be carrying a bomb?" Rodríguez would also say to the security chief with appropriate irony, "Look, you are a campesino and these people are poor." Eventually, he and the security chief "became good friends." For Rodríguez a democratic government had to be open to the people, and "security" could not be a rationale for limiting access to decision makers.

One particularly striking example of Rodríguez's leadership skills and forbearance concerned the former members of the civil patrols, some of whom had also been members of ORDEN. These men, who had cooperated with the government during the prolonged conflict, felt that they were being left out of the peace accords' provision that offered land to ex-combatants. Rodríguez points out that while many ex-soldiers had received land through ISTA, the ex-patrolmen had received very little land, because the ARENA party was using the possibility of getting land as a tool to get the support of the former civil patrol members. Also, ARENA wanted to include only ex-soldiers and ex-guerrillas in the land disbursement, since their key goal was to limit the land-redistribution program. After all, ARENA was the party of the same oligarchy that had fought tooth and nail to prevent land reform. The FMLN, on the other hand, wanted to distribute as much land as possible, even to civilians rather than just ex-combatants, regardless of whether they had cooperated with the FMLN or government. Rodríguez remembers that a number of people "with bad intentions" took advantage of the patrolmen, taking their money and promising to represent them. He found out about these scams and decided to attend some of the meetings of the patrolmen. He recalls that at one meeting he said,

> I am an FMLN deputy and I have come to tell you the truth about what is going on in the Legislative Assembly, and what programs we have, and that you do not have to pay even one cent [to get what you are entitled to]. You need to form your own organization, your own commission. Go [to the assembly] and we [the FMLN] will attend to you.

Remarkably, the former parish priest, who at one time would have been killed by some of these men, was now helping them to get organized so they could fight for their rights.

Emboldened, and since the legislature was now open to the public, some ex-patrolmen occupied the assembly and took some deputies hostage in order to make demands for land. The assembly agreed to give them more land, but, according to Rodríguez, the ARENA-controlled government did not follow through with the concession. Rodríguez remembers that relatively soon thereafter he was at a commission meeting on the fifth floor when the deputies present saw that once again a group of patrolmen were approaching the assembly. Because the gathering crowd was clearly visible from the window, the meeting was suspended quickly. The FMLN representatives decided to go outside and meet with the patrolmen. Eventually, the FMLN deputies arranged to allow the patrolmen to enter the assembly to discuss their demands. Rodríguez points out that now many patrolmen have switched sides and have become supporters of the FMLN, and in the department of La Paz the FMLN has helped to organize them. Those peasants who joined ORDEN or civil patrols and helped the government repress the church and the popular organizations did so principally because they needed assistance. The FMLN was now providing assistance, so they gladly accepted it.

In the Public Works Commission, the FMLN pushed for a program—Programa de Caminos Rurales Sostenibles (Sustainable Rural Roads Program)—to pave roads in rural areas where small and medium-size producers had the highest agricultural production, so that campesinos could get their produce to markets. The infrastructure in the country had been designed to serve almost exclusively the interests of large-scale producers, the oligarchy. If the campesinos were to improve their lives, they needed better infrastructure that would facilitate their commerce. Making matters worse, the war had wreaked havoc on the country's infrastructure. For example, a road called La Panorámica–La Paz starts at Santiago Texacuangos, just southeast of San Salvador, and runs along the mountains that extend just south of Lake Ilopango, east of San Salvador. The road then veers north and ends in the department of Cuscatlán, just to the east and north of the department of San Vicente. Rodríguez reminisces, "Jokingly, I would say, we call it Panorámica, but, since one has to look at the potholes in the road [as one drives], one does not look at the panorama." Three FMLN deputies—Rodríguez from La Paz, Amelia Díaz from San Vicente, and Manuel Melgar from Cuscatlán—joined forces in an effort to "organize the people from their departments to push the government to pave" the scenic, potholed, yet economically important road. This effort led to the rural roads program that the FMLN eventually proposed in the assembly. The legislature approved the program; and, as Rodríguez points out, "never before have so many roads been paved" to serve small communities. Political power in this case had produced a positive outcome that would help many small producers.

In a related program, the Public Works Commission considered a plan to develop roads in rural areas that were in disuse. For example, during the war a new road called the Carretera del Litoral (Coastal Highway) had been built to replace a road that had linked Zacatecoluca to San Salvador. The new road was much straighter than the old one, so segments of the old road were practically abandoned. During the war, many people built small shacks along those old road segments and also along the abandoned railroad line from San Salvador to the country's eastern port at La Unión. People had settled in these areas to escape the conflict and because these were state properties from which they would be less likely to be ejected. The railway—which ran east from the capital, wove its way through the departments of San Vicente and La Paz, and ended in the department of La Unión at the coast—had fallen into disuse during the war, principally because of FMLN economic sabotage. The people living along these roads and rail lines found some degree of safe haven from the conflict, but at war's end these settlements became a government problem. These displaced communities highlighted the need to find property for ex-combatants and people in general, since, owing to lack of funds, their only recourse was to squat on unused government lands.

The legislature decided to give land to the squatters along twenty-two miles of the old rail line in the eastern part of the country, since a new railroad would not traverse that particular area. Also, several rulings granted land to squatters along roads in disuse. However, the problem of squatters along these state properties persisted for other segments of the rail line and some roads, principally because the government did not have enough land to distribute (owing to lack of funds) and because a plan to reactivate the railroad was in the works. After the struggles of the 1970s and the long civil war, land tenure was still a major problem in the country.

The Public Works Commission also dealt with problems relating to public transportation. Rodríguez points out that the transportation system was in a "deteriorated" condition, with "poor-quality transport, particularly in the small towns." Another problem was that the system was composed of many individuals who owned "one, two, three, or four buses," resulting in almost no effective coordination. At the same time, centralizing the bus service would mean that public transport would most likely then end up in the hands of one wealthy family or company, since three families controlled the importation of cars and buses into the country. These families had been trying for some time to take the transport business away from the small owners. In fact, they had introduced microbuses into some of the same routes that the old buses were running in hopes of forcing the old buses out of the market. The transportation owners, however, had formed a number of organizations to defend their interests—the strongest being the Asociación de Empresarios de Autobuses Salvadoreños (Salvadoran Association of Owners of Autobuses) and the Asociación de Transporte de Pasajeros (Association of Passenger Transport). The leaders of these organizations, as Rodríguez points out, argued that "if a new fleet of buses was needed, then the government should give the small business owners long term credit so they could buy the buses." They also wanted the government to eliminate the competition from the microbuses and demanded an "end to the corruption in the Ministry of Transportation." Simply put, these organizations boldly argued that they were being forced to "offer a bribe to the ministry" in order to be authorized a bus line by the government. Rodríguez suggests that they were absolutely correct, but no one discussed this corruption openly. The public transportation system was a difficult and, at the time, unsolvable problem. This situation demonstrates that, as with coffee in the past, the oligarchy's support of competitive capitalism was weak at best, since what they seemed to desire was monopoly.

In the six years that Rodríguez served as a deputy in the Legislative Assembly, it was very difficult for the FMLN to achieve its goals. Rodríguez points out that after a decade of ARENA control, most of the government agencies were staffed by ARENA, PCN, and PDC officials, the latter two being beholden to ARENA for their positions. Without a majority in the legislature, the FMLN simply could not get the other parties to accept major changes. Rodríguez surmises that without sufficient political power, you "can't talk about rule of law or the institutionalization of the country, which was one of the aspirations of the peace accords." The Human Rights Office, the Supreme Court, the Supreme Electoral Tribunal, and the Attorney General's office were all compromised by their politicization. Rodríguez recalls, for example, that the country's prosecutor "lost almost all important cases."

One very fond memory that Rodríguez retains from his first two terms as a deputy is a visit that he made to Cuba. He had been offered a trip to Spain, which would have been very useful for him, since he had always wanted to get his official diploma from the Pontifical University at Las Comillas, where he had studied canon law. Rodríguez had left Spain before the academic term ended to attend the school for papal nuncios in Rome and thus had not been able to pick up his diploma. Nevertheless, he offered the trip to Spain to another FMLN deputy because there was a possibility to go to Cuba with the Public Works Commission, something that appealed to him even more. The trip was authorized by the ruling ARENA party, since one of its members, ironically enough, wanted to receive medical treatment in a Cuban hospital. Rodríguez eventually traveled to Havana as he had done in the 1980s. While in Cuba, he found the location of Tito's grave, a mass burial site, and was given a small plaque commemorating the death of his son. Rodríguez was always calm and collected when discussing personal matters; however, recalling the fate of his son visibly moved him.

Disunity within the FMLN

The FMLN's inability to achieve majority power via the ballot box was partly self-inflicted, owing to internal conflicts and schisms, beginning with the departure of Joaquín Villalobos. Rodríguez points out that during the civil war the five groups that composed the FMLN never really worked in unison, but owing to the presence of a common enemy a reasonable amount of cooperation existed. Once the FMLN became a legal political party, however, some serious differences emerged. Over time, the five groups no longer represented the key divisions, although the differences between the FPL and the PCS still persisted, each group seeing itself as the vanguard of the party. Rodríguez points out that the FPL and the PCS had "lived together in the mountains" and naturally some jealousies and mistrust emerged and a sense of division continued between the most orthodox members of each group. The PCS believed it deserved to be the ideological leader of the Salvadoran left, since it had the longest history. They saw the FPL as an offshoot of the party, which it indeed was. The FPL, however, had been by far the most important politico-military organization, with the largest popular front, the BPR. An important part of the FPL's broader appeal stemmed from its strong Christian dimension, thanks to liberationists like Rodríguez.

By the late 1990s, however, the key division within the FMLN was between two ideological tendencies. The Tendencia Revolucionaria (Revolutionary Trend) did not want to jettison the FMLN's socialist, revolutionary platform. The other tendency was more open to negotiating with other groups for a common purpose. Another division arose over how much time the FMLN devoted to popular organization versus what Rodríguez and others referred to as "electioneering." These critics believed that the party should never distance itself from its base, the people, and should never focus principally on winning elections. Electioneering had in many ways been part of the cause of the civil war, since elected officials always made promises during campaigns but never followed through once in office. Although the term no longer had precisely the same negative connotation, electioneering was still viewed as a problem, since it meant that leaders worried more about getting power than they did about solving people's problems. The rationalization was that only with sufficient power could real changes take place, and thus winning elections was the crucial first step. Rodríguez laments that, although he sympathized with the orthodox view, some members of Tendencia Revolucionaria "have an attitude [of which] I do not approve." At times these leaders would severely criticize others in the party and charge them with being "traitors or even CIA collaborators." Such "negative attitudes," Rodríguez says, "does not allow us [the FMLN] to debate the [country's] problems in depth." What Rodríguez feared most at the time was that the FMLN would embrace the electoral tactics of the right and that, instead of offering an alternative, the FMLN would become like them. This was not what he and countless others had struggled for when they supported liberationist ideas or the revolution.

One of the key controversies within the party lay in that some members wanted the FMLN to focus on creating a socialist country, while others believed the most important goal should be to improve "democracy, creating a rule of law, and simply ensuring that the constitution be enforced." Only after forging a truly democratic system could the party carry out the necessary transformations, such as "agrarian reform, the reactivation of agriculture and constitutional reforms." Rodríguez points out that if the FMLN could not achieve "the full backing of the majority of the people" to make fundamental changes, the oligarchy and the parties opposed to the FMLN would "leave the country with nothing," suggesting that they would pull their money out of the country as they had done during the civil war. For Rodríguez this meant that revolutionary changes could be achieved only if the FMLN effectively organized the people, gained their confidence and support, and developed a "strong foreign policy with links with Venezuela, with Nicaragua, with China." At the end of the civil war, most FMLN leaders had abandoned their goal of creating a Marxist revolution and, like Rodríguez, openly supported social democracy.[13] However, a number of less progressive party leaders seemed willing to distance themselves even more from that minimal revolutionary political commitment.

As in the civil war, therefore, the road to a better El Salvador in the new democratic system, as one astute peasant asserted, will be a "prolonged struggle." The problem was further intensified because some party members were now used to holding political or government office and, as Rodríguez laments, had "become used to their benefits." Some FMLN leaders and elected officials, says Rodríguez, would arrive in communities "in big cars with darkened windows." He worried that this type of behavior was "an affront to the people." His reasoning was that such behavior separated the leader from the people, but more importantly, it harkened back to the days when security forces arrived in the same way to small communities and to the days of "politicking," or electioneering. Rodríguez recalls that he became "enamored with the [original] movement because, in the past [1970s and 1980s], leaders worked with and lived like the people." He recalls that he would say to his catechists about the FPL leaders, "These compañeros are more Christian than us." For Rodríguez the FPL's sense of community, solidarity, and commitment to justice was much stronger than that of many Christians in El Salvador, particularly the conservatives within the church. And FPL members were more than ready to die, become martyrs, for a better, more just El Salvador. Rodríguez laments the fact that after the peace accords the FMLN accepted "some leaders who are mediocre" and who did not come in contact with the people. The FPL's and the FMLN's mystique and sense of empathy toward the poor seemed to be withering away.

During his first six years as a legislator, Rodríguez longed for the "method of inquiry and participation" that the party employed during the war, steeped in "analysis and self-criticism." He was hopeful that the party would return to such a method of reflection. The commitment to community, social justice, critical analysis, and self-criticism, however, was not the exclusive property of the FMLN, since liberationist leaders like Rodríguez had pioneered and developed these principles in the 1970s with the creation of CEBs and Bible circles. In general, Rodríguez's principal fear was that the FMLN would lose its commitment to the people and to social justice and that it would lapse into a centralized, elitist political organization. Rodríguez was still a liberationist at heart—an ideology formed by the church, not by the politico-military organizations. He had hoped that once democracy was inaugurated in El Salvador, politics would become participatory, inclusive, accountable, and responsive. Sadly, the democracy that had come to the country was certainly better than the military-dominated regimes of the past, but was still a far cry from the liberationist system he had hoped for.

If a better democracy was to be created, Rodríguez was sure it would have to start with the FMLN. He came to the conclusion, and argued at conventions and party meetings, as other leaders did, that the FMLN needed to change in several ways. First, it had to put an end to its "internal aggression," or what he called "cannibalism." Second, it had to stop isolating the leadership from the people and cease making important decisions with "small groups of people." Third, it should begin a dialogue "even with supporters of the other parties." Rodríguez points out that despite the needed corrections and internal turmoil, the party did not "self-destruct." For example, the PCN and the PDC, which were both practically dominant parties in the past, had virtually disappeared from the political scene, while the FMLN was improving its national position vis-à-vis the ARENA party, which was very well funded. The internal divisions continued, but the FMLN held together to compete effectively in future elections.

The Bout with Parkinson's

As early as 2001, Rodríguez had begun to feel his right hand trembling. At a special plenary session of the legislature in Santa Ana, a departmental capital in the western part of the country, Rodríguez finally realized that his health was in peril. The assembly happened to be debating what to do with a state-run sugar mill in the department of San Vicente that had been constructed during the Duarte government. The large mill had forced the smaller mills to close, and all sugar growers in the area were selling their harvest to the government mill. The ARENA government wanted to privatize the mill, and thus a debate had ensued. When he took the floor, Rodríguez's knees began to tremble, then his hand, and then his entire body. In distress, he said abruptly: "Excuse me, I'm a little ill of health; I will continue, but I will sit down." He recalls that, although losing control of his movements, he was not in any pain. He eventually had to stop talking and left the meeting place, borrowing a car and driver from another FMLN deputy. He was taken to a doctor, who after examining him, said: "This is Parkinson's." The doctor recommended rest, so Rodríguez decided to retire from the legislature.

At the end of his second term, in May 2003, Rodríguez returned to Marranitos—no longer a priest, a rebel, a legislator, or a political organizer—and decided to try his hand at agriculture. He recalls that this was a very difficult period: "I was living in the flesh what many ex-combatants go through now." His medical treatment and medication regimen were expensive, one test costing "about four hundred dollars," so Rodríguez, the citizen, began to sell off some of his farm animals. Although his salary had been high as a legislator, his compañera, Merci Henríquez, points out that "he would often give part of his salary away" to worthy causes or constituents in need. His efforts at agriculture were not very successful, despite the fact that he had grown up on a sugar plantation. He had, after all, embraced the priesthood full force rather than the life of a small farmer. Desperate to become more active and needing health coverage, he decided to look for a "paying job" once again. In April 2006 he landed a position in the mayor's office in Mejicanos, a town contiguous to San Salvador, as the director of the Oficina Municipal para el Apoyo de Microempresas de Mejicanos (Municipal Office for the Support of Microbusinesses of Mejicanos), meaning that he traveled to the capital often, a trip of more than an hour each way.

Rodríguez's popularity within the rank and file of the FMLN, however, was still quite high, and although he was officially "retired," a number of supporters urged him to run for the office of party coordinator in Zacatecoluca, only ten miles north-northwest of Marranitos. The FMLN coordinating committee in Zacate had eleven members, the coordinator and ten others, who had functional responsibilities in areas such as "education, youth, women, propaganda." It is important to point out that after leaving the assembly, Rodríguez felt that the orthodox members of the party seemed to have decided that he was no longer useful and somehow was not "sufficiently revolutionary." Although he never lost his desire to bring social justice to the people of El Salvador, some political leaders still saw him as a former priest and as someone who would dialogue with anyone. Rodríguez, however, felt that the FMLN would go to the people for votes and always "talk about the revolution but would not really listen to the people." The bottom line was that the FMLN had someone else in mind for the coordinator's job in Zacate. When the debates for the post of party coordinator took place, the candidate backed by the party accused Rodríguez of having "sold out and of moving to the right." When the internal party election was held, Rodríguez recalls that he "won by twenty-seven votes, but when the party announced the results it asserted that his opponent had won by four votes." Rodríguez sent a letter to the FMLN's tribunal asserting that he had won and requesting that the party investigate the election. The FMLN, to its credit, acceded to his request, and an inquiry demonstrated that the existing coordinating committee in Zacate, which favored the other candidate, had indeed tampered with the votes in order to give their candidate the victory. The tribunal ruled that the election be repeated. The local people knew and trusted Rodríguez, so he won the election again a second time, and thus the party leadership was forced to accept him as party coordinator. Interestingly enough, his opponent in that election "had some serious problems" subsequently and ended up aligning himself with Rodríguez, eventually letting him know exactly how the fraud was committed in the first election! Sadly, once in positions of power, some of the FMLN rank and file seemed to be operating in the same objectionable manner in which the right had functioned all along.

Rodríguez reminisces that during this time he felt as if he was in the Catholic Church once more because the hierarchy was cautious of him but the people embraced him. Moreover, as he had done before, he "found a space within the organization to continue working" for the good of the people. Rodríguez admits that at times he thought about "breaking with the party," as some others had done. The FMLN often accused those who broke with the party of "selling out or of treason," but Rodríguez asserts that some party members just could not take it anymore, owing either to the party's radicalism, ostracism, inflexibility, or elitism. Ironically, the individual whom the FMLN favored in this difficult internal election had never been in the front as had Rodríguez, who had a long history with the FPL and the FMLN. Rodríguez points out that in the past, when he worked in the finance committees, the FMLN leadership had "tremendous confidence in him." He recalls that, during those years, when he visited the leadership they would show respect toward him, but sadly "the confidence of the past was not there." Part of the problem stemmed from the fact that Rodríguez had criticized the party for not working sufficiently with the people—strong criticism which some in the FMLN "could not take."

A sad truth that partly explains the party's inability to maintain the moral strength of the past has to do with the simple reality that many of the most dedicated leaders in the revolutionary and popular movement had been killed in the war. Rodríguez states with sadness, "We lost magnificent leaders in the war who would now be helping greatly." Although the government repression of the 1970s helped to strengthen rather than to crush the popular and Christian movements, the long-standing repression and then the civil war effectively decimated the mid-level leadership of the FMLN and the popular blocs. The FMLN was not defeated by the government—it won the right to become a political party, forced the demilitarization of the country, and brought democracy to El Salvador—but at the end of the war it had lost countless leaders who might have helped to more effectively transform the country. In effect, the government, oligarchy, and repressive apparatus had exterminated a generation of leaders committed to bringing social justice, if not liberation, to the Salvadoran poor.

In November 2006 the Legislative Assembly established a satellite office in the City of Zacatecoluca, and Rodríguez was hired in December to be part of a section to oversee civic education. An FMLN leader, Gerson Martínez, said to him, "Look, you've been a deputy so you should be able to do good work." Despite his sense of isolation from the party, Rodríguez's selection for this "political position" showed that at least enough party leaders still felt that he was useful or at least that they owed him a debt. Rodríguez's principal responsibility at the assembly office was to provide civic education to young people, mainly offering classes and information on democracy, the workings of the Legislative Assembly, the making of laws, and the rights and responsibilities of citizens. The office offered civic education to government officials as well. Rodríguez points out that students would ask many questions, the most popular being, "Why do elected officials make so much money?"[14] Once again, twenty years after teaching at Centro Naranjos, Rodríguez was helping people understand their rights and the means by which they could promote their interests. This time, however, rather than doing it in a way that criticized the state, he was being paid by the state to educate citizens about the new democratic system. The director of the office was from the PCN and would often accompany Rodríguez to his classes, which would run for about three hours a day. At first the director perhaps simply wanted to keep an eye on him, since he represented the FMLN, but after a while he became quite friendly with Rodríguez and one day said to him, "You know, you should be getting two salaries," since Rodríguez would not only teach the classes but also attend to people's needs, which was the responsibility of others in the office. In fact, when citizens would come to the assembly's office in Zacate, they would often bypass the public assistance office, run by ARENA, and ask to see "Padre David."

Rodríguez emphasizes that, although the FMLN was at times unorganized and at times was becoming too detached from the people, ARENA officials tended to be completely "arrogant" and unapproachable. One day in early 2007, a group of cattle ranchers came to Rodríguez and asked him if he could get them an audience with the mayor of Zacate, a member of ARENA. Rodríguez points out that people would normally address ranchers as "señores" (gentlemen), since they had a reasonable degree of status and wealth. The ranchers were of course normally ARENA supporters. Rodríguez said to the ranchers, "Señores, how am I going to get you an audience, since he [the mayor] is from ARENA?" The ranchers responded that they had tried to see the mayor but he refused to see them. The cattlemen were concerned because they had heard that the livestock arena where they sold their cattle "was going to be sold off [privatized]." Rodríguez decided to help and then called the ARENA deputy from La Paz, using the speaker function of his phone so that the ranchers could listen to the call. Rodríguez told the deputy that the ranchers were in his office, listening to the call, and urged him to get them a meeting with the mayor. The deputy said, "Yes, tell them that I'll meet with them on Monday." On Monday, however, the deputy was not available. Once again the frustrated ranchers were in Rodríguez's office, who then decided to call someone he dealt with regularly at the ARENA-controlled ISTA. Once again, Rodríguez said, "Look, I have—" but was quickly interrupted by the ARENA official on the other line who said, "Yes, yes, I have the bastard [mayor] right here in my office and I've been counseling him [to listen to the ranchers]." Rodríguez and the ranchers broke out in laughter. The mayor then agreed to meet with the ranchers on Wednesday, but he never showed. The ranchers once again came to Rodríguez, who told them, "Look, you know the situation; I can't do anything else." Eventually, the ranchers went to the assembly and denounced ARENA. At base, the problem was that the ARENA government wanted to privatize the facilities where cattle were sold, but the small cattle ranchers, who were also conservative, did not want this to occur, since it would principally help the oligarchs rather than the smaller-scale cattle owners. Rodríguez points out that these kinds of anti-democratic actions by other parties "open up spaces for the FMLN." Those who had been supporters of ARENA learned that their interests were not necessarily with that party and that the FMLN—the dreaded "cow killers"—would often be more responsive to their needs.

While working for the civic education office, Rodríguez also set up forums for students to have discussions with their legislators from the department of La Paz. The idea was to bring together the four deputies so that students could learn about democracy and the constitution during a question-and-answer session with their elected representatives. After the first event, at which titular or substitute deputies from the FMLN, ARENA, and PCN attended, Rodríguez was summoned by the director of the civic education office, a PCN member, who said to him, "We are not going to hold these forums again." Naturally, he asked, "Why not?" The director hesitantly responded that it was too controversial and it was "better to have the deputies talk with the people one at a time, not all together." The problem was that if a particular deputy felt pressed by the crowd, as the ARENA deputy had been with the issue of dollarization (changing the national currency to the U.S. dollar), he or she would feel that the forum was being used by another party for political purposes.[15] Since the positions in the Zacatecolua civic education office were political appointments, the PCN and ARENA decided that the forums would not be productive for them politically. Rodríguez points out that the forum was "very educational, very productive, but it scared them [the PCN and ARENA]." Despite the problems that the FMLN was experiencing, overall the party seemed closer to the interests of the poor than any other party. And, it was also more willing to listen to those who had grievances.

The job in Zacatecoluca allowed Rodríguez to spend much more time in his home in Marranitos. Working as a deputy for six years in San Salvador had kept him away from his new home most of the time. Although doctors recommended rest, he now had the time to begin to work closely with the parish priest at the Iglesia El Calvario in Zacate. He also returned to political organizing and social work, and thus galvanized the sixteen small communities of Marranitos, establishing the Coordinadora para el Desarrollo Económico y Social de Marranitos (Coordination for the Social and Economic Development of Marranitos). Rodríguez also asked the church that the excommunication case against him be withdrawn now that his political work had ended. In November 2003 the church dropped the case, and Rodríguez began to work with the priests at San Nicolás Lempa, where Bishop Aparicio had placed him after being removed as parish priest in Tecoluca, on several civic and religious projects.

The FMLN in Power

According to Rodríguez, around November 2006 the FMLN made a concerted effort to reach out to the people, as he and others had advised. As a result, the party regained some unity and momentum in preparation for the 2009 legislative and presidential elections. He speculates that the FMLN has always had loyal followers as its core constituency and that a large number of Salvadorans, sometimes reaching 60 percent, although not solidly aligned with any political party, had voted in the past for the PDC, ARENA, or the PCN. Many of these Salvadorans had for years been hesitant to vote for the FMLN, but Rodríguez is certain that the FMLN's efforts to appeal to more people finally convinced many citizens to vote for the party in 2009. Also, as the fear of repression waned and the political climate improved, increasing numbers of Salvadorans believed that voting for the FMLN would not carry any negative consequences. Rodríguez points out that one strategy that ARENA used to scare voters was to argue that, if the FMLN won, Salvadorans living in the United States would not be able to continue sending remittances to their relatives in El Salvador. He recalls that even one of his relatives, who had always sympathized with the FMLN but never voted owing to her advanced age, voted for ARENA in one election because she feared that she would lose her remittances from relatives living abroad. Many Salvadorans also thought that U.S. economic aid would be cut if the FMLN won, something the U.S. Embassy in San Salvador cagily suggested. To some extent, only a less repressive state and the healing effects of time eventually assured some voters that nothing catastrophic would take place if they voted for the FMLN.

In addition to moving closer to the people, many FMLN leaders also believed that the party needed a new, more electable candidate. For the previous presidential elections, the FMLN had nominated key leaders from the contentious revolutionary period: Rubén Zamora in 1994, Facundo Guardado in 1999, and Schafik Handal in 2004. In the 2004 election, the ARENA candidate, "Tony" Saca, won handily in the first round with almost 56 percent of the vote, in a field of four presidential candidates. Schafik Handal came in second, garnering just under 36 percent of the vote. While the FMLN continued to be the second-largest party, it repeatedly failed to win over a majority of the voters. Rodríguez points out that even before 2004, many FMLN loyalists would say, "If they put up Mauricio Funes, we will win." The FMLN leadership, however, had chosen to run revolutionary leaders with "hard bones," as Rodríguez puts it. Nevertheless, he became more optimistic about the FMLN's chances around 2007, since the party was promoting grassroots efforts and fresh candidates who would appeal to the independent voters.

On November 11, 2007, in celebration of the 1989 offensive, the FMLN's presidential and vice-presidential candidacies were officially launched at the Cuscatlán Stadium in San Salvador, the largest soccer stadium in Central America and the Caribbean, holding forty-five thousand people. Presidential candidate Mauricio Funes had never fought in the war and was a journalist, but he was young, attractive, well known, and respected. His running mate, Salvador Sánchez Cerén, who had taken over the FPL after Carpio's demise, represented the old guard. The FMLN believed it now had a winning ticket—the old with the new. Rodríguez remembers that the FMLN "concentration" at the stadium had a "national impact." Rodríguez is certain that ARENA leaders decided not to hold a similar rally at the stadium because they were afraid of "looking ridiculous, not filling the stadium."

Rodríguez was filled with hope and enthusiasm. His Parkinson's seemed under control, his energy was at high levels, and he was still a very popular leader and organizer. How could he be left out of the final victory—the FMLN taking over the political reins of the country? Consequently, he made the decision to run again as a deputy from La Paz, something that many of his supporters continued to suggest. On January 18, 2009, elections were held for legislative deputies and mayors. The FMLN, which had been showing gains in the polls, partly because of its new national ticket, won a plurality of the vote, 42.6 percent, while ARENA garnered 38.5 percent. As a result, the FMLN won thirty-five seats, and ARENA thirty-two, in the Legislative Assembly.[16] Rodríguez would fill one of those seats and would once again represent the department of La Paz. The FMLN was brimming with optimism. They were right to be sanguine. On March 15, 2009, El Salvador held its national presidential election. Mauricio Funes won 51.3 percent of the vote and would thus become the first-ever FMLN president. The ARENA candidate received 48.7 percent of the vote. The rightist party, which had dominated the political system for twenty years, finally lost the reins of power. Even though the FMLN had now won the presidency and the largest bloc of seats in the assembly, they were still without a majority in the legislature, meaning that they would have to form alliances with the PDC and the PCN to pass legislation.

In the 2012 legislative elections the FMLN lost some gains, resulting in fewer seats in the assembly. ARENA garnered 39.8 percent of the vote, while the FMLN, in second place, dropped to 36.7 percent. As a result, ARENA won thirty-three seats, while the FMLN won thirty-one, a loss of four seats. Rodríguez, once again, won one of those seats, being reelected as a deputy from La Paz. The FMLN was still without a legislative majority and thus had to form alliances. This time, however, the political scene had changed: the PDC had not won any seats, and the ARENA party had split. Prior to the elections, former president Tony Saca had left ARENA and formed the Gran Alianza por la Unidad Nacional (Grand Alliance for National Unity). The alliance won eleven seats in the assembly. The FMLN was thus compelled to negotiate with legislators in Saca's alliance in order to pass legislation.

The FMLN continued to feel optimistic about its electoral chances and thus nominated Salvador Sánchez Cerén as its presidential candidate for 2014. Rodríguez points out that Sánchez Cerén may not have been as "good a candidate as Funes but would make a better president." Many within the FMLN had felt that Funes was the safe candidate—someone with which the party could win its first presidency. Sánchez Cerén, on the other hand, would be the more substantial candidate and would promote policies more in line with the FMLN's progressive social and economic agenda. Rodríguez asserts that at times "Funes had spent more time dialoguing with the opposition than with his own party." One big question remained, though: Could the former guerrilla and FPL leader win the presidency? The presidential election was held on February 2, 2014. Although Sánchez Cerén won a plurality, a second round was needed, since he did not win over 50 percent of the vote. On March 9, Sánchez Cerén ran against the ARENA candidate, Norman Quijano, who had been mayor of San Salvador. The official results put Sánchez Cerén in the presidency with a narrow margin, 50.11 percent against 49.89 percent for his opponent.[17] The FMLN could really not have hoped for a better political outcome—just over twenty years after the end of the civil war, they had won the presidency twice and had become a major political force in the Legislative Assembly. With these electoral victories, would the FMLN be able to carry out the revolutionary changes that had motivated the Christian, popular, and revolutionary movements in the first place?

A Democratic El Salvador

Despite the political achievements—free and fair elections and the FMLN becoming a key political party—the country and people of El Salvador remain in a state of economic crisis. Rodríguez suggests that from an economic perspective, "all we achieved was some transfer of lands. The economic reality has not changed; what has changed is the political reality." He fears that political violence has not only continued but may also increase in the future. He notes, "We see signs of death squads again;[18] wire taps are being used, and the rationale is to fight gangs, but they are used politically." "This might be fine in a normal country," he continues, "like Costa Rica, but not in El Salvador." Rodríguez is also concerned about corruption. He believes that "money is in abundance" but that graft either raises the costs of projects or prevents them from being carried out. The issue of debt and public works has divided the FMLN, because some party members believe the government should stop taking out large loans, while other members argue that the government needs money to fund projects for the poor. Rodríguez recalls that after the 2001 earthquakes the government borrowed about $162 million to rebuild hospitals that had been damaged, but as of 2007 none of the hospitals had benefited from the loan. As in the past, social programs and services in the country are woefully underfunded. Health costs are high, and retirement pensions are meager and not available to many. According to Rodríguez, all of these problems are exacerbated by the "high cost of living, dollarization and [the high cost] of fuel." As he thinks about whether the fight was worth it, Rodríguez is realistic: "Did we have to have such killing, such sacrifice for only this? But, it was necessary to do it, because if not we would still have our heads bowed and have boots on our heads. It was necessary to do it because they [oligarchy and military] were so recalcitrant that we had to make that effort." While acknowledging the limits of the movement and revolution, Rodríguez continues to hold a positive attitude and believes that the FMLN can continue to fight for a better future for all Salvadorans.

Rodríguez, of course, has kept in contact with the Salvadoran church, especially those priests who shared his liberationist vision. The church became more distant from the people particularly after Fernando Sáenz Lacalle, a conservative Spaniard, became archbishop of San Salvador in April 1995. His appointment generated some resentment among priests and bishops, who felt that a Salvadoran should have been appointed archbishop. Owing to the concordance between the Vatican and the Salvadoran government, both the Vatican and the ARENA government preferred a solid turn to the right in the Salvadoran church.[19] Nevertheless, according to Rodríguez, some priests continue to subscribe to a pastoral that promotes justice and popular interests. Many of the more progressive priests in the country are in the northern areas where there are plans to mine for gold, a potential health hazard for the local people. Popular organizations are also fighting against the building of more dams. The Lempa River already has three dams, and according to Rodríguez there is talk of building two more dams that will flood lands and force people to move to other areas, similar to what happened in the 1970s with the Cerrón Grande project. A priest in the community of San Antonio del Mosco has helped to organize people to fight for their rights and to challenge the new projects.

Despite some hopeful signs, the Salvadoran church is no longer the liberationist church of the 1970s. Rodríguez points out that CEBs have declined in number, because progressive messages need to be "developed slowly in reflection" with parishioners. At times, some of the progressive priests make statements that are just as "advanced" as pronouncements made by priests in the 1970s, but those messages can "scandalize people" if not absorbed slowly with reflection. In some dioceses and in the archdiocese, the church is turning toward a more conservative, Vatican line. Rodríguez regrets that the diocese of San Vicente is still "one of the most conservative" in El Salvador, principally because former bishop Óscar Barahona, who had tried to excommunicate Rodríguez, selected conservative young men to attend the Minor Seminary "Pío XII." And, if a seminarian showed some progressive attitudes, "he would try to find a way to expel him." It is clear that some religious leaders are politically engaged, but the focus of the institutional church is now on spirituality and institutional preservation.

Although the caustic divisions of the 1970s and 1980s are over, the church continues to experience some problems owing to the legacy of liberation theology. For example, in San Esteban Catarina, every August 4 the community commemorates the anniversary of Father Macías's death at the church where he is buried. In 2005 the celebration clearly demonstrated the continued fissures within the Salvadoran church. Rodríguez recalls that the bishop of San Vicente at the time, José Luis Escobar Alas, at the last moment, decided not to attend the ceremony, and instead sent two representatives who arrived at the church wearing traditional black cassocks and spoke to no one prior to the start of the mass. Several progressive priests were also in attendance. During the mass, the conservative parish priest[20] did not say one word about Macías, even though the people in attendance from CEBs and popular organizations were there mostly to pay respects to the martyred priest. Before the service ended, one of the priests of the diocese whispered to the parish priest that a fellow priest (who was progressive) wanted to say a few words before the end of the mass. The parish priest refused the request, saying that the "priest was not of the diocese." One older priest, who had been a colleague of Macías, was finally allowed to say a few words. When this priest began to speak of Father Macías the worshippers at the church "began to become enthused." After a few minutes, though, and before the priest was done speaking of Macías, the parish priest interrupted him by singing "Blessed is God" in an effort to end the service. Rodríguez remembers that the parish priest "was singing while Ramiro was speaking!" The people at the church then began to chant loudly, "We want priests at the side of the poor." Rodríguez points out the irony that at the end of mass people are enjoined to say "Peace be with you," yet the priests were at the altar in a visible "ideological" conflict. Rodríguez was at the rear of the church because at very visible masses like this one there would sometimes be a small group who might react negatively to his presence, and even shout, "Out, guerrilla priest!" Without doubt political divisions continue both within Salvadoran society and within the church.

Rodríguez is now a family man, but he still longs for his first love, the Catholic Church. Two barriers remain: the fact that he openly has a family, and his past and present political involvement. In Marranitos people have asked him, "Why don't you celebrate mass?" Rodríguez, however, wants to be respectful to the church and to the parish priest. At times, though, after the priest finishes a service, Rodríguez will take the microphone and "reflect" with some of the parishioners who stay behind, something any parishioner could conceivably do. The issue of celibacy is a frustrating one for Rodríguez. He points out that many priests and bishops have led and continue to lead double lives: "The bishops know it, everyone knows it." He believes that it is more Christian, true to the faith, to take responsibility for children than to ignore or pretend they do not exist. Rodríguez jokes, "The children of priests are the only kids who call their father uncle." He has told some bishops that he has no problem dedicating himself to a parish, even as a layperson, but he also wants to make sure that his daughter, Ana Ruth, receives a good education. Rodríguez believes that the most important problem is not his family, his compañera, or his daughter, since "people are no longer scandalized by that."[21] His principal problem is the "political question." The church is still very leery of priests or laypersons who "are too political."

As in the past, El Salvador's domestic policies are conditioned by its relationship to the United States. Rodríguez wryly admits that, while El Salvador cannot break relations with the United States, the notion of sovereignty is "a little bit romantic." He points out that El Salvador is now dollarized and that the United States has a "military base" for anti-narcotics purposes at Comalapa, where the international airport is located. In addition, El Salvador's economic policies are to a large extent determined by U.S.-promoted neoliberal policies. Although the FMLN has "not been in agreement with privatization," these policies continue to be promoted. The telephone system in the country has already been privatized. Many essential services, such as electricity, health care, even water, are susceptible to privatization.

As of 2007, the "commercialization" of electricity had been privatized, but not the production and distribution networks.

Failure in Success? Democracy and Social Justice

The FMLN, the FDR, and the popular organizations did not defeat the Salvadoran government, either during the mass mobilizations of the 1970s or during the civil war. In that sense, they failed to take power and make the reforms they desired in the 1970s or the revolutionary changes that they then demanded once the FMLN was formed and the civil war ensued. Likewise, the state and its allies, despite their strength, material resources, and massive external support, were unable to defeat the popular movement, the politico-military groups, and political opposition. The stalemate led to a negotiated settlement that gave political power to the FMLN but ignored the fundamental goal that motivated the opposition movements that emerged in the 1970s in the first place—economic justice. The justification for this compromise on the part of the opposition was that, once the FMLN was able to compete as a political party, most Salvadorans would gravitate to the party and then, once in power, important transformations could at last be carried out. As the electoral process in El Salvador progressed, the FMLN in fact became increasingly stronger, and in less than two decades won the presidency and the largest bloc of seats in the Legislative Assembly. The members of the movements of the 1970s, who demanded political rights and a more just economic order, had finally attained enough political power to carry out some of the changes they desired.

As Rodríguez and others point out, however, El Salvador remains a country mired in social and economic problems, where the poor struggle incessantly for survival. Economic justice is as far off as the Promised Land. Did the Christian movement succeed or fail? The answer is that it succeeded in bringing democracy to the country, eliminating military government and ending repression against the political opposition, but failed to force the state to bring about reforms that would benefit the poor, particularly land reform. This is a conclusion that Rodríguez and many others acknowledge. The important question then is, why did the Christian and popular movements that emerged in the 1970s, which then joined forces with the politico-military organizations, fail to achieve their goal of economic justice once democracy returned to El Salvador?

One potential answer to this question is that once democracy was achieved, those who wanted to carry out economic reforms that would help the poor attain better lives represented only a part of the electorate. Had the state been defeated in the 1970s or 1980s, the opposition could have carried out significant or radical changes in the aftermath of revolution, as happened in numerous revolutions in Latin America in the twentieth century. However, in a democratic process, only a tremendous amount of popular support would allow one political party to carry out significant reforms. Even the 2009 elections did not give the FMLN a sufficient mandate to transform the country, despite the fact that it won the presidency for the first time. Although the FMLN won the presidency again in 2014, the strength of the party in the legislature was still not sufficient to carry out bold reforms. This can be seen as a result of both the strength and weakness of democracy.[22] On one hand, democracy represents all points of view, and thus one point of view, no matter how moral or just it may be, cannot impose its will on a society. Under a democratic system, the FMLN can carry out transformative projects only if it gains enormous support from the population, which it has not been able to achieve. On the other hand, the failure of the FMLN to bring about economic justice can be attributed to the fact that democracy is still a political regime dominated by elites who are responsive mostly to the wealthy. The oligarchy still has tremendous political influence even in the democratic game.

The notion that elected political leaders respond principally to the needs of the economic elite rather than the poor gets us back to the study of leadership. One of the problems with reaching a stalemate in an armed conflict was the need for compromise. When the FMLN negotiated a settlement, rebel leaders opted for political power rather than demanding economic justice. This choice suggests that opposition leaders may have been more interested in attaining power than pushing for economic change. The government and oligarchy, of course, would probably have never accepted a reverse deal—economic changes instead of letting the FMLN become a political party—but the outcome suggests that the FMLN leaders as well as the opposition political parties (under the banner of the FDR) were mostly interested in gaining political power. Perhaps one of the lessons we can learn about leadership is that, although opposition leaders often use justice as a rallying cry, most political entrepreneurs in the final analysis are motivated chiefly by the quest for power. They can achieve that power mostly by accommodating the interests of the wealthy.

Even Padre Rodríguez ended up attaining political power while the poor of El Salvador awaited a better life. Yet Rodríguez appears to be a unique sort of leader who fought first for the liberation of his parishioners and then for the interests of his constituents. Once the war ended, his principal aim was to return to the Catholic Church, not to stay in the FMLN in hopes of becoming a government or political leader. Also, when he was elected as a deputy in the Legislative Assembly, Rodríguez donated much of his salary and continues to live very frugally. One lesson from his life story is that scholars who study leadership should examine the qualities of leaders who make greater efforts to represent the average citizen rather than those who are seeking mostly power and wealth.

7

One Priest's Quest for the Promised Land

"'El Chele' David has always been a leader"

Just north of Apastepeque, we turned off the Pan American Highway, which runs east-west through El Salvador, and entered a narrow dirt road that took us northeast toward the hamlet of Calderas, home to Los Huatales, the Rodríguez Rivera hacienda. Alex Bonilla, Rodríguez's driver, maneuvered the car, while David Rodríguez and Mercedes Henríquez shared the back seat. The curvy road is lined spottily by trees that prevented me from seeing very far into the distance, but not long after turning off the main highway and making a few soft turns I saw some structures in the distance. This was my first visit to Rodríguez's former homestead. "There it is!" he blurted out with enthusiasm. "There is the ermita." Ahead, on the right side of the road, we could now see the small church that Lisandro had built in Calderas. Rather than continue to his family home, we decided to stop at the chapel, painted off-white with rust-brown trim, a large, dark green door at its center. Although the structure is relatively small and modest, once inside I was taken aback by the elegance and beauty of the altar, made of rich mahogany and probably ten or twelve feet high. At the center was the colorful, iconic image of the Virgin of Guadalupe, Calderas's patron saint. Outside I noticed two iron bells at one side of the chapel. Rodríguez pointed out to me that the bells were named Raquelita and Lupita, after his sisters. These same bells, decades earlier, summoned the Rodríguez Rivera family and the people of the area to Sunday mass.

We continued down the road a short way, passing a row of small, humble wooden homes on our right, and Rodríguez expressed again, albeit with some hesitation, "There it is, there it is." All I could see was an old

Figure 7.1. The small church built by Rodríguez's father at Calderas. Photo by author, January 2008.

stone fence, but further down the road I could make out a black metal gate, with long spikes shooting skyward, and the tiled roof of a house that ran alongside the eroded fence. It was clear to me that this had not been a modest home, since the fence, though in an advanced state of deterioration, was made of expertly placed stones, with roof tiles lining the top. The gate was locked, but Alex, with his habitual enthusiasm and initiative, said he would see if someone would let us in. He returned quickly, and the gate was now magically open. No one greeted us, but Alex told us that we could enter the property and look around, having received approval from the current owner. Once inside the gate, I could see what Rodríguez had seen as a young man: a bucolic landscape with green rolling hills and numerous livestock. Rodríguez pointed out to me that the house had been reconstructed. "The corridor ran through here," he said with boyhood enthusiasm; and, pointing to an area where there was now a carport, he said: "This is where I had classes." We walked away from the house, toward a jutting hill in the distance, and Rodríguez pointed to where the old sugar mill, the *trapiche*, used to be. "This was the center of activity during the sugar harvest," he said with satisfaction. When we walked back to the main house he pointed out a structure that was but a pile of bricks and said quietly, "This used to be the small schoolhouse that my father had built." At this point, Rodríguez's mood began to change. He was visibly saddened and nostalgic. Henríquez noticed his change in mood as well, and said with tenderness, "David, don't get like this; it happened a long time ago." We decided to leave. I then found out that this had been Rodríguez's first visit to Calderas since the early 1980s, when the military burned and plundered his home. The memories of the tragedy that his family had experienced quickly overwhelmed him. A positive, cheerful, although at times stoic man was filled with grief.

It had been over thirty years since Rodríguez had made the fateful decision to join the FPL and take the revolutionary path. That decision cost him dearly. He lost his calling—the priesthood. Rodríguez will never again be a "pastor of souls," as he had written to his mother so many years ago. He lost

Figure 7.2. Remnants of the fence at the Rodríguez Rivera family finca in Calderas. Photo by author, January 2008.

his family home and, more importantly, his close-knit family. His mother, brother, and two sisters had moved away from El Salvador. The civil war had wrecked his life and those of countless others, but it was his liberationist activities to a large extent that had turned him from a respected priest to a wanted rebel. Why did Rodríguez take such a bold, dangerous, and eventually costly path?

Why Did Padre Rodríguez, Why Would a Campesino, Choose Rebellion?

In the 1970s, El Salvador was primed for political contention. The poor, particularly campesinos, had every justification to engage in contentious political behavior to demand a better life. Their economic situation was dehumanizing and desperate, and when they tried to express their concerns, they were ignored at best and repressed at worst. Professionals, students, leaders of political parties, intellectuals, and Catholic leaders all agreed that dramatic changes were necessary for the modernization of the country and for the good of the people. Salvadorans began to organize to oppose the status quo in the early 1970s, to a large extent because of the unjust economic and political systems in which the poor, and others, lived. This palpable injustice, however, cannot alone explain the rise of rebelliousness at this specific historical moment. For decades, the Salvadoran peasant had lived at the margins of the economy and political system, yet only on sporadic occasions did the poor participate in attempts at contentious political behavior, as happened in the Matanza of 1932, when an uprising led to the slaughter of about ten thousand Salvadorans.[1] Decades went by, and both peasants and leaders remained relatively passive. No doubt, hesitance to act contentiously had a great deal to do with the Salvadoran government's tight control of the society, allowing a potential opposition little opportunity to take form. This was particularly true for the campesinos and rural workers, who were legally prohibited from organizing.

Religious leaders had helped the poor for centuries. However, their efforts had been mostly rhetorical or through various charities. These actions certainly helped many poor families, but they never resulted in contentious actions or any widespread movement to promote transformative changes in the economic or political structure. And so, poverty, misery, and political exclusion continued as before. Then, in 1970, after Vatican II and the 1968 Medellín Conference had encouraged the preferential option for the poor, Archbishop Chávez y González convened the first pastoral week of reflection to bring together religious leaders so they could think about how to better serve the poor. The result of that watershed meeting was that the most progressive priests and nuns in the country, along with some from other countries, came away energized, and embraced a new pastoral plan—an injustice frame—that would shake El Salvador to its core. No longer would priests discuss the needs of the poor only in their sermons. No longer would nuns teach about the condition of the poor only in Catholic schools. From then on a large number of El Salvador's priests and nuns would teach lay leaders and the poor, using the Bible, that their condition of poverty was not God's will, as the church had suggested in the past. These priests and nuns did not just teach, but rather trained and organized the poor so they could help themselves. Religious leaders were able to do this because the Catholic Church as a respected global and national institution provided the political opportunity and key resources for effective organization in a country where political organizing was a dangerous endeavor. The group of ideas of Vatican II and Medellín thus served as a key causal factor in the rise of contentious political behavior starting in 1970 in El Salvador.

We have seen that Padre David Rodríguez was instrumental in this effort, since he trained lay leaders and created dozens of CEBs in his parish, and also taught classes at one of the national training centers, Centro Naranjos. Moreover, Rodríguez helped to found the Union of Peasant Workers of San Vicente, which became a national organization that eventually joined forces with FECCAS to create the largest peasant organization in Salvadoran history, the FTC. Although one of the most active and well-known leaders in this religious movement, Rodríguez was but one of dozens of priests and nuns who helped to galvanize poor Salvadorans into taking a greater political role. The extensive state repression against the church is testimony to the effective organizing work of Salvadoran priests and nuns. Why would the state repress a revered institution for more than a decade if it did not fear the actions of religious leaders? It was this focus on taking action that made the new pastoral truly revolutionary and represented a dramatic break from the traditional practices of the church. The pastoral week, therefore, helped a number of religious leaders in El Salvador to undergo a conversion or awakening that turned them into activists working on behalf of the poor, who were unable or unwilling at the time to demand their own rights. Once priests and nuns stood by the marginalized, the poor saw that they had a potentially strong ally on their side, which made it easier, more rational, for them to decide to engage in contentious political behavior.

El Salvador's revolutionary movement has been characterized as principally peasant-based, including both traditional peasants and rural wage earners. Since the vast majority of Salvadorans lived in rural areas in 1970, a large-scale contentious movement could emerge only if supported by the peasantry. Consequently, many analysts see the peasantry as the crucial force behind the popular movement of the 1970s and the revolutionary movement of the 1980s. Indeed, without the peasantry the leaders of the movements that emerged in the 1970s would have been isolated and ineffective. The two most important politico-military organizations, the FPL and the ERP, started out as urban-based revolutionary groups, because they did not believe that a rural guerrilla war could succeed in El Salvador, owing to the small size and high population density of the country as well as the absence of large mountain ranges. It was not until the Christian movement demonstrated its potential that the FPL and the ERP began to reach out to organized Christians in rural areas, roughly in 1974 when representatives of these organizations contacted Rodríguez. And it was not until 1980 that the FPL and the ERP moved their principal armed units to the countryside and became fully committed to carrying out a rural guerrilla war. The popular organizations, principally the BPR and the ERP's Ligas Populares (Popular Leagues), made it possible for the revolutionary movement to present a truly existential threat to the government in the 1970s, since their existence demonstrated widespread support for a desire to dramatically alter the status quo. Once the civil war commenced in earnest in 1981, it was these popular organizations that provided the experienced recruits for the FMLN. As we have seen, most of these recruits had been trained and gained experience as catechists and Delegates of the Word, or had been members of CEBs.[2] Salvadoran religious leaders had been the ones to "form" those same recruits, who had first demanded reforms and later, after the repression, decided to help overthrow the system. It was religious leaders, not the leaders of the politico-military organizations, who first awakened and raised the insurgent consciousness of the Salvadoran poor.

Padre Rodríguez, like other religious leaders, embraced the liberationist cause not with the hopes of becoming a revolutionary but with the expectation that the new pastoral would help the campesinos of his parish to achieve a better standard of living and some political enfranchisement. His goals were reformist and local, not revolutionary or national, and were guided by the church's new pastoral. Only after the state repressed his parishioners for their activism, most importantly at La Cayetana, and the state captured and tortured his fellow parish priest, Father Barahona, did Rodríguez make what he refers to as a "qualitative jump" to incorporate himself into the FPL and lead a clandestine, revolutionary life. His principal rationale for taking this bold decision was that he felt compelled to "accompany" the people he had helped to form. Additionally, he knew that joining the FPL was the best insurance policy against being captured, tortured, or killed, since he had become a wanted man himself. Rodríguez had little difficulty in justifying his decision: the church's just-war theory allowed for violence in unjust situations, and Pope Paul VI had stated that in cases of "long-standing tyranny"—which clearly fit the case of El Salvador—rebellion was justified. After the repression, many other Christians also came to the conclusion that rebellion was their best, if not their only, option. Consequently, state repression provided the breeding ground for the radicalization of both religious leaders and campesinos.

Rodríguez's decision to join one of the politico-military groups was a relatively unpopular one among nuns and priests, however. Of the dozens of liberationist priests, only a handful—perhaps six to eight—joined one of these organizations. Two of the clerics who joined a politico-military organization died in confrontations with government forces. The majority of the liberationists, priests and nuns alike, either left the country (some of them being expelled) or stayed in El Salvador and ceased to take an active role in the liberationist cause. Some of them, however, certainly sympathized with and even assisted the popular and revolutionary movement, but never to the extent the Salvadoran government claimed, as demonstrated by the failed effort to find weapons at the University of Central America when six Jesuits, their housekeeper, and her daughter were brutally murdered. No doubt Rodríguez was more willing to rebel than other religious leaders. A number of factors may help to explain his bold move and why other liberationists remained more on the sidelines. Since his brother was also a liberationist priest who did not accompany the people, we can rule out the upbringing of the two brothers. While they both had the same parents and religious training, Benigno did not attend the first pastoral week, did not attend the Christians for Socialism meeting, and did not have the close associations that his brother did with Juan Macho or Bernardo

Boulang, the two foreign priests who were bent on promoting the new pastoral. Benigno also was not involved in Campesino University, a veritable training ground for political awakening and contention. No doubt other factors may have also had an effect on David Rodríguez, including his natural boldness (Benigno was more timid), as well as his initial close associations with FPL leaders who courted him since he was a popular leader. Finally, because he became politically active early on, Rodríguez became an early target of the oligarchy and thus needed protection, which the FPL was more than willing to provide. His brother, on the other hand, was never in the gun sights of the state.

In summation, the decision to participate in contentious political activity is first and foremost driven and facilitated by the existence of unjust political or economic conditions that generate serious and legitimate grievances. Objective conditions of injustice alone, however, did not spark the wave of contentiousness that hit El Salvador in 1970. When the new ideas of Vatican II and Medellín washed over El Salvador like a volcanic eruption, a number of priests and nuns experienced a conversion, embraced a new pastoral mission that focused on liberating the poor, and then constructed and diffused a highly acceptable and motivational injustice frame. These religious leaders then in turn "awakened," trained, and mobilized the poor, who now felt they had a strong ally and thus could fight for their rights. New ideas, entrepreneurial leaders, and prevailing injustice all conspired in the early 1970s to yield a strong Christian movement in El Salvador. Since the church was at the time still considered to be a traditional institution, liberationist priests had the opportunity to organize themselves and their parishioners, enjoying a wide array of organizational opportunities and resources. These fortuitous circumstances allowed the Christian movement to grow in strength for five years before the government began to take notice and began to repress the movement. It was not until 1977, however, that the state chose to brutally attack the leaders and followers of the movement, and by then the Christian movement had achieved formidable strength. Organized Christians, however, became radicalized and eventually opted for rebellion only when the state engaged in wanton repression. Most Salvadorans in the 1970s paid little attention to, or cared little about, the repression of the state against the violent politico-military organizations. It was the state's repression of Christians and their religious leaders that enraged Salvadorans the most.

Why Did Traditional Catholicism Become Politically Engaged, and How Did This Choice Affect the Church?

The experiences of Padre Rodríguez and El Salvador suggest that the adoption of new religious ideas, which produced an acceptable, coherent injustice frame, was the first step toward fomenting widespread contentious politics in El Salvador. In 1970, the week of pastoral reflection introduced these ideas to many progressive Catholic leaders. No doubt a number of priests had heard about and even started to implement these ideas prior to 1970, particularly some of the foreign priests, like Juan Macho and Bernardo Boulang. However, it was the week of reflection that galvanized and inspired many progressive church leaders, at least partly because it became clear to them that the new pastoral was sanctioned by their archbishop, Luis Chávez y González. As we have seen, however, the ideas that inspired the pastoral week originated not in El Salvador but at the Vatican just a few years earlier, and then diffused to Latin America where they were validated by the 1968 conference at Medellín.

The pope and Vatican made the bold decision to revolutionize Catholic social doctrine both to improve the living conditions of the poor in the Catholic realm and for more selfish, institutional reasons. Theologians and many bishops, as well as countless local priests and nuns, had become increasingly concerned about the plight of the poor. In Latin America, particularly, the poor seemed to be in a constant state of precariousness, both economically and politically. Consequently, a desire for social justice, a key element of the church's social doctrine since the late 1800s, was an important driving force for promoting a doctrine that would attempt to distance the Church of Saint Peter from the powerful and move it close to the poor and the marginalized. A second motivation was institutional survival. The church was losing its flock in droves, particularly in Latin America, where secular ideologies and Protestantism were convincing some believers that Catholicism was of little relevance to their lives. Consequently, an important reason for embracing the poor was to return the church to a position that would appeal more to the vast majority of parishioners, who also happened to be those who were "poor" and "afflicted," as *Gaudium et Spes* announced. The move to a preferential option for the poor, then, also represented a desire to compete with both Protestantism and secular ideologies such as socialism and Marxism.

In effect, then, the objective conditions that bred contention—political marginalization and economic injustice—were also instrumental in indirectly inspiring new ideas that would later convince priests and nuns to challenge the status quo and mobilize the poor. While the ideas promulgated at Vatican II were the immediate cause of contention and mobilization at a particular point in time, the unjust political and economic conditions present in Latin America were instrumental in convincing the church that a preferential option for the poor was necessary, not only to bring justice to the poor but also to help preserve the church's role in Latin American society. Leadership was important at this point as well, since both John XXIII and Paul VI both embraced a new, bold paradigm for Catholicism that led to the preferential option for the poor.

Eventually, the bishops, priests, and nuns who actively pursued the new pastoral mission came into conflict with conservative prelates and the Vatican itself, the very source of the progressive doctrinal changes. By 1983, as the Salvadoran civil war was raging, the Vatican warned that some elements of liberation theology were dangerous and deviated from Catholic doctrine. The admonitions came from Pope John Paul II but were developed by Cardinal Joseph Ratzinger (later to become Pope Benedict XVI), who at the time served as the prefect of the Congregation for the Doctrine of the Faith, the group of bishops who determine what is and is not consistent with the tenets of Catholicism.[3] What happened between 1965, when Vatican II finished its work, and the mid-1980s to cause the Vatican to turn its back on the doctrine that placed the church on the side of the poor? The answer is complex and lies both in the new doctrine itself and in the institutional interests of the Catholic Church.

When Vatican II and the Medellín Conference called for the church to side with the poor, few prelates and clergy envisioned that by siding with the dispossessed some priest and nuns would find themselves calling for the same economic changes as socialist and Marxist groups, and that they would also end up favoring a socialist economic system. In addition to flirting with secular economic ideas, namely, Marxist-inspired class analysis, the Vatican eventually became convinced that liberationists had entered the realm of political activism. Rodríguez serves as a striking example, since he, like many liberationists, embraced socialism, actively organized the poor, and took sides in the Salvadoran civil war, eventually joining the FPL, a Marxist guerrilla organization. Although he serves as an extreme example, it was the actions of priests and nuns like him that most unnerved the Holy See. The Vatican therefore decided that liberationists had gone too far, in that their radical Catholicism had encouraged bishops, priests, nuns, and theologians to embrace socialist ideas and become too politically active. As a result, the Vatican warned that some aspects of liberation theology were inconsistent with Catholic doctrine.

The Vatican's displeasure with liberation theology had both doctrinal and practical dimensions. The church had always been critical of Marxism. As an atheistic, secular ideology, Marxism could never be reconciled with Catholicism. At the same time, since the encyclical *Rerum Novarum* of 1891, the church had also begun to impugn capitalism. Similarly, while the church abhorred the use of violence, it had also given rise to just-war theory, and Pope Paul VI had himself suggested that violence was legitimate under certain circumstances. The church's return to a more conservative stance therefore had as much to do with institutional preservation as with doctrinal (or ideological) questions. Once liberationist priests and nuns began to promote the interests of the poor, conservative and, particularly, wealthy Catholics began to distance themselves from the church. Not only did many conservative parishioners become estranged from Catholicism, but many of them stopped supporting the church financially. In El Salvador's rural areas, the church depended upon the generosity of the finca and hacienda owners, the country's oligarchy. In the areas where liberationist priests operated, the landed elite stopped giving donations to the church and even began to verbally attack liberationist priests. Soon after he embraced the liberationist cause, Rodríguez clashed with the wealthy landowners of his parish, and Bishop Pedro Aparicio said to him, "You are ruining the parish!" The Catholic Church's hesitance to continue siding with the poor, therefore, had a pragmatic, economic dimension.

The church's decision to eventually denounce certain aspects of liberation theology also derived from the questioning of authority and the internal divisions that liberationist ideas generated within the church. First, the liberationist cause led to what was eventually called the "popular church." In El Salvador the founding of CONIP represented this popular vision of Catholicism that harkened back to the original, persecuted church of the catacombs. Consistent with the ideas of liberation theology, supporters of the popular church believed that the heart and soul of Catholicism was the people and the Gospel, not the physical churches, not the Vatican, not the pope, not the saints. The popular church also challenged the authority of local bishops. We have seen how Rodríguez and lay leaders of the parish of Tecoluca questioned the authority of Bishop Aparicio, at times clashing with the prelate. In effect, liberationist ideas promoted popular participation in an institution that was highly hierarchical. The Vatican could not accept this bottom-up version of Catholicism, which dismissed and questioned papal authority and infallibility.

The liberationist cause, which was meant to revive the church, led to deep divisions within the church. Even before liberation theology emerged in the early 1970s, conservative bishops and theologians had started to criticize some of the changes introduced by Vatican II and Medellín. In fact, Vatican II had been a highly contentious meeting where bishops from various camps struggled to get their positions on particular matters to prevail. Even though most documents achieved nearly unanimous support from the bishops present, a small yet powerful group of bishops and cardinals were adamantly opposed to some of the changes made at the council. Some of those who opposed the progressive changes were bishops and cardinals with high-level positions in the Vatican.[4] Ideological divisions were also prominent in Latin America. Many of Latin America's conservative bishops did not attend the Medellín Conference, since they did not favor what they knew would be a move toward greater support for the progressive ideas that had emanated from Vatican II. Once liberation theology spread in Latin America and was perceived as being influenced by Marxist ideas, conservative bishops, priests, and nuns began to distance themselves from the ideas of the Medellín Conference and criticize those church leaders who promoted liberationist ideas. The Vatican became concerned not only about the financial losses of the church but also about the acrimonious divisions that were emerging within the church. In El Salvador, divisions among the bishops meant that the liberationist pastoral was not promoted by a segment of priests and nuns, since the majority of bishops were on the conservative end of the spectrum. The liberationists, nevertheless, enjoyed tremendous support in that Archbishop Chávez y González and then Archbishop Romero, after his rapid conversion, supported the new pastoral. No doubt, if all the Salvadoran bishops had been united in support of the new pastoral, the Christian and popular movements would have been monumentally powerful.

The Vatican was also concerned about the violence that had been unleashed against the church. While martyrdom is a badge of honor in most religions,[5] the Vatican recoiled from a situation where priests were killed on a consistent basis for what church conservatives viewed as misguided political involvement. When Archbishop Romero was murdered in 1980, the Vatican was eerily silent, refusing to publicly condemn the Salvadoran government. It is possible that the Vatican simply did not want to take sides or sacrifice its relationship with a government that was under siege by a liberationist church. In El Salvador between 1970 and 1993, right-wing death squads or Salvadoran security forces murdered or disappeared eighteen priests, Archbishop Romero, and four nuns (see table 1).[6] In addition, foreign priests were expelled from the country, religious leaders were tortured, churches were ransacked and bombed, the Catholic radio station was destroyed on several occasions, and thousands of lay leaders were murdered, often brutally. Such violence, directed against the church and its believers, had to be stopped. The Vatican must have felt that the best way to stop the persecution of the church was to get priests and nuns out of the political realm, out of the crossfire, and back to offering mostly spiritual guidance.

The outcome of these concerns was that the church pulled back from the progressive efforts of the 1960s and early 1970s, and the opportunities for political organization and mass mobilization that existed then quickly dried up. Pope John Paul II, with the help of Cardinal Ratzinger, reined in the liberationists, warning them that promoting the most radical version of liberation theology would result in reprimand and silencing. Several liberation theologians were called to Rome for consultation, and some were silenced, such as Bernardo Boff and, more recently, Jon Sobrino, who has lived in El Salvador since 1957.[7] However, even before the mid-1980s, in El Salvador, the murder of Óscar Romero greatly undermined the Christian movement in that most Christians lost the political opportunities and organizational resources they had enjoyed in the 1970s.

Today the church in El Salvador is much more traditional, although some priests, as Rodríguez points out, still try to focus on the interests of the poor. After the death of Archbishop Rivera y Damas in 1995, the Vatican appointed Fernando Sáenz Lacalle, a conservative Spaniard and member of Opus Dei, as archbishop. One priest who taught at the Major Seminary in San Salvador while Sáenz Lacalle was archbishop said that those who worked at the seminary felt that the archbishop was "trying to fill the institution with Opus Dei members." After the archbishop's retirement, the pope appointed the conservative bishop of San Vicente, José Luis Escobar Alas, as archbishop. Clearly, the Vatican wanted to ensure that the bishops in El Salvador did not stray from the newer, conservative line.

Table 1. Priests murdered in El Salvador, 1970–1993[1]

1970	Father Nicolás Rodríguez Aguilar, November 28
1977	Father Rutilio Grande, March 12
	Father Alfonso Navarro, May 11
1978	Father Ernesto Barrera, November 28
1979	Father Octavio Ortiz Luna, January 20
	Father Rafael Palacios, June 20
	Father Alirio Macías, August 4
1980	Archbishop Óscar A. Romero, March 24
	Father Cosme Spessotto, June 14
	Father Manuel Reyes, October 6
	Father Ernesto Ábrego, November 23 (disappeared)
	Father Marcial Serrano, November 28 (disappeared)
1986	Father César Valle, April 11[2]
1989	Father Ignacio Ellacuría, November 16
	Father Amando López, November 16
	Father Joaquín López y López, November 16
	Father Ignacio Martín-Baró, November 16
	Father Segundo Montes, November 16
	Father Juan Ramón Moreno, November 16
1993	Monsignor Joaquín Ramos, June 25[3]

Sources: Guerra, Tobar, Moran, and Villalobos, *Testigos*; and David Rodríguez.

1. A few of the murdered priests are not mentioned in the text. Rodríguez wanted to make sure that the names of all the murdered priests were included in the book, and I thought the best way to do it was in list form so that all the names could be seen in one place. He also expressed concern that El Salvador's diocesan priests, which represent most of those who were killed, had not been sufficiently commemorated.
2. No source that I know of mentions César Valle as a priest who was killed during the conflict, most likely because he left the priesthood in 1970. Rodríguez points out, however, that Valle joined the ERP in the late 1970s and was eventually killed in the San Salvador volcano after having been captured once and exchanged for the release of José Napoleón Duarte's daughter, whom the ERP had captured.
3. Ramos was the second bishop killed, and the government argued that the murder was perpetrated by someone who tried to rob him. Ramos was vicar to the military, but the armed forces never liked him and had wanted the conservative bishop Freddy Delgado instead.

Rodríguez points out that the church currently has two options: "a spiritualist pastoral, or a committed pastoral." The problem is that the committed path is "still dangerous," and the hierarchical church no longer seems to be very interested in this path, for the reasons expressed above. Rodríguez laments that the church has returned to a more "individualistic" pastoral, where priests work in "isolation," as before, and the joint pastorals of the 1970s are seldom applied and are mostly spiritualistic. The bitter divisions are gone, the popular church is no more, and priests and nuns are no longer targets, but the preferential option for the poor, as a church imperative, is pretty much in the dustbin of history. The poor of El Salvador, for the most part, have lost their powerful ally and may have to return to fatalism.[8]

Did Liberationists Help to Produce a More Just Society in El Salvador?

The battle for economic justice and the liberation of the poor was fought to a large extent in the ideological arena. Just as new ideas were essential for the emergence of rebelliousness among some religious leaders and Salvadorans, anti-communism was indispensable for the oligarchy and the United States to defeat the challenge to the status quo. When landowners called Rodríguez a communist, when the Salvadoran right-wing media labeled liberationist clerics "red priests" and "third-world priests," and when Bishop Aparicio stated that Rodríguez was teaching "communism" rather than the Gospel, the debate over whether the poor should have higher salaries, or better health care, or more land, or simply be treated like human beings was derailed into an argument over simplistic versions of competing economic ideologies, of communism versus capitalism. The strength of anti-communism is underscored by the fact that in Catholic El Salvador the oligarchy and military accepted the killing of priests who were deemed to be influenced by socialism even though those priests were following the ideas that had been promulgated by Vatican II and the Medellín Conference. Those who defended the status quo decided to label them Marxists rather than Christians. Archbishop Romero, in his homilies and pastoral letters, always cited key church documents to demonstrate that his admonitions were not the product of a wayward, radical perspective but derived directly from official Catholic doctrine. Likewise, Rodríguez's plunge into economic and political arenas came only after his church and his archbishop promoted the preferential option for the poor. The pleadings of the archbishop and the liberationists fell on deaf ears, however, and the quest for economic justice in tiny El Salvador became one more example of the perennial conflict over the proper distribution of resources, expressed in an ideological charade. The oligarchs "owned" the fertile land, which they had taken from the indigenous population over time and now held with ardent, moralistic tenacity.[9] Land was the source of their wealth, and they would keep it no matter the cost—savage repression, the murder of priests and nuns, economic ruin, and a civil war.

At the 1970 congress on land reform, even before the liberationist movement had started in the country, Father José Inocencio Alas forcefully presented the church's conviction that land reform was desperately needed in the country. As mentioned above, after his presentation Father Alas was kidnapped, beaten, drugged, and left naked on a mountaintop. The representatives of the oligarchy walked out of the conference, not wanting to even debate the topic. At that time, religious leaders like Alas and Rodríguez simply wanted a little social justice, so they supported land reform. The first politico-military organization that called for socialism—the FPL—was just emerging, so the oligarchs could not claim that land reform was the goal only of the revolutionaries. The dreaded Catholic-communist link, therefore, could not even be postulated at the time. Yet as early as 1970, the right-wing in El Salvador was already willing to attack religious leaders who interfered with their power and wealth. In the same year of Father Alas's ordeal, in November 1970, the first Catholic priest in El Salvador was murdered, Father Nicolás Rodríguez Aguilar, because he had called for social justice and confronted landowners.[10] At this time, the church did not anticipate the systematic attacks against priests and nuns that would ensue in just a few years.

In short, then, the church and other opposition groups that wanted reform prior to the civil war were unable to achieve their reformist goals because the oligarchy had a vice grip on power. They controlled the country's best arable land, the national wealth, the state, and the security apparatus. Nothing would pry the land from their hands. But military force and wealth alone did not allow the oligarchy to maintain its power. They also used anti-communism and support for capitalism to convince many other Salvadorans that the opposition, including the liberationist priests and nuns, were nothing more than the lackeys of international Marxism, bent on exterminating capitalism and democracy. Yet it was the oligarchy-controlled state that trounced on both democracy and competitive capitalism, since the key element of Salvadoran elections was fraud and the oligarchy represented an oligopoly. In the face of such strong resistance, and then harsh repression, many of those who wanted reform became radicalized and decided to follow the armed path to revolution. The Christian and popular movements that emerged and gathered tremendous organizational strength owing to political opportunities in the 1970s, therefore, were no match for a unified, powerful state, backed by a wealthy oligarchy, that used anti-communism to denigrate and invalidate reformist appeals. Even limited success for the liberationists was therefore frustrated by this vast power and the willingness to exterminate any challenges to that power.

During the civil war, many liberationists, both leaders and followers, supported the revolutionary, popular struggle. However, the FMLN, as the armed element of the revolutionary opposition, was unable to topple the Salvadoran state. There are a number of reasons for this. While it was not sufficiently unified, and certainly made many mistakes, as Rodríguez acknowledges, the FMLN had tremendous popular support and would most likely have defeated the Salvadoran government had it not been for the massive support that came from Washington. Many within the oligarchy had moved their money and families to Miami once the civil war started, their commitment to staying in their country quickly wavering. Within the armed forces, reformist elements were still present that may have been swayed to force changes, as happened briefly in the 1979 coup. Once the U.S. government made a strong commitment to shore up the Salvadoran government, however, the resolve of the armed forces and the oligarchy strengthened considerably. In addition to the resources and symbolic support, U.S. pressure on the Salvadoran government to hold elections in 1984 and to carry out some sort of land reform must have also defused some opposition to the Salvadoran state. Despite the tremendous flow of military and economic assistance and the political reforms, however, the Salvadoran government failed to defeat the FMLN. The FMLN's commitment to a prolonged struggle had a lot to do with the injustice that reigned in the country and the brutal repression, but for many of its members it must have also stemmed in part from the belief that the Gospels and Jesus were on their side. If the state and oligarchy had a superpower behind them, the insurgents had a much more powerful ally.

The state's refusal to reform and its willingness to use repression prevented success in the 1970s, while state and elite unity, along with the aid of a superpower, and the weakness and divisions within the FMLN, prevented revolutionary success in the 1980s; but why has there been a failure to establish a more just society in El Salvador *after* the peace accords, *after* the end of the conflict, *after* the installation of a democratic government? We have seen that one of the failures of the peace accords was the lack of a national land-reform program and the lack of a commitment to economic justice. The FMLN leadership viewed the accords as a great victory for a number of good reasons, mainly the end of the conflict, political inclusion of the FMLN, and demilitarization of the country. However, while political exclusion had certainly been a motivation for the war, the most frequently mentioned cause for war had always been the unjust economic system in El Salvador. Entry into the political system therefore trumped the call for justice. By 1992, if not sooner, FMLN leaders had given up on establishing a revolutionary government modeled after Cuba or Vietnam, owing principally to the fall of the Soviet Union in 1991. After all, many of these leaders, as already pointed out, were initially as much Christians and social democrats as they were Marxists. The great hope of the FMLN leaders was that political inclusion would yield political power that would then allow the FMLN as a political party to make substantial economic reforms. The FMLN therefore had given up on the single-party, socialist state model and gladly embraced democracy. Soon after the end of the civil war, most FMLN leaders expressed their support for social democracy.[11] It would be unfair to criticize the FMLN for not producing a more just economic system immediately after the war's end, since the ARENA party dominated the political system from 1994 until 2009. The FMLN had hoped that the people would vote for the new party in large numbers once the war was over, but that did not occur. Consequently, the FMLN had to work to build its links to the people, as Rodríguez and others repeatedly advised. Prior to the FMLN's victory in 2009, Rodríguez pointed out: "The economic reality has not changed, what has changed is the political reality." Would political power finally allow the FMLN to carry out substantial changes that would make the lives of the poor significantly better?

In 2009 the FMLN finally won the presidency, a truly watershed moment, but since it was unable to win a majority in the legislature it proved difficult to put through substantial reforms. The problem was much broader, however, than the number of seats in the assembly. The end of the civil war coincided not only with ARENA's dominance of the political system but also with neoliberal economic reforms that washed over Latin America. The so-called Washington consensus led to major economic changes: trade liberalization, promotion of foreign investment, reduction of state expenditures—the dreaded austerity measures—and privatization. These changes, promoted by the United States, other G-7 countries, and the International Monetary Fund, symbolized the triumph of globalization and global capitalism. The FMLN's social-democratic platform stressed state intervention in the economy and increased state expenditures on social programs. Neoliberalism proposed exactly the opposite. And so, just like the calls for land reform in the 1970s, new calls for social welfare programs and state assertiveness in domestic economic development have met with intense resistance.

To win this new ideological conflict, the FMLN and elected representatives like David Rodríguez will need to organize the people of El Salvador once more. As Rodríguez has pointed out, however, the solidarity of the 1970s has withered away and has been replaced by individualism. Many FMLN leaders have become accustomed to well-paying jobs in the capital and have lost touch with the people. One distressing aspect of revolutionary leadership is that many of the leaders who called for transformative changes to improve the lives of the poor fell into complacency once they attained power, becoming much like the leaders they wanted to displace.

Once elected to office, Deputy Rodríguez served constituents rather than parishioners. According to everyone I spoke with during interviews, Rodríguez has never forgotten the poor or marginalized and has always worked hard to represent their interests. Instead of focusing on what the church should do, he says, "We need to make state institutions work for poor people." For him, the state should adopt the preferential option for the poor, which, ironically, is still the official position of the Catholic Church's social doctrine. When Rodríguez and I talked in 2013 about the current situation in El Salvador, compared to the 1970s, it was clear that he was not happy with what was happening in his country. I said to him, "Then, it looks like the parties and elections and the political opening did not resolve very much." Rodríguez responded without hesitation, "No, they didn't resolve much. The repression, that's it." He continued, saying, "Before, the campesinos, for example . . . were exploited, but at least they had their little corn . . . they had their food. Not now, at this very time . . . it is a miracle that people can live . . . the vision of young people is to leave the country." As far as Rodríguez is concerned, El Salvador is still run by an oligarchy. He says, "El Salvador is no longer run by fourteen families but by only five families." The guerrillas were not defeated, and the FMLN finally achieved the presidency in 2009 and in 2014, but the poor in El Salvador are sadly still awaiting the Promised Land.

The Graying of a Priest, Rebel, and Political Leader

After over four decades of struggle to end injustice, and despite the current problems, David Rodríguez does not regret the long, difficult road he embarked upon in 1970. "Some people say, 'we fought for nothing,'" Rodríguez laments, but he stresses that the FMLN won a "political opening which [in the past] was impossible in El Salvador." Most important, he posits, is the "ability to have public meetings or to say what you want." In addition, Rodríguez points out that the peace accords "put the military in its rightful place and reduced it in size, established a procurator for human rights, and created the National Civilian Police." He asserts that "the biggest problems are economic," like "the abandonment of agriculture, the debt, and evasion of taxes." Rodríguez points to other problems that often have economic ramifications, like corruption, delinquency and gangs, narco-trafficking, the health-care system, and education. When I asked him if he thought that the initial goal of creating a more just society in El Salvador could still be achieved, the perennially optimistic Rodríguez responded, "I think it is possible because truth always conquers lies."

David Rodríguez and his compañera, Merci Henríquez, have never married. For a long time he hung on to a hope that his church would take him back without unacceptable conditions, although that hope has now evaporated. He would also want to be married by the church and knows that this can happen only if he rejects his vows as a priest. His compañera maintains a remarkably positive attitude. When I interviewed her, she opened up immediately and recounted their love story. She said to me, her face brimming with mischief, "Did you see the movie [TV mini-drama] *The Thorn Birds*?" The reader may recall that the TV show was based on a best-selling novel about a Catholic priest who chooses the church over the woman he loves.[12] When I responded that I had indeed watched it, she said to me, conspiratorially and with delight, "Well, our story was just like that, except that I got the priest!" We laughed for quite a while.

Padre and deputy, David Rodríguez Rivera continues to struggle to help the people of El Salvador. Even before becoming a revolutionary, "Padre David" had a charisma and leadership mystique that made him stand out as one whom the church, and later the FPL and FMLN, would classify as a "natural leader." One interviewee, who was a young girl when Rodríguez first went to Tecoluca and now works at an NGO, put it succinctly: "'El Chele' David has always been a leader in whatever time

Figure 7.3. Rodríguez at the abandoned hacienda La Chenga Sola. Photo by author, January 2008.

Figure 7.4. Rodríguez, Mercedes Henríquez, and their daughter, Ana Ruth, San Salvador, El Salvador. Photo by author, May 2013.

or space where he has been." Rodríguez has indeed been an influential leader, and part of his appeal came from his music. One of his most popular songs involved his namesake David, the future king of Israel, who slew the giant Philistine warrior, Goliath. The story of David and Goliath is of course the classic tale depicting the unlikely victory of the underdog over a powerful foe. Rodríguez wrote the song "David and Goliath" to symbolize the struggle between the people of El Salvador, who were weak, poor, and defenseless, against the powerful Salvadoran state, oligarchy, and U.S. government, representing the epitome of power and wealth. The song is a ballad, including spoken verse and a chorus. One of the verses, directed at Goliath, says:

> You felt so safe with so much armor
> On this day the world will know that it was God who made the earth
> and the sky
> Prepare yourself brother it [the stone] comes for you.[13]

Padre Rodríguez tried to slay Goliath, but the giant warrior proved to be too strong, too well armored, too well financed, too close to a superpower, too prone to violence, and now virtually immune to change. In this case "Padre David" was unable to defeat Goliath. And so the Promised Land for the people of El Salvador appears to be a mirage looming on the distant horizon. Padre Rodríguez, however, despite his advanced age and the toll of Parkinson's disease, retains his mystique, his charisma, his musical acumen, his love for the Salvadoran people, including his family, and yes, his undying love for the Catholic Church.

Appendix

The Personal Interviews

The most important interviews for this book are the unstructured conversations that I had with David Rodríguez Rivera at Loyola University Chicago during May 15–25, 2007, in El Salvador during January 1–12, 2008, and in El Salvador during May 13–17, 2013. Throughout the first set of interviews, Rodríguez and I would talk in my office at Loyola University from about 9:00 a.m. until noon, and then again from around 1:00 p.m. to 4:00 p.m. The interviews are recorded, and Rodríguez does the vast majority of the talking. My initial interviews with him were unstructured in that he simply narrated his life and I asked questions only when a particular point was unclear or when I felt that he was neglecting a time period of his life. I had to make it a point to ask him about his personal life because, although a very charismatic and gregarious person, he tended to focus on events and ideas rather than his emotions or his family. At the end of his stay in Chicago, Rodríguez gave me twenty-four pages of notes he had written in the evenings while at the Jesuit residence on the Loyola campus. These notes were also a rich resource, since they included what he perceived as the key events and most influential people in his life. Rodríguez pointed out to me that my interviews with him had encouraged him to write at night. In a sense, then, his handwritten notes were an indirect product of the interview process.

As the next part of my interview plan, I traveled to El Salvador to talk to individuals who had known David Rodríguez, but naturally I also discussed many things with him during my visits to El Salvador. I was in El Salvador for a relatively short time in 2008, fifteen days, but with the help of Rodríguez, Gene Palumbo, Mercedes Henríquez, and Alex Bonilla (Rodríguez's driver) I was able to conduct a relatively large number of personal interviews that ranged from several minutes to over three hours. I conducted some of the interviews during community meetings, which meant that people would take turns leaving the meeting so I could talk with them. Also, on a few occasions a number of people gathered in one place and I would interview them one at a time. When Rodríguez was with me, however (which was seldom), he always made it a point to leave the location at which I was conducting interviews. Rodríguez was present at only a few of the interviews, and these were interviews with close friends or family members. All in all, I interviewed ninety-five individuals, which included peasants, former catechists and Delegates of the Word, priests, FMLN deputies (legislators), boyhood friends, one former teacher, former and practicing clergy, and a few family members. Alex Bonilla recorded interviews with five additional people while I was occupied in San Salvador, and he gave me a cassette tape of those interviews. I also interviewed two additional people in May 2013. Finally, I conducted one telephone interview with a former liberationist priest, Father José Inocencio Alas, which I did not record. Thus I have a total of 103 interviews, all but one recorded, with people who have known David Rodríguez.

Locations were also important. During my two weeks in El Salvador in January 2008, I visited places that were important in Rodríguez's life. In the area of Calderas, where Rodríguez grew up, I visited his boyhood home, his father's chapel and gravesite, a relative, and a number of people who had worked for Lisandro Rodríguez and had known David Rodríguez as a child and later as a priest. I also visited Apastepeque, where Rodríguez finished elementary and middle school, and interviewed his third grade teacher. I visited Santo Domingo, Rodríguez's first parish, and interviewed about a dozen people, some of whom had joined the popular movement. A number of these people had known Rodríguez before he became a liberationist priest. In San Vicente, I visited the Minor Seminary "Pío XII" and the church of Nuestra Señora del Pilar, Rodríguez's second parish. Naturally, I visited the town of Tecoluca, the church where his problems began, and interviewed a number of people who knew Rodríguez when he converted to the liberationist cause. I visited Las Pampas, where Rodríguez and other former combatants were demobilized at the end of the war, and interviewed several people who had served in the FPL and FMLN with Rodríguez. I rode in the back of a truck, up the lower third of the San Vicente volcano, with six FPL ex-guerrillas (who showered me with war stories), to visit the remnants of the hamlet of La Cayetana. I was able to speak with individuals who still remembered that dreadful event and who lost family members there. I also traveled to Cinquera, an area where Rodríguez was well known both in the 1970s and later when he worked with the FMLN. I traveled to San Carlos Lempa, to which Bishop Aparicio had transferred his wayward priest in 1983. In Marranitos, I visited Rodríguez's small house and spoke with a number of people at a weekly gathering on his property, in a community center that he had built. In San Salvador, I visited the Major Seminary "San José de la Montaña," the Metropolitan Cathedral, and Liberty Plaza and spoke with a number of people, including former priests and church leaders, two of whom had been in an FPL cell with Rodríguez. Also in the capital, I visited a number of FPL safe houses that both "Flor" (Mercedes Henríquez) and "Joaquin" (Padre Rodríguez) used as they carried out their revolutionary roles. Visiting these locations was essential to get a feel for the places and landscapes that shaped Rodríguez's life.

During the January 2008 interviews, a number of people became emotional when recounting their lives in Calderas, both because of their fond memories of the Rodríguez Rivera family and because of nostalgia for a time before the war. Even though the 1960s and 1970s were difficult years for many campesinos, those who worked for Lisandro Rodríguez look back on those years as very happy times. One school friend of Rodríguez's even referred to Calderas in the 1950s and 1960s as "paradise." No doubt some of the individuals who looked back on those days in a positive light were privileged workers in Lisandro's property, since they had year-round employment. I did not interview any peasant who worked seasonally on the Calderas property. I suspect that they would not recall those times fondly, even though they may have been treated better than workers at other fincas or haciendas.

The interviews surprised me in a number of ways that helped me to develop some of my key conclusions. Very few of the informants discussed or even mentioned liberation theology or Marxism. Those who did were priests or were reasonably well educated. This suggests that ideologies—the ideas that form the logic behind a rebellion, the "injustice frame"—are the domain of leaders. Just as Rodríguez had stated that he learned more from the peasants than he did from the Bible, I was taken aback by the eloquence of some of the campesinos whom I interviewed. A number of them were still painfully shy and quiet. The majority were able to express themselves in very sophisticated ways, and some were exceptional storytellers, like one peasant from Cinquera who told me fascinating stories for over three hours! Naturally, most of the peasants I interviewed had been involved in the FPL or popular movement and were precisely those people whom Rodríguez and liberationists had identified as "natural leaders." These were the campesinos who had received religious, practical, and leadership training. After speaking to a number of campesinos, I started to realize that the accepted notion that priests and nuns "awakened" the poor was paternalistic and discounted the intelligence of the campesinos. Some of those whom I interviewed clearly pointed out that they knew there was injustice in El Salvador but that there was little they could do about it. Their submissiveness was not the result of fatalism but of a clear understanding that any form of defiance on their part would result in punishment. I became convinced that liberationist leaders themselves became awakened first and then they "awakened" the poor, by training peasants for political action and convincing them that they now had a strong ally. Church leaders therefore were indeed instrumental in creating an injustice frame and the popular movement, but not in the ways that others have explained it.

The interviews were sometimes difficult to carry out. On several occasions I found myself trying to discuss the conflict of the 1970s in a small, dirt-floored wooden shack, with chickens cackling in the background. Dogs barked and roosters crowed as I strained to listen to a man or woman in a very quiet voice recount why he or she decided to join the liberationists, or the FPL, or describe the horrible things that happened to them and their families during the "struggle." While I did not ask people about their personal difficulties—I primarily wanted to know about Rodríguez's actions and what they thought of him—many interviewees told me about the horrendous things they saw and the losses they suffered during the conflict. A number of them wept. Despite some difficulties and sad moments, no amount of reading could have come close to giving me the historical or personal perspectives that I gained from these interviews and visiting the places that shaped this history.

On my last evening in San Salvador in January 2008, I went out to dinner with Rodríguez, Mercedes Henríquez, their daughter (Ana Ruth), Gene Palumbo and his wife (Guadalupe), and Alex Bonilla. Toward the end of the dinner Rodríguez retrieved his guitar from the trunk of his car—miraculously enough, the same one he had purchased in Spain in the early 1960s—and started singing his revolutionary songs in the restaurant. After listening

A.1. Author (*left*), with (*clockwise*) Rodríguez, Mercedes Henríquez, their daughter, Ana Ruth, Gene Palumbo, and his wife, Guadalupe Palumbo. I am holding a book of popular songs, *El Pueblo Canta,* which contains several of Rodríguez's songs. Photo by Alex Bonilla, January 2008.

to just a few of his songs, my impression was that he was the epitome of a troubadour with a cause. Though sixty-seven at the time and suffering from Parkinson's, he was still skilled with the guitar, his voice was strong, and his songs were powerful and moving. This was the first time I had heard him play and sing. Imagining how popular and inspiring he must have been as a young priest, I thought to myself, *No wonder he moved so many people to action.*

Notes

Preface and Acknowledgments

1. Ueltzen, *Conversatorio con los hijos del siglo.*

2. Father Rafael Barahona is currently a priest in Guadalajara, Mexico. At some point, someone destroyed or took the original parish files, so all that remained are the copies made by Barahona. In 2013, when Barahona traveled to Tecolua to celebrate his fiftieth year as a priest, he provided copies of the files to the parish.

Chapter 1. A Man and Questions for All Seasons: Leaders and Ideas in Contentious Politics

1. Quotations without references are from the recorded interviews I conducted with David Rodríguez. When quotations come from other interviews, I identify the source. However, I have kept the vast majority of my other interviewees anonymous, because despite the political changes that have taken place in El Salvador, it is best to keep names out of the historical record as much as possible.

2. Almeida, *Waves of Protest,* 151; and Brockett, *Political Movements and Violence,* 294–306.

3. C. McClintock, *Revolutionary Movements in Latin America,* 45.

4. McAdam, *Political Process;* and McAdam, *Comparative Perspectives on Social Movements.*

5. Smith, *Emergence of Liberation Theology.*

6. McAdam, *Political Process,* 43.

7. Smith, *Emergence of Liberation Theology,* 59–60.

8. Ibid., 62; emphasis in source.

9. I am grateful to Leigh Binford for the term *transmission belt.*

10. Benford and Snow, "Framing Processes and Social Movements."

11. See, for example, Santiago, *Harvest of Justice,* 178–79; Peterson, *Martyrdom and the Politics of Religion,* 51–52; and Montgomery, *Revolution in El Salvador* (1995), 87.

12. González, "Iglesia, organizaciones populares y violencia sociopolítica," calls it a "religious mutation" that soon led to a political conversion (245–47).

13. In Spanish, "hablando de los pajaritos y angelitos."

14. Gladwell, *The Tipping Point*, 7.

15. O'Malley, *What Happened at Vatican II*, 310.

16. The first council had ended hastily in 1870, owing to Italy's unification, the Risorgimento.

17. Quoted in O'Brien and Shannon, *Catholic Social Thought*, 166.

18. O'Malley, *What Happened at Vatican II*, 288.

19. Latin American Bishops, "Poverty of the Church," paragraph 9; emphasis added.

20. Latin American Bishops, "Peace," paragraph 16.

21. Ibid.

22. The seminal work on liberation theology is G. Gutiérrez, *A Theology of Liberation*.

23. See Berryman, *Liberation Theology*, for a good overview of liberation theology.

24. For a theoretical debate, see Goodwin and Jasper, *Rethinking Social Movements*.

25. See Snow, Soule, and Kriesi, *Blackwell Companion to Social Movements*.

26. Selbin, *Modern Latin American Revolutions*, 27.

27. Barker, Johnson, and Lavalette, *Leadership and Social Movements*, 1.

28. Ganz, "Leading Change," 529.

29. For discussions on this bias and omission, see Erickson Nepstad and Bob, "When Do Leaders Matter?" 1; and Barker, Johnson, and Lavalette, *Leadership and Social Movements*, 1.

30. Rochon, *Culture Moves*, 31.

31. Westby, "Strategic Imperative, Ideology, and Framing," 290–91.

32. Snow and Benford, "Ideology, Frame Resonance, and Participant Mobilization," 198.

33. Morris and Staggenborg, "Leadership in Social Movements," 171.

34. Ibid., 172–73.

35. Bob and Erickson Nepstad, "Kill a Leader, Murder a Movement?"

36. Quoted in Goodwin and Jasper, *Rethinking Social Movements*, 241–43.

37. Ganz, "Leading Change," 528.

38. Binford, "Peasants, Catechists, and Revolutionaries," 105.

39. It is no secret that prior to 1977 Óscar Romero had close ties to the oligarchy and was not very sympathetic toward the church's preferential option for the poor. See Erdozaín, *Monseñor Romero*, 29.

40. On the history of the church, see Bokenkotter, *Concise History*.

41. MacNutt, *Bartholomew de Las Casas*.

42. Metaxas, *Bonhoeffer*, 155.

43. Schroth, *Bob Drinan*.

44. O'Malley, *What Happened at Vatican II*, 20.

45. Smith, *Emergence of Liberation Theology*, 90–94.

46. See Giuni, "Was It Worth the Effort?"

47. Amenta et al., "The Political Consequences of Social Movements," 302.

48. On the influence of outrage, see Wood, *Insurgent Collective Action*, 2, 8.

49. See Mason, *Caught in the Crossfire,* 213–17.

50. Goodwin, *No Other Way Out.*

51. Dahl, *Polyarchy.*

52. Burstein, "Social Movements and Public Policy," 3–12.

53. Álvarez, "From Revolutionary War to Democratic Revolution," 7.

54. Peterson, *Martyrdom and the Politics of Religion,* 28–30.

55. Byrne, *El Salvador's Civil War,* 23.

56. H. Alas, *El Salvador,* 27, 170.

57. Byrne, *El Salvador's Civil War,* 24–25.

58. Almeida, *Waves of Protest,* 6.

59. See, for example, Pearce, *Promised Land,* 112; Santiago, *Harvest of Justice,* 178–79; and Binford, "Peasants, Catechists, and Revolutionaries," 125.

60. Berryman, *Religious Roots of Rebellion,* 105. Rodríguez asserts that Rosario de Mora was not a combative parish. Instead, he states that other, more contentious parishes could be added, such as Cinquera and San Esteban Catarina, both in the diocese of San Vicente.

61. See, for example, Lernoux, *Cry of the People,* and Berryman, *Religious Roots of Rebellion,* who describe the early work of both priests.

62. Cáceres Prendes, "Political Radicalization and Popular Pastoral Practice," 118.

63. This statement, attributed to the liberationist priest Astor Ruiz, is quoted in Berryman, *Religious Roots of Rebellion,* 106.

64. See the appendix for a description of the personal interviews.

65. For a good discussion of this controversy, see "If Truth Be Told."

Chapter 2. The Training of a Traditional Priest: "I would like to be a pastor of souls"

1. In El Salvador, places are often referred to by several names, making identification difficult. In addition to this problem is the complexity of the names of departments, cantons, and municipalities. I have sought to identify all places correctly.

2. Lupita entered the Salesian order and eventually went to Costa Rica. However, she did not fare well as a nun, had troubles with the order, went back to El Salvador to be with her family, and in 1971 went to the United States to live with a cousin named Gladys.

3. *Aguardiente* is a strong, distilled liquor (similar to moonshine). In El Salvador campesinos made an aguardiente, called *chicha,* from corn, since they could not afford to buy beer or hard liquor and almost all campesinos planted at least some corn.

4. Rodríguez believes that the school his father established by donating land has now expanded to include ninth grade.

5. The academic year at Comillas had started in September 1963, but with help from the Jesuits, Rodríguez received credit for his entire first year.

6. Mayol became a member of Argentina's Third World Priest Movement and defied the Vatican's policy on celibacy by marrying. He eventually left the church and became a playwright.

7. O'Malley, *What Happened at Vatican II*, 310.

8. For the texts of the papal encyclicals discussed, see O'Brien and Shannon, *Catholic Social Thought.*

9. Ibid., 107.

10. Ibid., 139.

11. Ibid., 214.

12. After his installment as pontiff, Paul VI decreed that popes would no longer be crowned.

13. O'Brien and Shannon, *Catholic Social Thought*, 253–54.

14. Ibid., 247; ephasis added.

15. The Daughters of the Divine Savior maintain a web page at http://vd.pcn.net/es/index.php?option=com_content&view=article&id=548:hijas-del-divino-salvador&catid=21:in-focus&Itemid=28 that has information on, and photographs of, Bishop Aparicio.

16. Data on the diocese are for 1966. See "The Hierarchy of the Catholic Church: Current and Historical Information about Its Bishops and Dioceses," © David M. Cheney, 1996–2013, http://www.catholic-hierarchy.org/diocese/dsnvi.html.

17. See Smith, *Emergence of Liberation Theology*, 106–8.

18. Montgomery, *Revolution in El Salvador* (1995), 84, 87. On the CEBs and democracy, also see Van Vugt, *Democratic Organization for Social Change.*

19. The Bible, New International Version, Exodus 3:7–8. https://www.biblegateway.com.

20. Acts 4:32–35.

21. Luke 6:20.

22. Matthew 19:23–24.

23. Williams and Walter, *Militarization and Demilitarization*, 78, 88.

24. Rodríguez points out that the financial barrier to marriage resulted from the fact that those who married within the church tended to have large, costly fiestas. Thus, many people simply lived together rather than incur the cost of a fiesta.

25. Asamblea Legislativa, "El Salvador."

26. Father Alas was threatened and harassed repeatedly, his parish house was burned to the ground, and he was arrested twice over the next few years. Eventually, Alas and his brother, Higinio, also a liberationist priest, decided to leave the country. See J. Alas, *Iglesia, tierra y lucha campesina.*

27. A number of campesinos whom I interviewed recounted their mistreatment by landowners, caporales, government officials, and state security personnel.

28. The owners of large haciendas and fincas usually lived in a city or town (most often San Salvador) where they had large homes and could send their children to better schools. The absentee owners would thus be less likely to develop a patron-client relationship with their workers. Because Lisandro lived on his hacienda, he formed a more humane relationship with his workers, not just because he was a kind person but because he lived in close proximity to his laborers. The larger the landholding, the less likely it would be that a more humane, personal relationship would develop between the owner and his or her laborers.

29. Certainly, labor unions and opposition political parties also demanded changes. Nevertheless, powerful groups, such as the PCN, the state, the oligarchs, the church, and the armed forces, had no strong commitment, desire, or concerted unity to propose and carry out major changes. Moreover, the vast majority of the oligarchy were vehemently against any kind of reform, especially changes to the land-tenure system.

30. On La Matanza, see Gould and Lauria-Santiago, *To Rise in Darkness*.

31. The name of the military-dominated party changed over the years, but the basic fact of military domination of the political system, at the behest of the oligarchy, did not change. See Williams and Walter, *Militarization and Demilitarization*, for an excellent history of the Salvadoran armed forces.

32. See M. McClintock, *The American Connection*, 204–8, for background on the founding of ORDEN, Medrano, and on the U.S. role.

33. "Aurelio" is not his real name.

Chapter 3. The Awakening of a Priest: "You have ruined the parish!"

1. Chávez y González was archbishop for forty years (1938–77). He organized and promoted the pastoral week and also encouraged Salvadoran priests to study abroad. See Hammond, *Fighting to Learn*, 28; and Montgomery, "The Church in the Salvadoran Revolution," 70.

2. Lernoux, *Cry of the People*, 32.

3. Latin American Bishops, "Justice," paragraph 18.

4. Cardenal, *Historia de una esperanza*, 146.

5. Richard went to Costa Rica after the 1973 coup in Chile, but he also spent some time in El Salvador and would at times speak there at meetings of progressive priests.

6. In fact, La Nacional was founded prior to the pastoral week, since a number of priests had already met in late 1969. Father Macho invited Rodríguez to one of these earlier meetings.

7. Cardenal, *Historia de una esperanza*, 152.

8. The strategy of going as teams (several priests) to communities for a few days or even longer appears to have been first used by Father Rutilio Grande in Aguilares. For more on this practice, see ibid.

9. In Spanish the term *formación* is applied to people much more readily than in English. To form someone as a person involves not only providing education or training, but also inculcating a moral or social compass. The forming of peasants included *concientización* (consciousness-raising) and promoting an awakening.

10. Rodríguez did not wish to reveal the name and noted that, while serving as a minister after the civil war ended, the individual was removed as a result of a corruption scandal.

11. On the death of Father Rodríguez Aguilar, see Guerra et al., *Testigos de la fe*, 262–73.

12. See Arzobispado de El Salvador, *Estudio sobre la persecución de la iglesia*.

13. Quoted in H. Alas, *El Salvador*, 168.

14. At this time, Rodríguez did not know that the FPL published *El Rebelde*.

15. G. Gutiérrez, *A Theology of Liberation*.

16. Smith, *Emergence of Liberation Theology*, 182.

17. Quoted in Berryman, *Liberation Theology*, 28.

18. Parroquia de Tecoluca, 1973–1977, Algunos Acontecimientos, document #76.

19. Ibid., document #74.

20. Ibid., document #75.

21. Some Protestant ministers were also involved in the liberationist movement. However, evangelicals in El Salvador tended to be conservative and thus were highly critical of liberationist ideas.

22. Rodríguez referred to it in Spanish as "una sabiduría preciosa."

23. I suspect that many young Salvadoran women fell in love with Padre Rodríguez, who was energetic, friendly, young, compassionate, and highly charismatic.

24. Cardenal, *Historia de una esperanza,* details the work of Rutilio Grande in his excellent biography of the priest.

25. Rodríguez recalls that everyone believed that Sibrián had simply left the priesthood and gone into exile to Honduras. However, a few years later they found out that he was working in the guerrilla-controlled areas.

26. Seven pastoral plans and two evaluations of those plans are in the files of the parish. The last document is from 1976. It seems clear from reading the documents that after 1976 the situation was so problematic, mostly because of government repression, that the priests did not have time to write formal plans or maintain files. Father Barahona describes the development of the base communities in an unpublished autobiography; see Barahona Herrera, "Una historia especial en tiempos dificiles," 120–31.

27. Parroquia de Tecoluca, 1973–1977, Plan Pastoral, document #9.

28. Rodríguez did not remember where the programs originated, but since the archdiocese distributed them, they were most likely developed by a liberationist church institution, such as the Pastoral Institute of Latin America, in Quito, Ecuador.

29. Most of the people I interviewed said that they had become engaged in the movement because of Rodríguez.

30. Rodríguez recounts this story in M. López Vigil, *Piezas para un retrato*. Díez and Macho, "En Santiago De María me tope con la miseria," however, state that Romero actually said, "If Rodríguez is a communist, then I am Chinese."

31. Berryman, *Religious Roots of Rebellion*, 124.

32. In "Una historia especial en tiempos dificiles," Barahona points out that many Bibles were distributed to peasants in the early 1970s. For those who could read, it was the first time they had read the Bible.

33. Montgomery, "The Church in the Salvadoran Revolution," 71.

34. When Rafael Barahona left El Salvador, he took seven groups of files that had been preserved in the parish of Tecoluca. Rodríguez allowed me to copy these files. See Parroquia de Tecoluca.

35. Parroquia de Tecoluca, 1973–1977, Algunos Acontecimientos, document #73.

36. Ibid., document #74.

37. In the next few years, as state repression against the church exploded, the offices of both *Orientación* and YSAX were bombed several times.

38. See Berner, "Ideological Origins."

39. Quoted in Harnecker, *Con la mirada en alto,* 65.

40. Erdozaín, *Monseñor Romero,* 12.

41. Parroquia de Tecoluca, 1973–1977, Varios, document #19.

42. Ibid., document #18.

43. Quoted in Harnecker, *Con la mirada en alto,* 59.

44. One former rebel says of the key ideological thinkers of the ERP: "All of them were students of Father Miguel Ventura. . . . I don't believe there is a leading political cadre in Morazán who did not enter this struggle by the door of the Christian base communities." And the few who were not in base communities, like Villalobos, came to the ERP via the PDC. See J. I. López Vigil, *Rebel Radio,* 42.

45. No doubt the oligarchy's and military's concerns about communism were partly for effect, since what they feared most was a revolution that would undermine their dominance of Salvadoran society. The progressive church represented a similar threat. Even the U.S. government was concerned about the revolutionary stance of the church soon after the Medellín Conference, in that a link between progressive Christian leaders and leftists was anticipated. See Central Intelligence Agency, "The Committed Church and Change in Latin America," for an interesting early assessment of the revolutionary dangers of the progressive church.

Chapter 4. The Radicalization of a Priest: "You are now 'Joaquín'"

1. Quoted in Ueltzen, *Conversatorio con los hijos del siglo,* 252.

2. Many liberationists in Latin America saw Torres as a hero. Torres renounced his priesthood before joining the guerrillas.

3. Parroquia de Tecoluca, 1973–1977, Algunos Acontecimientos, document #71.

4. In describing this massacre I rely on Rodríguez's recollections, some documents in the files of the parish of Tecoluca, and Ortiz, "La Cayetana."

5. Parroquia de Tecoluca, 1973–1977, Algunos Acontecimientos, document #69.

6. Ibid., document #66.

7. A few campesinos at La Cayetana were already "incorporated" into the FPL. Nevertheless, campesinos made limited demands, their actions were not radical or violent, and the response by the local authorities was extreme.

8. I am being purposefully vague.

9. Rodríguez points out that Carpio did not have a good experience with the church, since he went to a Christian school that was a correctional school for wayward youths.

10. Parroquia de Tecoluca, 1973–1977, Algunos Acontecimientos, document #29.

11. Although Barahona does not describe this in his letter to Aparicio, Rodríguez says that his friend was put on a metal bed and given electric shocks, which gave him "health and psychological problems."

12. Parroquia de Tecoluca, 1973–1977, Algunos Acontecimientos, document #36.

13. Parroquia de Tecoluca, 1973–1977, Varios, document #15.

14. See Díez and Macho, "En Santiago De María me tope con la miseria," 49–51.

15. See J. Delgado, *Óscar A. Romero*, 67–68.

16. Montgomery, *Revolution in El Salvador* (1995), 67.

17. A priest who was present at this meeting told me that he could not remember whether it was he or Rodríguez who proposed the occupation of the cathedral, but both of them strongly favored this strategy.

18. The document lists the names of specific individuals: the minister of defense (Colonel Carlos Humberto Romero, who would become the next fraudulently elected president), the chief of the National Guard (Colonel Rosales), the chief of the Treasury Police (Colonel Alvarenga), and the rector of the National University (Alfaro Castillo). Parroquia de Tecoluca, 1973–1977, Varios, document #13.

19. Che Guevara's *foquista*-style revolution, where a small group of armed rebels would attack an illegitimate, exploitative state, and thus arouse a popular insurrection, had been discredited by 1968, after Guevara was captured and killed in Bolivia in 1967.

20. Parroquia de Tecoluca, 1973–1977, Varios, document #12.

21. Parroquia de Tecoluca 1973–1977, Algunos Acontecimientos, document #26.

22. Ibid., document #27.

23. See H. Alas, *El Salvador*, 58.

24. Latin America Bureau, *Violence and Fraud in El Salvador*, 6.

25. Ibid., 19–20.

26. Parroquia de Tecoluca, 1973–1977, Algunos Acontecimientos, document #23.

27. Arzobispado de El Salvador, *Estudio sobre la persecución de la iglesia*, 119.

28. Parroquia de Tecoluca, 1973–1977, Algunos Acontecimientos, document #25.

29. J. Alas, *Iglesia, tierra y lucha campesina*, 191–93; Armstrong and Shenk, *El Salvador*, 68.

30. Lernoux, *Cry of the People*, 71; Cáceres Prendes, "Political Radicalization and Popular Pastoral Practice," 120.

31. Latin America Bureau, *Violence and Fraud in El Salvador*, 20.

32. Parroquia de Tecoluca, 1973–1977, Varios, document #10.

33. Richard and Meléndez, *La iglesia de los pobres*, 90. When Chávez y González retired, he bravely volunteered to become parish priest in Aguilares, which had been left without a priest after Father Grande was murdered, indicating his commitment to the church, the people of El Salvador, and the liberationist cause.

34. Erdozaín, *Archbishop Romero*, 1, 29.

35. Arzobispado de El Salvador, *Estudio sobre la persecución de la iglesia*, 112.

36. Mena Sandoval, *Del ejército nacional al ejército guerrillero*, 79–82.

37. Latin American Newsletters, LTD, *Latin American Political Report* XI, #25, July 1, 1977, 195.

38. José Napoleón Duarte was still in exile.

39. Montgomery, *Revolution in El Salvador* (1995), 71–72.

40. Ibid., 72.

41. Ibid., 93.

42. Conferencia Episcopal de El Salvador, "Mensaje sobre el momento actual que vive el país."

43. Father Barahona is certain, based on sound information from a military official, that three priests were slated to be killed on that day: himself, Rutilio Grande, and Rutilio Sánchez, who was also a liberationist and eventually worked in FMLN-held territory. See Barahona Herrera, "Una historia especial en tiempos dificiles," 232.

44. Mena Sandoval, *Del ejército nacional al ejército guerrillero*, 11–12.

45. Erdozaín, *Archbishop Romero*, 15.

46. Almeida, *Waves of Protest*, 159.

47. Parroquia de Tecoluca, 1973–1977, Algunos Acontecimientos, document #20.

48. Ibid., document #9.

49. The archdiocese published a summary of the meeting in its publication *Boletín Informativo*. The document is in Parroquia de Tecoluca, 1973–1977, Varios, document #6.

50. Ironically, while people like Molina accepted the possibility that the leftists would kill a liberationist priest, Mena Sandoval, in *Del ejército nacional al ejército guerrillero*, 151, asserts that some military officers were responsible for at least some of the kidnappings of members of the oligarchy that were taking place.

51. Guerra et al., *Testigos de la fe*, 42–46.

52. H. Alas, *El Salvador*, 184.

53. Ibid., 187.

54. Parroquia de Tecoluca, 1973–1977, Varios, document #4.

55. Parroquia de Tecoluca, 1973–1977, Algunos Acontecimientos, document #5.

56. Arzobispado de El Salvador, *Estudio sobre la persecución de la iglesia.*

57. Quoted in H. Alas, *El Salvador*, 72.

58. Montgomery, *Revolution in El Salvador* (1995), 72.

59. Quoted in H. Alas, *El Salvador*, 72.

60. M. McClintock, *The American Connection*, 193.

61. Latin America Bureau, *El Salvador under General Romero*, 45.

62. Ibid.

63. Quoted in ibid., 44.

64. M. McClintock, *The American Connection*, 187.

65. The Salvadoran government offered Archbishop Romero a mansion in San Salvador in an obvious effort to tempt him to stop criticizing the government. He refused the offer and continued to live very modestly, thus undermining his security.

66. Richard and Meléndez, *La iglesia de los pobres*, 103.

67. The letter to Nuncio Gerada is reproduced in H. Alas, *El Salvador*, 191–93. Rodríguez's quote is not verbatim but certainly captures the tenor of the letter, which must have infuriated the nuncio and the conservative bishops. The phrase "margins of the faith" is found in the letter.

68. Romero, *Monseñor Romero*, 43.

69. Ibid., 105.

70. Romero and Hodgson, *Archbishop Oscar Romero*, 54–55.

71. Ibid., 69.

72. This is not his real name.

73. See Smith, *Emergence of Liberation Theology*, 209–31.

74. Erdozaín, *Archbishop Romero*, 54.

75. Ibid.

76. Aparicio, *Ante el momento histórico*, 128–29.

77. H. Alas, *El Salvador*, 193–94. Most likely the government and security apparatus had given Aparicio a great deal of information that they had gathered via intelligence operations and agents of ORDEN.

78. H. Alas, *El Salvador*, 200.

79. Guerra et al., *Testigos de la fe*, 109–44.

80. Quoted in Latin American Newsletters LTD, *Latin American Political Report* XIII, #19, May 18, 1979, 145.

81. Dunkerley, *The Long War*, 126.

82. Ibid., 124.

83. Duarte and Page, *Duarte*, 96.

84. Quoted in Williams and Walter, *Militarization and Demilitarization*, 112.

85. Guerra et al., *Testigos de la fe*, 146.

86. See Mena Sandoval, *Del ejército nacional al ejército guerrillero*, 15, for a fascinating account of these events; Erdozaín, *Archbishop Romero*, 67; and Williams and Walter, *Militarization and Demilitarization*, 99–100.

87. As the junta became more conservative and repression increased, Washington sent more, rather than less, aid to El Salvador's armed forces; see Bonner, *Weakness and Deceit*, 165, 168.

88. Williams and Walter, *Militarization and Demilitarization*, 97; and Dunkerley, *The Long War*, 135.

89. Mena Sandoval, *Del ejército nacional al ejército guerrillero*, 365–68.

90. Ibid., 15.

91. Williams and Walter, *Militarization and Demilitarization*, 101.

92. J. Delgado, *Óscar A. Romero*, 159.

93. Armstrong and Shenk, *El Salvador*, 123.

94. Williams and Walter, *Militarization and Demilitarization*, 102.

95. Duarte and Page, *Duarte*, 114–16.

96. Montgomery, *Revolution in El Salvador* (1995), 129.

97. Latin American Newsletters, LTD, *Latin American Weekly Report*, WR-80-04, January 25, 1980, 3.

98. Dunkerley, *The Long War*, 145.

99. Pearce, *Promised Land*, 190.

100. Quoted in Latin American Newsletters, LTD, *Latin American Weekly Report*, WR-80-04, January 25, 1980, 3.

101. In 1980, sixty-four PDC leaders were killed. See Stanley, *The Protection Racket State*, 184.

102. Quoted in Dunkerley, *The Long War*, 152–55.

103. H. Alas, *El Salvador*, 92.

104. Duarte and Page, *Duarte*, 114–16.

105. Quoted in Bonner, *Weakness and Deceit*, xvi.

106. Erdozaín, *Archbishop Romero*, 32.

107. Ibid., 80.

108. Ibid., 78.

109. Ibid., 79.

Chapter 5. A Revolutionary Priest: "The 'Che' of the Bible"

1. Benigno went to the United States and Barahona to Guadalajara, Mexico. Understanding the precarious situation in El Salvador, the bishop of Guadalajara had sent a letter to the bishops in El Salvador saying that "their doors were open" to Salvadoran priests who needed to leave the country. The Salvadoran bishops either felt that their priests were indeed in danger or, for the conservative ones, that it would be better for progressive priests to leave the country.

2. Rodríguez does not remember the exact number, but at one point La Nacional was also known as the Group of Thirty, for the size of its membership.

3. Erdozaín, *Archbishop Romero*, 91.

4. Dunkerley, *The Long War*, 160–61.

5. Lupita had left for the United States much earlier, in 1971, after leaving her religious order. Benigno is now retired after serving many years as a parish priest in Los Angeles, California, and has the honorary title of Monsignor. Both of Rodríguez's sisters and his mother settled in Los Angeles. Raquelita passed away in 2008; his mother, María, passed away in 2010.

6. Almeida, "Opportunity Organizations," 377.

7. Erdozaín, *Archbishop Romero*, 96.

8. On the life of the bold oligarch, see Lamperti, *Enrique Álvarez Córdova*.

9. "Death on a Twisting Dirt Road," *Time*, December 15, 1980, 54.

10. Forche et al., *El Salvador*, 61.

11. For an account of Father Ponceele's work as a priest in the ERP-controlled areas in the department of Morazán, see M. López Vigil, *Muerte y vida en Morazán*. Ponceele never carried a weapon and never formally joined the ERP.

12. Alma Guillermoprieto, "Salvador Leftists Buried, Coup Fears Mount," *Globe and Mail*, December 4, 1980.

13. Quoted in Juan M. Vasquez, "Salvador Funeral Unmarred by Violence," *Los Angeles Times*, December 4, 1980, B16.

14. Ibid.

15. On September 30, 1981, the newspaper *Diario de Hoy* published a photo of Bishop Marco René Revelo blessing a U.S. supplied helicopter amidst a group of military officers. See H. Alas, *El Salvador*, 192.

16. Quoted in Erdozaín, *Monseñor Romero*, 73.

17. The UN Truth Commission (United Nations, *De la locura a la esperanza*, 57–58) estimated that the government and its security apparatus were responsible for 85 percent of the human-rights violations, which mostly included extrajudicial executions, disappearances and torture; while the FMLN was deemed responsible for 5 percent. The report concluded that death squads were responsible for 10 percent of the violations, even though the U.S. and Salvadoran governments had both argued that the right-wing violence was the result of extremists rather than the state. We must keep in mind, however, that the thousands of people killed during the 1970s, many of them religious lay leaders, were not included in the UN report, because these deaths occurred prior to the official start of the civil war. At least one very serious case of extreme human-rights violations perpetrated by the FPL, which I discuss in chapter 6, was not included in the Truth Commission report.

18. The PRTC, like the RN, originated from the ERP.

19. Castellanos, *The Comandante Speaks*, 31.

20. Duarte and Page, *Duarte*, 162.

21. On the development and work of the PPLs, see Ventura, *El poder popular en El Salvador*.

22. For personal accounts on the life and activities of the armed insurgents, see, for example, Metzi, *Por los caminos de Chalatenango*; Alegría and Flakoll, *No me agarran viva*; D. Gutiérrez, *La persona, la fe y la revolución*; and, in English, Clements, *Witness to War*.

23. Tilly, *From Mobilization to Revolution*, 217.

24. The most significant, documented massacres are described in United Nations, *De la locura a la esperanza*. On the worst massacres committed by the government during the war, see Binford, *The El Mozote Massacre*; and Danner, *The Massacre at El Mozote*.

25. Interestingly enough, when I visited the ruins of the finca La Chenga Sola with Rodríguez in January 2008, we saw still-standing, outdoor latrines that the U.S. Army had built with funding from the U.S. Agency for International Development, the result of a U.S. government effort to pacify the population.

26. The contested zones were areas that neither the FMLN nor the Salvadoran state fully controlled.

27. "Salvadoran Troops Retake Town," *New York Times*, November 1, 1983, A3.

28. Ruiz, quoted in Berryman, *Religious Roots of Rebellion*, 106. Some forced recruitment on the part of the FMLN occurred during the civil war. However, most of the forced recruitment appears to have been conducted by the ERP in Morazán.

29. Only the more educated people I interviewed discussed ideology, whether it was socialism, Marxism, or liberation theology.

30. See Herman and Brodhead, *Demonstration Elections*, for a description of the term *demonstration election*, which they apply to El Salvador.

31. For the electoral results and the seat tallies, see Legislatina.

32. On the elections, see Montgomery, *Revolution in El Salvador* (1995), 155–62; and Williams and Walter, *Militarization and Demilitarization*, 122–23.

33. Williams and Walter, *Militarization and Demilitarization*, 133.

34. Ibid., 149.

35. La Montañona was a guerrilla stronghold during most of the war and home to the Radio Farabundo Martí radio station. It is now a guerrilla ecotourism location where visitors can see the underground tunnels that were built, akin to the tunnels built by the Vietcong in Vietnam.

36. I will not reveal the name, since he was a well-known priest.

37. Because some of these groups are still in existence, I will not name them here.

38. Mayor Newport's visit to El Salvador is discussed briefly in Medina Núñez, *El Salvador*, 104.

39. Mena Sandoval, *Del ejército nacional al ejército guerrillero*, 311, 321–22. Some weapons were even purchased from corrupt military officers, although the extent of this corruption is not fully known.

40. Benítez Manaut, *Teoría militar*, 305, 307–10.

41. Didion, *Salvador*, 39.

42. On the refugee and displacement crisis see Todd, *Beyond Displacement*; and Cagan and Cagan, *This Promised Land.*

43. For fascinating accounts of the FMLN's principal radio station, Radio Venceremos, see J. I. López Vigil, *Rebel Radio*; and Henríquez Consalvi, *Broadcasting the Civil War.*

44. See Legislatina.

45. Montgomery, *Revolution in El Salvador* (1995), 161.

46. Brett, "Archbishop Arturo Rivera Damas," 735–36.

47. Ibid., 737.

48. For a detailed account of these murders, see Whitfield, *Paying the Price.*

49. See Brett, "Archbishop Arturo Rivera Damas."

50. Todd, *Beyond Displacement*, 5.

51. For a summary of key factors in revolutionary success and failure, see Wickham-Crowley, *Guerillas and Revolution in Latin America*, 302–26.

52. On the "democratizing" effects of the elections, see Peceny, "Democratization by Elections."

53. For strong arguments suggesting that U.S. aid kept the Salvadoran state from collapsing, see Benítez Manaut, *Teoría militar*, 305, 307–10; and C. McClintock, *Revolutionary Movements in Latin America*, 221–35. See also the candid comments of U.S. government and military personnel, as well as Salvadoran officials, in Manwaring and Prisk, *El Salvador at War*, 144, 145, 149, 233, 238, 248–49, 284, 396, 398.

54. Quoted in Manwaring and Prisk, *El Salvador at War*, 396.

55. Lindo-Fuentes and Ching, in *Modernizing Minds in El Salvador*, 29–70, make a strong case for not viewing the oligarchy and armed forces as unified actors and argue that important differences existed in their worldviews.

Chapter 6. A Democratic Priest: "Padre David has the word"

1. Bishop Aparicio passed away in September 1992.

2. The cooperative provided small loans for projects and health needs, as well as for a priest's funeral. The members also had access to a seaside retreat.

3. In 1987 the Vatican established the diocese of Zacatecoluca.

4. Rodríguez points out that he was not the only popular candidate to cede to an influential leader from one of the smaller groups within the FMLN who did not have a candidacy.

5. Rodríguez states that he received 4.5 *manzanas* of land. A *manzana* represents about 1.75 acres, yielding approximately 8 acres.

6. During the war, the government and those on the right used a number of derogatory terms to refer to the guerrillas, such as terrorists, delinquents, *corta puentes* (bridge-cutters, since they blew up bridges in conducting economic sabotage), and *matavacas* (cow-killers). Naturally, guerrillas were in dire need of protein during the twelve-year civil war and would often kill cows when they took over a contested zone or town, earning the sobriquet cow-killers. On the other hand, the guerrillas would refer to the soldiers as *cuilios,* since they were always chattering or twittering like little birds.

7. Election results are available at Legislatina.

8. A very common role for young boys who collaborated with the guerrillas was that of carrying messages to various locations. If captured, these boys would be at grave risk.

9. For interviews with women who participated in the war effort, some of whom recount some very difficult times and highlight sexism within the FMLN, see Kelly Rivera et al., *¿Valio la Pena?*; and Vázquez, Ibañez, and Murguialday, *Mujeres-Montaña*.

10. FMLN leader Salvador Sánchez Cerén, elected vice president in 2009 and elected president in 2014, was the commander of the FPL while Sibrián committed these heinous crimes. For many, Sánchez Cerén and other FPL members of the high command during the war share much of the responsibility for not acting sooner, while some suggest that Sibrián's actions were tolerated or even authorized by the FPL commanders. For a recent account of the murders in the para-central region which argues that more than one thousand people were killed, see Galeas and Ayalá, *Grandeza y miseria en una guerrilla*.

11. Araúz and Aguilar, "Plática con David Rodríguez."

12. There are two amnesty laws: one was part of the peace accords, and the other was passed by the Legislative Assembly soon after the promulgation of the Truth Commission report.

13. See Ueltzen, *Conversatorio con los hijos del siglo*, for interviews of a number of revolutionary leaders, including Rodríguez.

14. Deputies in El Salvador at the time (and of course today) were paid very well. However, the FMLN developed rules to ensure that deputies would give back some of their salary toward helping the party as well as providing scholarships for poor children. Rodríguez points out that this generosity by the FMLN has "frightened the other parties."

15. In 2001, in a controversial move, El Salvador decided to adopt the U.S. dollar as its official currency.

16. See Legislatina for voting results.

17. For the results of the election see the Supreme Electoral Tribunal web page at http://www.tse.gob.sv.

18. In January 2008, while I was in El Salvador conducting interviews, an FMLN mayoral candidate was gunned down while campaigning.

19. After the mid-1980s the number of conservative bishops and archbishops throughout Latin America increased, since Pope John Paul II and then Pope Benedict had been critical of liberation theology and wanted to move the church toward a more conservative position.

20. Rodríguez discussed the particular individuals with me, but I have decided to leave out the names. The key point is that the divisions between traditionalists and liberationists continues to plague the church.

21. One bishop in El Salvador told me that Rodríguez's political involvement, rather than his family, was the principal problem keeping him from being able to return to the church in some formal role, and that his role as a legislator was more of a problem for the church hierarchy than was his past involvement with the FPL and FMLN.

22. Burstein, "Social Movements and Public Policy," 3–12.

Chapter 7. One Priest's Quest for the Promised Land: "'El Chele' David has always been a leader"

1. Many groups did indeed organize and demand their rights between 1932 and 1970, yet only in the 1970s did an important protest wave sweep the country, led by a sizable Christian and popular movement; and then, after intense state repression, a powerful revolutionary movement emerged.

2. Vázquez, Ibañez, and Murguialday, *Mujeres-Montaña*, interviewed sixty-one women who were incorporated into or collaborated with the FMLN, and the authors note that "all of them said they had been influenced by pastoral activities of the Catholic Church" (101). Moreover, as pointed out previously, most of the leadership of the FPL and the ERP had also been influenced in various ways by progressive church doctrine.

3. In the mid-1980s, the Congregation for the Doctrine of the Faith issued two documents that were critical of liberation theology: "Instruction on Certain Aspects of the 'Theology of Liberation'" (1984) and "Instruction on Christian Freedom and Liberation" (1986). The first document harshly criticized some elements of liberation theology, while the second toned down the criticism and pointed to many similarities between liberationist goals and church doctrine.

4. O'Malley, *What Happened at Vatican II*, offers a fascinating account of Vatican II.

5. On martyrdom in the Salvadoran church, see Peterson, *Martyrdom and the Politics of Religion*.

6. Sister Silvia Maribel Arriola was murdered on January 17, 1981. The four American women murdered in 1980 included three nuns and one lay worker.

7. In 2007, Sobrino received a notification from the Congregation for the Doctrine of the Faith stating that his writings were dangerous. Sobrino, who had been living and working in El Salvador since 1957, would have been murdered in November 1989, along with his six Jesuit colleagues, if he had not missed his flight to San Salvador.

8. Here I am referring to the institutional church as the strong ally. In a number of parishes, individual priests and nuns continue to embrace and apply the ideas of liberation theology and continue to help the poor. Had the institutional church supported liberation theology fully in the 1970s, tremendous changes may have taken place throughout Latin America.

9. In the late 1880s, as coffee became El Salvador's chief export crop, the oligarchy convinced the state to take land away from the indigenous people. See Montgomery, *Revolution in El Salvador* (1995), 30.

10. See Guerra et al., *Testigos de la fe.*

11. See Ueltzen, *Conversatorio con los hijos del siglo.*

12. McCullough, *The Thorn Birds.*

13. See *El pueblo canta* (no author), song number 201, n.p.

Glossary

ajusticiamiento. Applying the death penalty.
campesino. Peasant or rural person.
caporal. Supervisor at a finca or hacienda.
caserío. Hamlet or splay of houses.
chele. Light-skinned person.
cipote. Child.
colectivo. Collective; an organizational cell of a politico-military organization.
colono. Agricultural worker living on a hacienda or finca.
compañero/compañera. Comrade or partner.
corvo. Machete.
ermita. Small chapel.
finca. Coffee plantation or farm.
guinda. Civilian flight from military attacks.
hacienda. Estate, typically greater than 247 acres (100 hectares).
incorporado/incorporarse. To become involved, incorporate oneself, in the revolutionary struggle.
milpa. Small planting of a peasant, usually of corn.
pintas. The painting of slogans in public places by the FPL or popular organizations.
realidad. The political, economic, and social context in which the poor find themselves; this term was used extensively by liberationists.
responsable. One who is responsible for someone who enters a revolutionary cell.
tamagás. Type of poisonous snake in El Salvador; also, the nickname for Bishop Pedro Aparicio.

Bibliography

Alas, Higinio. *El Salvador:¿Porque la insurrección?* San José, Costa Rica: Secretariado Permanente de la Comisión para la Defensa de los Derechos Humanos en Centroamérica, 1982.

Alas, José. *Iglesia, tierra y lucha campesina: Suchitoto, El Salvador, 1968–1977.* San Salvador: Asociación de Frailes Franciscanos, 2003.

Alegría, Claribel, and D. J. Flakoll. *No me agarran viva: La mujer salvadoreña en lucha.* México, D.F.: Ediciones Era, 1983.

Almeida, Paul. "Opportunity Organizations and Threat-Induced Contention: Protest Waves in Authoritarian Settings." *American Journal of Sociology* 109, no. 2 (2003): 345–400.

———. *Waves of Protest: Popular Struggle in El Salvador, 1925–2005.* Minneapolis: University of Minnesota Press, 2008.

Álvarez, Alberto Martín. "From Revolutionary War to Democratic Revolution: The Farabundo Martí National Liberation Front (FMLN) in El Salvador." Berlin: Berghof-Stiftung für Konfliktforschung, 2010.

Amenta, Edwin, Neal Caren, Elizabeth Chiarello, and Yang Su. "The Political Consequences of Social Movements." *Annual Review of Sociology* 36 (2010): 287–307.

Americas Watch Committee (U.S.). *El Salvador's Decade of Terror: Human Rights since the Assassination of Archbishop Romero.* New Haven: Yale University Press, 1991.

Aparicio, Pedro. *Ante el momento histórico: Lo que dijimos ayer.* San Salvador, El Salvador: Diócesis de San Vicente, 1980.

Araúz, Sergio, and Jimena Aguilar. "Plática con David Rodríguez, ex capellán del ejército, sacerdote, ex guerrillero y diputado por el FMLN." *El Faro* online (www.elfaro.net). San Salvador, El Salvador, posted on 29 June 2009.

Armstrong, Robert, and Janet Shenk. *El Salvador: The Face of Revolution.* Boston: South End Press, 1982.

Arzobispado de El Salvador. *Estudio sobre la persecución de la iglesia en El Salvador.* San Salvador, El Salvador: Secretariado Social Interdiocesano, 1977.

Asamblea Legislativa. "El Salvador: Memoria del primer congreso nacional de reforma agraria, enero 5–10, 1970." San Salvador: Asamblea Legislativa, Departamento de Prensa, 1970.

Barahona Herrera, Padre Rafael Antonio. Una historia especial en tiempos difíciles." Unpublished autobiography. Guadalajara, México, 2013.

Barker, Colin, Alan Johnson, and Michael Lavalette. *Leadership and Social Movements.* Manchester, UK: Manchester University Press, 2001.

Benford, Robert D., and David A. Snow. "Framing Processes and Social Movements: An Overview and Assessment." *Annual Review of Sociology* 26 (2000): 611–39.

Benítez Manaut, Raul. *La teoría militar y la guerra civil en El Salvador.* San Salvador: UCA Editores, 1989.

Berner, Brad K. "The Ideological Origins of the 'Farabundo Martí National Liberation Front' (FMLN) of El Salvador." Amazon Digital Services: Kindle books, 2008.

Berryman, Phillip. *Liberation Theology: Essential Facts about the Revolutionary Movement in Latin America—and Beyond.* New York: Pantheon Books, 1987.

———. *The Religious Roots of Rebellion: Christians in Central American Revolutions.* Maryknoll, N.Y.: Orbis Books, 1984.

Binford, Leigh. *The El Mozote Massacre: Anthropology and Human Rights.* Tucson: University of Arizona Press, 1996.

———. "Peasants, Catechists, and Revolutionaries: Organic Intellectuals in the Salvadoran Revolution, 1980–1992." In *Landscapes of Struggle: Politics, Society, and Community in El Salvador,* ed. Aldo Lauria-Santiago and Leigh Binford, 105–25. Pittsburgh: University of Pittsburgh Press, 2004.

Bob, Clifford, and Sharon Erickson Nepstad. "Kill a Leader, Murder a Movement? Leadership and Assassination in Social Movements." *American Behavioral Scientist* 50 (2007): 1370–94.

Bokenkotter, Thomas S. *A Concise History of the Catholic Church.* New York: Doubleday, 2004.

Bonner, Raymond. *Weakness and Deceit: U.S. Policy and El Salvador.* New York: Times Books, 1984.

Brett, Edward T. "Archbishop Arturo Rivera Damas and the Struggle for Social Justice in El Salvador." *Catholic Historical Review* 94, no. 4 (2008): 717–39.

Brockett, Charles. *Political Movements and Violence in Central America.* New York: Cambridge University Press, 2005.

Burdick, John. *The Church at the Grassroots in Latin America: Perspectives on Thirty Years of Activism.* Westport, Conn.: Praeger Press, 2000.

Burstein, Paul. "Social Movements and Public Policy." In *How Social Movements Matter,* ed. Marco Giugni, Doug McAdam, and Charles Tilly, 3–21. Minneapolis: University of Minnesota Press, 1999.

Byrne, Hugh. *El Salvador's Civil War: A Study of Revolution.* Boulder: Lynne Rienner, 1996.

Cabarrús, Carlos. *Génesis de una revolución: Análisis del surgimiento y desarrollo de la organización campesina en El Salvador.* México, D.F.: Centro de Investigaciones y Estudios Superiores en Antropología Social, 1983.

Cáceres Prendes, Jorge. "Political Radicalization and Popular Pastoral Practice in El Salvador, 1969–1985." In *The Progressive Church in Latin America,* ed. Scott Mainwaring and Alexander Wilde, 103–48. Notre Dame, Ind.: University of Notre Dame Press, 1989.

———. "Revolutionary Struggle and Church Commitment: The Case of El Salvador." *Social Compass* 30, nos. 2–3 (1983): 261–98.

Cagan, Steve, and Beth Cagan. *This Promised Land, El Salvador: The Refugee Community of Colomoncagua and Their Return to Morazán.* New Brunswick, N.J.: Rutgers University Press, 1991.

Camacho, Daniel, and Rafael Menjivar. *Movimientos populares en Centroamérica.* San José, Costa Rica: Editorial Universitaria Centroamericana, 1985.

Cardenal, Rodolfo. *Historia de una esperanza: Vida de Rutilio Grande.* San Salvador, El Salvador: UCA Editores, 1985.

———. *La voz de los sin voz: La palabra viva de Monseñor Oscar Arnulfo Romero.* San Salvador, El Salvador: UCA Editores, 2006.

Castellanos, Miguel. *The Comandante Speaks: Memoirs of an El Salvadoran Guerrilla Leader.* Boulder: Westview Press, 1991.

Central Intelligence Agency. "The Committed Church and Change in Latin America." Directorate of Intelligence, Secret declassified report, RSS #0039/69, September 10, 1969.

Centro de Estudios y Publicaciones. *El Salvador, un pueblo perseguido: Testimonios de cristianos.* 2nd ed. Lima: Centro de Estudios y Publicaciones, 1981.

Cleary, Edward. *Crisis and Change: The Church in Latin America Today.* Maryknoll, N.Y.: Orbis Books, 1985.

Clements, Charles. *Witness to War: An American Doctor in El Salvador.* New York: Bantam Books, 1984.

Comisión Evangélica Latinoamericana de Educación Cristiana. *Iglesia de Jesucristo, iglesia de los pobres.* Cuadernos De Estudio 23. Lima: Comisión Evangélica Latinoamericana de Educación Cristiana, 1981.

Conferencia Episcopal de El Salvador. "Mensaje sobre el momento actual que vive el país." Episcopal letter, March 5, 1977. http://www.iglesia.org.sv, accessed on November 7, 2009.

Congregation for the Doctrine of the Faith. "Instruction on Certain Aspects of the 'Theology of Liberation.'" The Vatican, August 6, 1984. http://www.vatican.va/roman_curia/congregations/cfaith/documents/rc_con_cfaith_doc_19840806_theology-liberation_en.html.

———. "Instruction on Christian Freedom and Liberation." The Vatican, March 22, 1986. http://www.vatican.va/roman_curia/congregations/cfaith/documents/rc_con_cfaith_doc_19860322_freedom-liberation_en.html.

Dahl, Robert A. *Polyarchy: Participation and Opposition.* New Haven: Yale University Press, 1971.

Danner, Mark. *The Massacre at El Mozote: A Parable of the Cold War.* New York: Vintage Books, 1994.

Delgado, Freddy. *La iglesia popular nació en El Salvador: Memorias de 1972 a 1982*. N.p., 1982.
Delgado, Jesús. *Óscar A. Romero: Biografía*. 1990. San Salvador: UCA Editores, 2005.
Didion, Joan. *Salvador*. New York: Vintage Books, 1983.
Díez, Zacarías, and Juan Macho. "En Santiago De María me tope con la miseria: Dos años de la vida de Mons. Romero (1975–1976—¿Años del cambio?)." San Salvador: Imprenta Criterio del arzobispado de San Salvador, 1995.
Dorner, Peter. *Latin American Land Reforms in Theory and Practice: A Retrospective Analysis*. Madison: University of Wisconsin Press, 1992.
Duarte, José Napoleón, and Diana Page. *Duarte: My Story*. New York: Putnam, 1986.
Dunkerley, James. *The Long War: Dictatorship and Revolution in El Salvador*. London: Junction Books, 1982.
Dussel, Enrique D. *A History of the Church in Latin America: Colonialism to Liberation (1492–1979)*. Trans. and rev. Alan Neely. Grand Rapids, Mich.: Eerdmans, 1981.
Ecumenical Program on Central America and the Caribbean. *Condoning the Killing: Ten Years of Massacres in El Salvador*. Washington, D.C.: EPICA, 1990.
Erdozaín, Plácido. *Archbishop Romero: Martyr of Salvador*. Foreword by Jorge Lara-Braud. Trans. John McFadden and Ruth Warner. Maryknoll, N.Y.: Orbis Books, 1981.
———. *Monseñor Romero: Mártir de la iglesia popular*. San José, Costa Rica: Departamento Ecuménico de Investigaciones, Editorial Universitaria Centroamericana, 1980.
Erickson Nepstad, Sharon, and Clifford Bob. "When Do Leaders Matter? Hypotheses on Leadership Dynamics in Social Movements." *Mobilization* 11, no. 1 (2006): 1–22.
La fe de un pueblo. 3rd ed. San Salvador: UCA Editores, 1988.
Figa Sastrengener, Ma. *De la utopía a la acción: Cuatro experiencias de promoción popular*. México, D.F.: Universidad Iberoamericana, 1995.
Forche, Carolyn, Harry Mattison, Susan Meiselas, and Fae Rubenstein. *El Salvador: Work of Thirty Photographers*. New York: Norton, 1983.
Galdámez, Pablo. *La esperanza de un pueblo*. San Salvador: Equipo Maíz, 2012.
Galeas, Geovani, and Berne Ayalá. *Grandeza y miseria en una guerrilla: Informe de una matanza*. 2nd ed. San Salvador: Centroamérica 21, 2008.
Ganz, Marshall. "Leading Change: Leadership, Organization, and Social Movements." In *The Handbook of Leadership Theory and Practice*, ed. Nitin Nohria and Rakesh Khurana, 527–68. Boston: Harvard Business Review Press, 2010.
Giuni, Marco G. "Was It Worth the Effort? The Outcomes and Consequences of Social Movements." *Annual Review of Sociology* 98 (1998): 371–93.
Gladwell, Malcolm. *The Tipping Point: How Little Things Can Make a Big Difference*. Boston: Little, Brown, 2000.
González, Luis Armando, "Iglesia, organizaciones populares y violencia sociopolítica." In *El Salvador: La transición y sus problemas*, ed. Rodolfo Cardenal and Luis Armando González, 232–58. San Salvador: UCA Editores, 2002.
Goodwin, Jeff. *No Other Way Out: States and Revolutionary Movements, 1945–1991*. Cambridge, Mass.: Cambridge University Press, 2001.

Goodwin, Jeff, and James Jasper. *Rethinking Social Movements: Structure, Meaning and Emotion*. Lanham, Md.: Rowman and Littlefield, 2004.

Goodwin, Jeff, James M. Jasper, and Francesca Polletta. *Passionate Politics: Emotions and Social Movements*. Chicago: University of Chicago Press, 2001.

Gould, Jeffrey L., and Aldo Lauria-Santiago. *To Rise in Darkness: Revolution, Repression, and Memory in El Salvador, 1920–1932*. Durham, N.C.: Duke University Press, 2008.

Grenier, Yvon. *The Emergence of Insurgency in El Salvador: Ideology and Political Will*. Pittsburgh: University of Pittsburgh Press, 1999.

Guerra, Walter, Benito Tobar, Reino Morán, and Efraín Villalobos, eds. *Testigos de la fe en El Salvador: Nuestros sacerdotes y seminarista diocesanos mártires, 1977–1993*. San Salvador: n.p., 2007.

Gutiérrez, Dagoberto. *La persona, la fe y la revolución*. San Salvador: Ediciones Ven y Sígueme, 1993.

Gutiérrez, Gustavo. *A Theology of Liberation: History, Politics and Salvation*. Maryknoll, N.Y.: Orbis Books, 1988.

Hammond, John. *Fighting to Learn: Popular Education and Guerrilla War in El Salvador*. New Brunswick, N.J.: Rutgers University Press, 1998.

Handal, Schafik. *Una guerra para construir la paz*. Buenos Aires: Ocean Sur, Editorial Morazán, 2006.

Harnecker, Marta. *Con la mirada en alto: Historia de las Fuerzas Populares de Liberación Farabundo Martí a través de entrevistas con sus dirigentes*. San Salvador: UCA Editores, 1993.

Hennelly, Alfred. *Liberation Theology: A Documentary History*. Ed. Alfred T. Hennelly. Maryknoll, N.Y.: Orbis Books, 1990.

Henríquez Consalvi, Carlos. *Broadcasting the Civil War in El Salvador: A Memoir of Guerrilla Radio*. Austin: University of Texas Press, 2010.

Herman, Edward S., and Frank Brodhead. *Demonstration Elections: U.S.-Staged Elections in the Dominican Republic, Vietnam, and El Salvador*. Boston: South End Press, 1984.

"If Truth Be Told: A Forum on David Stoll's *Rigoberta Menchú and the Story of All Poor Guatemalans*." *Latin American Perspectives* 26, no. 6 (1999): 5–68.

Kelly Rivera, Ana, Edy Arelí Ortiz Cañas, Liza Domínguez Magaña, and Maria Candelaria Navas. *¿Valió la pena? Testimonios de Salvadoreñas que vivieron la guerra*. San Salvador: Editorial Sombrero Azul, 1995.

Kincaid, A. Douglas. "Peasants into Rebels: Community and Class in Rural El Salvador." *Comparative Studies in Society and History* 29, no. 3 (1987): 466–94.

Lamperti, John. *Enrique Álvarez Córdova: Life of a Salvadoran Revolutionary and Gentleman*. Jefferson, N.C.: McFarland, 2006.

Latin America Bureau. *El Salvador under General Romero: An Analysis of the First Nine Months of the Regime of President Romero*. London: Latin America Bureau, 1979.

———. *Violence and Fraud in El Salvador: A Report on Current Political Events in El Salvador*. London: Latin America Bureau, 1977.

Latin American Bishops. "Justice." Medellín, Colombia, September 6, 1968. http://www.shc.edu/theolibrary/resources/medjust.htm.

———. "Peace." Medellín, Colombia, September 6, 1968. http://www.shc.edu/theolibrary/resources/medpeace.htm.

———. "Poverty of the Church." Medellín, Colombia, September 6, 1968. http://www.shc.edu/theolibrary/resources/medpov.htm.

Lauria-Santiago, Aldo. *Landscapes of Struggle: Politics, Society and Community in El Salvador*. Pittsburgh: University of Pittsburgh Press, 2004.

Legislatina: El observatorio del poder legislativo en América Latina. Salamanca, España. http://americo.usal.es/oir/legislatina/el_salvador.htm.

Lernoux, Penny. "Christians for Socialism Challenge Catholicism and Communism." Rome: APF Newsletters of Penny Lernoux, 1976.

———. *Cry of the People: The Struggle for Human Rights in Latin America—The Catholic Church in Conflict with U.S. Policy*. New York: Penguin Books, 1982.

Levine, Daniel H., ed. *Religion and Political Conflict in Latin America*. Chapel Hill: University of North Carolina Press, 1986.

Lindo-Fuentes, Héctor, and Erik Ching. *Modernizing Minds in El Salvador: Education Reform and the Cold War, 1960–1980*. Albuquerque: University of New Mexico Press, 2012.

López Vigil, José Ignacio. *Rebel Radio: The Story of El Salvador's Radio Venceremos*. Trans. Mark Fried. London: Latin America Bureau, 1994.

López Vigil, Maria. *Muerte y vida en Morazán: Testimonio de un sacerdote*. 3rd ed. San Salvador: UCA Editores, 1987.

———. *Piezas para un retrato*. San Salvador: UCA Editores, 1993.

Lungo, Mario. *La lucha de las masas en El Salvador*. San Salvador: UCA Editores, 1987.

Lungo, Mario, and Arthur Schmidt. *El Salvador in the Eighties: Counterinsurgency and Revolution*. Philadelphia: Temple University Press, 1996.

MacNutt, Francis Augustus. *Bartholomew de Las Casas: His life, Apostolate, and Writings*. Cleveland: Arthur H. Clark, 1908. Kindle e-book edition, 2011.

Mainwaring, Scott, and Alexander Wilde, eds. *The Progressive Church in Latin America*. Notre Dame, Ind.: University of Notre Dame Press, 1989.

Manwaring, Max G., and Court Prisk. *El Salvador at War: An Oral History of Conflict from the 1979 Insurrection to the Present*. Washington, D.C.: National Defense University Press, 1988.

Martínez Peñate, Oscar. *El Salvador: Del conflicto armado a la negociación, 1979–1989*. San Salvador: Editorial Nuevo Enfoque, 1997.

Mason, T. David. *Caught in the Crossfire: Revolutions, Repression, and the Rational Peasant*. New York: Rowman and Littlefield, 2004.

McAdam, Doug. *Comparative Perspectives on Social Movements: Political Opportunities, Mobilizing Structures and Cultural Framings*. Cambridge, UK: Cambridge University Press, 1996.

———. *Political Process and the Development of Black Insurgency, 1930–1970*. Chicago: University of Chicago Press, 1982.

McClintock, Cynthia. *Revolutionary Movements in Latin America: El Salvador's FMLN and Peru's Shining Path.* Washington, D.C.: United States Institute of Peace Press, 1998.

McClintock, Michael. *The American Connection.* Vol. 1, *State Terror and Popular Resistance in El Salvador.* London: ZED Books, 1985.

McCullough, Colleen. *The Thorn Birds.* New York: Harper and Row, 1977.

Medina Núñez, Ignacio. *El Salvador: Entre la guerra y la esperanza.* Guadalajara, México: Universidad de Guadalajara, 1990.

Medrano Guzmán, Juan Ramón. *Memorias de un guerrillero—Comandante Balta.* San Salvador: n.p., 2006.

Mena Sandoval, Francisco. *Del ejército nacional al ejército guerrillero.* San Salvador: Ediciones Arcoiris, 1990.

Menjívar Ochoa, Rafael. *Tiempos de locura, El Salvador 1979–1981.* 3rd ed. San Salvador: FLACSO, 2008.

Metaxas, Eric. *Bonhoeffer: Pastor, Martyr, Prophet, Spy—a Righteous Gentile vs. the Third Reich.* Nashville: Thomas Nelson, 2010.

Metzi, Francisco. *Por los caminos de Chalatenango: Con la salud en la mochila.* 2nd ed. San Salvador: UCA Editores, 2003.

Montgomery, Tommie Sue. "The Church in the Salvadoran Revolution." *Latin American Perspectives* 10, no. 1 (1983): 62–87.

———. *Revolution in El Salvador: From Civil Strife to Civil Peace.* 2nd ed. Boulder: Westview Press, 1995.

———. *Revolution in El Salvador: Origins and Evolution.* Boulder: Westview Press, 1982.

Morris, Aldon D., and Suzanne Staggenborg. "Leadership in Social Movements." In *The Blackwell Companion to Social Movements,* ed. David A. Snow, Sarah A. Soule, and Hanspeter Kriesi, 171–98. Oxford, UK: Blackwell, 2004.

O'Brien, David J., and Thomas A. Shannon. *Catholic Social Thought: The Documentary Heritage.* 1992. Reprint, Maryknoll, N.Y.: Orbis Books, 2006.

O'Malley, John. *What Happened at Vatican II.* Cambridge: Belknap Press of Harvard University Press, 2008.

Opazo, Andrés B. "El movimiento religioso popular en Centroamérica: 1970–1983." In *Movimientos populares en Centroamérica,* ed. Daniel Camacho and Rafael Menjívar, 143–99. San José, Costa Rica: Editorial Universitaria Centroamericana, 1985.

Ortiz, Miguel Ángel. "La Cayetana: Lecciones de la historia para El Salvador." San Vicente, El Salvador: n.p., November 2002.

Parroquia de Tecoluca, 1973–1977. Algunos Acontecimientos [Some Events]. Parish files (79 documents). Parish of Tecoluca, Department of San Vicente, El Salvador.

———, 1973–1977. Catequesis [Catechesis]. Parish files (5 documents). Parish of Tecoluca, Department of San Vicente, El Salvador.

———, 1973–1977. Incidentes Politicos [Political Incidents]. Parish files (26 docs.) Parish of Tecoluca, Department of San Vicente, El Salvador.

———, 1973–1977. Liturgia [Liturgy]. Parish files (13 documents). Parish of Tecoluca, Department of San Vicente, El Salvador.

———, 1973–1977. Plan Pastoral [Pastoral Plan]. Parish files (9 documents). Parish of Tecoluca, Department of San Vicente, El Salvador.

———, 1973–1977. Varios [Various]. Parish files (20 documents). Parish of Tecoluca, Department of San Vicente, El Salvador.

———. 1975–1980. Financiamento de Cursos [Financing of Courses]. Parish files (47 documents). Parish of Tecoluca, Department of San Vicente, El Salvador.

Pearce, Jenny. *Promised Land: Peasant Rebellion in Chalatenango, El Salvador*. London: Latin America Bureau, 1986.

Peceny, Mark. "Democratization by Elections: A New Mode of Transition." *Latin American Politics and Society* 52, no. 4 (Winter 2010): 160–63.

Peterson, Anna. *Martyrdom and the Politics of Religion: Progressive Catholicism in El Salvador's Civil War*. Albany: State University of New York Press, 1997.

Peterson, Anna, Manuel Vasquez, and Philip Williams. *Christianity, Social Change, and Globalization in the Americas*. New Brunswick, N.J.: Rutgers University Press, 2001.

El pueblo canta: Libro de cantos. San Salvador: Imprenta Criterio, n.d.

Richard, Pablo, and Guillermo Meléndez, eds. *La iglesia de los pobres en América Central*. San José, Costa Rica: Departamento Ecuménico de Investigaciones; Editorial Universitaria Centroamericana, 1982.

Rochon, Thomas R. *Culture Moves: Ideas, Activism, and Changing Values*. Princeton, N.J.: Princeton University Press, 1998.

Rodríguez Rivera, José David. Personal interviews with author. May 15–25, 2007, Loyola University Chicago; January 1–12, 2008, and May 13–17, 2013, San Salvador, El Salvador.

Romero, Óscar. *Monseñor Romero: Sus cartas pastorales*. N.p., n.d.

Romero, Óscar, and Irene Hodgson. *Archbishop Oscar Romero: A Shepherd's Diary*. Cincinnati: St. Anthony Messenger Press, 1993.

Santiago, Daniel. *The Harvest of Justice: The Church of El Salvador Ten Years after Romero*. New York: Paulist Press, 1993.

Schroth, Raymond A. *Bob Drinan: The Controversial Life of the First Catholic Priest Elected to Congress*. New York: Fordham University Press, 2011.

Selbin, Eric. *Modern Latin American Revolutions*. Boulder: Westview Press, 1994.

Sigmund, Paul E. *Liberation Theology at the Crossroads: Democracy or Revolution?* New York: Oxford University Press, 1990.

Silber, Irina Carlotta. *Everyday Revolutionaries: Gender, Violence, and Disillusionment in Postwar El Salvador*. New Brunswick, N.J.: Rutgers University Press, 2011.

Smith, Christian. *Disruptive Religion: The Force of Faith in Social-Movement Activism*. New York: Routledge, 1996.

———. *The Emergence of Liberation Theology: Radical Religion and Social Movement Theory*. Chicago: University of Chicago Press, 1991.

Snow, David A., and Robert D. Benford. "Ideology, Frame Resonance, and Participant Mobilization." *International Social Movement Research* 1 (1988): 197–217.

Snow, David A., Sarah A. Soule, and Hanspeter Kriesi. *The Blackwell Companion to Social Movements*. Malden, Mass.: Blackwell, 2004.

Stanley, William. *The Protection Racket State: Elite Politics, Military Extortion and Civil War in El Salvador*. Philadelphia: Temple University Press, 1996.

Tilly, Charles. *From Mobilization to Revolution*. Reading, Mass.: Addison-Wesley, 1978.

Todd, Molly. *Beyond Displacement: Campesinos, Refugees, and Collective Action in the Salvadoran Civil War*. Madison: University of Wisconsin Press, 2010.

Tula, María. *Hear My Testimony: María Teresa Tula, Human Rights Activist of El Salvador*. Boston: South End Press, 1994.

Ueltzen, Stefan. *Conversatorio con los hijos del siglo: El Salvador del siglo XX al siglo XXI*. San Salvador: Editorial III Milenio, 1994.

United Nations. *Acuerdos de El Salvador: En el camino de la paz*. San Salvador: Editorial Arcoiris, 1994.

———. *De la locura a la esperanza: La guerra de 12 años en El Salvador: Informe de la comisión de la verdad para El Salvador*. New York: United Nations, 1993.

Van Vugt, Johannes P. *Democratic Organization for Social Change: Latin American Christian Base Communities and Literacy Campaigns*. New York: Bergin and Garvey, 1991.

Vázquez, Norma, Cristina Ibañez, and Clara Murguialday. *Mujeres-Montaña: Vivencias de guerrilleras y colaboradoras del FMLN*. Madrid: Horas y Horas, 1996.

Ventura, José. *El poder popular en El Salvador*. México, D.F.: Editorial Mexico-Sur, 1983.

Westby, David L. "Strategic Imperative, Ideology, and Framing." *Mobilization* 7 (2002): 287–304.

Whitfield, Teresa. *Paying the Price: Ignacio Ellacuría and the Murdered Jesuits of El Salvador*. Philadelphia: Temple University Press, 1994.

Wickham-Crowley, Timothy. *Guerillas and Revolution in Latin America: A Comparative Study of Insurgents and Regimes since 1956*. 1992. Reprint, Princeton, N.J.: Princeton University Press, 1993.

Williams, Philip J., and Knut Walter. *Militarization and Demilitarization in El Salvador's Transition to Democracy*. Pittsburgh: University of Pittsburgh Press, 1998.

Wood, Elisabeth Jean. *Insurgent Collective Action and Civil War in El Salvador*. Cambridge, UK: Cambridge University Press, 2003.

Wright, Scott. *Promised Land: Death and Life in El Salvador*. Maryknoll, N.Y.: Orbis Books, 1994.

Index

Page numbers in *italics* indicate illustrations.

Peter M. Sánchez is professor of political science at Loyola University Chicago. His research focuses on Latin American politics and U.S.–Latin American relations. He has published numerous articles and book chapters, as well as the book *Panama Lost? U.S. Hegemony, Democracy, and the Canal.* He lives in Evanston, Illinois.